SECOND EDITION

CARD *Talk*

Winning Communication Games

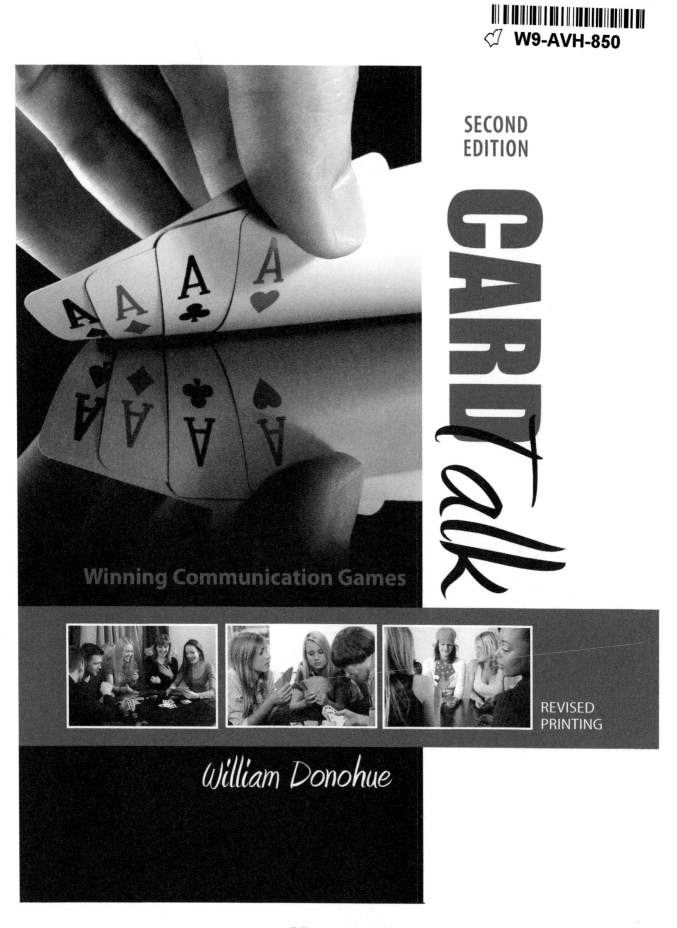

REVISED
PRINTING

William Donohue

Kendall Hunt
publishing company

To Denise for all her love and support

Kendall Hunt
p u b l i s h i n g   c o m p a n y

www.kendallhunt.com
Send all inquiries to:
4050 Westmark Drive
Dubuque, IA 52004-1840

Copyright © 2010, 2012 by William Donohue

ISBN 978-1-4652-2181-0

Printed in the United States of America

10 9 8 7 6 5 4 3

Contents

♠ ♦ ♣ ♥

Like *Card Talk* on Facebook!

♣ Setting the Stage with Texas Hold-Em

The Game

Maybe you've seen it on TV: Texas Hold-Em. This is a high-stakes poker card game where two cards are dealt face down to each player. Then five community cards that both players share are placed face up between the players by the dealer—a series of three ("the flop"), then two more single cards ("the turn" and "the river"). Players have the option to check, bet, or fold after each deal. Betting may occur prior to the flop, on the flop, on the turn, and on the river.

The Players

Four people sit facing one another under a low-hanging shaded light, concentrating on each other's every move. One bearded, middle-aged man wears a cowboy hat pulled low over his eyes. He intensely studies the two cards in his hand and scowls. Is it a bad hand (his set of cards) or an act designed to manipulate the others' perceptions of his hand?

Across from him sits a 20-something man—hoodie pulled low. He takes one look at his hand, makes no expression, and carefully lays his cards down. Is he portraying confidence, youthful cockiness, or just being cautious?

To his right is a sharp-dressed woman of about 27 who looks over her cards, then begins studying each of the other players for clues about how this game will play out.

Opposite her sits a sophisticated gentleman in a fedora—well polished and professional looking. He fidgets his cards and signals to the dealer that he is ready to play—he wants the flop.

© 2012 by Elnu. Used under license of Shutterstock, Inc.   © 2012 by Elnu. Used under license of Shutterstock, Inc.

Suddenly, the dealer complies by turning over three cards. Each player looks at the other. It's the cowboy's turn to bet. He lays down $20,000 in chips to open the betting—he's in.

Poker is all about the betting and what the betting communicates. If you eagerly throw in a large amount of money, you are signaling to the other players that either you have a good hand or you're bluffing.

Next, it's baseball boy's turn to bet. He must decide if the cowboy is bluffing or has good cards. After baseball boy bets, then the foxy lady must bet. She has to interpret the other bets in relation to her cards. When the older gentleman bets, he must look at the whole table and all the players' mannerisms and approaches before placing his wager.

And this is just the first round of betting on the flop. This process is repeated with the turn card and the river card until a winner is declared. It's a challenging game because it's all about studying one another and paying close attention, in addition to the cards you've been dealt.

♣ Communication Hold-Em

Talk Cards

Communication is like a Texas Hold-Em card game, but instead of using playing cards we play **talk games** with **talk cards**. To understand this analogy, let's focus first on talk cards.

Whenever we craft a message by talking, writing, calling, or texting someone, we frame that message from the role we're playing in relation to the other person. I might be talking to a student as a professor or sometimes as a friend. I can talk to my wife as her husband or her business partner. When I craft a message playing the husband role, in essence I am playing my Husband Card. I select a certain topic from that card to discuss, depending on what I want to accomplish. Then I add a style or tone to the message to get my point across.

I play many roles in my life, and each one demands a different card with varying approaches (styles) and tones (emotions). I have a Friend Card, a Professor Card, a Colleague Card, and so on.

Talk Games

Now, what are Talk Card Games? A Talk Card Game is a message exchange between people associated with a specific goal. For example, if I want to calm my wife after a rough day, I might start by asking her questions about her day to help her debrief the troublesome events. She responds with observations thoughts about her day.

The goal of this exchange becomes the name of the **Talk Card Game** we want to play. I call this particular game the Chill Game. When she reciprocates and plays her Wife Card she begins to debrief her day and calm down, we are playing a talk card game.

As we move through our days, we play many games with all kinds of people. The key is playing the games well and winning those games.

Winning Talk Games

In playing Texas Hold-Em, the goal is to win the game by taking the pot of money. Only one player can win, and the others lose. Most talk games, like the Chill Game, are different. Most talk games are cooperative events in which both people want to win by achiev-

© 2012 by Sanzhar Murzin. Used under license of Shutterstock, Inc.

ing their goals. I want to calm my wife after a tough day, and she wants to be calmed as well. If the exchange is successful, we both win the game.

Of course there are games in which people try to gain an advantage over another, as in poker card games. These talk games are typical in negotiated business dealings or in interpersonal conflict. One might win and accomplish his or her goals, while the other loses. But, in general, most talk games are cooperative events in which both parties try to help one another win by accomplishing their goals.

To review, a **talk card** is the package of messages communicated in playing a specific role. To play any role competently the communicator needs to have a strong list of messages ready to go that others believe effectively reflects that role. In essence, I can't be a good husband unless I can "talk" like a good husband. A **talk game** reflects the goal the messages are designed to accomplish. Winning means both parties have accomplished their goals.

♣ The Strategic Advantage

The complexity of playing talk games becomes apparent when people play different games than they think they are playing. A guy might be playing the game of Casual Conversation with a Facebook friend, but she might think he's playing the game of Stalking a Girl. Sometimes when people send a Facebook message, they have to label their game and indicate clearly that they are not stalking. I recently saw in an example from urbandictionary.com in which a guy sent this message to a female friend of his: "No stalk, but I noticed you changed your quotes on your profile."

The point is that if we view the process of communication as a talk card game, we can **think more strategically** about our moves, and whether we are making the right moves to be effective.

I conduct research on physician-patient communication. When doctors communicate with patients, they play their Doctor

A
♥

Winning most of your communication games—whether speaking in public or chatting with a friend—is the goal of this book.

A
♠

© 2012 by Alexander Raths. Used under license of Shutterstock, Inc.

Cards. The game they play is Diagnosis and Treatment. Playing the game well involves learning as much as possible from patients about their health issues, and then teaching them about proper healthcare, while maybe persuading them to change their bad habits.

When playing their Patient Cards, the patient tries to be understood and possibly learn to address their health issues. But he or she might also try to deceive the doctor into prescribing some desired medication. The best strategy for a successful doctor is getting the right information to craft the right diagnosis to prescribe the right treatment plan for the patient. If the game is not played well, the patient's life is at risk.

This scenario captures the goal of this book: to think about communication strategically. What talk cards do you have? What games can you play successfully? How can you more easily connect with others to win those games? We move through some critical communication concepts to understand how games are played in those contexts. Winning most of your communication games—whether speaking in public or chatting with a friend—is the goal of this book.

♣ The Organization of This Book

The card games we choose to play not only depend on our specific goals but on the contexts surrounding our communication. We might be talking to a friend in a coffee shop, meeting with several people at work, uploading some pictures on our Facebook pages, or broadcasting on our YouTube channels. Each context demands different card choices. Since these contextual factors are so important in determining our card play, this book organizes the chapters into six sections, largely by context.

Part 1: Communication Foundations

The first four chapters provide the foundations for a Card Talk approach to understanding communication.

- **Chapter 1:** What are talk cards and how do they work?
- **Chapter 2:** How do the characteristics of language influence card play?
- **Chapter 3:** When does culture influence our choice of talk cards and talk games?
- **Chapter 4:** How does our social identity or self-image shape how we choose our card games?

Part 2: Interpersonal Card Games

The second group of chapters focuses on understanding how we use card play to grow and manage our interpersonal relationships.

- **Chapter 5:** How do card games both grow and erode personal relationships?
- **Chapter 6:** Since much of our card play is aimed at persuading others to comply with our requests, how can card talk help us accomplish our goals?
- **Chapter 7:** Card games that manage conflict constructively are vital in building effective relationships.

Part 3: Group and Organizational Communication

The third group of chapters moves beyond personal relationships to understanding how communication functions in groups and organizations.

- **Chapter 8:** How do we use card play to fit into various groups?
- **Chapter 9:** How do people coordinate and share information effectively in groups and organizations?
- **Chapter 10:** How should we structure card talk to promote good decision making?
- **Chapter 11:** How do leaders use card play to influence and direct groups?

Part 4: New Media Card Games

The fourth set of chapters looks at how we play talk games in a new media world. The concept of media 2.0 is that different media work together and are both broadcast to everyone and narrowcast to specific individuals at the same time.

- **Chapter 12:** How do we select the right cards when using social media?
- **Chapter 13:** When can card play influence how new and old media affect change in our society?
- **Chapter 14:** How do we learn from and how are we entertained by new and old media?

Part 5: Public Speaking Card Games

The final chapters were developed to help you craft public speaking messages by guiding the way you plan and deliver your speeches.

- **Chapter 15:** How can we analyze audiences and develop a strategy to connect?
- **Chapter 16:** What messages will best inform and persuade the audience?
- **Chapter 17:** What delivery considerations will help you look more professional when giving your speech?

Part 6: Appendix, Course Assignments
Getting Started

To better understand the importance of how context influences our card play, consider this example. Recently a student named Kaitlin presented me with a difficult card talk problem she faced at work. She had just been promoted to supervisor of several friends she had worked with for two years.

With these friends Kaitlin developed and played her Friend Card in most social chit-chats to reinforce their friendship. But suddenly she became their boss. How does she communicate with them? Does she continue to play her Friend Card and talk to them like she has for two years or does she play a Supervisor Card so she can discuss work topics to get the job done? After all, Kaitlin can't be a supervisor unless she learns to talk like one.

Kaitlin's dilemma illustrates how we grow into our talk cards. Most of us begin with family-related cards, such as a Son or Daughter Card, a Brother or Sister Card, and perhaps a Niece or Nephew Card. Then we learn to create a Friend Card as we go to school and play with friends. These are interpersonal cards. When we join groups at school and then at work, we are challenged to create cards that show us how to fit into these groups, share information, make decisions, and even lead these groups.

© 2012 by auremar. Used under license of Shutterstock, Inc.

A ♥ The main challenge for achieving personal and professional success is developing a full deck of talk cards for each role and learning how to use them.

Kaitlin had to learn fast. She was challenged to build a Supervisor Card and learn how and when to play it, depending on the talk game being played at any given moment. Kaitlin will also need other professional cards in that deck when she starts to step into professional situations, such as conferences and meetings. And she'll need to know how to use social media talk cards as well. In short, being a professional means talking like a professional.

In fact, the main challenge for achieving personal and professional success is developing a full deck of talk cards for each role and learning how to use them to play talk games. Whether the games are personal associated with being a good friend, sister, or wife, or whether they are professional and involve learning to talk like an employee or a boss, research results are clear: Success and card choice are synonymous. If you don't have the card, you can't play the role.

The goal of this book is help people overcome communication challenges. Everyone needs to think about their talk card deck, create more and better cards to adapt effectively to different situations, and learn how to play talk games successfully. Using the Card metaphor is important because it provides a simpler path toward communication growth than merely listing skills and hoping people improve.

We begin by focusing on gender games and how characteristics of language influence the way those games are played. Then we move from interpersonal through group and organizational communication issues to mass media contexts and finally to giving speeches.

On a personal note, I have been teaching public speaking and conducting communication research for many years. I have come to know many of the people whose ideas I present in the course of the book. From time to time I share personal recollections about these individuals and their ideas to give some added dimension to the ideas.

I hope you enjoy the book and have fun growing your card talk decks!

PART One

Communication Foundations

♠ Talk Cards and Talk Games

♦ Language Card Games

♣ Culture Card Games

♥ Social Identity Card Games

CHAPTER One

Talk Cards and Talk Games

♣ Introduction

In the introduction, I described the three important components of the card talk idea.

- A **Talk Card** is the package of messages that is communicated in playing a specific role. To play any role competently, the communicator needs to have a strong list of messages ready to go that others believe effectively reflects that role. In essence, I can't be a good husband unless I can "talk" like one.
- A **Talk Game** reflects the goal the messages are designed to accomplish. Winning means both parties accomplish their goals.
- A **Card Deck** is the set of cards we have available to play a card game at any given moment. We have both a Personal Card Deck and a Professional Card Deck, and we must develop both of them well to succeed as communicators.

To understand better about how and why we play card games let's turn first to some examples of card games in real-life examples.

The Scheduling Game

Imagine Kaitlin, the student supervisor who is new on the job and has not yet developed an effective Supervisor Card. One of her first duties is to create a work schedule for student employees and enforce that schedule to make sure all hours are covered. She must talk with each student and determine when each can work.

Imagine that one of her employees, who happens to be a good friend, comes in to get some special time off to attend a wedding. This person makes the request using her Friend Card. Yet the supervisor cannot relent. She must play her Supervisor Card and refuse the request. This is a tough lesson in learning to be a supervisor; Kaitlin will be making some unpopular decisions, possibly losing friends along the way.

The Parenting Plan Game

I conduct a lot of research in the area of divorce mediation. In this context a neutral third party sits down with divorcing parties and helps them create a parenting plan for their children after the divorce is finalized. This facilitator must have an effective Mediator Card to deal with the parties who will alternately play Husband and Wife Cards and Mom and Dad Cards. Typically, the mediator's goal is to encourage parties to play Mom and Dad Cards so they can focus on the task of building a parenting plan. If they play Husband and Wife cards repeatedly, they move away from playing a Parenting Plan Game and more toward a Marital Argument Game that the mediator prefers to avoid.

The Patient Care Plan Game

A third game of interest that I referenced in the Introduction focuses on how physicians play their Doctor Cards to create effective treatment plans for their patients. The challenge is that doctors must play the game so that patients open up and provide accurate information about their feelings, their history with the health issues, their family, and even their job pressures. This information is vital if the physician is able to win the game by creating a plan to help the patient get better.

Let's use these three games to illustrate some key principles about talk cards, talk games, and card decks. We begin by diving deeply into the concept of talk cards.

♣ Talk Cards

Two of my good friends in the field of communication are Drs. Jim Dillard and Denise Solomon, both scholars at Pennsylvania State University. One of the important questions that Jim and Denise seek to answer in their research is: What goals drive interpersonal communication?

Their research has shown that people have both **primary** and **secondary goals** when they interact. The communicator's **primary goal** focuses on the response he or she wants to achieve from the target of the message. Does the communicator want the message target to understand something, change an attitude about something, or perform some specific behavior? We tend to think of these primary goals as reflected in the topic or purpose of the message. **Secondary goals**, according to Denise, Jim, and their colleagues, focus on defining the relationship between the communicators. The three important relational factors that are key in defining a relationship are affiliation, involvement, and dominance.

Affiliation adds messages about how much people like or dislike one another. **Involvement** messages reveal how much interpersonal distance or formality the person is trying to create in the relationship. **Dominance** projects a desire to control or direct the person to do something.

What Denise and Jim also learned is that we combine these goals into a whole message presentation or package as we communicate. In this book, we refer to this as **card talk**. Thus, a **talk card** is the package of messages that is communicated in playing a specific role. To perform a personal or professional role well, the communicator needs a strong list of messages ready to go that others believe effectively reflects that role.

The message "package" consists of two elements: **content** and **style**. **Content** is the primary goal of the message or the topic you want the other person to understand or the thing you want them to do: Go here, play there, I want this, I care about that. **Style** concerns how friendly, how formal, and how powerful you want to appear in presenting that topic or idea. Style gives emphasis and fills in meaning about the topic. They work together in the message package.

Card Style

Our **secondary goals** in communication focus on adding relational information to our message. Jim and Denise tell us that we mix and match three elements in formulating our style.

The first element is **liking**. We include words, gestures, eye movements, and other facial expressions to show how much we like or dislike someone. Showing extreme liking might involve smiling, getting physically close to someone, or even touching. Showing extreme dislike might start with a scowl and an angry tone.

When divorcing parties in mediation play the Marital Argument Game, they often show this extreme dislike for one another that the mediator must redirect to keep the focus on the Parenting Plan Game.

The second style element is **formality**. A very formal message is one that creates distance between parties. It shows less involvement in the relationship. When we want to show less involvement we use big words, proper grammar, and long sentences. On the other hand, a more informal style aimed at showing more involvement might include shorter words, slang, sentence fragments, and perhaps an exaggerated accent. People are often informal when they want to show they like someone. When they are angry, sometimes they are also informal and use profanity, for example. But they might also use formal language, for example, if they are scolding someone.

The third style form is **power**, or **dominance**. Messages always include information about the speaker's status, or power, in the relationship. Big power messages try to establish dominance and might include threats, demands, or other attempts to impose the speaker's will. When the divorcing male plays his Husband Card, he might try to intimidate his ex-wife by yelling or using threatening language to dominate the conversation and impose a solution on the parenting plan.

One high-power strategy that some people use to establish dominance is shoving a talk card in someone's face. That means playing a role forcefully. For example, the student supervisor might need to do that if the student she's talking to refuses to play an Employee Card and continues to play her Friend Card to get time off to attend the wedding. The supervisor might have to say, "Look, here are the hours you're going to work because you have the lowest seniority. I don't have any choice!"

An analysis of the supervisor's message at this point reveals low liking, low formality, and high power. This is a typical profile for a message of this kind. She could have said, "I appreciate your concern but I must insist on scheduling you at this time." This message shows medium liking, high formality, and medium power. It certainly contains a different style than the previous "Look" message.

> **A ♥**
>
> We include words, gestures, and facial expressions to show how much we like or dislike someone.
>
> **A ♠**

© 2012 by Patrizia Tilly . Used under license of Shutterstock, Inc.

Relational Negotiation

As it turns out, our topic and style selections make specific relational proposals. When the student played her Supervisor Card in responding to her friend, she was negotiating the relationship between the parties, her secondary communication goal. Playing that card and using a high-power style suggests that the relationship between the friends should shift from friend-friend to supervisor-employee.

If her friend accepts this proposal by playing an Employee Card in response to her friend's comments, then the relationship negotiation is over. A new relationship has been established. If the friend rejects the proposal and plays a Friend Card in response by getting mad, then the negotiation is still on. The friend is basically saying, "I don't want to be your employee; I want to be your friend."

When there's extended disagreement about what card should be played, it's difficult to win any communication games. To win, people need to play cards that work together, rather than against one another.

As you might imagine, sometimes these negotiations get tricky. When her friend asked for time off to attend her cousin's wedding, the supervisor was probably caught off guard. She thought her friend/employee was coming in to play the Casual Conversation Game, and suddenly the friend changed it to the Scheduling Game and asked for time off. Now the new supervisor must play her Supervisor Card and talk about the policy that says no special time off is allowed.

To keep her friendship alive, the supervisor has to discuss the topic with the relational goal of not alienating her friend. That's difficult to do. As she becomes more skilled at her job and develops her Supervisor Card, she will grow more comfortable playing the Business Meeting Game. She will know when to play a card and how to adjust her topics and styles so that her friends don't reject her Supervisor Card.

This raises the point about the size of our cards. A card is large if we have command of many topics and many styles in expressing those topics. Once the supervisor learns to develop her Supervisor Card, she will know how to shift back and forth easily between her Friend Card and her Supervisor Card when talking with her employee friends that she has worked with for some time. In fact, learning a job means developing the card associated with that job.

© 2012 by iofoto. Used under license of Shutterstock, Inc.

Personal and Professional Decks

As the supervisor example illustrates, card decks are generally divided into two categories—**personal** and **professional**. The **personal** cards are typically those we develop first between family members and friends. We use them most often when we communicate. In contrast, **professional** cards focus on job-related duties.

You can probably empathize with the student supervisor who has to overcome the challenge of developing her Supervisor Card. Not only must she explain policies to people, she must learn how to train new employees, talk to customers, resolve customer complaints, and deal with her boss, the owner of the establishment. These are all topics she is expected to be able to discuss, and she must make the right style choices with each to be effective in her position. For example, when a customer comes in and plays the Customer Complaint Game with her, she has to know how to (a) present herself as a competent problem solver, (b) send positive relational messages to avoid alienating the customer, and (c) creatively solve the problem to keep the customer happy.

Physicians have these same challenges. When talking with a patient the physician must often switch between personal and professional cards. The physician might play a Friend Card with a patient he has known a long time by sharing personal information about his family. That kind of conversation sets a relaxed, friendly tone to the interaction so when the physician switches to the Doctor Card, he can more easily interview his friend/patient about his health concerns.

♣ Card Play Is Reciprocal

The Physician-Patient Card Game illustrates an important point about card play. When someone plays a card, he or she is asking the other person to play a card that typically matches or complements the card the person is playing. In other words, card play is always **reciprocal**. For example, when playing the Doctor Card, the physician is asking the patient to play a Patient Card and to carefully listen to the physician's instructions.

Often when playing a Patient Card, a person might get nervous and not listen well or not feel comfortable asking questions. That's when the physician is wise to switch to a Friend Card, which asks the patient to also switch to a Friend Card and start opening up more as a friend. When a person talks casually he or she reveals a lot of important information to the physician that might help create a good treatment plan.

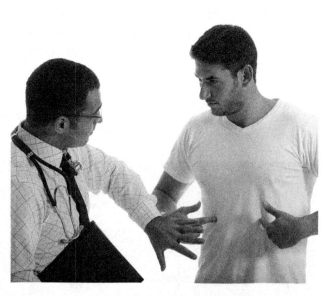

© 2012 by Ronen Boidek. Used under license of Shutterstock, Inc.

In our other example, when the student supervisor's friend came in to ask for time off, she was playing her Friend Card, which essentially asked the supervisor to play her Friend Card in return. But the supervisor had to play her Supervisor Card to do her job and had to deny the friend's request. The denial could certainly be friendly, and the supervisor could show a little of her Friend Card. But the supervisor had to reject her friend's request to only play her Friend Card and give the employee the time off.

The key point is this: Don't think only about the card you should play. Think also about the card you're asking the other person to play. Is it the card that will allow you to accomplish your goals?

♣ Talk Game Goals

Types of Goals

What drives us to play talk games? My friend Jim Dillard and his colleagues have some answers to this question. His research finds that every time we form a message to communicate there are several goals we work to successfully achieve.

The first goal is related to our **identity**, or how we define ourselves. This is called a **self-presentation goal**. Each person wants

> A♥
>
> The strategic question is whether the card you're asking the other person to play will help you accomplish your goals.
>
> A♠

to be perceived in a particular way to be accepted and respected by the other person and his or her peer or social group. Or the person might want to show that he or she is not a part of that group. But whenever we exchange information in whatever medium, we have self-presentation goals. We talk more about these self-presentation goals in chapter 4, which focuses on self-concept and identity needs.

The second kind of goal we pursue in talk games is **relational**. Each person inserts information in a message that's designed to pull the other closer or push them farther away. Pulling closer is accomplished by using a friendlier, informal style of communication. We work to establish relationships that enable us to accomplish our primary message goals. The first judgment people generally make toward an individual is how "friendly" the person looks or acts.

The third aim of every message is the goal that the communicator usually focuses on most directly—our **achievement** goal. This goal relates to the task we want our message to accomplish—some job that must be accomplished. I want to give you some information, persuade you to change your mind, or entertain you with a story. These material goals provide the labels we use to describe the purpose of a message. For example, someone might want to tell you about their new job, or persuade you to share a cup of coffee. These are achievement goals and they are often the main motivator for communicating with another.

Messages can be motivated primarily by self-presentation or relational purposes. For example, for the newly appointed supervisor whose employee/friend asks for time off probably wants to play her Friend Card to her newly designated supervisor. She wants to present herself as a competent employee (presentation goal), reestablish her friendship (relational goal), and get time off for the wedding (achievement goal). These goals work together for the employee. By playing her Friend Card she emphasizes the relationship that she thinks should afford special privileges. She also shows that she's a good employee by asking for time off rather than calling in sick.

What's interesting about this request is that it illustrates how these three motivations combine to play a communication game. To achieve her goal of getting time off, the employee/friend wants to emphasize the Friend Card while playing the Employee Card, again to get special consideration. Using the Friend Card, she picks a topic from the card that she and her new boss have probably talked about when they were just friends. Pulling a familiar topic from the Friend Card indicates that she wants to play the Casual Conversation Game first to set the tone for the request. She might say, "Hey, did you hear my cousin is getting married? I think you guys met. She's really cool." After a few exchanges, the employee/friend might begin to show her Employee Card and say, "By the way, I would really like to go to her wedding, so I need some time off."

Winning Card Games

How should the new student supervisor handle the request to "win" the game? (Recall that winning means both people accomplish their goals in the conversation.) The supervisor can only win if she is successful in accomplishing her achievement goal (getting the employee to work), relational goal (keeping the friendship), and presentation goal (being a competent supervisor). On the other hand, her friend probably has the same relational and presentation goals but a different achievement goal (get time off). The best the supervisor can hope for in this exchange is to accomplish her own achievement and presentation goals, but she might sacrifice her relational goal of keeping the friendship. She has to play her Supervisor Card in such a way to minimize that, if possible.

Card talk games are difficult to play so that all players achieve their goals. In this context, "winning" a card game means that both parties play the cards in their hands to accomplish their self-presentation, relational, and achievement goals. We "lose" a game if, after the cards are played, one or both parties fail to achieve their goals. For example, the supervisor would **lose** if she has to say no to her friend in a way that really makes her mad. She can only **win** by playing the Supervisor Card carefully while also playing some of her Friend Card, gently saying no, and explaining the policy in a friendly way.

As this example illustrates, talk card games start by one person showing a specific card, the other person seeing the card, and either reciprocating or not reciprocating with the same card. As this process evolves people get a sense of what they're doing—they define the activity. This activity then becomes "the game." This example also illustrates that games can change quickly. What started as a Casual Conversation Game quickly turned into a Scheduling Meeting Game. Just as in conventional card games, leading with the wrong card can end in disaster. It was unfortunate that the friend/employee played her Friend Card to try to use her friendship to get a favor from her new boss. Leading with that card may have cost her a friendship just to get a day off.

In many circumstances, misreading cards and, by extension, misreading proposed games can have severe consequences. In the Parenting Plan Game, the mediator's goal is to read the couple's cards and figure out if they are playing the Husband and Wife Cards or their Mom and Dad Cards. Then, when they are showing the right cards, are they playing a game that will result in winning the game, which is creating a parenting plan for the children. A key skill in effective communication is reading the other's cards. That awareness is essential in then playing a game that will result in achieving the goals and winning the game.

♣ Card Development

Style Switching

As you recall, the underlying motivation to create cards is to satisfy our self-presentation, relationship, and achievement goals. Striving to accomplish these goals when faced with diverse communication settings creates a need to be able to switch quickly from one style to another and, thus, develop bigger cards.

My senior roommate in college was an African American guy who was adept at switching styles (friendliness, formality, and power). When Ron played his Friend Card with me, he used a typical Standard English accent. However, when his African American friends entered the room, Ron immediately adopted their more urban accent when playing his Friend Card with them. That accent is important in establishing friendliness, informality, and equal power. It honors the culture and establishes a connection.

He and I talked about this switching extensively. He felt that is was important to switch styles to show solidarity and respect for his African American friends. He believed his ability to hang out with them hinged on using that style in their presence. Similarly, he

felt that using the Standard English style was important when hanging out with his white friends.

Everyone learns to make subtle shifts in their style to satisfy their needs. High school students often use the word like every fourth or fifth word in communicating with one another. Including this word shows solidarity with friends. When these students speak to older folks they often avoid this word to play a more Adult Card. Women play their Female Card by introducing subjects and styles that appeal to their female friends when exchanging social topics. Men display similar quirks in their speech to appeal to their buddies when they play their Man Card.

Card Origins

As people mature and spend more time outside their families, they learn to expand their cards because they have to fit into more groups. Our identities become more complex as we age. Kids go to school and must create Friend and Student Cards when they get to school. As friend and family groups expand, they put more cards into their deck as a way to fit in. By the time we mature into adults, we require an elaborate set of cards to effectively relate to our increasingly diverse world.

The story about Ron, my college roommate, illustrates where cards come from. We know what cards we have from two sources. First, we play cards and see how people react to us. If they respond to the cards we play and we achieve our goals, then we know we can hold and play those cards. If they don't respond well, then we probably figure we don't have or can't play those cards well.

I am constantly reminded that I don't have a Youth Card when I can't participate in conversations about new bands or video games. I don't care much about those issues so my cards are small or even non-existent. I feel sorry for people trying to go back to school and learn a new craft after being laid off. They have to learn to communicate in an entirely new way for that new career. Many people get comfortable playing the same cards over and over, and never find new ones to play.

Second, we learn about our cards when people reflect on our personalities. They might comment on the style with which we play our cards, for example. "That Sara is really sensitive," means she prefers to play her Friend Card frequently by taking time to listen to people she really cares about. Or "That Bill is a good dad" means to that person, Bill's Dad Card impresses the casual observer.

Card Deck

Your card deck consists of all the cards you have available for any and all communication situations. An easy way to think about your deck is to look in your closet. What sets of clothes do you have for which situations? If you're typical, you have various outfits for different situations. You have dress-up clothes for formal occasions, business clothes for your job, casual clothes for going to class or hanging out. You can think of these clothes as part of your Card Talk deck. For example, you put on your business

A♥ Many people get comfortable playing the same cards over and over, and never find new ones to play.

clothes for your job and you play your Business Person Card at work. When you help customers or talk to the boss in your work clothes you present the whole professional business package to these people.

It's important for everyone to have a large deck of talk cards to manage the broad range of communication challenges we face. By virtue of my crazy, exciting life, I have been in many situations and learned to build a big deck. I work with people who are pleased to tell me about my cards and how they're working, so I have many opportunities to learn about my cards.

Imagine what the doctor's card deck looks like. Personally, he may need to create a Dad, Husband, Friend, and Son Cards. Professionally, he may need to create Doctor, Colleague, and Employee Cards in working at the hospital. If you have a busy life and jump in and out of many situations, then you probably hold many personal and professional cards. And you often switch quickly among these cards as you switch among card games. One minute the game is Casual Conversation and then next minute it's a Family Chores Game, discussing who does what around the house.

Card Tricks

What about card tricks? A card trick involves playing a card or initiating a card talk game with the intention of hiding true self-presentation, relational, or achievement goals. People do this all the time when they want to fake interest or attention. For self-presentation purposes I might play the card that I'm asked to play, as I want to get along, but in my heart I really don't want to play that card. These are innocent diversions that are common in conversation.

This was the challenge that the student supervisor faced when her friend asked for time off. Her friend came in and played her Friend Card and initiated a Casual Conversation Game. Then she switched immediately and played the Scheduling Game. The switch was a bit of a trick because the Casual Conversation Game was a cover for the real achievement goal of getting time off. When both parties show the same or compatible cards over several exchanges and both parties believe they are playing the same game, they have achieved **synchrony**.

When it becomes clear they are not playing the same game, it is called **dissynchrony**. In extreme circumstances individuals can trick others into believing they are playing one game when in reality they are playing something else. If the mediator allows either divorcing party to play a Husband or Wife Card while the other is trying to play a Mom or Dad Card, then dissynchrony might emerge. The party changing the card works to change the game to accomplish different goals rather than cooperatively creating a parenting plan. The mediator must keep watch for this trap and redirect it when necessary.

Winning for both parents depends largely on achieving synchrony by: (a) reading one's own and the others' cards correctly, (b) determining if parties are playing the same game, and (c) knowing how to expand the game rules to widen synchrony opportunities. While we have covered (a) and (b), we have not focused on game rules and how they work. Let's take a look at rules and how to play with them.

♣ Talk Game Rules

What Are the Rules of the Game?

Another colleague with whom I have interacted over the years is the late Dr. W. Barnett Pearce, a scholar at the University of Massachusetts. He developed the **Theory of Coordinated Management of Meaning**, which says that the meaning of messages is coordinated among communicators—or negotiated as discussed above. The idea is that each talk game is organized around a set of rules required to play it properly. These rules, created by the communicators themselves, both define the game being played and the ways to play the game fairly. But when parties have different definitions of the game and can't coordinate their understanding of the game, it is difficult to play the game and communicate effectively. The question is, what are game rules and how do they work?

Card talk rules regulate the topics and styles that are acceptable in playing the game. If the game has a formal definition, like the Patient Care Plan Game, then the rules are clearer, but also more constraining. When a doctor interviews a patient, the purpose of the talk is to understand the issues and create a patient care plan to improve the patient's health status. In a rigid situation like this, the rules are pretty strict; it's only acceptable to discuss a relatively few number of topics to ensure that no time is wasted and the doctor is able to solve the problem. For example, it would be all right to talk about medically relevant issues but not all right to talk about the relative success of various sports teams.

Styles are also constrained in card talk. In casual conversation, using bad grammar or mildly profane language signals an informal situation. But in a job interview, if a candidate uses this style combination, it suggests the candidate does not know how to communicate properly in formal situations. The interviewer might even say, "We don't use that kind of language here."

© 2012 by Monkey Business Images . Used under license of Shutterstock, Inc.

Bending the Rules

Rules are constraining because the person might be prevented from using a style that is more effective in that situation. For example, the doctor might notice that the patient seems overly nervous playing the Patient Care Plan Game. The doctor might decide to break out of the formal interview mode to put the patient more at ease. So the doctor might play a Friend Card and talk about family issues with the patient.

People bend game rules all the time. Mediators are constantly on guard for parents who try to bend the rules during a mediation session to gain an advantage. One of the important rules that mediators try to enforce is the "no interruption" rule.

Interrupting is a power style move aimed at establishing dominance in a conversation. To avoid such a show of dominance, mediators establish the rule that when one person is talking, he or she is allowed to complete the thought. But instead of overtly interrupting, the "listener" might make a noise, roll his or her eyes, or do some other disruptive act that isn't "technically" interrupting. Since people aren't always cooperative, the mediator must constantly watch for these rule violations.

Communication Style Survey

Do you typically pay more attention to the *topics* you select when playing card games or to the *styles* you use when communicating? Since style choices (friendliness, formality, power) reflect relationship priorities, paying more attention to the topics suggests you are less tuned in to your relationship priorities as you communicate.

Directions: Take this survey to find your tendencies. When you have completed the survey, total your scores for each dimension (Friendliness, Power, Formality, etc.). Then total all three dimensions on each page.

Relationship Style Awareness Items

QUESTIONS	1	2	3	4	POINTS
1. I am able to be friendly when it's important to do so.	NO!	no	yes	YES!	
2. I know how to show friendliness nonverbally.	NO!	no	yes	YES!	
3. I try to maintain appropriate eye contact when speaking with others.	NO!	no	yes	YES!	
4. I am encouraging to the others when it's helpful.	NO!	no	yes	YES!	

Total Friendliness Score: _____

5. I am aware when I talk too much for the situation.	NO!	no	yes	YES!	
6. It bothers me when people don't know that they're being pushy.	NO!	no	yes	YES!	
7. I can put my foot down and direct the situation when necessary.	NO!	no	yes	YES!	
8. I also know how and when to give in to achieve a more important goal.	NO!	no	yes	YES!	

Total Power Score: _____

9. I am comfortable switching from a formal to an informal tone.	NO!	no	yes	YES!	
10. I know when it's necessary to become more formal in my speech.	NO!	no	yes	YES!	
11. I am comfortable joking around from time to time.	NO!	no	yes	YES!	
12. It bothers me when people are being too informal when it's inappropriate.	NO!	no	yes	YES!	

Total Formality Score: _____

Total Relational Style Awareness Score for Items 1–12: _____

Communication Topic Awareness Items

QUESTIONS	1	2	3	4	POINTS
13. I like to focus on the topic until it has been explored completely.	NO!	no	yes	YES!	
14. I always give good reasons for my opinions.	NO!	no	yes	YES!	
15. I am not afraid to explore a wide range of topics in conversation.	NO!	no	yes	YES!	
16. I have the patience to learn details about topics others discuss.	NO!	no	yes	YES!	

Total Topic Focus Score: _____

17. I am detail oriented when the conversation is important.	NO!	no	yes	YES!	
18. In important conversations I insist on precise definitions.	NO!	no	yes	YES!	
19. I like to be accurate when I speak to avoid misunderstanding.	NO!	no	yes	YES!	
20. Often I insist that others give examples for what they are saying.	NO!	no	yes	YES!	

Total Precise Score: _____

21. In most situations I try to explore the full range of issues under consideration.	NO!	no	yes	YES!	
22. I try not to rush to a conclusion before all the issues have been explored.	NO!	no	yes	YES!	
23. I make a conscious effort to understand the other party's most important issues.	NO!	no	yes	YES!	
24. I make sure that the other party understands my priorities during interactions.	NO!	no	yes	YES!	

Total Topic Development Score: _____

Score for Items 13–24: _____

Score for Items 1–12: _____

_____

_____

_____

_____

Results:

If your total score was over 36 for the relationship style and topic awareness style dimensions, then you are confident in your ability to function strategically about the topics you select and develop as well as your style choices when communicating. If your total score for all 24 items was over 80, then you are very confident in both dimensions and probably are able to play talk cards effectively.

If one score was about 10 points higher than the other score, then you have a definite tendency to pay more attention to the area in which you scored higher. For example, if you scored higher on the relationship style items, then you probably monitor your relational messages more carefully than the topics you select from your talk cards. In theory, your score should be over 40 for each of the two dimensions for you to be confident in the effectiveness of your topic and style choices.

♣ Modeling the Card Talk Elements

Let's take a broader look at the card talk process by modeling its components. Every communication event contains these elements, and we refer to them throughout this book.

Sources and Receivers

Every communication event includes at least one source and one receiver. The communication process is not simply sending information to unknown receivers. That process is information dissemination.

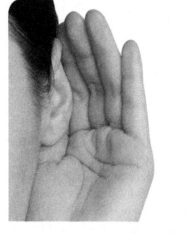

The communication process occurs at a higher level. It means that a **source** wants to impact a **receiver**—changing attitudes, beliefs, values, or behaviors in some way. When the source has impacted the receiver even minimally, then we can say communication has occurred.

A source whose self-presentation goal is looking "cool" and walks into a room with a

© 2012 by Sukhonosova Anastasia. Used under license of Shutterstock, Inc.

"hot" outfit and gets the desired reaction (people staring at the source) is communicating. The source had a goal, the clothes and outfit were the message, and receivers were impacted.

Messages

Every communication event involves a **message**. It could be verbal, written, or nonverbal in nature. Using the language for this book, the message shows the talk card the person is playing, and probably the game as well. This means that messages ask us many questions that must be answered. What is the person trying to say, what card or cards are they playing, what game is happening, and what is the goal?

Many factors impact how we answer these questions , and we talk about those in the model as well. It's important to note that the receiver's first job is to figure out what the source is communicating, then what the message means, and finally, what should be done (if anything) about it. The source's main job is to send messages, or play cards and games most likely to impact the receiver in the intended way. The wrong messages at the wrong times, as we have seen, do not connect with receivers or are taken the wrong way.

The Channels

The **channel** is the method you use to communicate, whether it's face-to-face, electronic media, or snail mail, for example. If you were a television star, you could say "hi" to your mom using television. Channels are either broad or narrow. **Broad channels** carry a lot of information, whereas **narrow channels** carry much less information. A channel is broad if it involves most of your five senses; it's narrow if it involves only one sense.

Most people control their channels strategically depending on what card they want to play. If the card requires maximum impact, then the face-to-face channel might be best. If self-presentation or relational issues are not critical, then a text might be fine. The key is to match the message with the channel. If you send a message through a channel the other person does not use or if you select a channel that is inappropriate to the message, your communication will most likely fail.

Noise

Noise is anything that distracts from or competes with the intended message. For example, a patient might have a nervous twitch or look around the room while the doctor tries to conduct an interview. Anything that distracts from playing the intended game is noise. You can think of noise as a ratio—the **signal-to-noise ratio**.

The **signal** is the message sent to accomplish intended self-presentation, relational, or achievement goals. It is the numerator, or top part of the ratio. **Noise** is the denominator, or bottom part of the ratio. The goal in communicating a message is to have a strong signal and minimal noise. Playing a card that sends a clear message with little interference is likely to get through more successfully than a confusing message or a weak message that cannot be heard above the noise.

Culture

Every message given from every card contains information about the sender's cultural orientations. As we discuss in a later chapter, **culture** is represented by an individual's values and behaviors. As an individual plays her cards, she might use a specific accent or wear a particular outfit to satisfy self-presentation goals that will be viewed positively by her peers.

The cards people select and the styles with which they choose to play the cards always reflect their cultural orientations. People want to be categorized into some group to obtain acceptance by that group, so people display their cultural orientations accordingly.

If I want to be viewed as a member of the hip-hop culture, what cards would I need in my deck, what styles would I use to discuss certain topics, what would I have to wear, and what accent would I need to use to present myself as a member of that culture? Gender membership asks the same questions. To be seen as male or female, what cards should I hold, how should I play them, and in which settings should I play them? We talk more about culture and gender later in the book.

A ♥

The cards people select and the styles with which they choose to play the cards always reflect their cultural orientations.

Contexts

Every time you play a card, you adjust to the **context**. Just as in Texas Hold-Em, you read the situation and figure out what game people are playing, what card you've been asked to play, and the rules for playing that card to accomplish your goals.

What are the elements you analyze? You look at the relationship between yourself and the other party to determine what style to use in covering the topic you play on your card. You scan for the amount of noise in the situation and adjust your card talk accordingly. If there's too much noise, you keep your play shorter or wait for a different situation. It is important to note that while you are playing cards, you are also creating context as you go. The longer a game goes on the rules for playing it become clearer.

Impacts

We have talked extensively about the impact of playing cards. The most visible **impact** of playing a card is **reciprocation**. Did the other person play the same card you played? Did this exchange satisfy your self-presentation, relational, and achievement goals? We tend to look first for evidence of these intended impacts.

We should also scan the environment for **unintended impacts**. For example, I might play a card to accomplish the self-presentation goal of being viewed as an authority on a subject. But the audience might not respond as intended.

I had a colleague who was perceived as attractive by many female students. Even though he played his Professor Card during lecture, it was obvious that some of the female students were not responding to that card. The point here is that controlling communication means having a *clear* idea about what goals you want to accomplish with your communication. Many people fail because they do not really know what impact they want their communications to achieve.

© 2012 by Zurijeta . Used under license of Shutterstock, Inc.

Chapter Summary

- A **talk card** is the package of messages communicated in playing a specific role. The message package consists of two elements: **content** and **style**. **Content** is the primary goal of the message or the topic you want the other person to understand. **Style** emphasizes and fills in meaning about the topic and establishes the relationship as being friendly (or unfriendly), formal (or informal), dominating (high power) or submissive (low power). Topic and style work together in the message package to play talk games.
- A **talk game** reflects the goal the messages are designed to accomplish. Winning a talk card game means that both parties accomplish their goals.
- A **card deck** is the set of cards we have available to play a talk card game at any given moment. We have both a personal deck and a professional deck of cards and we must develop both decks well to succeed as communicators.
- **We negotiate relationships as we talk.** If communicators agree on style choices as they talk, they are better able to win their communication games. If they disagree, it's difficult for them to achieve their goals.
- **Card play is reciprocal.** When someone plays a card, he or she is asking the intended message receiver to play a card that matches or goes along with the card played. In other words, card play is always reciprocal. The strategic question is whether the card you're asking the other person to play will help you accomplish your goals.

- **We choose talk cards and games to accomplish our goals.** When we communicate we set out to accomplish our identity goals (how we want others to think about us), our relational goals (how close we want to become), and our achievement goals (what task we want to accomplish).
- **The cards we create come from many sources.** We create cards to fit into our families, schools, and communities. They are influenced by our personalities and cultural orientations.
- **Card play has rules.** These rules both constitute the games we play (e.g., in our neighborhood this is how we trash talk) and regulate what plays are fair or foul (e.g., in our home, we don't swear).

Lessons Learned

Here are some key lessons from this chapter that should help you understand talk card games and play them effectively:

- **Understand what cards you have in your deck.** To play a role competently, the communicator needs a strong list of messages ready to go that others believe reflect that role. It is also important to have the right cards in your deck so you can switch talk games quickly and effectively.
- **Understand the game you're playing at all times.** By looking at the other's card and how he is playing it, you can guess the game he is playing. If it's a game you like, you can continue to play. Sometimes people pull card tricks and switch games. It is difficult to win if you aren't playing the right talk game.
- **Understand the cards you're asking the other person to play.** Remember, whenever you play a card, you're asking the other person to play a card. Is the card you're asking the other person to play going to help win your talk card game?
- **Understand the rules for playing that game.** Once the game becomes clear, a set of rules is established for how to play the game properly. When you play the game long enough, you understand the rules and how to bend them to give you a better chance of winning.
- **Try to win the game for both parties.** Ideally, communication is played as a cooperative event. The more you can approach communication with that goal, the more you can select cards and play games that help everyone accomplish their goals. Sometimes that's not possible, but we should work hard to do so.
- **Try to minimize noise in the communication process.** Concentrate on organizing the communication process so there is little noise or interference in getting your message across. The signal strength should be strong and noise minimal.

It is difficult to win consistently if you don't have good talk cards and don't know the rules for playing the game. This book walks you through a number of situations that present challenges to most people in daily life. Hopefully, you emerge from this book playing with a full deck and winning more games!

References

Dillard, J. P., Segrin, C., & Harden, J. M. (1989). Primary and secondary goals in the production of interpersonal influence messages. *Communication Monographs, 56*, 19–38.

Pearce, W. B. (1976). The coordinated management of meaning: A rules-based theory of interpersonal communication. In G. R. Miller (Ed.), *Explorations in interpersonal communication* (pp. 278–290). Oxford, UK: SAGE Publications.

Solomon, D. H., Dillard, J. P., & Anderson, J. W. (2002). Episode type, attachment orientation and frame salience: Evidence for a theory of relational framing. *Human Communication Research, 28*, 136–152.

© 2012 by Solaria/Shutterstock.com.

CHAPTER Two

Language Card Games

♣ Introduction

Have you ever met someone who you thought would display a specific ethnic style because of his or her skin color or appearance, yet the person could not use that style? I have talked with many students facing this challenge. They want to connect with other students who look like them physically, but those students won't readily accept them because they sound different—the accent, slang, and other elements of card talk style are just not there. Some students report that it takes a long time to become accepted by others with whom they do not share an ethnolinguistic heritage.

Language, in its broadest sense, is the tool we use to build our talk cards. The question is, How does language work? Let's begin to answer this question by talking about three interesting card games that illustrate key functions of language.

The Ethnic Proof Game

President Obama gives many speeches every day. For the most part he uses Standard English for his speeches without much linguistic variation that would hint at any particular ethnicity. Yet he is America's first African American president. Which ethnic card is he playing when he speaks? Is it a Euro-American Card, an African American Card, or some other card?

In a story that ran in a South Carolina newspaper, *The State*, during the 2008 presidential election, the Rev. Jesse Jackson sharply criticized Barak Obama for "acting like he's white." In a follow-up article, *Washington Post* (February 16, 2007) columnist Marjorie Valbrun expressed concern that others had accused Mr. Obama of not being "black enough." She argued that this accusation is narrow minded. While Rev. Jackson later apologized for his remarks, it suggests that some folks are expected to prove their ethnicity by showing an Ethnic Card.

The Small Talk Game

Later in this chapter we have some fun with gender differences in communication. In fact, we have a gender quiz to see if you understand gender biases in communication. One of the most difficult communication tasks for men is to engage in the Small Talk Game. This game, which women tend to like more than men, consists of simple topics about the events of the day with no particular goal in mind; it's all about sharing. Men typically don't play this game well because they are biased to believe that messages are reserved for accomplishing a specific goal like solving a problem or contributing an idea. When women share small talk men often check out and don't pay attention. In fact, many women will ask, "Are you listening to me?"

> Men don't play the Small Talk Game well because they are biased to believe that messages are reserved for accomplishing a specific goal.

The Factory Talk Game

I remember meeting my roommates in college for the first time. I had worked at a car factory that summer before coming to school, and I'd learned to cuss a lot. About every third or fourth word was the F-word in this particular factory. (It might be characteristic of how men talk to each other, but I'm sure women use this word a lot, too.) In the factory we would even split up words and put the F-word in the middle. On my first day in college I had just come from the factory floor the night before so I was still in factory talk mode. After using that same intense language during my first encounter with my roommates, one of them quickly remarked, "You sure swear a lot!" I had played my Factory Friend Card, a standard part of which included the F-word because swearing in the factory was how you acknowledged friends. I backed off and, from that point on, formulated a Roommate Card that did not include profanity.

♣ The Characteristics of Language

Each of the situations above involves some element of being misunderstood. I am sure you've been misunderstood in some card talk game. You thought you said one thing, but the other person thought you said something else entirely and responded in a manner you did not anticipate. Sometimes this happens when you try to be funny. Maybe you played a Friend Card by telling a new friend a joke that you previously told one of your old friends in a different situation. But the new friend didn't understand or appreciate the joke as you had intended.

One of the main reasons this kind of misunderstanding occurs is that we mistakenly assume that language holds objective meaning. Language isn't objective at all. Rather, the meaning we derive from language is personal and subjective, or more precisely, language is negotiated between communicators.

One of my colleagues and good friends is Dr. Scott Jacobs, a professor at the University of Illinois. Scott explains why misunderstanding often occurs in communication in a chapter he wrote on language and communication (Jacobs, 2002). He makes the point that meaning is one of the central problems in language. And for the other person's language to mean something or be sensible, we listen and fill in what is left unsaid.

For example, in playing the Small Talk Game, a friend might say, "Hey, what's up?" In listening to that comment you fill in what the friend really means. You might conclude that the person is playing a Friend Card by greeting you. The style is friendly and informal with low power. The person wants you to play your Friend Card in return. You conclude that your friend's intent is a simple greeting and not an attempt to learn everything about what's really up with you at that very minute. Your friend probably expects a short response like "Not much."

This filling-in process can get us in trouble when we don't fill in meaning correctly for the situation. Your friend might have been looking for a sympathetic response like "You look like something bad has just happened." If you didn't accurately interpret the greeting by listening carefully to the style of the greeting, then your friend might conclude that you don't care about him or her. Filling in meaning takes a lot of skill to listen not only superficially, but to really pay attention to subtle style choices by the message sender.

What this filling-in process suggests, according to Scott's chapter, is that we continuously build the meaning and significance of any given card talk exchange. Understanding his idea that the meaning of cards is co-created derives from what we know about the characteristics of language. This understanding is easier when you realize that language is symbolic, abstract, arbitrary, and conventional.

Language Is Symbolic

Language is a system of symbols we string together to create a picture in another person's mind. A symbol represents something else, like an object, person, idea, or place. Compare it to symbols on a road map. Maps provide a visual representation of some geography using symbols for roads, rivers, and airports to help us find our way. Words function in the same way.

For example, when Rev. Jackson characterized President Obama as "acting like he's white," he was trying to provide people with a map to navigate or understand Rev. Jackson's perceptions about then–candidate Obama. In every message each word has meaning, but when all the words are strung together in a sequence they create a symbolic map to help the recipient navigate the speaker's thoughts.

© 2012 by sonia.eps. Used under license of Shutterstock, Inc.

Do your words always help the recipient navigate your thoughts as precisely as you intend? Almost everyone has had the experience of raising a topic that ends up triggering an unintended reaction. Afterward, we wonder if we should have created a different map to the ideas bouncing around in our heads. Humanity has gone to great lengths to build all kinds of symbolic maps from cave drawings and biblical scrolls to the Declaration of Independence. Each of their creators intended to create a language map that presented some important ideas.

Language Is Contextual

In his chapter Dr. Jacobs makes the point that formulating the meaning of any message is always bound by the context in which the message is received. Every message is delivered and received at a particular point in time, through a specific medium (e.g., in a text or in person) while we're in a specific location doing something.

Context is an important consideration of card play. If you select the wrong talk card, you risk offending people and undermining your communication goal. For example, playing a Comic Card at a funeral would be offensive. The same card played at a party would be applauded. This logic applies to topic and style choices as well. Any card you play or any card you ask someone else to play for any card game must be appropriate to the context or situation.

Language Is Abstract

As a symbol system, language uses letters and words to represent ideas in our heads or things in the physical world, such as baseball, hot dogs, apple pie, and Chevrolet. These **referents** name the ideas or thoughts we have about the external world. They're what we use to build our maps for people when we play our talk cards. Referents essentially tag our psychological or emotional thoughts and feelings when we infuse our topics with style elements. To communicate my interest in fitting in at the summer factory job, I would go over to the guys and say in a casual way, "How the F is everybody?" Each of these style elements chosen to communicate liking from the tone of voice to the inclusion of the F-word is a referent. Each style element puts a behavioral tag on the speaker's emotions as the message seeks to build a map to help the listener explore the speaker's psychological world.

Language is **abstract** because it refers to things we can't see or point to. Abstractness is a useful characteristic of language. What would happen if we couldn't refer to "love," for example? Of course, when you play the Love Game with your Boyfriend or Girlfriend Card, you need to express your love in many abstract ways. The abstractness of language allows you to express these concepts even though they have no referent you can touch, not in the way I can touch a computer or this book.

Another reason language is abstract is that symbols can refer to any number of specific referents in a whole class of items. For example, the symbol B-O-O-K can refer both to the novel I just purchased and to any novel of any size in any location. This aspect of abstraction is the source of many misunderstandings. People confuse whether our referent indicates one specific thing or a general group.

When a woman is playing her Girlfriend Card and playing the Small Talk Game with her boyfriend, men often interpret that game as something other than it is. They might hear it as a Need Advice Game and interrupt the small talk just to solve her problems. Sometimes the woman will say, "I'm just talking—no need to respond." There might need to be some talk about clarifying the game because for the man it might be too abstract.

> A♥ Any card you play or any card you ask someone else to play must be appropriate to the context or situation. A♠

Language Is Arbitrary

Because language is symbolic, it is necessarily **arbitrary**, but that makes it flexible. The symbols that we conventionally assign to objects, people, or ideas are given to us by tradition without any objective rule for its assignment. My coffee cup could have easily been called C-H-A-I-R rather than C-U-P. The French word for cup is T-A-S-S-E. Which is correct? All symbols are correct if everyone agrees that the symbols represent the objects. After all, the symbols were chosen arbitrarily in the first place to represent their respective objects, feelings, and ideas.

This flexibility is valuable because people are free to name things or emotions as they wish and make up new labels if they don't like the old ones. If the new label catches on, that's great and it becomes a better term than the old one. Tweet used to refer to a bird's sound, but now it also refers to a Twitter post. Of course, the downside of this flexibility is that there is no necessary connection between a symbol and its referent, thus no objective way to make sure that symbols mean only one thing. Some people have tried to develop a universal language with objective meaning, but all attempts have failed.

By using the term "white" to characterize then–candidate Obama, Rev. Jackson was using a term that could mean a range of things to many people. It was an abstract term to refer to some nebulous cultural concept held by Rev. Jackson. The key point, once again, is to ensure that when communicating an idea, the listener understands it in the way it was intended to be understood. Feedback is the check for that.

Language Is Conventional

Remember that symbol referents are given to us because of the history of language. It is through convention that certain symbols refer to certain things or ideas. A **convention**, or **norm**, is a pattern of behavior that we implicitly agree to follow. In the case of language, we agree to call a referent by a given name. For example, let's refer to the act of talking for 10 minutes in front of a group of students as S-P-E-A-K-I-N-G. We certainly could call it D-O-I-N-K-I-N-G, but we don't. These conventions can change dramatically over time. As another example, the word "gay" used to refer to a lively, happy, exciting event. Now it refers most commonly to sexual orientation.

> The key point is to ensure that when communicating an idea, the listener understands it in the way it was intended to be understood.

The problem with convention is that when immigrant Americans acquire English as a second language, they typically learn only the formal English conventions in their homelands. They don't learn slang, or idiomatic communication, until they spend some time with native speakers. **Slang** is the unique language that friends, groups, or societies create that has meanings unique to those groups. It's fun to make up words for old ideas or objects.

We used slang all the time in the factory and made-up words constantly. We used to call anyone who was not a native English speaker a honyak. I am not sure what that referred to, but it was a made-up word. Of course, when you play a card using slang, it is important to know that the other person is likely to understand the referent for the unique symbol attached to the slang. Otherwise, misunderstandings are likely to occur.

The take-away from this discussion is that because language is symbolic, it is necessarily abstract, arbitrary, and conventional. That makes it fun to play with, but also frustrating. Choose your language wisely when you play your talk cards. Pick terms and styles that make sense to the person or people with whom you're playing.

♣ The Talk Elements of Language

These foregoing five characteristics of language provide the framework for creating our talk cards. Now let's descend from those abstract, tall trees for a moment and get closer to the ground. Let's explore the specific elements of language that form the building blocks of messages we assemble on our cards.

Phonetics

One of the first elements of our language that becomes apparent to others when we play a talk card is **phonetics**, or the sounds we produce when speaking. The English language consists of 26 letters, but about 44 sounds. For example, five of the six vowels can be either short or long. The letter "a" can be pronounced as a short sound as in the word cat, or in its long sound as in the word cane. Standard and nonstandard English uses different sounds, and they are important to use in proving one's ethnic identity, for example.

Semantics

A second key element of language that impacts how we play our cards is **semantics**. It refers to the *meaning* of a specific sound or word. This is an important issue for how topics and styles combine to form a message when a card is played because it relates to the issue of understanding. In fact, there is a field called general semantics devoted to repairing or preventing misunderstandings by discovering how words distort or complicate meanings.

> The key in crafting a message from any card is ensuring the meaning of each word has the intended impact on the receiver.

The key in crafting a message from any card is ensuring that the meaning of each word has the intended impact on the receiver. Will that person interpret the words you use in the way you want them to be interpreted? The first step in building confidence that you will be heard as intended is learning as much as possible about the receiver's message filters. What are the filters that impact meaning?

Upon hearing or reading messages, receivers evaluate them from their subjective positions. They apply their attitudes (like or dislike the message), values (this is a good or bad message), beliefs (this is a true or false message), and knowledge levels (here's what I know about this message) to the job of understanding your message. More knowledge about receivers means you can tailor a card talk message that is more likely to be interpreted accurately by them.

Think for a moment how difficult it is for some men to understand women. Much has been written about this topic, and we explore it later in the chapter. Understanding each other's message filters is usually difficult, particularly when someone is from another cultural orientation.

Complicating this already difficult task is that meaning is broken into small units. The smallest semantic unit of language is called a **morpheme**. Morphemes are units of meaning that can either stand alone or are attached to words to clarify their meaning.

For example, prefixes and suffixes change the meaning of a word. The word "call" can be changed by adding -ed. The word "called" now means that the calling occurred in the past. The prefix dis- changes the meaning of a word by negating it. "Dissatisfied" means that satisfaction did not occur. How many morphemes are in the word "unbeatable?" The first is un-, a bound morpheme (bound to the meaning of the word "beat"), "beat," which is a free, standalone morpheme, and "able" which is a bound morpheme and a suffix. The word unbeatable has three morphemes.

Such subtle features of language as morphemes are typically taken for granted. We use them all the time when we play with verb tense or even when we make a nonverbal gesture while saying a word. If I wink at my friend while making an insulting comment about his outfit, maybe I want to tell him that I am joking or teasing him about the outfit. The wink is a nonverbal morpheme but adds a great deal to the semantic meaning of the comment, and transforms it from an insult to a joke.

Syntax

A third element of language is syntax, or how we assemble morphemes into strings that most often form sentences. **Syntax** is the process of chunking language into meaningful clumps. We use punctuation for that chunking job. For example, my son showed me a photo he found online with a group of baby seals apparently dancing at a nightclub. The caption under the photo read "Stop clubbing, baby seals." Without the comma (Stop clubbing baby seals.), the caption is a protest against hunters clubbing and killing baby seals for their pelts.

Adding the comma changes the syntax of the caption. Instead of a protest sign, the photo becomes a funny play on words.

One of my other favorite examples of syntax changes is a sign outside a motel pool that read: Private. No swimming allowed! Someone had changed the punctuation of the sign with a black marker to read: Private? No. Swimming allowed. Instead of a warning sign, the syntax changes, brought about by punctuation, converted the sign to an invitation! That's a clever change, but it illustrates both how flexible language is, and how important punctuation and syntax are to the meaning of our card talk messages.

Pragmatics

The final element of language is **pragmatics**, which focuses on the work we want the messages to perform. We often think about pragmatics in terms of achievement goals. In writing this book I want to play my Professor Card to inform you about some key communication ideas. If you play your Student Card and dutifully absorb this riveting information, then the message is viewed pragmatically as a lecture. In other words, it's the label we apply to the message that defines the pragmatic purpose the message is trying to accomplish.

♣ Standard and Nonstandard Card Talk

One of the first judgments people make when listening to a card being played is whether it is standard or nonstandard English. Is the speaker presenting standard or nonstandard phonetic, phonemic, syntactic, and pragmatic elements of language when playing a card? The Ethnic Proof Game is a good example of how these judgments impact the perceptions of others. In his admonition that candidate Obama was "not black enough," was Rev. Jackson really saying that he believed Obama did not use enough nonstandard speech to validate his black ethnicity? **Standard English**, like the kind of language you might hear on a TV news report, is crisply enunciated, does not include slang, and is delivered in carefully modulated tones. Standard English is so labeled because it is the social gauge for achieving "perfect" language use.

Nonstandard English typically involves other dialects of English. For example, in the United States, we can distinguish Southern English, East Coast English, Midwestern English, Latino English, and Ebonics (an American urban dialect). These dialects are language systems in their own rights, but are governed by syntactic, semantic, and phonemic rules that differ in identifiable ways from Standard English.

It is important not to confuse standard vs. nonstandard English with clear communication. In many communities speaking standard English would be confusing and would hinder understanding. The opposite is also the case: Nonstandard English can introduce a lot of noise into the system. The point is, the extent to which the language facilitates connection and understanding with the receiver, not the form the language takes.

As we know from the Ethnic Proof Game, people attribute a great deal of significance to the language forms that people use. For many groups, applying a label to one kind of language as the standard of perfection sets up an inevitable comparison. The implication here is that those who speak the nonstandard version of a language may be labeled as nonstandard people. This is precisely what happens in social interaction. Research shows that we feel greater trust for others whose speaking style is similar to our own. Therefore, it is a natural and perhaps unconscious response to mistrust or even dislike those who speak differently.

The goal of playing a nonstandard card to others who use the same dialect is self-presentation. The dialect is a key element in demonstrating membership in that language community. Problems arise when people cross these language communities and try to play talk cards with different styles. When the language used in that talk card is perceived as different, it can result in negative judgments or racism, sexism, and class distinctions, all of which get in the way of successful communication. On the other hand, playing a card displaying nonstandard language adds to the cultural diversity of any given communication experience.

♣ Four Theories of Language

Language scholars have developed several useful theories to explain how we decide what language to use in playing cards. For example, do you recall Dr. W. Barnett Pierce's **Theory of the Coordinated Management of Meaning** from chapter 1? It describes how communicators interpret messages when we play various cards. The theory explains that:

1. Over time, as people exchange messages, they develop norms about what talk is acceptable or unacceptable when a card is played.
2. These norms evolve into card talk rules about what messages mean (constitutive rules) and which card talk topics and styles are acceptable (regulative rules).
3. People use these rules to coordinate their talk or synchronize their interaction.

Does this theory sound familiar? It describes the process laid out in the last chapter about how card games develop rules. The smart card player understands the rules and then tries to change them to present topics and styles that are needed in any given situation to win the talk game.

The student supervisor example is relevant here. That student needed to negotiate with the employee-supervisor about what cards should be played to deal with the special time-off request. The supervisor needed to play her Supervisor Card, while also acknowledging the Friend Card. Negotiating these rules to regulate the conversation and turn it from a Casual Conversation Game into a Job Talk Game is tricky but important to understand.

Another important principle is the **Symbolic Interactionism Theory**. Developed by sociologist Dr. Herbert Blumer and others, this theory explains the role of language in how we come to know or define ourselves. The theory says that:

1. In the process of learning our native language, we also learn our culture's values through the special meanings that our parents and teachers assign to symbols.
2. As we use language we see how others react to us and develop a sense of ourselves as others see us. In other words, we use feedback from receiver as a kind of mirror to see what we look like as we're communicating.

A♥ The smart card player understands the rules and negotiates them to present topics needed to win the talk game. A♥

3. We rely on significant others in our lives to give us the most important feedback that we take to heart in defining ourselves in particular ways.

As we play cards and see how others play in response to us, we begin to understand who we are—we establish an identity, or self-concept. The key is that we rely on significant others, such as parents, friends, or coaches to establish that self-awareness. Next time you are around someone who significantly influences you, notice how you pay more attention to the talk cards that person plays in response to yours.

A third principle of language that bears discussion is **Communication Accommodation Theory**. For years, my colleague Dr. Howard Giles and his associates have explored the issues of synchrony and dissynchrony discussed in the last chapter, and why people are more or less motivated to converge their communications (Gallois, Ogay, & Giles, 2005; defined below).

© 2012 by Charles Knox Photo. Used under license of Shutterstock, Inc.

Accommodation means matching or synchronizing with one another's conversational partners in speed, tone, volume, pitch, rhythm, profanity use, and formal or informal language. The theory says that:

1. When we play the same cards and discuss the same topics with similar styles we are **converging**. We are **diverging** when we intentionally play different cards or select different topics to accomplish some goal. And, we are **maintaining** when we keep our own style because we can't shift our communication for some reason.
2. The more we rely on our own language community for our identity, norms, and values, the more we tend to **diverge** or **maintain**, particularly with "outsiders," because diverging and maintaining emphasizes our identity to outsiders.
3. People tend to diverge more when they (a) perceive their language community is under attack, (b) use language as a show of strength, or (c) show solidarity with their community.
4. When we are less dependent on our own language group for our identity or when we see our conversational partner more as an individual (than as a representative of some outside group), we are more likely to converge with that person to establish common ground.

These accommodation concepts were definitely in play in the Factory Talk Game. By changing my language to cuss a great deal when I played my Friend Card, I was converging into my own factory language group. Since I did this all summer it was difficult for me to break out of the habit when I went to college. It took a while to make the full switch.

The fourth and final principle of language that in many ways encompasses the other three language theories is the **Code Switching Theory**. We know from the coordinated management of meaning theory that, as we interact with someone, we coordinate our talk and over time build constitutive and regulative rules that govern which topics and styles are acceptable or unacceptable in any given situation. These rules ultimately create a look and feel to the language we are creating called a **code**.

Skillful code-switchers reach their communication goals more often because their ability to code-switch makes them more flexible.

The basic features of the theory are:

1. Codes develop over time in language communities (like my summer job) and situationally (like telling a joke in the factory).
2. When we want to change goals while communicating, we might switch the code (diverging, according to Communication Accommodation Theory). For example, when lecturing on an important topic as I play my Professor Card, I might switch the code and play a Friend Card to reengage listeners in the topic. After all, too much professor talk can be boring, as most students know.
3. Skillful code-switchers reach their communication goals more often because their ability to code-switch makes them more flexible. They have a greater range of communication strategies to employ across social situations.
4. Code-switching should not be confused with insincerity. Rather, it should be seen as evidence that we know how to adapt to our listeners' needs. We know when to converge, when to diverge, and when to maintain. We have greater control over the messages and the impact of our messages.

♣ Gender and Language

Are you aware of any language differences between men and women? Research tells us there are male and female language codes—or typical ways that men and women use language. We can call them Male and Female Cards. Let's see if you can distinguish between Girl and Boy Cards. Here are two Facebook wall postings: Can you tell which was written by a teen boy and which from a teen girl?

1. "Seriously, countdown to p's and c's!? We can even skip our birthday haha, and it can be March madness/spring training tomorrow, I'd be more than fine."
2. "Hey. I'm good. Working a lot and hopping around different TV shows. Its fun. Just looking for that break. It's good to hear from you and I hope the job search goes well."

These are two of my students, both older teens. Break down the code. Notice there are grammatical errors in these two postings because that's what you get on Facebook walls. So which one is male and which one is female? If you look at the first entry, the topics include p's and c's (whatever those are), birthdays, March Madness, and baseball spring training. Now look at the style elements on display in the first posting. Look at the use of the words "seriously" to begin and "haha" in the middle. These communicate high liking and informality, and low power. Are boys or girls more likely to use this language?

Contrast the second posting with the first. Notice that the second posting begins with the expression "Hey. I'm good." Would a boy or girl be more likely to say that? What about the topics? In the second posting, the person is talking about hopping around different TV shows. Is that more male or female?

The first posting is from a young teen-aged female and the second from a young male. The point is that every person carries a gender card to tell others how they would like their gender to be displayed. If we could see the parties, they would give us even more clues as to their gender. If you look at Facebook, can you notice any differences between the way females display pictures from males? Is the dress any different, are there more people in the photos—what are they doing in the photos?

Two communication professor friends, Drs. Dan Canary and Kathryn Dindia, edited a book on sex differences and similarities in communication (Canary & Dindia, 1998). They point out that sometimes men and women talk alike, particularly if their status and social roles are similar. Other issues such as the goals of the communicators and to whom they're talking also tend to wash out differences between the sexes.

© 2012 by Darrin Henry. Used under license of Shutterstock, Inc.

Of course, in many homes there is little differentiation between male and female talk. Perhaps a female might come from a home with all boys or from a home promoting little or no gender differences. Perhaps you know people who cannot play their gender cards. They can't "talk like a girl," or "talk like a guy." While you may know people who don't hold Man and Woman Cards, most people carry a gender card and play it on a regular basis.

To see how much you know about gender cards, complete this quiz. Below are a number of findings from various sources about gender communication trends. Indicate whether you believe that the trends are True or False.

Results:

Here are the answers to the quiz. If you got four or more wrong, you'll need to attend gender re-education camp!

1. **False.** Men like to focus on topics and styles of communication aimed at asserting themselves, establishing their identity, and making sure people know who they are and what they know. Women, on the other hand, have different goals. They select topics and styles aimed at showing interest in others, learning about their needs, and responding to those needs.

2. **False.** Men are more likely to bring up topics that focus on competition as a way to prove themselves, gain attention from others, and interrupt others to keep topics focused on them. Women select more cooperative topics by inviting others into the conversation, following up on their topics, and responding to what others say.

3. **False.** Men believe that talk should accomplish something, such as solving a problem, giving advice, or taking a stand on issues. Men believe small talk is boring and stupid, so they often tune out with these topics. Women are more likely to bring up topics that deal with feelings, personal ideas, and problems. They believe talk should be used to build relationships with others. Women believe small talk is good because it both reveals and solidifies the relationship.

4. **False.** At work, women select different communication partners than men. Men communicate with the boss as much as possible to establish their identity. They select more business-related topics, again to compete—to move up the ladder. Women select more personal topics, and seek out other women who value these topics regardless of their relative roles in the company. Consequently, women are more likely to engage in personal communication with subordinates and peers at work.

5. **False.** Men believe that activities are the foundation of close friendships and romantic relationships. They like to cement friendships by doing things together (playing or watching sports) and doing things for one another (trading favors, washing a car, doing laundry). For women, close friendships and romantic relationships are all about the talk. That is, talk is not only a means to an end, but an end in itself. Topics focusing on feelings, personal issues, and daily life are the way women build and continuously enrich relationships.

6. **False.** First, men don't like to talk about troubles because it shows weakness. If they do, the goal of the talk is to search for solutions. Men are socialized to use messages as tools to accomplish specific goals so they tend to offer advice or solutions. Thus, women often interpret men's advice as communicating lack of personal concern. Men are often frustrated if they hear empathy and support instead of solutions. In contrast, women like to talk about what's troubling them because they want to validate their feelings about these issues. So the first thing women look for when discussing problems is empathy and connection—old-fashioned listening and not necessarily advice.

7. **False.** Men prefer to disclose infrequently. The rule is, Keep your issues to yourself. Men don't want to look weak or powerless to solve their own problems. For women, the rule is, Disclose often. Sharing confidences is an important way to enhance closeness.

8. **False.** Men are silent listeners—women are noisy listeners. Women tend to make listening noises such as "hmm," "yeah," and "I know what you mean," while others talk to show interest. However, the listening noises don't necessarily mean agreement. For men the rule is, Be quiet while listening." Affirming isn't part of the listening contract. Men often misinterpret women's listening noises as indicating agreement (versus attention) and are surprised if women later disagree with their ideas.

9. **False.** Men perceive that the "relationship" is the woman's job or concern, so it's not a topic men want on their cards. For men, the rule is, Let's not talk about us. Talking about *us* means trouble or a problem to be resolved. If you want to be close, let's *do* something together. If there is a problem, the man will wait for her to bring it up. Men often don't understand that for women the rule is, Let's talk about us. This means, Let's celebrate and increase closeness. But if there is a problem women believe they must take the lead in resolving it because the men simply won't. They'll ignore it.

10. **False.** Women touch people to show liking and intimacy. Women are often socialized to be deferential and nice to others, which explains why some women don't voice objections to unwanted touching. Men touch people to assert power and control. In fact, research indicates that parents touch sons less often and more roughly than they touch daughters.

11. **False.** Men talk about twice as much as women in mixed-sex dyads (two-persons). In fact, a woman who talks for more than one-third of the available time may be regarded by others as talking too much. Men assert their power by talking more.

12. **False.** Women are more likely to overlap one another's speech than men are. Women highly value cooperation and collaboration in their conversations. For men, overlapping is seen as interrupting. Remember, talk is not necessarily a cooperative act. It is an opportunity to assert identity.

13. **False.** Women are more likely to use hedges, or words that "dilute" an assertion by saying things like "sort of," "like," "I think," or "kind of." They also use words that hedge their certainty about a concept, such as saying "should," "could," "would," "may," or "might." In contrast, men are less likely to hedge or qualify their speech, or ask permission to be certain in their speech like using the word "OK" at the end of a sentence.

14. **False.** Women are more likely to discuss personal topics in more detail than men as a way to get people more involved in their lives. Men speak in general terms. They move more sequentially through points, which is more formal and less intimate, while reinforcing the conversational goal of information exchange rather than relationship development.

15. **False.** Women give orders differently than men. Women often soften their demands and statements. Women tend to use tag phrases, such as "If you don't mind" or "Don't you think?" following a comment or request. Men are more direct and less tentative in their communication than women. It doesn't mean the person is bossier or feels superior; the style is simply different.

16. **False.** Women are more likely to give praise than men and are more likely to use it before giving bad news. Women are frustrated when male managers are slow to give praise.

♣ Summary of Gender Findings

Topic Differences

So what have we learned about the contents of each person's gender card? First, men and women prefer to include different topics on their cards. Women like to talk about feelings, personal issues, and daily life—topics that build more comprehensive relationships. By extension, this relational talk also includes discussions about personal troubles or challenges. Of course, men want to avoid talking about troubles since they don't want to seem weak and incapable of handling these challenges.

Women want to disclose personal issues and they expect others to reciprocate. That means they also want more specifics on topics. Men, on the other hand, want to be more general about personal issues, since going deeply into them is too "touchy-feely." Women like topics of general interest across people's lives; men want to focus on specific problems or issues to use communication as a problem-solving tool.

Style Differences

Second, men and women differ on the styles they use to present their topics. Women appear to have a wider range of ways to express liking. They will touch more, listen more actively, and show more expressions of approval and praise. They typically show more excitement than men.

Regarding formality, men are more formal listeners—they don't provide much verbal or nonverbal feedback when listening. In contrast, women are more responsive listeners. They give noisy feedback and overlap one another's speech to add informality to the situation. Men are more formal in how they organize conversation. Men move sequentially through points as a way to use communication to solve a problem while looking like a strong contributor.

© 2012 by Dmitriy Shironosov. Used under license of Shutterstock, Inc.

Power differences among the sexes are apparent. For example, even when men are the minority in a meeting or conversation, they are more likely to dominate the interaction by talking more (again, in mixed-sex interactions) and interrupting more. They want their topics to take precedence. Women often form habits that *project* a lower-power status. They hedge their thoughts and are more tentative in conversation. They try to soften bad news first with praise as a way to be less superior and more conscious of the other's feelings.

Don't Overgeneralize

It's important to recognize that these general findings from communication research do not apply to everyone. As we know from the Canary and Dindia book, there is tremendous variability in each person's gender card. In fact, men and women can exchange gender cards with women talking like men and vice-versa. Or people can adopt features of another person's card as they wish. Listening to how individuals communicate as they interact with one another is the best way to determine whether individuals have and play a Male or Female Gender Card.

Chapter Summary

- **Language is the raw material** we use to construct our messages in card talk. The trick in using language is to make sure your language is being interpreted as you intended, to produce the result you want.

- **Language has many characteristics.** It is symbolic, contextually bound, abstract, arbitrary, conventional, and subjective. Because of these characteristics, the good news is that language is flexible. It lets you say what you want in an infinite number of ways. The bad news is that there are also an infinite number of ways to *interpret* what you say. That leaves a lot of room for misunderstanding and not connecting with your message receiver.

- **Language has many structural components.** Phonetics is the sound component of language; semantics refers to the meaning component; syntax focuses on how symbols are strung together; pragmatics deals with what we want the language strings to accomplish. Every message contains these components, and we are successful only if we know how to manage each of these components.

- **Language exists in both standard and nonstandard forms.** The form that most people use in any society is the standard form, and any other form is called nonstandard. Both forms are useful for displaying certain cards that might be effective to play in winning your talk card game. An ethnic card generally displays nonstandard topics and styles.

- **There are many theories of language.** Some theories talk about how we create, coordinate, and synchronize the meaning of our language choices. Others describe how we use language to develop our social identities. The point is that understanding how language works helps us make better card talk decisions as we communicate.

- **Gender matters.** Sometimes there are significant differences in how males and females play their talk cards, and sometimes there are few differences. These changes depend on the role and status of the communicators, their specific goals, the context of the interaction, and the target of their messages. It's best to think of gender from a cultural perspective. Sometimes men and women create different cultural orientations that impact how they relate to one another.

Lessons Learned

Here are the lessons you should have learned from this chapter about language use as it pertains to card talk:

- **Meanings are in people, not words.** Thus, we must strive to use more concrete, not more abstract language when playing our cards. Concrete language tries to directly identify a referent, whereas abstract language uses generalities. Remember, the style part of your card consists of nonverbal communication cues, as well. Can you keep those concrete to avoid misinterpretation?

- **Check your perceptions to be sure you've understood what the speaker intended.** This is a key lesson because it will help you interpret the card the other is playing and the card the other is asking you to play.

- **Consider how your language lines up behind your goals.** We are always sending messages about our self-presentation and our relational and achievement goals. Are you creating impressions of yourself and sending relational signals consistent with your achievement goals? Using language inconsistent with your goals can cause others to play card games you don't want them to play.
- **Changing to more inclusive language can expand our perceptions of the world.** Therefore, we should be open to new ways of expressing ideas. Experimenting with new terminology for events, people, groups, and other phenomena expands what we have on our cards while asking others to expand their perceptions of the world. It can also increase our sensitivity to the perceptions of others.
- **Be aware of the rules in play** at any given point in time and how they impact your card games. Language is a code system governed by rules and norms. As explained in chapter 3, norms are usually situationally determined. Procedural knowledge tells you how to handle yourself in particular situations. Increase your sensitivity to procedural norms by watching others.
- **Be aware of the biases, judgments, and stereotypes** you apply to the language you use. Everyone is biased in some fashion, because we all have preferences for certain kinds of speech, different kinds of people, or communicating in different situations. The danger when we communicate is that we are unaware of our biases and unwilling to be flexible. That can result in negative stereotyping, which is thinking someone is inferior because they're different.

References

Blumer, H. (1969). *Symbolic interactionism.* Englewood Cliffs, NJ: Prentice Hall.

Canary, D. J., & Dindia, K. (1998). *Sex differences and similarities in communication: Critical essays and empirical investigations of sex and gender in interaction.* Mahwah, NJ: Lawrence Erlbaum Associates.

Gallois, C., Ogay, T., & Giles, H. (2005). Communication accommodation theory: A look back and a look ahead. In W. Gudykunst (Ed.), *Theorizing about intercultural communication* (pp. 121–148). Thousand Oaks, CA: SAGE Publications.

Jacobs, S. (2002). Language and interpersonal communication. In M. Knapp & J. Daly (Eds.), *Handbook of interpersonal communication* (pp. 213–239). Thousand Oaks, CA: SAGE Publications.

Culture Card Games

♣ Introduction

If you looked up Hip-Hop Culture in *Wikipedia*, in 2012 you found this graffiti from Eugene, Oregon. *Wikipedia* describes hip-hop as a cultural movement growing from the working class communities in New York City in the late 1970s. According to the entry, one of the movement's founders, DJ Afrika Bambaataa, outlined five pillars of hip-hop, including MCing, DJing, breaking, graffiti writing, and knowledge. Other elements are beatboxing, hip-hop fashion, and slang. The movement began as an expression of African American urban life through language, art, music, politics, fashion, and technology. What began as an urban cultural expression spread throughout the United States and now extends worldwide through rap music, movies, and dress.

Do you know this culture? Have you ever tried to build it into your life, or would you rather escape from it? I like talking about hip-hop culture because it has endured, grown, and become interesting and influential. It tells us a great deal about how culture works, directs our lives, and most important for our purposes, exemplifies key principles of card talk.

Remember in chapter 2 focusing on language that we talked about standard and nonstandard English and the Ethnic Proof Game? Every card we play seeks to tell the other person how we want to be labeled culturally and socially. These parts of our cards help with our self-presentation goals. We want to be seen in a particular way to help us fit into some groups and separate ourselves from others. Over time, we create an identity, or self-concept, that forms the beliefs and attitudes about ourselves needed to sustain membership in this group. This identity issue is the subject of chapter 4. For now, let's dive into this idea about culture to better understand its influence on card talk.

♣ Culture Card Talk Games

A♥

They didn't understand each other's cultural orientations, and were unable to play the same kind of talk game to a successful conclusion.

A♠

The Business Negotiation Game

Because business deals often span continents, it's common for cultures to clash during negotiations. Much has been written about U.S. businesspeople trying to negotiate with Chinese or Japanese businesspeople. Before they developed some savvy in the international Business Negotiation Game, American businesspeople would fly to Japan and begin meeting with Japanese executives looking to close a deal. U.S. businesspeople are accustomed to completing deals within two weeks or less, with intense negotiations over complex details.

Yet the Japanese, being people who enjoy the process, are more flexible with deadlines and prefer to get to know their partners thoroughly before making a business deal. Consequently, while the U.S. people pushed for greater detail and immediate results, the Japanese delayed and wanted instead to focus only on the big picture, with a closing handshake instead of a contract.

In card talk terms, the Americans played their Executive Cards differently in the Business Meeting Game while the Japanese reciprocated with the Get Acquainted Game. At the beginning, they didn't understand each other's cultural orientations and were unable to play the same kind of talk game to a successful conclusion.

The Trust Game

This same kind of game mismatch can occur when people from more task- and relationship-based cultures try to work together. For example, police agencies are often relationship-focused cultures. Police stick together to function as a team to deal with crises that might threaten the community. To be trusted, officers must earn their way into the police fraternity. Outsiders are not trusted immediately and must earn their way in.

I remember the first time I tried to work with a police agency on a project. I played my Professor Card thinking they would be interested in my ideas. But while I was playing the Business Meeting Game, they were engaged in the Trust Game. Playing their Police Cards, they were listening to me and trying to determine if I could be trusted. They were not particularly interested in my ideas at that point. If I'd understood their culture well enough to recognize the Trust Game, I would have approached the project differently. I would have gotten to know them first in a social setting, persuading an insider to vouch for me and be my sponsor, thereby showing my support for police culture. I've worked successfully with police agencies many times since that first culture clash, but I'll always remember the lessons learned from it.

The Culture Test Game

Can you prove you're a member of the cultural group that most defines you? If your entire college experience is focused on being an athlete, then you probably dress in athletic clothes every day and hang out with other athletes. You're also expected to walk and talk like an athlete specific to your chosen sport. What you're doing is showing off your Athlete Card. You want to clearly label yourself as belonging to a specific culture.

Think of this process as a test. How can you "prove" you're a member of a specific culture—the athlete culture, for example? What tests would you give someone to prove membership? Perhaps knowing how to dress, discuss certain sports topics, or walk in a particular way would be sufficient to pass your test.

Other membership tests relate to how outsiders view the athlete culture. If an outsider can easily view you as an athlete, then your membership status is solidified. Once you've been labeled an athlete, one of the first things people probably ask you about is your sport. They want to talk about the team, so they ask you to play your Athlete Card. They tend not to ask you to play your Student Card and do not inquire about your major, when you will graduate, or what kind of job you want.

The Fit In Game

Unfortunately, sometimes being able to pass these culture tests has significant consequences. Perhaps you have had the challenge of trying to fit in somewhere and found it challenging. To illustrate the Fit In Game, I'll tell you about a new freshman from Somalia who came to my office hours. I asked how he arrived from Somalia to attend classes at Michigan State University. He began by telling me that in Somalia he belonged to the minority tribe that held little power and was persecuted constantly by the major-

ity tribal leaders. There was no central government in Somalia capable of protecting anyone. One day when he was about 6 years old, members from the majority tribe came to his small house. They dragged away his father and older brothers, never to be seen again. That day his mother decided they should escape to neighboring Kenya or they would suffer a similar fate. They walked hundreds of miles through hostile territory, finally reaching Nairobi, Kenya, where they stayed with a relative in a small hut with a dirt floor. They wanted to avoid the local refugee camp, which was dangerous.

To survive in Nairobi, this young man had to play the Fit In Game. He had to look and talk like a Kenyan and not a Somali, or he would be tossed into the refugee camp or worse. He had to quickly learn Swahili, the official language of Kenya, and use a Kenyan accent. He had to pass this intense culture test every day. When he turned 13, his mother got together enough money to smuggle him into Canada via the United States. He arrived in Chicago with the smuggler, and took a bus headed for Canada and safe haven with a distant relative. While he was sleeping in the Detroit bus terminal, the smuggler abandoned him. There he was, alone, 13 years old, no money, in a dangerous area at night, and with only a smattering of English he had picked up in Kenya. Again, he was faced with having to rapidly fit in and pass even more difficult culture tests, or face deportation back to Somalia.

After spending time in a homeless shelter in Detroit for a couple of years, my student was informally adopted by a teacher at a school he was attending. He was able to stay with that family until graduating from high school. He was ultimately voted president of his senior class, graduated with honors, and received a scholarship to Michigan State. Imagine the Fit In Games he had to play to become successful in school! Not only did he need to learn English, he had to make friends and continue his education in a new language.

His inspiring story of survival and success is first and foremost a testament to his courage and his mother's courage, guidance, and caring. He used this foundation to make the **knowledge and relational and communicative transitions** necessary to adapt fully to his new country and its cultures. He learned how to communicate to pass many culture tests and survive in precarious life-and-death situations in Africa, and how to thrive in new, yet difficult academic and social situations when he ended up in Michigan. A key to his success was playing his talk cards well enough to fit in and quickly adapt to his many new environments.

♣ Culture Defined

The word culture is often overused as a way to explain human behavior in general and the evolution of interpersonal relationships specifically. To better understand its role in card talk, we turn to the classic text written on the subject by two of my colleagues, Drs. Bill Gudykunst and Stella Ting-Toomey. In their book *Culture and Interpersonal Communication*, they define culture as a system of knowledge (i.e., attitudes, beliefs, values, and behaviors) shared by a group of people over a long period of time.

This definition suggests that culture exists in two places. First, culture is an internal, psychological force, a system of knowledge we carry around in our heads daily. Second, culture is an external, behavioral force displayed through our actions, what we wear, how we speak, and how we live. As we share these actions with one another, our cultural knowledge is constantly reinforced and altered at the same time. The English language is a good example. We use it to express our cultural orientations, but we are constantly adding words and expressions to our card play as a creative way to strengthen our culture.

Over time this shared cultural knowledge creates a set of rules for playing card games. When people are viewed as operating within the knowledge system, they receive approval from one another. It shows respect for the culture. When people are playing outside those boundaries, they are breaking the rules. The more frequently people act within the rules, the stronger the culture becomes and the more influence it has over its members. The Culture Test Game shows how these rules play out every day. People "test in" to the culture by showing they can follow the rules with their card play.

Remember in chapter 1 we discussed how card play is always governed by rules? Now we learn that these rules are really cultural standards that help individuals decide which cards to play and how the receivers will interpret the cards. The tighter the card play rules, the more influence the culture has over the card play as the Trust Game clearly shows. Police officers are, by necessity, a tight-knit group. They create and constantly reinforce a tight culture in terms of their communication rules.

I hope these examples make it clear that everyone belongs to many groups, each of which creates its own system of knowledge or culture. We each spend a great deal of time creating our own unique cultures. We have a culture at work, in our home towns, in our families, and in our countries of origin. Each culture creates its own rules to determine how people can act to show knowledge of and respect for the culture. To make these ideas clearer, let's break down the culture idea into its parts:

The term culture means a **system of knowledge** with the following attributes:

1. **Culture is shared among a group of people who have common characteristics.** In other words, members of any given culture are constantly searching for cues about their commonality with one another. When someone plays a talk card around friends, must that person pass the Culture Test Game? In most cases, part of being a friend means showing respect for the culture. Is the person using the language, wearing the clothes, and walking the walk as expected? When these consistent behaviors occur, members feel they belong to a unique group of individuals called a culture.

    A — When people are viewed as operating within the knowledge system, they receive approval from one another.

2. **Culture appears unique to outsiders.** The external face of the culture is important. The culture must be visible from the outside because the insiders want everyone to know how they're different, so they must display their differences clearly and visibly. A shared sense of cultural identity is a vital part of each individual's persona. Common language and dress are critical in holding the hip-hoppers, the police, or the Somali tribes together as a group. They want to show their pride and attachment to the culture through language, dress, music, and other unique actions.

3. **Culture forges a common destiny among members.** Not only is it important that outsiders know who belongs to the culture, it's also important to communicate that these members share a common destiny. They share goals, a mission, a set of strategies for accomplishing their goals, and a common fate. If the culture exists to fight crime (police) or claim legitimacy for a lifestyle (hip-hop group), then everyone who claims membership shares that destiny. The common destiny issue is important for the police because they must know whom they can trust among their peers. Their ability to take risks in life-threatening circumstances depends on knowing they will be backed up when necessary.

4. **Culture stretches cross several generations.** Cultures are enduring. They certainly change and shift, but the common elements remain fairly stable over time. Members of some cultural groups take great pride in transferring their language, customs, and rituals to future generations. The Japanese and American executives believe that their cultural orientations are best because they have endured for hundreds of years. Both of these cultural orientations run deep. I visited Japan recently and was impressed by their commitment to strongly held cultural orientations.

    A — The culture must be visible from the outside because the insiders want everyone to know how they're different.

♣ Functions of Culture

One of my favorite authors, Dr. Deborah Cai at Temple University, brings the concept of culture to life by arguing that culture defines the social context within which people communicate. Deborah is one of my former doctoral students. While she grew up in Michigan, she spent a great deal of time in Asia learning the languages and getting to know the people. She learned firsthand how we use cultural knowledge in our card play to understand and respond to every situation.

© 2012 by Andresr. Used under license of Shutterstock, Inc.

Her article with Dr. Steve Wilson at Purdue University, another friend and colleague, illustrates this point (Cai & Wilson, 2000). They found that Japanese and U.S. cultures have dissimilar rules for how people try to influence one another. Subjects from Japan were more concerned about the image of the person they were trying to influence than the U.S. subjects, and the Japanese incorporated those concerns into their card play. This study illustrates that culture serves some important functions. Let's look at some of the more critical functions.

Linking

When we make our cultural judgments about one another, we are looking for people who might quickly and willingly include us in their group. They apply their membership test and if we mostly pass, we become a good candidate to form a relationship with these group members to link up with. People who understand your own culture are easier to talk to so it's easier to be yourself around them. Men and women have unique cultural orientations. We've already talked about their gender cards. If a man wants to link to a woman, he must understand and adjust to her culture (language, beliefs, behavior)—her talk cards. Men are usually less able or willing to make this adjustment than women.

Common Identity

As social creatures we need to know that we are not alone. There are others out there like us. That makes me normal and a regular social being. People of like cultures seek out one another to give them a common identity and validate themselves as being normal people. Being a member of a culture also provides people with a common destiny. It provides a set of goals, a place in society. As a college student, your goals are pretty clear. You take classes to amass your credits in something cool, interesting, and marketable, and then start your future. After graduation students who don't get jobs right away have a hard time adjusting because their cultural identity is up for grabs. Who are they? They're no longer students, they're not employed, they're not parents, and they certainly don't want to be kids living at home again. So what are they—unemployed job seekers? That's neither very cool nor interesting.

Interaction Context

Once you pass the membership tests by pulling out and playing a few talk cards that will convince everyone you belong, what other functions does culture play? Culture gives us rules for how to play our talk cards and our card games. Remember in chapter 1 that we talked about regulative and constitutive rules for card games? **Constitutive rules** tell us how to interpret card plays. **Regulative rules** tell us when and how we can play our cards.

For example, in some cultures establishing eye contact during interaction with another person of higher status is considered an insult. It is expected that the lower-status person will look down. During a job interview in this cultural context, if the lower-status person establishes eye contact, the interviewer would interpret the person's card style as threatening (constitutive rule). Then the interviewer might tell the person to look away or even dismiss the person (enforcing a regulative rule). In this case, both constitutive and regulative rules were violated because of cultural orientations. The interviewee didn't first respect the culture before selecting topics and styles to play the Interviewing Game effectively.

♣ The Five Value Clusters

© 2012 by Ambrophoto. Used under license of Shutterstock, Inc.

Many authors have tried to shed light on how culture influences behavior. One of the most widely cited authors on this subject is Dr. G. Hofstede (1980), who argues that cultures are organized around **five value clusters** that people use to form deep-seated social identities that bind them together and drive behavior. Let's take a look at each of these clusters.

Context

The first cluster focuses on how much group members value togetherness. A **high-context culture** is a densely layered support network of individuals that emphasizes unity and conformity. The individual's fate is closely linked to the good of the group. To do anything negative would first bring shame to the group, and second to the individual. The person might then risk being shunned by the group. This is not to say that people in high-context cultures have no sense of individuality. Surely they do, yet the primary goal in high-context cultures is the good of the group. For people in these cultures the extended family is central. It would not be unusual for a better-off relative to sponsor the schooling and provide a place to live for several distant, poorer relatives from rural areas. Consensus is the preferred norm, while conflict and criticism are avoided. Japan, China, and India exemplify high-context cultures.

In a **low-context culture** the individual's needs are seen as separate from the group, and if forced to choose, individual needs come first. Being immersed in a low-context culture creates an **"I" identity**. Group membership changes a lot in low-context societies, meaning allegiance to the group is not as important as allegiance to self. People belong to many groups for short durations to accomplish specific tasks making membership in any one group less important. Members are loyal to themselves because of these shifting social structures. Debate and discussion that challenge the norms are welcome and regarded as healthy by individuals from any political orientation. England, Australia, Germany, and the United States are examples of low-context cultures.

Context has a profound impact on talk card play. In high-context cultures all the information for interpreting the card is in the context itself. It creates more of a **"me" identity**. Inside jokes and slang are only funny or sensible to people who understand the unique languages the group members have developed. In low-context cultures, all the information for interpreting the card or the game is in the message itself so people can communicate across groups. When you give your speeches you want anyone from any group to understand your messages. The point is that card play in high-context cultures for individuals not familiar with the culture is difficult. It takes a long time to get access to the group and to understand the communication shorthand.

Individualism and Collectivism

Driving the need to form a high-context culture is a value for **collectivism**, or a desire for group cohesiveness, uniformity, and common identity. People from collectivist cultures hold an insider-outsider view of the world. Everyone within their own group or society has a bond of togetherness and a loyalty to uphold the goals and traditions of the group, family, religion, town, or profession. These group members may not trust or even like people from outside their accepted groups, tribes, or societies. The prejudice is that members are good, and nonmembers are bad.

Individuals do not hold this same in-group/out-group mentality. They belong to many groups and value their individual success over group success. They measure their own value not by what the group accomplishes as collectivists do, but by what the individual accomplishes. They are expected to display their individual personalities and to choose their own affiliations. These folks want to separate themselves from the group and rise above the crowd, not be part of the crowd.

These values also dramatically impact talk card choices. People from individualistic, low-context cultures tend to use more direct, dominating, and task-oriented conflict styles, for example. In playing an Employee Card, for example, the individual would feel free to disagree with a less friendly, more informal, and higher-power style on the card. He or she might even encourage open disagreement. This is not so in collectivistic cultures. People in these high-context groups prefer conflict avoidance as a way to show respect for one another's face or identity. Any disagreement is seen as a threat to positive and negative face, disrespect, and a threat to group cohesion. It is frustrating for a person from an individualistic culture to get "straight talk" from a collectivistic person. Collectivists don't want to risk the face threat.

Card play differences in the Business Negotiation Game illustrate this challenge. When someone from an individualist culture like the U.S. goes to a collectivist culture like Japan to craft a deal, the U.S. people will expect periods of direct agreement and disagreement. If U.S. negotiators cannot discriminate between the two, they will have difficulty figuring out what the Japanese businesspeople want in the ultimate contract. The Japanese could be ambiguous or hard to read because they don't want conflict or disagreement, even though they truly may not agree.

> A♥ Everyone within their own group has a bond of togetherness and a loyalty to uphold the goals and traditions. A♠

Power-Distance

Power-distance focuses on the issue of status or inequality. High power-distance groups and societies value status and social rank. To them it is important to equate someone's status as a measure of their social worth. In low power-distance groups and societies, status is less important. People are more informal and are viewed more as equals. People from these low-power distance cultures value independence, loose supervision, consultative management, and friendly disagreement, and they have a positive value toward wealth and reward. Most Euro-American countries maintain low power-distance values.

© 2012 by Vadym Drobot. Used under license of Shutterstock, Inc.

High power-distance countries include many equatorial, Spanish-speaking countries, like Ecuador, Columbia, Venezuela, and Mexico, and Asian countries, including Korea and Japan. Their peoples value conformity, close supervision, autocratic and paternalistic managers, and conflict avoidance. They have a negative association with individual wealth; they prefer coercive power strategies to keep people in line; and they have more centralization and broader acceptance of authority.

You can imagine how power-distance might impact card play. In high power-distance cultures playing the Trust Game is difficult for a person who does not enjoy much social status. If the person is not "important," then authorities have less value for communicating with him or her, making it difficult to establish any trust. As a result, higher-status people generally mistrust lower-status people. There are many scenes from movies (*Aladdin* comes to mind) in which a commoner (low-status person) dresses up in high-status garb to impress, and secures the trust from some upper-class person. The key challenge is to recognize the high power-distance nature of the culture and concentrate on spending time building interpersonal relationships rather than getting down to business too quickly.

Masculinity and Femininity

Fourth, some cultures are more masculine, while others are more feminine. A male-focused culture values competitiveness, assertiveness, ambition, and the accumulation of wealth and material possessions. Members of female cultures value relationships, quality of life, and more fluid gender roles; they are not stuck in the idea of man's work or woman's work. They have more flexible ideas about what constitutes appropriate behavior for men and women.

If you are a woman and you were told as a child that "Girls can do anything," then you were likely raised in a more female-focused household that emphasized fluid gender roles. If you were told that "Men should be tough and do what's necessary to get ahead," then you grew up in a male-focused household emphasizing competitiveness and ambition. Strict boundaries laying out "women's work" and "men's work" or emphasizing competitiveness and ambition characterize a male-oriented culture.

High power-distance cultures tend to be more masculine in their cultural orientation. The idea of status is often associated with gender. It is common to see men in positions of power and women in positions of service. For example, in conservative Muslim countries, such as Saudi Arabia, women are forbidden to drive and must wear conservative clothing. In Japan, men are more likely to be leaders while women tend to work in service positions.

You can imagine how someone from a more feminine culture might react to another person competitively playing a talk card. If someone used a powerful style while playing a talk card in the Fit In Game in a feminine culture, he or she would risk offending everyone and not fitting in well. That person should use a more "affiliative" style when raising a topic.

It is important to note that a value cluster describing attitudes and behaviors about masculinity and femininity is a concept associated with gender and not necessarily with biological sex. **Gender** refers to one's orientation about the roles men and women play in society, while **sex** is simply a biological trait. Both men and women can exhibit *either* masculine or feminine gender qualities. More masculine people look for opportunities to compete and assert themselves in search of their ambitions regardless of whether they are men or women. That said, there is a high correlation between gender and sex, so that most men act like the male gender sex role, and most women act like the female gender sex role. But I'm sure you know women who act like men and vice-versa.

Future Orientation

Cultural groups develop a psychological orientation about time. Some focus more on the future while others focus more on the past and present. In long-term oriented societies, members are more patient, focusing on actions, beliefs, and values that impact the future: persistence/perseverance, thrift, and saving. Groups that are more focused on the past or the immediate present think in more short-term time frames. They value immediate stability, protecting one's own face, respect for tradition, and reciprocation of greetings, favors, and gifts.

Some people feel the U.S. lost the Vietnam War in 1975, in part because the Vietnamese have a long-term view of their culture. They are patient and measure their success over decades and centuries. In contrast, the U.S. culture is "now" oriented. Everyone wants results now for instant gratification. In some countries, time is used as a way to communicate power-distance. In some Hispanic cultures, the longer someone is asked to wait to see someone, the more status they have. It is not uncommon to make an important person wait for a couple hours to see someone. Only the low-status folks are seen right away. Of course, in the U.S. time is viewed differently, so that lower-status people are asked to wait while higher-status people are seen immediately.

The issue of how a culture thinks of time and punctuality impacts talk card play. In the Business Negotiation Game, it would be important not to request an immediate solution to a problem in negotiating a business deal with someone who takes a long-term view of the business arrangement. The longer-term thinker would want to think about the deal and lengthen the process because they see the deal as a multiyear arrangement.

Two of my colleagues at Michigan State University, Drs. Hee Sun Park and Tim Levine (also a married couple), write about these value clusters and how people see themselves in relation to these clusters. Hee Sun was raised in South Korea and works in the United States as a professor in our department. She has learned to adjust her card play to adapt to these dissimilar cultures. Interestingly, she and Tim wrote in one of their articles (Park & Levine, 1999) that the extent to which people from different countries demonstrate these values depends on the communication context. In other words, people can show more or less of these values in their card play when the situation calls for it.

♣ Cultural Orientation

Communication scholar Dr. George Borden (1991) believes that these five value clusters combine to create some interesting cultural orientations that are a little easier to remember when thinking strategically about which cards to play as you're interacting. Basically, there are three orientations that will assist you in **winning card talk games**. These global cultural orientations focus on how people view time, schedules, information, planning, and interacting. I talk about Borden's orientations and then reveal the countries most likely to exhibit these characteristics.

Task Oriented

Cultures that value a **task orientation** are more individualistic, low context, low power-distance, feminine, and focused on the past and present. They work with strict time limits and time schedules. They have a plan and stick to it. They believe in facts, and obtaining statistical and verifiable information. There is a correct, logical procedure for doing things, and a high priority on finishing the job. They are ambitious and competitive, materialistic, and they want it all *now*. People follow rules when they communicate and interrupt infrequently. Countries whose majority populations demonstrate these orientations are the United States, England, Australia, Germany, and Sweden.

© 2012 by auremar. Used under license of Shutterstock, Inc.

People Oriented

Cultures with a **people orientation** are more collectivistic, high context, feminine, status conscious, and future oriented. These cultures don't fixate on time and rigid, formal schedules. They work when it suits them or makes sense. Schedules are flexible and unpredictable. People change plans when they want, and may or may not tell anyone about it. They value information that is communicated orally and comes from first-hand sources. It's got to be verbalized to be real or important.

For process people, there are no hard facts. Facts can change because people see things differently. Relationships are the most important aspect of this orientation. Finishing human interactions, but not necessarily tasks, is a key expectation in people-oriented cultures. People-oriented cultures are more confrontational and use highly emotional communication styles. They interrupt often and don't have much use for formal communication rules. Countries whose majority populations demonstrate these orientations are Mediterranean, Eastern European, Latin American, Arab, African, Indian, and Pakistani.

Process Oriented

Individuals in **process-oriented** cultures are also more collectivistic, low context, masculine, status conscious, and future focused. While the task- and people-oriented individuals are more proactive in causing change to happen, these folks are more reactive, focusing instead on following rather than leading. They work with flexible time orientations. Yet, they believe in schedules to better structure the process; they prefer small changes to the schedules. When they make a statement, it is a promise, so there is little need for formal contracts and details. Rather, they are interested in the whole, big picture, not negotiating every detail up front. They like small changes, not big ones, and use both verifiable facts and firsthand information from others. They react to others quietly and like to sweep controversy under the rug. Process folks avoid confrontation at all costs and never interrupt since it would be rude. Countries whose majority populations demonstrate a process orientation are Japan, China, Taiwan, Singapore, Korea, and Finland.

What happens when people from task-oriented cultures try to work with others from people-oriented cultures? The task-oriented folks want to use more high-power styles and raise topics associated with doing the work. However, the people-oriented folks prefer to talk more about personal topics to develop the relationship. Americans have had to face these kinds of issues for years when working with business partners in Japan, China, and South Korea. These Asian partners prefer to spend time developing group relations, while the Americans want to get down to business.

♣ Direct-Indirect Communication

One of the more interesting communication variables that reveals someone's cultural preferences is how directly or indirectly they communicate their thoughts. (see Bresnahan et al., 2005) People who like to communicate more directly prefer to state messages clearly, revealing their real opinions. They don't like to beat around the bush. In card talk terms, they are more interested in raising controversial topics and using high-power styles when necessary. In contrast, indirect communicators like to be ambiguous. They prefer to reveal messages that are open to interpretation as a way of sparing the other's feelings. They don't like to reveal controversial subjects or use high-power styles.

Research suggests that people from more task-oriented cultures use more direct communication styles, whereas those from more people- and process-oriented cultures like a more indirect style. Being too direct risks showing disrespect to someone or threatening group cohesiveness, so being indirect helps preserve relationships for these collectivistic cultures.

Being too direct risks showing disrespect to someone or threatening group cohesiveness.

Results:

Take a look at your scores. Which score is higher, direct or indirect communication? If your highest score is over 40 for either scale, then you have a clear preference for more direct or indirect communication. If your score was over 40 for the direct style, then you are probably more task oriented in your cultural preferences. Does your card play reflect this cultural orientation? If neither of your scores is over 40, then you probably have a mixed style and no clear preference.

♣ Cultural Adaptation

We live in an increasingly global business climate. Executives regularly fly all over the world to build business partnerships. As they work, these executives face the daunting challenge of adapting to multiple cultures. The first task of forging these partnerships is to learn how to adjust our card talk strategy to adapt more quickly to a different culture. Let's look at the steps that people use in adapting to different cultures.

Before we explore the steps, it's important to point out that moving through them one after the other is not necessarily required for everyone to adapt to a different culture. Some people jump into a new culture and adapt quickly with minimal difficulty. Others get exposed to a new culture, become dissatisfied, and want to leave it immediately without trying to adapt. The adaptation steps in this model reflect a typical process people might experience if they immerse themselves in a different culture for a significant time.

Anticipation

Adaptation begins by gathering as much information as possible to learn about the new culture in **anticipation** of joining it. Are people from this culture likely to be more task, people, or process oriented in their outlook? Of course, the second part of that information search is self-reflection. Are you a match for those cultural orientations or will you need to learn more to adapt? If you had been asked to list the top three cultural issues that you expected to face when starting college after high school, what would they have been? You may be more adapted to culture change than you realize.

The Somali student would certainly be able to list more than three issues he confronted when adjusting to life in the U.S., Detroit, and college. In addition to learning a different language to win the Fit In Game when he arrived from Somalia, he had to adjust to the task-oriented culture typical on campus. Usually at the end of this anticipation phase, people are excited about becoming part of the culture they're about to enter.

Honeymoon

Once the anticipation is over, it's time to jump in with both feet. Because the anticipation process usually ends with a positive attitude and sense of excitement for entering the new culture, the first few contacts in the new culture create a kind of **honeymoon** experience. The new people see differences as exotic and fun in much the same way you might feel when visiting an amusement park like Disney World for the first time. However, in time these differences become less amusing; they might even seem

© 2012 by AISPIX by Image Source. Used under license of Shutterstock, Inc.

annoying. You came to college with a sense of excitement, but then the day-to-day grind took over. It takes a long time to get to class, people might not be as friendly as you thought, and your roommate is weird.

Frustration

The point at which annoyances outweigh positives in the new culture is the point at which a visitor is likely to experience **frustration**, the third phase of cultural adaptation. We end up taking the positive aspects of the new culture for granted and start focusing more on the disturbing elements. On a trip to Hong Kong, I met several American families who were living in Hong Kong and doing business in China for a couple of years. They are called expatriates, or expats, for short. When they first came to Hong Kong they were excited. But after a while, they started to miss their families back home, a yard for their kids to play in, and extra freedoms that they took for granted in the U.S. that were unavailable in Hong Kong. As a result, they were eager to return home to the American culture.

Readjustment

The frustration people feel when they stay in a different culture for a while causes them to develop a coping strategy. Their strategies can evolve in one of four directions. They can: (1) decide to learn the language and customs and **fully participate** in the new culture, (2) **make accommodations** to survive in the culture, but make friends only with people from their home culture, (3) **fight** any form of adaptation by spending as little time as possible there, or (4) **leave** the new culture and return home. Each of these **readjustments** is an adaptation of sorts to the new culture. For most people learning to fully participate is the best option for getting the most out of the new culture. There is so much to learn from others. Unfortunately, our biases often prevent us from making this kind of fully integrated commitment.

Think about your cultural adaptation to college. I see many students at each level of readjustment. Most students get into the culture and fully participate, but others never grow comfortable here. Instead they attend classes and go home as often as possible. Some become overwhelmed and simply leave.

The key to adapting to college or any new culture is to learn the **card talk** as quickly as possible so you can see the world as others see it and gain perspectives you never knew existed. You will then add new cards and new styles to your card talk deck, which will help you throughout life. That's probably the real benefit of attending college.

> A♥ ♠A
> The key to adapting to a new culture is to learn the card talk as quickly as possible so you can see the world as others see it.

♣ The Business Negotiation Game Revisited

In light of everything we've just learned about cultural adaptation, let's revisit the Business Negotiation Game to see how we might develop a better strategy for playing this game successfully. Consider the following issues when deciding how to play your cards in this kind of situation.

Confrontation

If you are negotiating with someone from a **people-oriented culture**, would they appreciate confrontation? They certainly would get upset with a topic introduced using a power-oriented card talk style. They value relational harmony and want to preserve face. Any direct face attack with a power play would be rejected. The people-oriented folks would shut down. Remember that they might not want to negotiate in the first place and risk confrontation. They might prefer indirect communication mediated by someone they trust rather than direct negotiations. It would be vital to get information up front to learn about their negotiation preferences and their problem-solving styles before charging ahead.

Information Sharing

What if the people you're negotiating with don't like direct, open information sharing or they don't like a lot of facts and figures at all? They could be **people-oriented** and want to focus on building trust before sharing proposals that would reveal information about their preferences. Another possibility is that you are more people-oriented and your business counterpart is more **task-oriented**. This situation requires you to play talk cards that directly share information and are specific with facts. Again, learning the cultural preferences of the other negotiators is important.

Influence

Sometimes people from **task-oriented** cultures try to directly influence or push their counterparts in a specific direction. They are not afraid to use their power when necessary. If this kind of culture clash happens, it often results in an impasse or a significant conflict spiral. Those people valuing **people-** or **process-oriented** cultural perspectives are not generally amenable to direct influence. They only respond to less direct influence attempts or forming more creative solutions to the problem. It is generally a bad idea to walk into any negotiation with only one preferred outcome. That sets you up for failure, particularly in a **multicultural** setting in which high-powered tactics are viewed as disrespectful.

© 2012 by Yuri Arcurs. Used under license of Shutterstock, Inc.

This small case study of the Business Negotiation Game illustrates two points about the importance of understanding the cultural orientations of your co-negotiators. First, **test the other's culture**. Most people learn about the other's cultural orientations by seeing what card they play and guessing what game they're playing. Remember, when the other person talks first, he or she is playing a card and asking you to play the same card. If they are playing a Friend Card, they want you to play a Friend Card. That helps locate the other's cultural orientation. If they do that repeatedly, perhaps they are more people oriented and less task oriented. Figure out what card the other person is asking you to play. Then make some decisions about their cultural orientation and how it should influence your approach to achieving your goals.

Second, **planning** and **flexibility** are important in any communication situation, but particularly in a negotiation. Just like the **cultural adaptation** process, anticipate whom you are negotiating with, their cultural orientations, their key issues, and their most important needs. Then see how you match with these preferences and orientations. Remember that a win-win card-talk game is one in which both parties benefit and creatively address their needs.

Chapter Summary

- **Culture is defined as** a group of people who believe they share common values, beliefs, and behaviors; are viewed by outsiders as having common characteristics; and who share a common destiny.
- **Culture serves many functions.** It helps us link with others, creates a common identity, and guides our interaction. Not understanding another's cultural orientation causes confusion and inhibits effective communication.
- **Culture is shaped by adherence to certain values.** These values relate to how people value context when interpreting information, how they view the individual in relation to others in the group, the extent to which they value status and power, and whether they are more masculine or feminine in their orientation. Views about time are also critical in defining cultural values.
- **These values create broad cultural orientations.** They combine into shaping people's perspective as being more task, people, or process oriented. These orientations have important implications for how people should play their talk cards.
- **Ultimately, understanding culture is about effective adaptation.** There is a process for how people typically adapt to new cultures. Sometimes the process is easy, and people move through the phases quickly. More typically, the process is challenging, as the individual reconciles his or her own preferences with the preferences of the different culture.
- **Finally, planning is the key** to working effectively in a multicultural environment. The more you plan and think through your communication challenges, the more effective your card talk will be.

Lessons Learned

Here are the lessons learned from this chapter that should help you improve your cross-cultural understanding:

- **Culture is about tests.** For any culture in which you claim to be a member, others will constantly subject you to tests to earn your membership. Do you hold the cards indicative of membership? Can you play the talk card games in a way that gives you the right to continue holding your membership status? Do you know the tests you'll be expected to pass and are you willing and able to make the commitments required to pass them?
- **Cultures take different forms.** Some are task oriented, others are more focused on relationships, and still others prioritize process concerns. As much as possible, learn about the cultural forms you are likely to encounter when you visit a place that has a different orientation than your own. Learn the tests you'll be required to take and make sure you know how to pass them. Passing these tests is difficult because cultural expression is difficult for us to easily adapt to.
- **Avoid snap judgments.** Keep an open mind about values and orientations that differ from your own. It is easy to be judgmental about how others view time or tasks because they don't make sense to you. The strategy is to listen first, then understand, and ultimately adapt. You may never embrace the differences but you can at least learn from them.

- **Cultural adaptation is easier with a mentor.** Find someone who is a respected member of the culture and earn that person's respect. Then this person will vouch for your credibility, giving you a gateway into the new culture. Cultural insiders can provide a rich perspective on their culture and, if you are at all curious, they will be pleased to educate you.
- **Be adventurous.** Learn the talk card games that you are expected to play and immerse yourself in the local communities to learn how "real people" play their unique cultural games. Most large cities around the world are westernized. Get off the beaten path and learn. This gives you the best way to learn about yourself and about others.

References

Borden, G. A. (1991). *Cultural orientation: An approach to understanding intercultural communication.* Englewood Cliffs, NJ: Prentice Hall.

Bresnahan, M. A., Levine, T. R., Sherman, S. M., Lee, S. Y., Park, C., & Kiyomiya, T. (2005). A multimethod multitrait validity assessment of self-construal in Japan, Korea, and the United States. *Human Communication Research, 31,* 33–59.

Cai, D. A., & Wilson, S. R. (2000). Identity implications of influence goals: A cross-cultural comparison of interaction goals and facework. *Communication Studies, 51,* 307–328.

Gudykunst, W. B., Ting-Toomey, S., & Chua, E. (1988). *Culture and interpersonal communication.* Thousand Oaks, CA: SAGE Publications, Inc.

Hofstede, G. (1980). *Culture's consequences.* Beverly Hills: SAGE Publications, Inc.

Park, H. S., & Levine, T. (1999). The theory of reasoned action and self-construal: Evidence from three cultures. *Communication Monographs, 66,* 199–218.

© 2012 by Monkey Business Images .Used under license of Shutterstock, Inc.

Social Identity Card Games

♣ Introduction

As we learned in the previous chapters, playing cards means displaying information about the way we want others to see us, what relationships we want to promote, and what achievement goals we want to obtain. When both parties synchronize around those three elements, they are more likely to understand each other and "win" the card talk game.

Recall that the first set of messages people focus on when they interpret your card is your self-presentation goals. How do you want to be seen by others at that moment? In general, these specific goals are driven by your identity, or self-concept. You see yourself—and you want others to see you—in a particular way, and that serves as the foundation for playing the rest of your card. What you wear, how you cut your hair, how you display your gender and how you phonetically form words all reflect on your identity.

♣ Social Identity Card Talk Games

The Gangster Game

In preparing this chapter I ran across the following website, which is a step-by-step guide on how to be a gangster: www.hubpage.com. According the website's creator, the first step is talking like a gangster, which involves constantly cursing and using the F-word as often as possible. Next it is important to use the pimp walk, which is more like a limp. "So, if you can limp, then you're a pimp," the website says. Clothes are also a key element in the transformation. A gangster wears baggy pants that are at least 10 sizes too big and extra-large shirts that have the Coogi label. The Gangster Card begins with these elements that are aimed at reflecting a clear self-presentation.

The Clan Game

Most Americans have little understanding of tribal or clan identity. For us, being an American supersedes our ethnic identities. Do you recall the Fit In Game from chapter 3 about the student from Somalia? To give you some background, Somalia is war-torn country in East Africa where tribal identity is more important than national identity. It is split into many clans and subclans, with the Hawiye clan dominating the capital of Mogadishu, and the Darod clan spread throughout northeastern and southwestern Somalia. My student was from the Darod clan but lived in Mogadishu.

One day a member of the Hawiye clan came to his home and simply abducted his father and brothers, who were never seen again. Frightened, he and his mother escaped the capital and moved to Nairobi, Kenya. Because my student looked like a Somali refugee he was constantly at risk of being arrested as an illegal immigrant. He finally made it to Detroit where he faced further discrimination as an illegal immigrant. Now that he is a naturalized U.S. citizen, his American identity has displaced his clan identity.

The Respect Game

Research in the areas of conflict and violence prevention indicates that conflict escalates into violence largely as a way of showing strength and restoring respect. In some communities one's very survival depends on being seen as strong and respected. When respect is challenged, the person must respond.

Generally the game plays out in the following way: If, in a casual social event like a party, a young male bumps into another young male, the person being bumped first looks into the other's eyes to define the event as either a challenge to his respect or as an accident. If the person apologizes or simply looks away, then it is an accident. But if no apology is offered and the person looks into the other's eyes, then it is a challenge and demands a response of some kind. The challenge is typically verbal at first as each studies the other to determine the level of the threat. If the infraction cannot be resolved verbally, then the situation is likely to escalate to violence, particularly if others are watching. The goal of the violence is to restore respect and an identity of being "large and in charge."

♣ Social Identity: Who Am I?

To understand why we play games related to our self-presentation goals, we turn to Dr. Henri Tajfel, a Polish Jew who grew up in Europe during the rise of the Nazis leading up to World War II and the Holocaust. Fellow Polish Jews were being rounded up and executed simply because they were the "wrong" race. Henri survived and went on to pursue an academic career to understand what drives prejudice, discrimination, and intergroup conflict of the kind my Somali student experienced. Henri felt the need to move beyond explanations focusing on personality to focus instead on the idea that these social ills stem from an individual's social identity.

Henri defined **social identity** as "the individual's knowledge that he belongs to certain social groups together with some emotional and value significance to him of this group membership" (Tajfel, 1974).

Types of Social Identity

Henri argued that identity consists of two sets of attributes: what I think of myself **personally that is separate** from everyone else in my group, and what I believe I **share in common** with all the other members of my group. Thus, we have both a **personal** and a **group** identity. Clearly, each person believes he or she is different or unique in some way from others in the group; perhaps the person believes he or she is smarter, faster, or more articulate than the others in the group. But the person might also believe that he or she shares some attributes in common with everyone else. "We all like hip-hop music," a member might say when asked to describe the group members.

This combination of separate and common attributes constitutes the individual's personal identity, or **self-concept**. In other words, my self-concept is a psychological understanding of what I believe to be true about myself, both separately from the group and in common with my group. If you were to describe yourself to others, what five terms would you use? How about these?

1. Smart
2. Caring
3. Funny
4. Persistent
5. Likable

These might be five terms that you would reveal on a Facebook page or in an email in response to an acquaintance's request to describe yourself. If these were your five terms, how might they impact the kinds of cards you would play, what topics and styles you would apply to them, and how you might play them? If you see yourself as smart, you might build your card with many interesting topics related to your academic interests that would allow you to play with other smart people. If you think you're caring, you might decide to play cards with people who appear to have some social problems so you could slip into the comfortable role of providing social support.

In addition to a self-concept (which combines personal and group perceptions of one's self), we also have a **relational self**, or set of perceptions about significant dyadic relationships in our lives, such as two great friends, a husband and wife, or a spousal partnership. When these relationships are close, people focus on attitudes and beliefs about what the parties have in common. A partnership might believe that, as a couple, they are effective parents and excellent friends to other couples they know. It is a collective sense of self that grows over time from the closeness of the relationship.

Bruce Rolff. Used under license of Shutterstock, Inc.

The Significance of Social Identity

Your vision of yourself as an individual or as a group member drives your card talk strategy. It guides how you perceive others, how you select people to communicate with, and how you play your cards. For example, playing the Gangster Game is all about projecting an identity that allows the gangster to hang out with other gangsters and to share their culture. In other words, showing the card is like a **ticket** to enter the group. If you are proud of your ethnic heritage and it was at the top of your list, then you might want to wear clothes and use language that proudly displays that heritage. Most students want others to see them as students, so they dress in casual student clothes to fit in.

Because self-concept is subjective, it is neither right nor wrong. It is simply how we see ourselves. This subjective view can be significantly distorted or extremely different than how others see you. A person suffering from an eating disorder, such as anorexia nervosa or bulimia, has a view of his or her own body that is inconsistent with both reality and others' perceptions. Such a victim typically looks in the mirror and evaluates him- or herself as being too fat. This biased self-perception, in turn, often leads to further attempts at weight loss and devastating physical consequences.

Who do you see when you look in the mirror? We see things on the outside such as our attractiveness, cultural orientations, and expressiveness. For example, you might say, "I am hot looking and a cool jock." We also see things on the inside. For example, you might say to yourself, "I am smart, I care about people, and I am fun to be around." The terms and phrases you use to describe yourself constitute your social identity.

Because **social identity** is so important to individuals in terms of guiding how they talk, dress, and hang when playing talk cards, it also happens to be the first judgment people make about one another. It's a simple judgment to make because it's visual. People look at age, skin color, facial features, dress, and other personal displays to decide if the person is like them or not. Then they make a prediction about how the other is likely to respond if spoken to. It's a quick judgment, but it takes priority over other judgments, including whether you are a nice person or an honest person.

Most people, including the person playing the Gangster Game, give many cues about how they want to be evaluated as a person. Of course, if the person is a not a stranger and we know his or her identity, then other initial judgments are made. The point is, social identity judgments are important because they are immediate and influential in guiding behavior.

The point is, social identity judgments are important because they are immediate and influential in guiding behavior.

♣ Origins of Self-Concept

Psychologists have thought for some time that our self-concept comes from communicating with others. Since we cannot watch ourselves communicate with others, we instead focus on their reactions to us. Other people function as mirrors to our social behavior. Do you recall from chapter 2 when we talked about the **Symbolic Interactionism Theory**? This is the same reflective process we use in learning language described by psychologist Dr. Herbert Blumer (1969).

People let us know if we're funny, caring, smart, or useful as we read their reactions to our card plays. This feedback can be negative through overt criticism, gestures and looks of annoyance, or people avoiding us. Through repeated exposures to this feedback over time, we begin to get a feel for what we do well and not so well. Of course, we have to be open to that feedback, which for some people is a tall order.

Psychologically, what drives the fundamental need to form a social identity? According to research pioneered by psychologist Dr. William Schutz (1958), every person from birth on strives to satisfy three basic interpersonal needs:

Other people function as mirrors to our social behavior.

1. **Inclusion,** or the desire to be accepted and respected within some group, family, or relationship.
2. **Control,** or the desire to impact the environment to get others to pay attention to us so we can get our message across, get fed, or get help.
3. **Affection,** or the desire to receive intimacy and civility from others.

William tells us that, while individuals vary on the extent to which they must satisfy these needs, everyone strives to achieve them to some extent. We must be part of a group, be included, and be accepted for who we are in that social structure as well as receive some emotional support from that group. We turn first to our families for this kind of acceptance and membership. However, if our families reject us, then we look to peers to provide this kind of acceptance. In fact, people will do almost anything that the group demands to be included. The gangster is a good example of the extremes to which a person will go to fit in. In fact, children seldom want to be separated from their abusive parents. The desire to belong to a family overpowers their need for survival.

What role does social identity play in satisfying these needs? Our identity is the primary tool we rely on to satisfy these needs. The talk cards we play and the manner in which we play them constitutes the expression of our identity. We forge and then protect our identity so that we can communicate and present ourselves in a way that the group will accept. If our social identity does not conform to what the group is looking for, as evidenced by the fact that we're playing the wrong talk cards or using the wrong topics on those cards, the group rejects us. The Somali student was from the "wrong" clan or tribe in his country. He was unable to play the card of the majority tribe and was rejected by that majority tribe—even risking the fate his father and brothers suffered.

These are powerful needs. When we perceive that someone is disrespecting us, not listening, or being mean, we believe it is an attack on our social identity. "They don't like me as a person. They are attacking me personally." This realization makes people emotional, because the one gift we hold most dear is our identity. When threatened, we are willing to do most anything to defend and protect it.

© 2012 by Monkey Business Images. Used under license of Shutterstock, Inc.

Self-Concept Structure

The **content** of my identity is the collection of beliefs that I have about myself. It contains the substantive information about me. But these beliefs are also organized in a **structure**. We organize these ideas into a system called the **self-schema**. A schema is the psychological scheme or organization for all the beliefs and attitudes we have about ourselves. We have a:

- Physical self *(How do I view my physical appearance?)*
- Moral-ethical self *(How religious, moral, or ethical am I?)*
- Relational self *(How do I see myself as a friend or mate?)*
- Professional self *(How do I see myself professionally?)*
- Family-oriented self *(What vision do I have about my place in my family?)*
- Personal self *(How smart, cute, or interesting am I?)*
- Social or group self *(What social, tribal, or clan beliefs and attitudes do I have?)*

Each self contains a large number of individual beliefs and attitudes. They overlap a great deal and are interconnected. It's not easy to simply break away this schema. For example, if you think you're attractive physically, you probably also think that personally you're cute and interesting, and socially you're a member of the cool group. We only truly understand how people view themselves when we step back from the conversation and look at the talk cards they're playing and the games they choose to play or not play.

♣ Self-Esteem: Do I Like Myself?

As it turns out, the answer to this question is crucial. For many years prominent psychologists, such as Dr. Abraham Maslow (1987), have argued that answering this question positively is an important human need. Self-esteem is a positive or negative **evaluation** of one's self. It is the difference between where I am and where I would like to be as a person—my **real self** and my **ideal self**. It is the subjective judgment about the gap between these two selves.

For example, let's say you want to be really smart as a key part of your ideal self. Then you take a class in calculus and fail it. If you needed that class for your major and you also failed some other classes as well, you might conclude (probably falsely) that your real self is not smart. This gap might produce low self-esteem about your calculus ability.

On the other hand, your real self and ideal self might match up well in your moral/ethical self-concept domain. You would like to be ethical and moral and you see yourself that way. In that particular area there is not a big gap so your self-esteem is higher as it pertains to the moral/ethical self.

Can you imagine the self-esteem issues the Somali student faced when arriving in Detroit? He might have lacked social confidence because he didn't know the English language well. On the other hand, he might have felt personally confident knowing that his mother gave him a sense that he was smart and capable, and had already successfully navigated several countries. Using confidence that came from his family he was motivated to overcome the gap between this ideal self (knowing English and succeeding in America) and his real self (not knowing much English). Over time, as he learned to communicate well in English, this gap disappeared so he was able to play a wider range of cards more comfortably.

Self-esteem is also a product of comparing one's self to others. Students conduct these kinds of social comparisons all the time when they want to know how well they scored on tests in relation to their friends. If you consistently score higher than your friends, you might conclude that your real self and ideal self are pretty close together. "I'm doing fine!" These social comparisons may also be the source of sibling rivalries. My older brother was always good at talking with girls, and I was less skilled in this area. He was also bigger, and I felt he got more attention from our parents. This self-esteem gap started to diminish as we grew older and closer personally. Our relationship matured, and we forgot about all those old growing-up issues.

Self-Esteem Effects

What is the effect of self-esteem on the cards we build, which cards we play, and what talk games we play?

The higher our self-esteem (the smaller the gap between real and ideal selves), the more likely we are to develop and play cards associated with that part of our self-concept. For example, if I am personally and relationally more confident, I am probably going to risk disclosing personal information to important people in my life. I am going to open up more when the time is right, and play cards that express riskier and more personal topics.

As self-esteem grows, people are more likely to take risks in expressing their personal attitudes. They are going to have more topics on their cards and be willing to play them when necessary. If they believe they are well informed, they may be willing to play a Political Debate Game with a friend. If they lack professional self-esteem and are supervisors, they may not be able to construct a Supervisor Card or play the role well.

People with higher self-esteem make better friends and lovers. Friends and lovers listen to one another, but also share their thoughts constructively. It is a balanced give-and-take. They don't try to attack one another. They are able to empathize and help one another work through their issues. One of the most important cards that anyone can hold and develop is a Friend Card. Being a good friend means you can show your support when needed, and that you are willing to talk about any topic of interest to your friend. The better developed this card is (good listening, honest discussion) the stronger the friendship becomes.

A healthy self-esteem consists of only a small gap between our real and ideal selves. There's always room for improvement. We should learn to live with the idea that we can grow bigger and better cards. We can add topics, we can be flexible in the styles we apply to those topics, and we can learn to play card games more constructively.

> A ♥
>
> People with higher self-esteem make better friends and lovers.
>
> ♠ A

Identity and Behavior

How does identity drive behavior? Dr. Sandi Smith and Dr. Jennifer Butler Ellis (2001) wrote an interesting paper describing the thinking process we use match our self-concept with our card play. The process is actually a three-step flow:

1. We create an identity along the dimensions listed above. *(I'm tough!)*
2. We develop principles or policies to protect our identity. *(Don't give in to an attack.)*
3. We select cards and play games that implement the policy. *(Resist or fight back.)*

Essentially, identity drives the development of the principles we use to protect it. After all, identity must be protected because it defines us. The principles are general guidelines for behavior. "Don't yield to attack" bolsters the identity of being tough. "Tell the truth" protects the personal identity characteristic of being honest. "Wear your pants low" protects the identity of belonging to an urban community. These principles state our intentions to act in a specific way in response to a certain situation.

© 2012 by CREATISTA. Used under license of Shutterstock, Inc.

Facework and Identity

One of the more interesting ways in which identity becomes visible in card play is through politeness. The pioneering study in this area was done by two linguists, Dr. Penelope Brown and Dr. Stephen Levinson (1978). They found that people adjust their politeness during conversation to manage their "face," or how they are viewed by others. They categorized face into two forms: positive and negative.

Positive face focuses on our self-presentation goals when we play our cards. It is the desire to be viewed in a positive, attractive, and competent light by others. You might play a card that makes people laugh so they will view you as a funny, interesting person. On the other hand, if you are trying to look tough, then you play cards that have topics and styles showing that look to others. The goal is to present a face that gets positive reviews and more respect so you can be accepted into the group that values such a face.

Negative face is the desire not to be controlled or pushed around in any way. It is the desire to maintain autonomy or freedom of choice. Do you remember your mom ever asking you to clean your room? Did she say, "If you have a moment and it's convenient for you, can you please straighten up your room a bit, dear?" Or was she more likely to say, "This room's a mess! Clean it up right now or else!" The second example is the full Mom Card shoved in your face with high power and an attempt to threaten your **negative face**. You have to do something right now that severely restricts your autonomy, to say the least!

Our positive and negative face goals are frequently negotiated when we play our talk cards. Let's take the Mom Card example. When mom plays her full Mom Card in the second example, she is engaging in a full **face threat**. She is threatening your negative face or desire to do what you want. But in the first example, mom plays her card differently. She is giving you the option of cleaning your room; she is asking if you're willing to do it, which avoids a direct negative face threat. Clearly, the full Mom Card with a high-power style attached to it is meant to threaten negative face.

When mom plays that card, how do you respond? You might comply and accept her right to play that card by playing the compliant Son/Daughter Card. Or you could reject the full Mom Card and push back, "I'll get to it when I'm done! I'm busy." Or you might respond with: "It's my room, and I'll clean when I want!" Mom may not have wanted this confrontation, but nevertheless, she got it. The negotiation is on and the card game is as well.

Could mom have played her card more constructively to avoid this confrontation? Perhaps she could have by using a **face support** strategy. Rather than playing the full

Mom Card with high power, she might have tried to support your positive face needs by saying: "I am really proud of you for doing so well at your swim meet. Dad and I are bragging about you to everyone! By the way, I wonder if you could straighten up in here a bit before tomorrow. Thanks, hon!"

Notice that mom first plays the Mom Card by bringing up the swim meet to support positive face, which is important to her child. Then she makes a soft request to avoid threatening **negative face** too much. There are options for cleaning up the room. This negotiation tactic still has some minor face threats, but begins by building up or supporting face. That improves the relationship messages while avoiding a confrontation.

Face maintenance is a self-presentation strategy intended to build up one's face to make it less vulnerable to face threats. We try to make ourselves look good by building up positive face and showing policies to others that it is unnecessary or unwise to threaten our negative face. The purpose of the Respect Game is to build up positive face and avoid negative face threats. The people playing the game must look tough and capable of taking care of themselves in a fight. Most of the time in casual conversation games, we might brag about something, use big words, or raise topics we know will impress others. These are attempts to build up our positive face to ensure that we can accomplish our self-presentation goals of inclusion, control, and affection.

Face saving involves warding off face attacks. Notice that the child's response to the mom's direct face attack was to push back. "I'll get to it when I'm done. I'm too busy." If the face attacks are strong and severe, they are generally met with attempts to save positive face and negative face—to not look bad or to not allow others to restrict autonomy or control. Thus, by playing the full Mom Card, she invited her child to play a face-saving card, which resulted in an argument.

A ♥ ♠ A

We try to make ourselves look good by building up positive face.

♣ Self Monitoring: How Do Others See Me?

So far we have talked mostly about how individuals see themselves. We've also raised the issue of how we compare ourselves with others. We haven't really explored the important issue of how we take others' perceptions into account in developing our self-esteem. In other words, how do we incorporate this information about others' perceptions into our self-concept and self-esteem?

The answer lies in understanding that our self-concept consists of two sets of perceptions: **How I see myself** and **how others see me**. We can call them the "I" and the "me." I see the characteristics of my identity by the cards I play. But when others observe me, what do they see? Is there a gap, or are they consistent? Are you more concerned about what you think about yourself, or more concerned with others' opinions of you? Your answers to these questions define you as either a **high** or **low self-monitor**. Let's look at this idea more closely and explore its impact in developing your talk cards.

© 2012 by Andrei Vorobiev. Used under license of Shutterstock, Inc.

We begin with the premise that most people want to act in a socially appropriate manner. The question is, What is socially appropriate? Clearly, people use different criteria to answer this question.

High self-monitors base their judgments of appropriateness on external factors. These are people who constantly scan the environment to determine what people think about them. How are others evaluating them? Those external factors might be other people's behavior or what's going on around them. High self-monitors base appropriateness judgments on cues they observe from the situation; they are very "me"-oriented. They are mostly concerned with how others see them.

In contrast, people who are **low self-monitors** are "I"-oriented. They are mostly concerned with how they see themselves. So they tend to base social appropriateness judgments on internal factors such as their own attitudes, moods, and values. After all, they are looking only at themselves, while high self-monitors are looking at how others see them.

High self-monitors have excellent cognitive, or thinking skills in that they are skilled in scanning the social situation to determine what behaviors are appropriate. They monitor the cards everyone is playing and are good at figuring out what games are being played as well. Second, high self-monitors can better adapt their behavior in ways that are viewed as appropriate to a particular situation. They are going to play the most effective cards in the card game because they see what's needed to win.

Low self-monitors pay less attention to the social setting and the cards that others are playing. They are focused on their own feelings and attitudes about what they are seeing around them. Because they have more difficulty figuring out what games people are playing, they are less adept at modifying their behavior to meet changing situational demands. They act the way they feel.

As you might imagine, self-monitoring has a significant impact on card play. High self-monitors can present whatever image they consider appropriate. If they need to play a card that makes them look good in some way, they know how to do that because they are focused on the external situation. As a result, they can present a variety of "selves" as needed when selecting and playing a card. In contrast, low self-monitors react generally to their underlying beliefs, attitudes, or feelings and play whatever talk card they want, regardless of how others might view those cards.

Who is more likely to exhibit the true characteristics of their identities: high or low self-monitors? Clearly, low self-monitors more accurately display their underlying attitudes and feelings than high self-monitors. Low self-monitoring individuals talk more and tend to control conversation in an effort to present multiple selves that would be viewed positively by others. They also seek more personal and private information when selecting a topic from their cards than do low self-monitors. It should come as no surprise, then, that high self-monitors are perceived as more competent communicators than are low self-monitors.

The high self-monitor is "me"-oriented (*How do others see me?*) while the low self-monitor is more "I"-oriented (*How do I see myself?*). Which is best? Research seems to suggest that a balance is best, with a slight bias toward being more of a high self-monitor. You are concerned with both how you see the world and how others see it. You are able to read the audience and the situation more carefully, but not allow the audience to turn you into a social chameleon who is unwilling to express personal opinions.

Results:

If you scored over 60, you are more of a high self-monitor and more me-oriented. If you scored between 35–50 you probably display a balanced sense of I and me. If you scored below 35, you are probably a low self-monitor.

What are the implications for how you play cards? If you are a low self-monitor, you are more I-oriented. You play cards based on your feelings, not what cards the other person is asking you to play. You tend to play the card you want, when you want it. It may or may not be the right card to accomplish your goals, but that's the card that made you feel good at that moment.

If you are a high self-monitor, you are more plugged into what talk card the other person wants you to play. If you are an extremely high self-monitor, however, you are cautious in how you play your cards. You play the one that you think makes you look the best since your self-presentation goals are probably your most important personal goals. Maintaining a strong positive and negative face is critical to you.

If you are a high self-monitor, you are more plugged into what talk card the other person wants you to play.

♣ What Influences Social Identity Development?

What factors shape our identity, or self-concept? What shapes how we develop a sense of I and a sense of me? Let's look at each factors and their impact on how we play our cards.

Culture

Culture strongly influences the development of self-concepts as we know from Henri's work, and even from the author of the gangster example at the beginning of the chapter. Once we become a member of that group or culture, we create a self that allows us to continue to be accepted and respected by that group. But keeping that membership means adding that cultural information to our cards so others will recognize our membership.

One of the most profound cultural influences is the issue of **high-** and **low-context**. This concept refers to how we interpret the cards another person plays. How can we understand the other's message? In a **high-context** message, the only way to accurately interpret it is to understand the context in which the card was played. Slang is a good example. All slang is essentially insider talk—made-up words and phrases that only insiders who live in the culture really understand. To understand someone playing a Gangster Card, it's important to become immersed in that culture.

In contrast, a **low-context** message is one in which all the information for interpreting the message is in the message itself. It is essentially context free. It is Standard English. Your speeches and presentations in this course are low-context messages designed for anyone who speaks English either as a native speaker or a non-native speaker. The point is, everyone must be aware of their cultural biases as they construct their cards and interpret the cards that others are playing.

© 2012 by Morgan Lane Photography. Used under license of Shutterstock, Inc.

Family

Since it is such an important part of our self-concept development, the family is often called a **primary group**. Family is the first group from which we seek to satisfy our needs for inclusion, control, and affection. We look carefully at what cards we need to create, what topics should be on them, and what cards we should play to be a member of the family. When we bond with our families, it is our first and most important reference point.

Of most importance is the relationship we create with our primary caregiver. We pay close attention to this person and allow them to help shape our cards. Did your parents ever tell you to say some things and not others? Did you have rules about how to label or interpret certain phrases uttered by others? More importantly, the primary care giver's job is to help us create a self-concept or identity that we're happy with. It is to give us the self-esteem we need to take the risks necessary to play the card games that help us grow.

If the mother does not treat the child in a loving and caring way, it is less likely that the child will exhibit feelings of self-worth. Those feelings about the self are thought to influence adult social identity as well as the nature of adult relationships.

Roles

Once we begin moving outside the family context, we look to others like peers, teachers, and employers to shape our identities. Once we get to school and compare ourselves to other kids, we get a real feel for the shape of our identity. Am I as smart or as attractive as the other kids? Do I get the kind of attention they receive? These issues are important in families, but once we get outside of the family context these issues become even more vital in shaping our identities. We learn to be friends, students, teammates, and employees on our life paths. We create these multiple identities that enable us to function in multiple contexts.

Each role you play requires a unique card. The student supervisor example in chapter 1 illustrates this point. Those students facing a new role must learn to create that role through their talk. They must acquire the topics and the styles necessary to play the games that supervisors must play with employees. For example, how should the supervisor play the Job Interview Game? What topics are appropriate to raise, what styles should be used to raise those topics, and what games should be played to learn as much as possible about that potential employee?

Identity Transitions Ranking Survey

Your identity changes over time. You make many transitions as you mature.

Directions. To really understand your multiple identities, take a minute to rank order along the seven dimensions that we described previously. To complete this task rank, order these dimensions from 1–7 with 1 being the most important and 7 being the least important to you.

SELF-CONCEPT DIMENSIONS	RANK ORDER 1–7
Physical self *(How do I see myself physically?)*	
Moral-ethical self *(How religious, moral, or ethical am I?)*	
Relational self *(How do I see myself as a friend or mate?)*	
Professional self *(How do I see myself as a student and ultimately as a professional?)*	
Family-oriented self *(How do I see my role in my family?)*	
Personal self *(How smart, cute, interesting am I?)*	
Social or group self *(What social, tribal, or clan beliefs and attitudes do I have?)*	

Results:

What do your rankings tell you about how you see yourself today? Is your moral-ethical self most important or perhaps your family-oriented self? If you see the family-oriented part of your identity as most important, what beliefs do you have about yourself as a family member? For example, my role as a dad to my children is probably my biggest priority. I want to get that role right. Whatever you select serves as a core driver of your vision of yourself and what's important to develop and to defend. These ratings change over the course of your life, but right now they present a good snapshot of how you see yourself now.

Finally, as you develop your character as a student, professional, spouse, or parent, it's important to see how these priorities will impact some of the key card talk challenges you'll face while making the transitions. These transitions will define how you grow. Do you control the growth and make these transitions in a positive way, or will you just let them happen to you? Let's explore each one and how your self-concept impacts each one.

Knowledge

The first transition we make in life is knowledge growth. As soon as you could see or hear, you began learning. Continuously learning and seeing connections among concepts is vital for your personal and professional growth. Only when you challenge yourself can you grow in knowledge and understanding of ideas, places, people, and events.

How does your identity impact your ability to make these important transitions? If you believe you can make them, that you are personally able to learn and grow, you can. If you believe you can work in a team environment with others and take advantage of their perspectives, learning continues. We live in a knowledge society in which your job is creating knowledge and passing it along. You are only valuable professionally if you can do this effectively.

© 2012 by Brian A Jackson. Used under license of Shutterstock, Inc.

Spiritual

The spiritual transitions in your life focus on the extent to which you believe in a higher power. That power may have religious roots or it may have scientific roots, or both. Our family believes in Christianity, and it guides our views of our close relationships and our place in the world. You may have similar traditional religious beliefs, whether Christianity or another belief system. If you rated the moral or ethical dimension of your self-concept as important, what belief system is important for you? Should you attempt to explore it further? Should you allow it to guide your relationships?

Relational

The next chapter focuses on our relational cards and talk card games. Everyone lives in a web of relationships, some stronger than others. We make many transitions relationally in our lives. We begin as children of parents, and perhaps brothers and sisters. Then we expand our web of relationships with friends, teachers, bosses, and others.

Of course, the big challenge we face relationally is mate selection. Can we acquire the kind of relational maturity to make a good choice? Self-concept is a big driver of this decision. If you see yourself as emotionally engaging, sensitive to others, and able to be a little higher self-monitor, then you may have the ability to make a good choice of a life partner.

Communicative

A fourth transition is that people change the way they communicate. Our talk card decks expand, and our cards become more complex as we learn different roles and become challenged to speak with individuals from many cultures. This chapter talked at length about how identity shapes our communication strategies.

The key in making transitions is keeping ahead of the communication contexts you face. For example, you know you're entering a professional role soon after graduation. You probably already have a part-time job. Do you feel confident that you can play cards with the correct topics and styles needed to connect with other professionals in your area of expertise? Develop them now if you can by participating in professional groups or internships.

Physical

Finally, we make many physical changes in our lives. We typically grow larger (on average people add about a pound per year to their bodies after age 20). But more important, we generally alter our appearances to adapt to new situations and challenges as well as the changing styles and norms in society. The trick is to control your physical development instead of ignoring it.

These transitions work together, of course. As your communicative transitions evolve, so can your relational transitions. You become more adept at connecting with people and playing the kinds of card games that result in success in social, professional, personal, and moral situations. Becoming more knowledgeable develops your communication cards, and your spiritual growth also impacts your knowledge quests.

In other words, all these work together, driven by your identity to form your character going forward. Travel well on your journey!

Chapter Summary

- **Social identity is the individual's knowledge that he or she belongs to certain social groups** that have emotional and value significance related to this group membership. We select cards, topics, and styles to protect and build our social identities.
- **We create an identity to satisfy our social needs for inclusion, control, and affection.** These are powerful needs, and we always try to satisfy them in every situation. When someone prevents you from satisfying these needs by showing disrespect, disinterest, or distance, you feel as if your identity is being attacked.
- **We have many dimensions to our social identity.** We craft thoughts about our physical self, moral-ethical self, relational self, professional self, family-oriented self, personal self, and social or group self.
- **Self-esteem is the extent to which we like ourselves.** The more self-esteem we have, the more likely we are to open up and play riskier cards, express more personal topics, and forge stronger relationships.
- **Facework consists of strategies we use to manage how others view us.** Positive face is the desire to be viewed in a positive or attractive light. Negative face is the desire not to be controlled or pushed around in any way. We are sensitive to face threats and try to recover quickly by bolstering our face to keep our identity strong.
- **Self-monitoring is a personal preference for how sensitive you are to others' opinions of you.** High self-monitors tend to be me-oriented. Low self-monitors tend to be I-oriented. A balance between the two shows maturity in card play.
- **There are many influences to your social identity.** Culture, family, and the various roles we play at work and with friends constitute the key factors that forge our identities. We make many identity transitions over the course of our lives as we mature.

Lessons Learned

Here are the lessons learned from this chapter that should help you improve your understanding of social identity in card talk:

- **Take care to understand your own identity.** This chapter begins with the question "Who am I?" Most of us develop life transitions naturally without paying much attention to the changes that happen to us. But people like Dr. Henri Tajfel or my Somali student, who were confronted with identity challenges early in life, had to know who they were and use this information to survive. The point is that all of us should reflect on our identities and see how they help or hinder our ability to make productive transitions.
- **It's important to understand where your identity comes from.** Remember that your social identity is formed around your needs for inclusion, control, and affection. Your identity is shaped largely to satisfy the requirements you believe are in place to belong to your preferred groups. So pick your groups carefully, because they will determine what kind of person you become as you make life transitions.
- **Make sure you like yourself, but not too much!** This seems like a bizarre lesson. How can you like yourself too much? If your self-esteem is high, it's because you believe your real self and ideal self match perfectly. There is no gap. That means you don't want to improve. The fact that you're in college suggests that you do want to improve, and there is a gap. The real challenge is to not let this gap get too wide or too small. Keep learning and growing to make more productive transitions in life.
- **Face issues are important in card talk.** One of the first considerations when playing cards is, how does your card impact the other's face? Most critically, does it threaten the other's positive or negative face? Generally, it's more effective to support the other's face rather than threaten it.
- **Balance in the I and me components of your identity helps card talk.** You are more effective in card play if you are a moderately high self-monitor. If you're too I–oriented, you tend to ignore other's reactions to your card play. If you're too me–oriented, you lack confidence to say what's on your mind. Balance is key.
- **Be aware of what influences your social identity development.** We began this section of Lessons Learned by asking you to reflect on your identity. Take a broad look at this question regularly by asking whether you have sufficiently broad cultural, professional, and relational experiences to develop your identity productively.

References

Blumer, H. (1969). *Symbolic interactionism*. Englewood Cliffs, NJ: Prentice-Hall, Inc.

Brown, P., & Levinson, S. (1978). Universals in language usage: Politeness phenomena. In Ester Goody (Ed.), *Questions and politeness* (pp. 56–289). London: Cambridge University Press.

Maslow, A. H. (1987). *Motivation and personality*, 3rd ed. New York: Harper & Row.

Schutz, W. C. (1958). *A three-dimensional theory of interpersonal behavior*. Oxford: Rinehart.

Smith, S., & Ellis, J. B. (2001). Memorable messages as guides to self-assessment of behavior: An initial investigation. *Communication Monographs, 68*, 154–168.

Tajfel, H. (1974). Social identity and intergroup behaviour. *Social Science Information, 13*, 65–93.

Interpersonal Card Games

♠ Relationship Card Games

♦ Persuasion Card Games

♣ Conflict Card Games

PART Two

© 2012 by RazoomGame. Used under license of Shutterstock, Inc.

Relationship Card Games

♣ Introduction

In a recent study conducted by the Pew Internet & American Life Project (www.pewinternet.org) researchers found that 55 percent of teens who use the Internet have created a personal profile online using sites such as Facebook. Older teens, particularly girls, are most attracted to these sites and they use them mostly to reinforce existing friendships. Boys were more likely to use these sites for flirting and making new friends, according to the study. About 48 percent of teens make these sites a part of their daily interpersonal communication routines to keep in touch with friends, make plans with friends, and in some cases, flirt with others.

Why are so many people using these social networking sites? We want to be plugged in! We are satisfying our need for inclusion—to be part of a group. Even better, part of a network. Social networking is an easy, fun way to stay connected with current friends or make new ones, as the Pew study found. The success of these sites stems from their ability to build relationships through card talk.

Remember, we learned in the first chapter that every time people communicate they present three kinds of information in their messages: self-presentation, relationship, and achievement cues. In chapter 4 we focused on self-presentation cues that reflect our social identities. This chapter focuses on relational cues and how we play our cards to accomplish relational objectives.

To begin, let's look at some relationship card talk games to illustrate what we mean by the terms **relationship** and **relational communication**.

♣ Relationship Card Talk Games

The Facebook Game. Here's a typical Facebook post that shows how people inject relational communication messages into the styles they select. Read this actual wall posting and try to figure out what assumptions this person is making about the relationship:

"Alrighty roomie love—I think I went 0 for 2 today on exams (kill me now) and I am not ready for this next one tomorrow. If you don't mind will you sign me in to 450 tomorrow morning? Sorry but I will be around the rest of the week....oh and tomorrow afternoon too (I have that exam—fingers crossed!) Keep me posted on the interview and I will let you know how things are on my end! Love you and have a great night at work!"

- Is the target of the posting male or female?
- What is the assumed level of intimacy and attraction between the parties?
- What is the assumed role relationship or status between the parties?
- What is the assumed level of trust?
- What is the assumed level of commitment to the relationship?
- What talk cards are being played?
- What are the topics and style choices, and how do they contribute to the relationship between the parties?

This post is from a female to her female roommate who clearly cares a great deal for her, trusts her to "sign me in to 450," and shows commitment to the relationship by doing the wall posting in the first place. Looking at the language, how can we draw these conclusions? Let's examine the topics and the styles used to convey these impressions as this roommate plays her **Friend Card** on the posting:

- **Topics:** (a) Exam performance, (b) class attendance in 450, (c) scheduling about being "around next week;" (d) the interview progress for both folks, and (e) having a great night at work.
- **Style 1: Liking.** There are several cues starting with "Alrighty roomie love." She ends with "Love you." There are also signs of caring by asking about how well the roommate performed on the interview.
- **Style 2: Formality.** The posting contains many signs of informality, beginning with the informal greeting, the shifting around of topics that resemble casual conversation, and the phrases "kill me now," and "I have that exam—fingers crossed!" There are also several exclamation points used in the post to convey emotion.
- **Style 3: Power.** The posting clearly conveys equal power by asking about the interviewing process and offering to share information about her own progress. To some extent, the roommate even shows a bit of deference by apologizing for being around next week.

A♥ A♠ *In the early stages of a relationship, it's important to understand how committed both parties are to one another.*

Clearly, the roommate plays primarily a Friend Card, and also shows a bit of her Roommate Card as evidenced by the apology for being around the apartment all week. If it were only the Roommate Card, there would be no need for all the chatter about interviewing and well wishes for work. The primary card played is a Friend Card meant to advance all the impressions that (a) she likes her (b) roommate and friend, (c) trusts her, and (d) is committed to the relationship.

Intimacy Games. A second set of interesting games relates to how couples express their intimacy through talk. It is not easy talking about intimacy issues. In the early stages of a relationship, it's important to understand how committed both parties are to one another. One common game that couples play to define their commitment is called Love Talk. This game typically begins when one party introduces a topic about where the relationship is headed or how she feels about the relationship. Her goal might be to strengthen the relational commitment and the level of intimacy. To accomplish this goal she must pull out her Girlfriend Card and start a conversation about this topic while using styles that look like she wants to escalate the relationship.

For example, she would probably use verbal and nonverbal messages that displayed **high liking** (maybe a low, sexy voice), **low formality** (she might

© 2012 by iofoto. Used under license of Shutterstock, Inc.

use touch while she's talking), and **low power** (she might ask a question or hint around about how he feels about her). If he reciprocates with his Boyfriend Card and plays along, then the game is on and the Love Talk begins. If he fails to see what she's doing and instead plays his Friend Card, he is essentially asking her to play a different game, perhaps the Sharing Talk Game that's described next. For this game to be successful, he's got to accurately label the card she's playing and identify the game she wants to play.

A second intimacy game is called Sharing Talk. The goal of this game is to simply talk about events of the day or general perceptions about issues of common interest. It's an intimacy game because couples use this time to indirectly say they like spending time together. This game might begin with her playing a Friend Card and talking about what happened in class today. Style-wise, she might use moderate levels of liking, low formality, and low power to have this sharing conversation.

Will he pick up on this game and reciprocate by playing his Friend Card and also sharing? We know from chapter 2 that men are more biased toward viewing communication as a tool for problem solving. When communicating they expect there to be a reason other than "It's time to share." Women often initiate this game, men tune out, and women ask, "Are you listening to me?" The men will say yes, and the Sharing Talk Game continues to some extent. A couple that learns to share their thoughts as a means of exploring intimacy in the relationship is more successful in strengthening it.

> A
> ♥
>
> A couple that learns to share their thoughts as a means of exploring the intimacy in the relationship is more successful in strengthening it.
>
> ♠
> A

Relationships and Card Talk

The Facebook game and the intimacy games tell us a great deal about how relationships work. The first point they tell us about relationships is that our understanding of the relationship is found in two locations. The most commonly understood location that people use to reference relationships is in their heads. My colleagues at Pennsylvania State University, Drs. Denise Solomon and Jim Dillard, tell us in their **Relational Framing Theory** (Solomon, Dillard, & Anderson, 2002) that people form relationships in their heads based on two kinds of judgments: dominance-submissiveness and affiliation-disaffiliation. The **dominance-submissiveness frame**, or perceptual set, focuses on the issue of control. How much do we want to impose ourselves, or submit to the other? The **affiliation-disaffiliation frame** focuses on how much we like, appreciate, and respect the other.

The theory argues that our interactions are always framed in our heads from these two main perspectives. Whenever we share information, we make judgments about these two main issues as we try to understand or make sense out of a relationship. This understanding forms the foundation of both communicators' interdependence.

What Is a Relationship? A **relationship** is defined as set of beliefs about the level and type of interdependence between ourselves and others. We constantly scan each other's card play to form beliefs about what our relationship is or is not at any given time. Once we decide what it is, then we apply a label to those feelings and beliefs, and call ourselves lovers, friends, coworkers, or colleagues. This definition process is continuous. We are always reevaluating thoughts about our relationships because they are so important in our lives.

There are four dimensions to this understanding of our interdependence:

1. The level of **intimacy** and personal attraction parties share *(How strongly are parties emotionally bonded, attracted to, or caring about one another?)*
2. Their type of **role status** *(Are they friends, coworkers, employer/employee, customer/ client, marital partners?)*
3. The level of **trust** between parties *(Do parties feel that the other will act in his or her best interest?)*
4. Their level of **personal commitment** to the interdependence *(What is the relative importance of the interdependence to the individual?)*

For example, playing the Love Game requires that each party in the relationship plays his or her relationship card like a Boyfriend/Girlfriend, Husband/Wife, or Partner/ Partner Card. Then they must discuss topics and use styles that communicate intimacy, reinforce their relational status as an intimate couple, and demonstrate trust and personal commitment. That's a lot to ask card talk to accomplish, but couples must learn to *talk* like intimate couples to *be* intimate couples. The feeling and the talk must be consistent.

Relationships Live in Talk. The issue of consistency brings us to the second location in which relationships reside. Relationships not only live in our heads; *relationships are also in our talk*. They are constantly being shaped and reshaped through the message styles we select. As we exchange messages, we deliver lots of cues through our style choices about the relationship we have or want to have with that other person. Over time, as relational messages stabilize, we start to form solid beliefs (or frames, according to Solomon, Dillard, & Anderson, 2002) about the psychological nature of our interdependence. How much do we like, trust, and care about one another? What is our role relationship?

For example, let's take a look at the Facebook Game and map the moves:

1. Strangers start exchanging messages on Facebook.
2. They select an Acquaintance Card and play the Casual Conversation Game.

> A♥
>
> *Couples must learn to talk like intimate couples to be intimate couples.*
>
> ♠A

3. They stick with safe topics like campus events or music preferences because they share that in common.

4. They select styles that show some liking, some informality, and equal power.

If the message exchange is between a male who is flirting with a female on Facebook, then he might try to change the game from Casual Conversation to a Flirting Game. Let's map these moves:

5. He starts talking about personal topics, such as likes and dislikes in a friendly, informal way.

6. She discloses personal information in return and then teases the person about something he wrote.

7. He discloses more personal information and teases her back, and then in time, he asks her to meet him someplace.

In essence, this is how we use language to grow relationships. We build in the style cues capable of accomplishing our relational goals when we select topics from a specific talk card we want to play. If we see the other person using similar language in response, we come to believe that the other feels the same way about the relationship. In the Facebook Game, the roommates have a conversation playing their Friend Cards with reciprocated topics and styles that confirm a friendship relationship that goes deeper than a roommate relationship. In the Flirting Game, the topics and styles reflect different and more intimate intentions.

♣ Interpersonal Communication

I hope you now have a feel for how relationships are created and reinforced through language and the talk cards we play. There is another important process we've yet to talk about in explaining how we form our card talk messages to build relationships. We know what topics and styles are present and how the relationship messages are communicated. But when they were playing the Facebook Game, how did the roommate know her message would be interpreted positively? How did she know which topics to discuss and which styles to use?

To her, the answer is simple: She's talking to her friend, and they have a history. Based on her knowledge of her friend/roommate, she made a prediction about what kind of topics would be most meaningful to her friend, and which styles would have the most impact before she began writing her post. She thought, "I'll talk about these subjects with these styles and I think she'll like that."

This is a key point. According to my long-time colleagues Drs. Gerald Miller and Mark Steinberg (1975), whenever we formulate a message, we predict how the other person is likely to interpret it even before we create the message. We make these predictions based on three kinds of information in every communication situation: cultural information, social information, and personal information.

Cultural Information. The first judgment anyone makes about someone they don't know when trying to predict how that person will hear or interpret a message is cultural information. We look

© 2012 by wong yu liang. Used under license of Shutterstock, Inc.

at the person's gender, age, ethnicity, clothing, and/or body language and guess what cultural orientations they might have. We don't necessarily stereotype because that means automatically evaluating someone negatively and prejudicially. Rather, we label people culturally, reach into our past experiences with similar people, and act accordingly.

Once we label someone culturally and decide to play a card, like a Casual Acquaintance Card, and a game like Casual Conversation, then we have to pick topics and styles. Perhaps we talk about the weather using a friendly, yet somewhat formal tone since we're not sure how the other will respond. If the person responds, then we can see what card they play in return and if they're interested in playing the Casual Conversation Game. That provides more cultural information and improves our ability to predict what other topics the person might like to discuss, or whether we even want to continue talking with them.

Social Information. After making cultural judgments, we look for more information to refine our ability to predict how the person will interpret the messages we want to present. We look for cues in both appearance and language to determine what groups or organizations the person might belong to that would make some topics and styles more relevant than others. Are you a student in a specific school, an employee of an organization, or a member of a club or a family that I might know about? We also look for other social cues in the specific communication context to determine if the timing is right for what we want to say.

Sometimes people wear clothes that have slogans, logos, or team names that define group membership. Most of the time people are open about what groups they belong to, and that helps us better predict the topics and styles that would appeal to them. After all, we know that people belong to groups because they share certain beliefs, attitudes, and values. These are tools people use to filter messages and make them meaningful, as we learned in chapters 1 and 2. If we know what these filters are, we can make better predictions about how they are going to respond.

Personal Information. The most refined piece of information needed to make better predictions is on a personal level. What separates the person you're talking to from all other students, employees, or group members? What are his or her unique likes and dislikes, attitudes, and values? Once we have this kind of personal information we can accurately predict how our specific messages are likely to be interpreted. Notice that once you have achieved this level of knowledge, you have already identified the individual culturally and socially. You know what cultural orientations they have and what group memberships they have. Now you can speak to them on a personal level like the roommates/friends did when playing their Facebook Game.

Communication at a personal level is called **interpersonal communication**. These are messages that individuals tailor to each other's personal profile. Notice how specifically the roommate tailored her comments to her good friend. Everyone would clearly recognize that the roommate was not speaking to a stranger or someone who was just a co-member of a club.

> A♥
> Whenever we formulate a message, we make a prediction about how the other person is likely to interpret it even before we create the message.

© 2012 by fstockfoto. Used under license of Shutterstock, Inc.

This was her friend, and she knew that when she crafted the post. Thus, any message exchanges we make using personal information by definition create interpersonal relationships. Sustained interaction between parties that involves personal information results in interpersonal relationships.

Now that we know how interpersonal relationships are formed and how language works to change them, let's talk about the range of relationships we create and how we build cards to manage them successfully.

Types of Interpersonal Relationships

Families. The first group of interpersonal relationships we learn to create is with our families. The first card that we form is a Son or Daughter Card to receive nurturance from mom, dad, or other caregiver. Then we might also form Brother and Sister Cards or Niece and Nephew Cards. Creating these cards with specific topics and styles can be a challenge because families have changed a great deal over the years. Instead of mostly traditional families with moms and dads raising kids, we now have single mothers and fathers, grandparents, or even foster parents raising children and serving one or both parental roles. Families now include people who are not related through any legal connection. Some people even refer to their close friends as "family."

Perhaps the best way to think about family is to conceive of it as a network of people who share their lives over a long time, who are bound by marriage, blood, or some formal or informal commitment, and who share future expectations of being connected to one another.

Of course, the type of family of which you are a member is going to influence the kinds of cards you need to thrive in that system. For example, if you are from a **closed family** in which members keep to themselves and are less involved in larger social networks, your communications are probably going to be fairly reserved and regulated. In these kinds of families, decision making is hierarchical and concentrated in one parent.

For example, if dad is the decision maker, he is expected to play his Dad Card that is likely to include topics related to disciplining the children, performing tasks around the house, and setting policies about friends and other issues related to growing up. In such families, moms are expected to hold Mom Cards to organize the household, enforce rules, and manage the system. The rules are known, and everyone is expected to follow them. In these families, negotiating is frowned on and conflicts are solved through predetermined rules and are authority based. If a child asks why, the parent might answer, "Because I said so!"

What kind of topics and styles might be expected in a closed family? Certainly, the topics might be limited by the rules. You learn quickly what topics you can and cannot discuss, and when and where you can discuss them. If you live in a closed family, you probably could not talk about your love life to your parents or even your siblings. Styles would also be more limited. While you might be friendly, you would probably be a little more formal, and you would communicate low power. You would need to continuously reinforce that others in the family have power over you as a child.

At the other end of the continuum is the open family, guided by values for novelty, creativity, and individuality. Members of these families have a more expansive set of cards to play. They express affection in spontaneous, enthusiastic, and public ways, vary in their time commitments to the family, and have fewer specific rules with even fewer of them rigidly enforced. Negotiation is seen as a positive and useful tool in this system. Mom and Dad Cards are unlikely to be very different in open families because their roles can

A♥

Sustained interaction between parties that involves personal information results in interpersonal relationships.

♠A

© 2012 by Gelpi. Used under license of Shutterstock, Inc.

interchange significantly. In this family, if a child asks why, the parents might answer, "What do you think?"

The topics and styles played by the children in an open family would be different than in the closed family. You could probably talk about your love life with your parents/caregivers and your siblings. You would not need to be as formal or as worried about showing low power. Power in open families is always being negotiated and is more fluid. As a result, people in these families adapt more easily to challenges that face the family.

The movies *Meet the Parents* and *Meet the Fockers* illustrate the differences between closed and open. The Burns family was closed and traditional. The Focker family was open and nontraditional. It is important to emphasize that *no one type of family is inherently better than another*. They vary mostly in process—how they're organized and how family members interact with one another.

Friendships. Once we develop family cards, we venture out into the world and start to develop friendships. These require different cards altogether. We must create Friend Cards that enable us to talk with male and female friends, older and younger friends, and friends whom we meet at different locations, such as in the neighborhood, at school, or at work.

How are friends different than family, and how will that impact our cards? Of course, friends are created voluntarily. If I see a person who is similar to me, and I play a talk card and the person responds with a similar card, we continue communicating and may become friends. My son is a history buff and loves to talk about war battles. If he finds another boy interested in such subjects, they become fast friends.

The voluntary nature of friendships is important because the rules for how we must develop and play our cards are different than for families. Friendships are more open and flexible, and probably look a lot like open family cards. In fact, kids from open families might consider their parents to be friends also, because the cards between parents and friends look similar.

Another important feature of friendships is assumed equality. People affiliate with others who are similar culturally, socially, financially, and often spiritually. They hang out with people who share their activities and who are willing to help with various tasks. Once these patterns have been established we also expect friends to act as confidants and provide us with emotional support. In other words, friends are a lot like open families in the sense that people voluntarily hang out together because they like each other and share lots of activities. They can even act as confidants and support givers.

Intimate Relationships. As we discussed in chapter 1, we move along in life through various transitions, including building intimate relationships with a few select individuals. We need these relationships to satisfy our **drive for intimacy** that is satisfied by hugs and kisses as children, but extends into many other kinds of intimacy expressions as we mature into adults.

A ♠ The voluntary nature of friendships is important because the rules for how we must develop and play our cards are different than for families.

Over time we tend to think of intimate relationships in terms of emotional bonds associated with closeness, passion, and commitment. We are close when we feel bonded and connected to someone. We feel passionate when we are physiologically aroused and have an intense desire to be with another person. Commitment involves both the short-term decision to love another person and the longer-term commitment to maintain that love.

If you think about it, the Sharing Talk and Love Talk Games can only be played successfully if each party is willing to play his or her Boyfriend/Girlfriend, Husband/Wife, or Partner/Partner Cards. If one person refuses to or cannot reciprocate with the appropriate card, the game changes. For example, if a female plays a Girlfriend Card and initiates a Love Talk Game, she is asking him to play a Boyfriend Card to play along with her. He might not play that card, because he doesn't know how or doesn't want to do that.

After all, a Boyfriend Card would need to consist of topics like "My feelings about you," or "My feelings about myself and about others." Accompanying these topics would need to be styles that reinforce them. The styles would need to show high friendliness and intimacy, low formality and low power. It's called being vulnerable and sharing. If he never was a boyfriend and had never discussed these topics, he could not play the game.

This description of the Love Talk Game illustrates the idea that relationship card talk has rules. There are rules about topics, when and how often people must communicate these topics, and what styles they should use for each of these topics. If the people in the relationship don't want to be accountable for these rules, they're essentially rejecting the escalation of the relationship to a more intimate level. Each partner has to establish priorities in his or her life, and perhaps an intimate relationship is not desirable at this time. This raises the point about how and why relationships escalate. Let's look at some theoretical frameworks to better understand these processes.

Theories About Relationships

A Stage Theory of Escalation and De-escalation. My good friends and colleagues Drs. Mark Knapp and Anita Vangelisti (2005) have written an excellent book on interpersonal communication. One of the more interesting ideas in their book describes how relationships progress through stages. Let's explore each stage and see how relationships move up and down the development staircase. Here are the stages:

Contact. When we first meet someone our goal is to develop an understanding about his or her cultural, social, and personal characteristics. We might consciously or subconsciously ask ourselves if we like this person, if we think he or she is physically attractive, and whether we should continue this conversation.

Experimenting. Playing the Sharing Talk Game is an indicator that parties have moved beyond the simple contact stage. Now they are experimenting with different talk games, seeking potential similarities, searching on multiple levels for more information about the other person, and deciding if they want to create Boyfriend/Girlfriend or Partner/Partner Cards.

Intensifying. Playing the Love Talk Game reflects movement into the intensifying phase of the relationship. It might involve sitting close and holding hands while talking about the relationship, or requesting psychological and physical favors from one another.

Integrating. Movement to this stage is marked by sharing some kind of physical symbol of unification like a ring or necklace. During integration, social circles may merge and couples may refer to things as belonging to both of them (e.g., our song, our restaurant).

Bonding. Public rituals institutionalize the relationship, such as marriage or having a child together. However, going steady, engagement, or using the term dating are other forms of institutionalization, depending on age.

Differentiating. Couples at this stage find themselves expressing differences about the level of commitment to the relationship. These discussions are useful in helping them grow as a couple, because there are issues that must be sorted out for them to continue to grow. As a result, couples often go back and forth between bonding and differentiating as the relationship intensifies.

Circumscribing. The hallmark of circumscribing is constricted (circumscribed) talk games. Couples no longer play Love Talk or Sharing Talk Games. Their communication focuses on superficial topics that avoid intimate discussions. Topics that address logistics or other non-involving issues are typically brief. Phrases like "It's none of your business" are common.

Stagnating. At this stage, couples are going through the motions of the relationship by doing routine activities, but not trying to confront conflict or communicate meaningfully. Since the intimacy is gone, couples are just trying to survive.

Avoiding. Couples move to this stage when they actively seek to be away from one another or even separate physically. Parties maintain some contact, however superficial, as a means of carrying on child-rearing or other common tasks.

Terminating. The final stage of coming apart implements the decision to end the relationship. The movement to this phase typically involves undoing the institutional label that formed the relationship, such as getting a divorce. Parties may be still involved, but the relationship has been redefined into different institutional forms.

Each phase is marked by parties playing different games at different times. As relationships escalate, the partners work to fill their talk cards with an ever-increasing number of topics and styles. They learn to play fun and interesting talk games that signal their desire to escalate intimacy. Love Talk Games and Sharing Talk Games are two examples. Others might be Teasing Games or Couples Sharing Games played with other couples to validate the institutional strength of their relationships.

De-escalating games also mark those stages. Parties often invent games, like the Fight Game, that might include the Hurt Feelings Game or the Lying Game. Perhaps you have seen couples play these games—some of which are fun to watch, while others are painful to observe.

Marital Types Theory. Another of my impressive colleagues is Dr. Mary Anne Fitzpatrick (1988), a communication professor and researcher focusing on communication and marriage. Her research looks at grouping married couples based on their communication patterns. She identified four types of marriages:

1. **Independents.** Independent couples (22 percent of the total) accept uncertainty and change, but do not pay as much attention to schedules and traditional values. They are more autonomous, work to confront conflict and negotiate autonomy issues, while sharing extensively. These folks work to develop fairly sophisticated games that are useful in managing a full range of differences. They are more flexible in terms of decision making and housework than the other types.

2. **Separates.** Separates (17 percent) tend to maintain more distance between each other than other couple types. They are typically not together very much and are not very good at the Sharing Talk Game. Also, they are not very skilled in arguing as they tend to avoid conflict. These folks are typically not growing as much in the

kinds of topics they have on their cards and are not playfully constructing new card games. Separates don't integrate their physical spaces very much and maintain separate schedules. They are also more rigid in who makes decisions and does chores around the house.

3. **Traditionals.** Traditional couples (20 percent) need routine. They like consistent card games played in routine ways. They hold conventional belief systems about what husbands and wives ought to do in relationships and actively resist changing those ideas. Yet they share more physically and psychologically than the other types. While these folks argue, their disputes are limited and played out routinely when they happen.

© 2012 by Yuri Arcurs. Used under license of Shutterstock, Inc.

Uncertainty and change upset Traditional couples, similar to Separate couples.

4. **Mixed.** Forty percent of couples represent some mixed type in which the husband and wife differ on their values and talk card skills. One party might be a Traditional and the other a Separate, for example. This ambiguity often threatens these relationships, particularly if these values clash often.

Marital Attitudes Theory. Drs. Ellen Braaten and Lee Rosen (1998) developed a scale to measure attitudes toward marriage. The Marital Attitude Scale measures the extent to which you view marriage positively or negatively at this point in your life. If you view it positively, you probably find yourself attracted to the Fitzpatrick's Traditional marital type. If you view it negatively, you might find yourself pursuing a more Independent or Separate style of marriage. The question is, What is your vision for your marriage?

Results:

If your score on the positive items is above 50, you have a generally positive impression of marriage and are probably destined for a more Traditional marital type, particularly if your score on the negative items is below 30. If your score on the negative items is above 50, you are probably less interested in marriage. But if you try it, you might find yourself pursuing a more Independent or Separate marital type.

If your score on both dimensions is in the 30–50 range then you're ambiguous about your marital vision. You are not really sure what to expect. You've probably seen some successful marriages and some that are unsuccessful. Consequently, you're not sure. That's fine, of course. The key is that if and when you're ready for a permanent relationship that you commit to it and do it well.

Relational Success Theory. As discussed by Knapp and Vangelisti (2005), couples fall into routines as they age, regardless of their marital type. Some routines pull them together, while others allow couples to drift apart. Talk games play a significant role, since couples use these games to express and perform their intimacy and commitment to one another. Other scholars have also conducted studies to better understand the factors that predict relational success. Results indicate that there are five major predictors of whether partners would maintain their relationship. See how these factors might be influenced by playing various card games.

- **Greater Certainty.** When couples have a clear picture about one another's commitment to the relationship and that commitment is high, they are more likely to stay together longer. Card games help with this process. Couples who play the Sharing Talk Game are able to see these issues more clearly.
- **More Routine Sharing.** Partners who routinely communicate are better able to stay together. These couples develop rules for sharing such as when to talk and what games are best at what times. Have you ever seen couples develop actual routines in their communication? For example, eating dinner together nightly or taking talking walks together.
- **Support from Family Members.** Support helps couples cope with stressors. For example, the grandparents can take the kids for a week while the couple takes a vacation together.
- **Support from Friendship Networks.** Couples need to play talk games with other couples so they can share their thoughts and fears. Successful couples regularly reserve time to spend with others, for example, bowling leagues, church committees, or golf outings.
- **Similarity.** Successful couples find ways to expand the contexts in which they play with one another. They might learn to play tennis together or volunteer or work out together. The more joint activities they perform together, the more they can understand and become attracted to one another.

© 2012 by Kzenon. Used under license of Shutterstock, Inc.

Self Disclosure Thory. One of the key talk games that successful couples play is the Sharing Game. The card we play is our Boyfriend/Girlfriend, Husband/Wife, or Partner/Partner card Among the key topics on those cards are items that are personally important to us. They may be attitudes, deep dark secrets about our past, or important feelings. The only way to escalate a relationship is to reduce uncertainty about one another. **Self disclosure** is the term used to reveal those key thoughts in the context of the Sharing Talk Game.

Most people know they must continue to reveal personal information about themselves, but it can be frightening. Telling another person your most embarrassing moment, what you are afraid of, or your intimate thoughts is intimidating. Nevertheless, we cannot help but disclose ourselves; even without words, our nonverbal communication can reveal to people how we feel or what we are thinking.

People who have trouble playing the Sharing Talk Game have difficulty self disclosing. It's important in escalating relationships for two reasons. First, it makes people more self aware. By revealing the information I also explain it to myself. The other person helps me understand it. Second, revealing information communicates trust in the other partner and commitment to the relationship, both of which are important success factors.

Not all self disclosures are equally revealing. The hallmark of self disclosure is that the information being shared is unique in that only a few other special people know it. These are personal items that allow the other to better understand key personality traits so the person can judge compatibility. Yet research tells us there are rules for playing the Sharing Talk Game and self disclosing. Personal information must be shared with only a few people, and only in small doses relevant to the topics at hand. If the information comes out of the blue and there's too much of it, the self disclosure will not be special. People who do mind dumps like that can be sort of creepy.

Physical Attractiveness Theory. So far we have not talked much about physical attractiveness. You probably have the sense that attractiveness is an important issue in developing relationships. Research tells us that most people will publicly say that they form relationships based on internal factors such as a person's values, beliefs, personality, and character. Research has repeatedly found that we form relationships with people primarily on the external factor of physical attractiveness and not on character dimensions. We like attractive people better, and we believe they have better social skills. We also think they are more fluent, faster speakers, and more confident. In addition, people are more likely to date people they find physically attractive and avoid people they find unattractive.

Why do we do this? First, people are taught from an early age about who is attractive and who is unattractive from parents and peers. For instance, children who are viewed as more physically attractive tend to receive less harsh punishments when they misbehave than less attractive kids. This halo effect, (the idea that kids can do no wrong) finds that people are willing to overlook misbehavior from attractive kids because they find it cute. Misbehavior from unattractive children is not typically overlooked. In fact, these kids are punished more than attractive children. Later in life, unattractive people are viewed more negatively in general and are perceived as less interesting and less successful than attractive people.

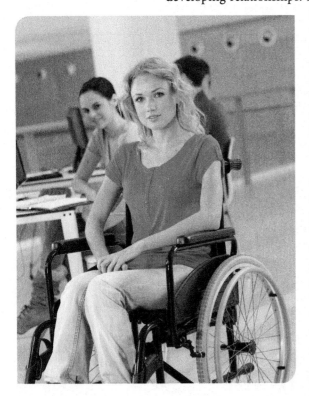
© 2012 by Goodluz. Used under license of Shutterstock, Inc.

As these studies reveal, people who are perceived as more physically attractive receive far more social rewards than those who are not. Moreover, society views attractive people as able to provide social benefits. Thus, we prefer to be surrounded by others who are physically attractive.

Interestingly, people have a strong tendency to deny that they value attractiveness in other people. This denial may be viewed as taboo within our societal norms. By admitting that physical attractiveness is important, people may risk being viewed as shallow and superficial. Furthermore, another study showed that people tend to make negative evaluations of those who rely heavily on physical attractiveness in choosing a dating partner. In general, it appears that individuals want to date physically attractive people, but do not want to admit that physical attraction affects their dates' desirability.

Social Exchange Theory. Based on a rational, economic model of relationships, the Social Exchange Theory views relationships in terms of their costs and rewards. This concept is discussed at length in the Miller and Steinberg (1975) book. The idea is that we seek relationships with people who provide more rewards than costs. Rewards are both physical and emotional. When we begin relationships with people, we may unconsciously think, "Is this worth the effort?" For instance, the term emotional baggage is often used with people who take more (emotionally) than they give back. It is difficult to maintain a friendship with a person who takes and rarely gives.

At its most basic level, the concept of social exchange might appear too rational in contrast to relationships based on emotional attachment and intimacy. Social Exchange Theory argues that emotions are one of the factors we use to calculate our cost-benefit ratio. If someone is emotionally attached to another person, that feeling is factored into his or her thinking as one of the rewarding aspects of the relationship.

What are the implications of this theory for card talk? When we're in a relationship with someone, we tend to play the cards and express the topics that are most rewarding, while avoiding those cards and topics that are painful. The point is that we get into card-play habits. I have routine topics that I express when I play my Husband Card as I talk with my wife. These are fun topics that she likes to discuss with me as she plays her Wife Card. Social Exchange Theory provides a framework for predicting which cards people play and which ones they avoid.

Chapter Summary

- **Relationships exist in our heads and in our talk.** Relationships are not only thoughts we have about other people. We send relationship messages through our card talk as we play games.
- **Relationships are about interdependence.** We think about relationships in terms of interdependence. The four issues that comprise interdependence consist of intimacy, role status, trust, and personal commitment.
- **Interpersonal communication requires information about the individual's unique characteristics.** That information goes beyond what is known about the person culturally or socially.
- **We live in many kinds of interpersonal relationships.** We live within families, friendships, and intimate couple relationships. Each requires different cards to play these relationship games successfully.
- **Relationships escalate and de-escalate.** Whether we're moving up or down the relationship ladder, we face card talk game challenges at each level. It is important to know when we are moving from one level to the next.
- **There are several theories about how relationships function.** Each suggests that as we develop the relationship, we create communication patterns that constrain how we respond to and develop the relationship. For example, more self disclosure typically leads to more intimacy.

Lessons Learned

Here are some important lessons we've covered about how card talk defines and develops relationships:

- **Carefully guard your language cues.** You feel a certain way about someone, then you put cues in your messages reflecting those thoughts and feelings. Therefore, carefully guard your language cues. Are you able to send the kinds of cues you want for the kinds of relationships you are trying to create?
- **There are many kinds of relationships.** Each requires separate cards and conscious thought about the important games that are expected in those relationships. Do you have the cards and do you know the games?
- **There are several theories about relationships.** In terms of the process of relational development we know that relationships grow in predictable stages. Because shifts to the next level are often driven by changes in card talk patterns, it's important to explore whether you can or even want to adjust your card deck to create the kinds of relationships you want.
- **When relationships evolve into marriage they can take different paths.** These paths have important implications for the kinds of talk cards we can and should play to be successful. Look around and see if you can identify the kind of marriage you want. Then ask whether you have the cards or styles needed to create that marriage.
- **Communication plays a key role in reducing the ambiguity that can threaten relational success.** Self disclosure is a key part of relational escalation, but there are rules for how to do it properly. Do you know the rules to perform effectively?
- **Physical attractiveness is important in relationships.** Because people find it rewarding, attractiveness plays a key factor in determining their desires to escalate relationships. Work to improve your physical attractiveness by transforming yourself into a more interesting person who can also communicate effectively.

References

Braaten, M. A., & Rosen, L. A. (1998). Development and validation of the Marital Attitude Scale. *Journal of Divorce & Remarriage, 29,* 83–91.

Fitzpatrick, M. A. (1988). *Between husbands & wives: Communication in marriage.* Thousand Oaks, CA: SAGE Publications, Inc.

Knapp, M. L., & Vangelisti, A. L. (2005). *Interpersonal communication and human relationships* (6th ed.). New York: Allyn & Bacon.

Miller, G. R., & Steinberg, M. (1975). *Between people: A new analysis of interpersonal communication.* Chicago: Science Research Associates.

Solomon, D. H., Dillard, J. P., & Anderson, J. W. (2002). Episode type, attachment orientation, and frame salience: Evidence for a theory of relational framing. *Human Communication Research, 28,* 136–152.

Persuasion Card Games

♣ Introduction

One of the more interesting set of card talk games I have observed was in the context of hostage negotiations. I've studied communication patterns in this context for years by analyzing actual hostage taker–police negotiator interactions. What makes these games interesting is their diversity.

The first game the police seek to play with the hostage taker is the Getting to Know You Game, the purpose of which is for the police negotiator to establish a relationship with the hostage taker so they can work out a surrender deal. Then the police negotiator switches to various bargaining games to try to trade food or other necessities for hostages. The final set of games involves the hostage taker giving up and coming out, which is an intense time; everyone gets emotional at the end because one wrong move could be fatal.

I am fascinated by these games because they illustrate some principles of how persuasion changes people's minds and alters their behavior. In fact, persuasion is common in most communication contexts. We have seen persuasion at work in many of the games from other chapters, like the Love Talk Game from chapter 5. In that game relational partners try to persuade each other to escalate the relationship. The topic of this chapter—how people craft persuasive messages to effect change—focuses on how persuasion works in all talk card games.

Perhaps the most comprehensive book exploring the topic of persuasion is Dr. Dan O'Keefe's book *Persuasion: Theory and Research*. O'Keefe tells us that determining what causes people to change their attitudes has dominated the study of communication from the ancient Greeks to the present. Aristotle, one of the ancient Greek philosophers, argued that people were persuasive if they were personally credible, presented emotionally engaging topics, and crafted logically reasoned arguments.

From that time forward, scholars have been interested in why and how people change their minds. To understand how persuasion works, let's present some card talk games that people play in which one person tries to promote change.

♣ Persuasive Card Talk Games

The Soft Sell Game. Everyone has experienced a sales pitch at some point. The typical sales talk game is fairly easy to identify. We go into a store to purchase something, and a salesperson comes to help with the decision. If that person immediately starts to show a Salesperson Card, which stereotypically involves aggressively pushing products, it's a real turn-off to most people.

As a result, professional salespeople are trained to avoid the "hard sell" and instead take a "soft-sell" approach. The soft-sell process involves being friendly and helpful—developing a relationship with the customer or being a resource. Similar to hostage negotiation, the seller's relational goal is to play a Friend Card first to build rapport and learn the buyer's needs. The seller can then use this knowledge to show a little bit of the Salesperson Card and start making recommendations for other purchases. "I know just the tie that would go with that shirt," as an example.

The Buckle-Up Game. You can probably recite the commercials by heart. Health officials create public service announcements (PSAs) to encourage us to engage in healthier, less risky behavior. For example, the government has spent millions of dollars to persuade motorists to use their safety belts when driving. Most of the TV commercials tell you to buckle up because it's the law. The commercial plays the Police Officer Card that tells you to buckle up or risk getting a ticket. The slogans include "Buckle Up or Pay Up!" or "Click It or Tickit."

Of course there are similar campaigns aimed at persuading people to stop smoking, taking drugs, or engaging in risky sex. Instead of playing a Police Card or even a Public Health Officer Card, these campaigns might present, for example, a typical teenager playing a Friend Card to tell you about the dangers of these bad behaviors—again, soft sell vs. hard sell.

The Party Pickup Game. Perhaps you have been to a party or social gathering and gotten hit on by someone interested in a more intimate relationship. The game often begins with a pickup line like, "Girl, you must be tired because you've been running through my mind all day." This approach is not generally successful because it is a play from a typical Sleazy Guy Card—it's tacky and immature. The better strategy is to first play a Friend Card, initiate a conversation, and get to know the other person informally. If the person reciprocates with a Friend Card, a pleasant conversation might follow that ultimately evolves into a friendship or even more.

The Persuasive Speech Game. When you give a persuasive speech in class, you must play a talk card. Many students get in front of the class and play a Student Card to accomplish their persuasive goals. Is that the right card to play to win acceptance? Students are typically receivers of information and are not usually seen as experts qualified to give information on any subject. My advice is to play an Expert Card instead. Begin by presenting your credentials as an expert in your subject and someone who is passionate about an issue. Start by playing the wrong card, as in the other examples, and your effectiveness drops dramatically and immediately.

From Aristotle's time forward, scholars have been interested in why and how people change their minds.

Definition of Persuasion

One of the foremost authorities on persuasion is Dr. Dan O'Keefe at the University of Illinois. His book on persuasion (O'Keefe, 2002) does a great job of helping us both define it and understand how it works. He tells us that **persuasion** is defined as a specific communication situation that involves (a) a source creating (b) messages that intentionally seek to (c) arouse meanings in the targeted receivers of those messages, which results in the receiver (d) freely choosing to change their attitudes, beliefs, values, and behaviors, and (e) the receivers having a clear path to comply. Let's take a closer look at these five elements.

The Message Source. Each of the social influence games described in this chapter tells us something about the source. The first judgment a targeted receiver makes about complying with another's request is to assess that source's credibility. A credible person is perceived as **knowledgeable, trustworthy,** and **dynamic.** Playing the hard-sell Sales-person Card initially fails because it is not genu-ine and trustworthy. The same is true of the Sleazy Guy Card. The first impression is negative, so no one listens further. The source must read the situa-tion and determine which card to play that is most likely to be effective in that situation for those tar-get receivers. They must play the card in a dynamic, nonboring way. Dull people are generally not very persuasive.

© 2012 by Sergej Khakimullin. Used under license of Shutterstock, Inc.

Intentional Messages. We know from O'Keefe's definition that persuasion is an intentional act. The source sets out to change the receiver's mind. As that intention becomes clear to the receiver, and he or she is still willing to listen, then the receiver's focus turns to the source's message. Is the message attention getting, emotionally engaging, logically and clearly argued, and easy to understand?

If the answer to these questions is yes, then the intentional nature of the message is clear. The source is trying to persuade the receiver to change. For example, in the Soft Sell Game, the clerk shifts from playing a Friend Card to playing a Salesperson Card when the seller suggests additional items to purchase. That shift signals the intentional shift to a persuasive situation. If the seller's message is clear, logically reasoned, and compelling, the buyer is likely to take the additional items if they can afford them. But if the messages are unclear or the source never changes from play-ing a Friend Card to a Salesperson Card, then persuasion is likely to fail because there is no shift from communication to persuasion.

Arouse Meanings. As we know from chapter 2 on language, messages are symbolic. They seek to **create meaning** or **build an image** in the target receiver's mind. In the Party Pickup Game, what meaning is conveyed with the bad pickup line? In the Buckle Up Game, what meaning is triggered when the officer says, "Buckle Up or Pay Up!"?

When a message arouses meanings, the receivers apply their own set of **filters,** or psy-chological beliefs, attitudes, and values, to interpret the message. In other words, it's not enough to send a clear, logical, and well-reasoned message; *the only thing that matters is how the audience interprets the message.* Will they like it or not? Knowing their **message filters** is a must. If the audience dislikes police, then the audience is likely to interpret the message as a threat and might react emotionally to the Buckle Up Game. Similarly, when giving a speech, you may offend the audience by introducing a certain fact or opinion.

That's why knowing the audience's message filters is so important. You must learn what turns them on and turns them off!

Changing Attitudes, Beliefs, Values, and Behaviors. An **attitude** is a judgment about likes and dislikes (e.g., *I like football.*). A **belief** is a judgment about truth or falsity (*Football is dangerous.*). **Values** are about what's right and wrong (*Football should be banned.*). And **behaviors** relate to a person's actions, including their communications (*I am not going to play football.*). If the intended meanings are aroused in the receivers, they are more likely to change their thoughts and actions.

In the Soft Sell Game, the clerk wisely begins with a Friend Card to learn about the customer's needs. That allows the clerk to reflect the intended ambiance of the store as a fashionable, friendly, and popular place to shop. Of course, the customer knows the clerk is interested in selling items so the intention to persuade is out in the open. Playing the Friend Card before the Salesperson Card is being nice and friendly.

O'Keefe's other key point is that in defining persuasion, receivers must have a free will to comply. They must have the freedom to decide whether they want to change their attitudes, beliefs, values, and behaviors. Coercion is not persuasion. In the Soft Sell Game, the customer is free to purchase or reject the merchandise. As long as the salesperson presents it as a free-will situation, then it is all about persuasion and not coercion.

> **A♥**
> *Message receivers must have the freedom to decide whether they want to change their attitudes.*

A Clear Path to Comply. Finally, the last judgment that a target receiver makes about the message is whether he or she has the ability to comply with the final request. Is the path toward compliance clear or does it have roadblocks? The receiver's thinking goes something like this: Do I know how to comply? Am I willing to comply? What will happen when I comply? What will others think of me if I comply?"

The Buckle Up Game is a good example. If receivers find the source credible, the messages clear, and they change their minds to believe that buckling up is a good thing, then the question is, Can they comply? The receivers might think, "Yes, it's easy to buckle up—it just takes a couple of seconds. Yes, I am willing to buckle up and I believe that buckling up won't make me uncomfortable while driving.

"But what if my friends make fun of me for buckling up?" If this thought sequence happens, then maybe the person becomes less willing to do it. The path to compliance is blocked by the perception of social rejection. However, if the path is clear, and the person believes that friends won't be a problem, then buckling up is more likely. They are officially persuaded at that point.

Psychological Motivations for Change

These examples and the definition of persuasion suggest that there are several psychological reasons that people change their minds. Let's review a few of the reasons that seem most influential in driving change.

Psychological Needs. Dr. Abraham Maslow's (1970/1954) classic book on motivation and personality says that individuals can be motivated to change when we appeal to their fundamental needs. Many individuals try to influence others by either threatening to withhold key psychological needs or appealing to these needs in some way.

Recall that we talked about social needs in chapter 4 in the context of defining social identity and self-concept. Social needs are included in this list, but they exist within a broader framework and function hierarchically. That is, once the first set of needs is met, then the second set becomes important, and so on. The needs Maslow focused on include:

1. **Physiological needs.** Survival needs for food, water, and air.
2. **Safety needs.** The need to be protected from harm and become physically and emotionally secure, while having structure and order in life.
3. **Belongingness and love.** The need to achieve the relational goals of socialization and inclusion with people and groups, and form bonds with others for reasons other than meeting physiological or safety needs.
4. **Self esteem.** The need to accomplish the self-presentation and achievement needs of being viewed as competent (positive face), able to accomplish tasks well, and enhance status and reputation.
5. **Self actualization.** The need to make some type of lasting contribution to the world and make the most of yourself.

Interpretation of Maslow's hierarchy of needs.

Notice how these needs are referenced in the card talk games listed above in the context of persuasive appeals. The Soft Sell Game appeals to our self-esteem needs. The Buckle-Up Game references our safety needs. The Party Pickup Game relates to our need for belonging and love. The argument is that if you do these things, you can be safe, be loved, feel good about yourself, and even make a lasting contribution to society. These arguments have been used since the beginning of time and they are all needs based.

Psychological Balance and Consistency. In his review of the psychological forces that encourage us to change, O'Keefe reveals that another powerful motivation to change is our deep-seated drive for psychological or mental consistency. People strive to live a stress-free life and reduce any inconsistencies they encounter. Everyone holds many sets of beliefs, opinions, attitudes, and ideas about people, places, objects, and issues. We strive to keep all these diverse cognitions consistent and in balance with one another to maintain a stress-free state of mind. Cognitions related to one another that are inconsistent cause stress, and we work hard to eliminate those inconsistencies.

For example, you might like horror movies but your best friend hates them. This awareness creates an inconsistency or imbalance in your mind that needs to be consciously addressed. You can choose to (a) live with this relatively trivial inconsistency, (b) change your mind (or your friend's mind) about the movie preferences, or (c) change your mind about the friendship. Of those three, which would you choose? Most people choose the easiest path to consistency, which in this case would involve learning to either live with it or changing movie preferences. Eliminating the friendship would not usually be an option for such a trivial issue.

Appealing to the need for consistency is a common tactic in persuasion. In playing the Soft Sell Game, the clerk might say, "This outfit makes you look sharp, just like your friend." In other words, it's inconsistent that your friend would value his or her attire

© 2012 by Mark Stout Photography. Used under license of Shutterstock, Inc.

© 2012 by Mopic. Used under license of Shutterstock, Inc.

more than you. The easy fix to create consistency is for you to buy the outfit so you can look good, too. Another example is the Persuasive Speech Game. In that game you might tell people that their actions should be consistent with their words. If they say they want to help save the rainforest, then they should join your organization dedicated to that cause.

Learning and Reinforcement. Attitudes and behaviors are shaped by conditioning processes or getting positively or negatively reinforced for thinking and behaving in particular ways. This is how we learn. Our actions bring about a change—positive or negative—in our environment. If we study and get a good grade, we may learn to study. The positive outcome (the good grade) reinforces the behavior (studying).

Similarly, negative outcomes cause us to decrease the behavior associated with them. If every time we ask for a date we're turned down, we may stop asking for dates or at least stop asking for dates using the same failed approach. Over time, this learning molds our behavior in that we want to do more things that result in positive reinforcements and fewer things that result in negative reinforcements.

Learning plays an important role in trying to influence someone. When the Party Pickup Game is played well, each play made from a Friend Card is reciprocated. Each person receives a pleasant response from the other, positively reinforcing the prior comment. The friendlier the play, the more reinforcing it is, and the more it continues. When the sleazy pickup lines are used, they are met with a negative reaction which, hopefully, causes the person using the lines to take stock and try a more genuine approach. The general strategy is to make plays from talk cards that the message receiver is likely to find rewarding.

Fear and Emotion. Emotional appeals are often used in persuasive messages to arouse feelings of pride, love, pity, nostalgia, concern, anger, or fear. The Buckle-Up Game is often played by using a fear appeal. Perhaps you have seen commercials in which viewers are shown how people die when they get into a crash and are not buckled up. The dummies get thrown from the vehicle and die instantly.

You can probably think of many other fear appeals you have seen showing the negative consequences of drinking and driving, unsafe sex, smoking, or taking drugs. A fear appeal stimulates emotional reactions by linking negative consequences with a failure to accept the message's recommendation. "If you don't buckle up, you'll die." An effective fear appeal has several important elements:

1. **The fear appeal establishes a threat.** For example, the crash dummies TV commercials demonstrate the threat of what will happen to our bodies if we don't buckle up.

2. **The fear appeal shows that the threat is real for the receiver.** For the fear appeal to be effective, listeners have to see that the threat could actually happen and they are vulnerable. For example, several safety belt campaigns show testimonials from real people about their friends who died in traffic crashes. The people and the stories are real to show that the threat is real.

3. **The fear appeal should show that the proposed action will stop or reduce the threat.** "Buckling up will solve the problem" is the message from the crash dummies. The commercials show the dummies in a crash with and without the belts. The dummies are fine when they wear belts and smashed up when they're not worn.

4. **The fear appeal should show that the proposed action is easy.** Not only will the belt solve the problem, it's easy to use. It only takes a couple of seconds to snap a safety belt. And the belts are adjustable to make sure they're comfortable for any body size.

5. **The fear appeal should show that the proposed action is doable.** Cars used to be made without seat belts. To tell someone to buckle up and that it's easy is great, but if there are no seatbelts in the car, the proposal is not very doable. An effective fear appeal should show the steps necessary to comply in a way that makes each step seem capable of being performed.

To summarize, when someone plays a card to persuade the other to change, it evokes a **psychological response**. The message might threaten or reinforce a basic human need, it might stimulate a perceived inconsistency, or it might evoke fear and emotion. If the card threatens someone's **need for security**, the other might want to know how to avoid that. If the card **creates inconsistency**, the other will want to know how to resolve it easily and quickly. The same is true of a fear reaction. When the listeners are scared, they want to know how they can feel secure once again. The key is knowing in advance what kind of psychological reaction is most likely when you play a card. That means understanding as much as possible about the listeners' attitudes, beliefs, and values—their **filters**.

Social Motivations for Change

In addition to psychological reasons to change, there are many social reasons why individuals might choose to comply with a request to change. In terms of psychological needs, we've already seen that the need to be included in some group or belong to that group is fundamental for everyone. That need is a private, internal drive innate within everyone. As the individual looks beyond their specific personal needs to the environment, some additional social motivations begin to assert themselves. Let's look at these social motivators.

Social Norms. Perhaps the broadest form of social influence is a social norm. A **norm** is a behavioral expectation, or social rule, that members of a group or society use to define appropriate and inappropriate attitudes, beliefs, values, and behaviors. As we reflect on what we think or do, we try to figure out if it is acceptable to people that matter to us. "Is that how we do things around here?" is a question that reflects whether we're operating within the rules or outside the rules as we perceive them.

Remember in chapter 1 when we talked about constitutive and regulative rules for playing card games? These rules are really social norms and they tell us when we are in bounds or out of bounds with respect to our card games. One of the funniest movies I've ever seen is *Borat*. The movie was about someone from another culture constantly breaking the rules, but people excused him (at least initially) because they perceived he didn't understand the rules.

© 2012 by Eric Broder Van Dyke/Shutterstock.com

Group Conformity. These norms become particularly powerful when they are made explicit within specific groups or collections of people. As they become more explicit they produce pressure to conform to the norms—to adhere to the rules. As discussed in the chapter on socialization, we all need to be a part of groups and need to feel accepted by others. At times, however, the need to be accepted can result in taking on the attitudes, beliefs, and behaviors of the group members without considering whether doing so is a good idea.

In a classic study on group conformity by Dr. Solomon Asch (1956), participants were presented with three lines drawn on a piece of paper and asked to judge which of the lines matched a fourth line in length. The study was conducted in a group setting, where all but one of the participants was a confederate, or someone working for the experimenter. The only real participant was the last person to answer. One by one, group members answered that the same wrong line matched the fourth line.

Results showed that most of the participants were influenced by the group and conformed to the majority opinion, even though it was obviously incorrect. Only about one-fourth of the participants were not influenced by the group. In this setting, the norm became explicit and was repeated over and over. This same principle applies to dress and language. To be a part of the hip-hop culture, it is important to conform to their appearance and language rules to show respect for these cultural values.

Social Contagion. Sometimes group conformity becomes so intense that people can't resist the pressure. **Group contagion** occurs when individuals behave within a group in a way that would be unlikely if they were on their own. For example, on their own initiative, people are unlikely to stand up in the middle of an auditorium, throw their arms up in the air, and sit back down. But when the wave comes around the football stadium, people conform. Within a group, individuals become uninhibited and follow the lead of others. **Contagion** can cause harmless behavior like the wave, as well as disruptive behavior like mobs of people who loot stores during a riot. People caught up in the moment do things they would not normally even consider.

> A♥
>
> *Group contagion occurs when individuals behave within a group in a way that would be unlikely if they were on their own.*
>
> A♠

♣ Persuasion Theories

Social Influence Strategies. Several prominent scholars have combined these psychological and social motivations to build models explaining how communicators try to socially influence others. For example, psychologist Dr. Robert Cialdini (1993) found there are essentially six strategies people use in various combinations to influence one another:

1. **Reciprocity:** One of the more powerful social norms is reciprocity—the expectation that people repay in kind when they receive a gift or favor.
2. **Consistency:** People align their behavior with their stated commitments, particularly when they are public and voluntary.
3. **Social Proof:** People want to be part of the crowd and conform to peer pressure. Testimonials from well-liked or famous people often activate this conformity.
4. **Liking:** People like those who like them. Liking increases when people uncover real, genuine similarities between one another. Genuine praise also increases liking.
5. **Authority:** People defer to experts. Exposing expertise that an audience respects builds its perception of the speaker as a subject authority.
6. **Scarcity:** People want more of what they can have less of. When persuaders indicate that an item is scarce or only available for a limited time, they're appealing to scarcity. And research shows it works.

What psychological motivators are at work in these strategies? Scarcity appeals to the fear of withholding physiological or safety needs if the scarce items are perceived as key for survival. Social proof deals with our drive for inclusion and the need to belong. Consistency, of course, focuses on the need to restore balance and eliminate uncertainty in one's life. Liking appeals to reinforcement as we want to be around others who give us rewards of some kind.

Social motivators are also evident in these strategies. The idea of social norms and group conformity are behind the reciprocity and social proof strategies. The need to defer to an authority figure is a learned reaction from our families because we were positively reinforced for adhering to authority and punished for not complying.

Theory of Reasoned Action. A second theory widely used in persuasion attempts is a good example of how psychological and social factors combine to influence people. The **Theory of Reasoned Action** (Fishbein & Ajzen, 1975) argues that persuasion is a result of careful, reasoned reflection about the speaker's key points. The theory contends that:

1. Listeners' intentions to comply are driven first by their general attitudes and beliefs toward the behavior the speaker is seeking to alter and the listeners' specific desires about how much they want to change their behavior.
2. After looking first at their own internal thoughts, listeners turn to their social surroundings. If they perceive that others who are important to them (e.g., friends and parents) want them to engage in the behavior, they are likely to change their behavior.

© 2012 by Anton Gvozdikov. Used under license of Shutterstock, Inc.

If the speaker is successful in attracting the audience's attention with the message, then the listeners first think about whether they agree with the speaker and like what the person has to say. Second, they think about whether the change would be popular with their friends. Again, the psychological properties of satisfying needs and getting rewarded for compliance, along with the social elements of conforming with norms, are reflected in this theory.

The key implication for playing card games is that good arguments are needed to first change peoples' attitudes and then make compliance a popular, socially acceptable choice. Take careful note of the order of these recommendations. Make good arguments and then make them appear popular.

Elaboration Likelihood Theory. A third theory does not take for granted that people automatically listen carefully to a speaker's message. In fact, **Elaboration Likelihood Theory** (Petty & Cacioppo, 1981) says that the amount of persuasion the speaker achieves depends on how well the audience listens to the key arguments. If they listen, they are more likely to change their behaviors. The key elements of the theory include:

1. The more listeners **elaborate** on or think about an issue the more they will change their opinions about that issue.
2. Listeners can listen or mentally elaborate on an issue in two ways. **Central elaboration** means they weigh the issue carefully and extensively—they give it full consideration.
3. **Peripheral elaboration** means they use a simple decision rule to judge the message, such as appearance or credibility. If they believe the speaker is not credible, the messages are uninteresting, or the concept is too weird, they will not listen nor will they change their minds about the issue.

Basically, the **Elaboration Likelihood Theory** argues that audiences must find the speakers and the information sufficiently rewarding that they are willing to listen and pay full attention. So, picking out a topic on a card aimed at influencing others should be done carefully. The topics and the styles must be attractive and rewarding to the audience if the persuasive attempt has any chance of success.

Research tells us that we're more likely to elaborate on, or think more about an issue when we are situationally more aware of what's going on around us as we communicate. More aware people are more tuned into their environment and think things through more thoroughly. In a sense, people who are more situationally aware are more open to persuasive arguments. That doesn't mean they are more easily persuaded, but it does mean they pay more attention and listen more carefully.

Results:

If your score is over 60, then you're fairly attuned to yourself and your surroundings. You are more likely to pay attention to people and listen to their messages. Your card play is helped since you are probably better able to understand the needs of your audience and can adapt your topics and styles needed to get their attention.

Social Norming Theory. This theory builds directly on the powerful idea that people need to conform to social norms. When deciding how to behave in most situations, individuals try to locate a social norm to guide their behavior. What's normal? What are the rules and expectations that guide the behavior of other group members? Once the individual locates those norms, he or she is motivated to comply with them to fit into the group.

Once individuals have located the norm, they look to see if the norm provides a lot of flexibility in how to act, or if it is restrictive. If the norm is perceived as flexible, people feel they have permission to behave any way they want to. However, if the rules are perceived as restrictive, individuals feel more compelled to observe them.

The Buckle-Up Game is a good example. If people perceive that hardly anyone wears a safety belt, then there is little social pressure to conform to a speaker's request to wear a belt. "After all, no one else is doing it, so why should I?" reasons the listener. But, if the listener thinks that nearly everyone else is buckling up, then he or she would feel weird not complying with the request to buckle up.

My good friends and colleagues at Michigan State University, Drs. Sandi Smith and Charles Atkin (2006) used **Social Norming Theory** to reduce student drinking around our campus. The idea is that if students believe other students drink a lot, then they believe they're normal if they also drink a lot. In their research, Sandi and Charles found that 64 percent of students reported drinking five

© 2012 by Lisa F. Young. Used under license of Shutterstock,Inc.

or fewer drinks "the last time they partied." Yet the perception was that 49 percent of typical students consumed five or more drinks. Consequently, if students consumed five or more drinks at any given event, they were drinking more than the average student—not less. Once students were made aware of the true norm they reduced their drinking to be more in line with it.

Which Theory Is Best? No theory is the best in any absolute sense. Each one is used to understand different persuasive communication card games. For example, the **Influence Strategies** are used often to explain how advertising seeks to influence buyers. The **Theory of Reasoned Action** is used to help health professionals design health campaigns. The theory tells us that a two-pronged approach is needed—attitude change plus social pressure—to change the public's health behavior.

Elaboration Likelihood Theory is more narrowly focused on explaining how specific attitudes change in response to persuasive messages. It focuses on the importance of ensuring that people pay attention to the key arguments encouraging change. **Social Norming Theory** is most valuable when it's clear that the audience is misinformed about some important social norm, like drinking or engaging in other risky behaviors. The theory points the way for how to change the perception of those norms and reduce risky behavior.

If we combine the theories into a set of recommendations about what motivates people to change their minds we might come up with the following list:

- A key part of any message is the source's credibility. Make sure you bolster your credentials so people will want to listen to you. Be likable, well informed, and interesting. Play more than one talk card when speaking.
- Make sure people pay attention to your message. Don't give them any excuses to ignore you as a speaker or the key points of your message. Remember, give good reasons the audience should change their attitudes and beliefs toward your position. A clear, simple message is always best.
- Social pressure is important. Make sure your message contains information about what's normal and that most other people are taking your path.
- Finally, are you asking people to do something they are capable of doing? It's important to ask for things that are within someone's grasp. Extreme requests are difficult to fulfill.

♣ Message Composition

When selecting a topic to communicate we don't think much about the structure of the message. But O'Keefe's (2002) summary of the research tells us that message structure is important for it to be effective. Essentially, the structure of the message should be determined by how the audience is likely to perceive it. Let's look at some of the key structural issues that determine message effectiveness.

One-Sided versus Two-Sided Messages. A **one-sided message** presents only those arguments that favor the persuader's recommendation. This type of message is best used when the audience already favors the proposal or is not well informed about it. For example, if the audience is unfamiliar with the organization you want them to join in

your persuasive speech, there is no reason to tell them any negatives about the organization.

However, if the audience feels negatively toward your organization, present a **two-sided message** that sets out arguments for your position and refutes or disparages arguments that oppose your group's position. Two-sided messages are best used when the audience is well informed about the issues being addressed or when the audience initially opposes the position being advocated. In these cases, the persuader should counter the possible negative positions by refuting them, in addition to presenting the advocated position. The Soft Sell Game is a good example. Once the seller learns that the buyer knows about competitive products, it is important to show how the seller's product outperforms the competition.

Explicit vs. Implicit Conclusions. A good persuasive message suggests one or more beliefs or attitudes the audience should agree with or behaviors the audience should adopt or avoid. The proposed conclusion can be either **explicit**, laying out clearly what the recommendation is that should be adopted or held, or **implicit** by leaving the audience to draw its own conclusions based on the evidence provided by the persuader.

The Party Pick-Up Game is best played by making the conclusion implicit. The goal of the game is to spend time getting to know one another. There is no specific proposal the person can advocate; or rather, any proposal other than "Let me get you a drink" would probably be inappropriate.

On the other hand, a message attempting to persuade listeners to vote a particular way on a technical proposal related to healthcare insurance may be more difficult for them to process; it's a complex issue. In this case it is more difficult for listeners to draw their own conclusions, particularly if new and unfamiliar evidence is presented. The persuader would need to provide an explicit recommendation.

Primacy vs. Recency. In situations in which two speakers have the opportunity to present opposing viewpoints, is it better to go first or second? The answer depends on the topic being debated. For certain topics, the audience remembers what it hears first. This idea is called a primacy effect. When a topic is controversial, it is better to present your arguments first because the audience is more likely to recall the first arguments it hears. When the topic is more interesting, when your arguments are stronger than your opponent's, or when the audience is familiar with the topic, a primacy effect is likely, making it best to go first in these situations.

In contrast, when the topic under debate is noncontroversial, is uninteresting, or is unfamiliar, then a recency effect emerges; that is, the audience is likely to remember what it hears last. In addition, if there is a long delay between the messages from first persuader and those of the second persuader, the audience is more likely to recall what it heard last. Remember this when you are playing the Persuasive Speech Game. Give your most persuasive reasons last because most students' presentations are noncontroversial. The audience is most likely to pay attention to what you say last, so make it good!

The point is that knowing your audience is essential.

Analyzing the Audience

Throughout this chapter we have talked at length about what listeners are likely to feel, know, or believe to be true. The point is that *knowing your audience is essential.* Whenever a card is played with a persuasive message, it is important to know (a) the size of the audience; (b) demographic information about the audience in terms of its education, income, cultural orientations, age, and knowledge of the issue; (c) its interest and commitment to the issue; and (d) whether it agrees or disagrees with the issue.

Consider these recommendations in adjusting your talk cards to an audience:

- If the **size** of the audience is large, it is important to be dynamic to keep them engaged in the message. If it is small, refer to individuals by name or get the audience involved in your presentation to connect with them as individuals.
- Understanding the **demographic** characteristics of the audience is important because of the filters it's likely to use in interpreting messages. If the **cultural orientation** of the audience is important, by celebrating its ethnicity or commitment to a cause, then referencing the cause or showing respect for the ethnicity is vital. The speaker needs to first earn the respect of the audience before delivering a persuasive message.

- If the audience is **hostile** to the speaker's message, the best strategy is to reduce any interference the audience might present and get it to listen to the message. Hostile audiences don't like to listen to opposing views.
- If the audience is **critical**, but not hostile, then a two-sided message is best. Recognizing the audience's opposing views not only shows respect for the position, but shows an understanding of the issues. The goal is to create doubts in the audience's resistance to the persuasive message.
  - If the audience is **uninformed** about, but interested in the topic, then the goal is to provide enough information to educate it about the issue so the message can be processed. It is also likely that the speaker is unknown to the audience, requiring him or her to build credibility by talking about credentials, or drawing their own similarity to the audience so it listens. Building a sense of excitement about the issue is also important.
    - For a **well-informed** audience that agrees with the speaker, the key is being well prepared to reinforce the group's position with evidence that will be deemed credible. After all, the audience knows a lot about the issue, so being prepared is important.

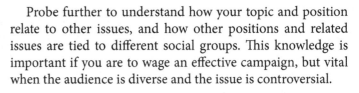

Careful consideration of the attitudes currently held by the audience helps you to tailor your talk cards appropriately. A good persuader, whether addressing one person or a thousand, knows about his or her audience and adapts the persuasive message to the attributes of the audience. One way to plan a persuasive campaign is to interview several people who are similar to the audience for your persuasive message. You might want to ask them:

- What are the words, ideas, or concepts that come to mind when you think about your topic?
- Why do you think some people favor your position? And why do you think some people oppose your position?
- Who do you think favors your position? Who do you think opposes your position?

Probe further to understand how your topic and position relate to other issues, and how other positions and related issues are tied to different social groups. This knowledge is important if you are to wage an effective campaign, but vital when the audience is diverse and the issue is controversial.

A good persuader, whether addressing one person or a thousand, knows about his or her audience and adapts the persuasive message to the audience.

© 2012 by iofoto. Used under license of Shutterstock, Inc.

♣ A Word About Ethics

After you master the basics of persuasion, you have a tool that can be used honestly or deceptively. As already discussed, one component of source credibility is trustworthiness. Anyone known for being deceptive loses trustworthiness and effectiveness as a source in the long run. Although there are certainly moral and religious reasons for being honest, there is also a practical one: *We don't believe people who have deceived us.* In the long run, we should expect deceptive practices to fail. *Be ethical and moral. Always!*

Chapter Summary

- **Persuasion involves sending messages that arouse meanings** that encourage change. Persuasion is a difficult goal to achieve because everything must line up. People must pay attention to the message, it must resonate with them, and they must be able to comply with it. That's a lot to ask.
- **There are many psychological motivations for change.** Not only do basic needs drive our desire for change, but mentally we're wired to keep all our attitudes and beliefs consistent. We're motivated to pursue positive reinforcement, avoid punishment, and resolve our fears. Messages that stimulate these reactions are more likely to be successful.
- **We are driven to satisfy our social motivations for change.** We like to conform to social norms and sometimes get caught up in a contagious event that makes us want to follow the crowd into extreme behavior. Messages that move us in these social directions have proven effective.
- **There are many important theories of persuasion.** Collectively they tell us that persuasive messages are likely to be effective when people are given incentives to pay attention to the message, good arguments to change their attitudes, and are made aware of social pressure to change.
- **Creating persuasive messages depends on audience needs.** When audiences are uninformed, a one-sided message with explicit conclusions and important arguments given at the end of the message works best. When audiences disagree or are informed, then a two-sided message with implicit conclusions and important arguments at the beginning works best.
- **Above all, analyze the audience!** When the audience is well understood, it is easier to craft persuasive, effective messages.

> A ♥ ♠ A
>
> *Anyone known for being deceptive loses effectiveness as a source in the long run.*

Lessons Learned

Throughout this chapter we have taken the position of the sender or source of messages. As you know, card games involve multiple people with multiple perspectives. When you play a card, the other person must decide what card to play in response. Persuasion is all about understanding how to structure your card to elicit the intended response from the other player. Based on the concepts in this chapter, here are some lessons learned:

- **Persuasive card play requires careful thought.** Make sure you understand the audience's views of the topic, what message is most likely to accomplish your goals, and what cards should be played in the persuasive context. Persuasion requires careful thought and preparation.
- **Plan the kind of psychological reaction that will best motivate the audience to change.** In structuring the message, decide if it's best to reference needs, create inconsistency, deliver positive reinforcement, or simply scare the audience into action.
- **Plan the desired sociological reaction to effect change.** Referencing social norms can trigger conformity needs that are powerful in changing an audience's behavior.

- **Any persuasive attempt should be theoretically driven.** Decide which theory best matches the occasion. If the audience is hostile, the **Elaboration Likelihood Theory** tells us the goal is to encourage careful consideration of the message—getting people to listen. If it is receptive to the message, creating logical arguments to change attitudes and build social pressure to conform to norms are likely to be most persuasive.
- **Message structure is important.** Based on audience analysis, decide whether the message should be one-sided or two-sided, whether the conclusions should be explicit or implicit, and whether it is best to go first or last with the most persuasive argument.

References

Asch, S. (1956). Studies of independence and conformity: 1. A minority of one against a unanimous majority. *Psychological Monographs, 70*(416).

Cialdini, R. B. (1993). *Influence: The psychology of persuasion.* New York: William Morrow and Company, Inc.

Fishbein, M., & Ajzen, I. (1975). *Belief, attitude, intention and behavior: An introduction to theory and research.* Reading, MA: Addison-Wesley.

Govern, J. M., & Marsch, L. A. (2001). Development and validation of the Situational Awareness Scale. *Consciousness and Cognition, 10,* 366–378.

Maslow, A. H. (1970/1954). *Motivation and personality.* New York: Harper & Row.

O'Keefe, D. J. (2002). *Persuasion: Theory and research* (2e ed.). Thousand Oaks, CA: SAGE Publications, Inc.

Petty, R. E., & Cacioppo, J. T. (1981). *Attitudes and persuasion: Classic and contemporary approaches.* Dubuque, IA: Wm. C. Brown.

Smith, S. W., Atkin, C. K., Martell, D., Allen, R., & Hembroff, L. (2006). A social judgment theory approach to conducting formative research in a social norms campaign. *Communication Theory, 16,* 141–152.

© 2012 by mast3r. Used under license of Shutterstock, Inc.

CHAPTER Seven

Conflict Card Games

♣ Introduction

Conflict games are particularly challenging, largely because they are emotionally draining and stressful. Most people try to avoid conflict. Avoidance often results in parties sidestepping important issues that are critical to discuss for the health of their relationship. In other words, conflict is about change or a shift in direction. That shift can be troublesome and threatening, but it can also be a growth opportunity.

Let's look at three conflict card games and explore both their dangers and opportunities. These games examine communication challenges at the interpersonal, organizational, and international levels.

The Sniper Game. When intimate couples fight, they're often not good at it. One of the least productive talk card games they play is the Sniping Game. It involves one person trying to pick a fight with an intimate partner. Perhaps she is upset about something. She walks into the room where he's watching TV and yells as loudly as possible, "You bastard!" Then she stomps out of the room. He might sit there and respond, "What?" The idea is that she takes a shot to "kill" her target with a remark and then quickly exits.

The **danger** in sniping is that it risks irreversible damage to the relationship. The **opportunity** presented by her sniper attack is an opening to address issues dividing them. This opportunity is only realized if she stays in the room and tries to work through her concerns.

A
♥

Most people avoid conflict. Avoidance often results in parties sidestepping important issues.

A
♠

The Job Review Game. Imagine a veteran employee of a company. He just got called into the boss' office for his annual job review. He anticipates that it will be tense since he and the boss have not been getting along well. As he walks into her office, the boss seems upset. She begins the conversation by pulling out her full Boss Card and shoving it in his face, saying, "What the hell do you think you're doing? Don't you know that we're in trouble here, and all you do is send me bad information about what's going on in the field? That doesn't do me any good. You better straighten up and do your job!"

The **danger** in yelling at the employee is that she risks alienating him from working there, while threatening a positive working relationship. The **opportunity** created by her outburst is raising some important issues about his performance and the organization's goals. As in the Sniper Game, these opportunities will only surface if she calms down and shifts the discussion to the specific issues causing her outburst.

The Diplomatic Slight Game. Politicians play lots of card talk games. In 2010, Vice President Joe Biden traveled to Israel on a diplomatic mission aimed at stimulating peace talks between Palestinians and Israelis. One of the big issues was and is development of Jewish settlements in East Jerusalem, which Palestinians claim as their capital. The day Vice President Biden arrived, Israeli Prime Minister Netanyahu announced more government-supported settlements in East Jerusalem, which U.S. officials took as a slap in the face to the vice president's peace mission.

A few weeks later, the Israeli prime minister visited Washington, and President Obama did not have dinner with him, which the Israeli press interpreted as a diplomatic slight, or insult. Normally the president would have a state dinner with the Israel prime minister, but President Obama chose not to. Was he trying to send a message by playing his President Card?

The **danger** presented by President Obama's diplomatic slight is a less cooperative relationship with Israel. The **opportunity** presented by the slight is increased motivation to help each country decide what kind of relationship they want in order to bring peace to the Middle East. To take advantage of that opportunity, they would need to address the issue directly and not run from it.

♣ Conflict Defined

To understand these three games, let's first see how they qualify as conflicts. According to an earlier book of mine (Donohue & Kolt, 1992), there are four elements that define a card talk exchange as a conflict:

> The key is to keep the conflict focused on the material interests and away from social identities.

1. **An Expressed Struggle.** Each of these games reveals a struggle that all parties recognize. We are not talking about conflicts that only one person acknowledges. These conflicts are out in the open. All parties must see that a conflict has emerged and have a stake in its outcome so they are motivated to resolve it.

2. **Between Interdependent Parties.** Notice that in each example individuals are highly involved with one another, either as relational partners, employer/employee, or individuals involved in a diplomatic exchange. One factor that feeds conflict escalation is the difficulty of walking away. The more interdependent parties are, the more they can impact one another personally and even economically.

3. **With Perceived Incompatible Needs and Interests.** All conflicts involve issues related to both social identity needs *and* material interests. Let's first explore the social identity component, since it is the

most challenging to address. Recall from chapter 4 (focusing on social identity) that we talked about how people build identities to enable them satisfy their social needs for inclusion (being respected by the group), control (getting people to listen), and affection (getting people to be nice). Every time someone plays a talk card, we evaluate the extent to which the card supports or threatens these three needs.

Would you feel disrespected and personally offended if your boss yelled at you as in the Job Review Game? If yes, then you would feel she attacked your social identity, because she denied your needs for inclusion and affection. **Needs-based conflicts** like this one quickly become emotional when people feel personally attacked. Your positive and negative face needs have been denied, and you may try to strike back to restore them. This **attack-defend cycle** is what makes conflicts escalate.

Also notice that in the Job Review Game the boss raises the **material interest** issue of how the employee communicate with her. She complains about not getting enough of the right kind of information. If she had raised that interest without first attacking the employee's social identity, they could have talked about it calmly and constructively. Instead, she chose to yell. In conflict, satisfying our social identity needs is mandatory. *These needs are not negotiable.* We must satisfy and defend them.

Material interests are different. These issues are negotiable since there are many ways to resolve them. All conflicts contain issues related to social identities and material interests and, therefore, have the potential to get out of control if parties focus only on identities. The key is to keep the conflict focused on the material interests and away from social identities.

4. **And Perceived Interference.** Not only do parties perceive that they have incompatible identity needs and material interests, they also perceive the other is actively **interfering** and standing in the way of satisfying those needs and interests. After all, if you perceive the other is showing disrespect, then that person is interfering with your right to be addressed respectfully, honestly, and pleasantly.

Perceived interference was a big factor in the Diplomatic Slight Game the politicians played. By announcing settlements in East Jerusalem, the United States perceived that the Israelis were actively interfering with the peace process. The Israelis refuted this perception by claiming the timing of the announcement was purely coincidental. Whatever the case, perceived interference played a big part in the dispute.

Problem Solving vs. Conflict. It is important to note the difference between problem solving and conflict. **Problem solving** involves the parts 1, 2, and 3 of the conflict definition above. We have a problem when we have an expressed struggle between interdependent parties who perceive incompatible needs and interests. In problem solving, there is no perceived interference since both parties are working together to resolve the differences.

However, a situation **escalates to conflict** when the **perception of interference** becomes obvious. Most interference appears in the form of social identity attacks. Showing disrespect, not listening, or being rude is a sign the other is less interested in helping you address your material interests and more interested in attacking your **positive and negative faces**.

Vice President Joe Biden.

Conflicts Are Stressful

Social Identity Protection. One of my favorite perspectives about conflict issues is reflected in Felson and Tedeschi's (1992) book focusing on aggression and violence. Dr. Richard Felson makes the point that social identity is at the heart of intense conflict. On the one hand, people often run from conflicts because they are personally threatening. This sense of personal threat is created by the sense of perceived interference. When the interference is apparent and a social need is violated, the identity threat becomes real. Many feel it's best to avoid that problem and look the other way.

On the other hand, when conflict can't be avoided, the strategy for managing conflict is aimed at restoring identity. Take a look at the conflict games described at the beginning of this chapter. All of them involve someone "yelling" at someone else. In each case, this yelling (metaphorical yelling in the case of the Diplomatic Slight Game) is viewed as a personal attack. In the Sniping Game, the woman attacks her boyfriend, probably in response to something he did that she perceived as an attack on her social identity. In the Job Review Game, the boss yells at the employee, and in the Diplomatic Slight Game, the Israeli prime minister perceived that President Obama disrespected him. When social identity needs are violated, it's like telling someone that he or she is a bad person.

To protect our social identity, we often strike back **to restore positive and negative face needs**. We want to look good and we don't want to be controlled.

Disputants can reduce stress by **granting positive and negative face** needs and focusing on material interests. This is not an easy task because face issues are always present in communication and they are particularly important when parties perceive interference from one another. Later in this chapter we talk about using constructive conflict strategies to take advantage of the opportunities presented by the conflict.

Surprise. Conflicts often arise from an unintentional triggering event. Although it may seem that we have done nothing to provoke a dispute, people in conflict with us can usually point to an incident that set them off. We are perceived as having done something unacceptable. In the Diplomatic Slight Game, the offending event was a statement about settlements in East Jerusalem. Since there was no prior warning that such an announcement might be coming, it caught the United States by surprise.

Scarce Rewards. People are often emotional when they are afraid. Fear is a factor when people really want something and they can't get it. Or when people try to protect something they already own. You can imagine that the boss' yelling in the Job Review Game could have been caused by her fear of losing an important contract. That fear probably caused her to get emotional and attack the employee. Conflict can also emerge from being denied resources others have that people feel they need or deserve. When people believe they have been deprived relative to others, they can respond aggressively. Those who have resources will likely defend their right of ownership and resist giving them up without compensation.

Personal Values. Values are a person's thoughts about how things should be. In a sense, values are goals that we want to achieve, and we often expect others to pursue them as well. This means that when another's behavior is perceived as inconsistent with our value system, conflict can occur. If you think about it, our values are very personal. We integrate them into our self-concept, and they become a part of our identity. Anyone who attacks your values attacks you personally. In the Sniper Game, the woman probably yelled at her boyfriend because he violated some key value that she held strongly, and she took the violation as

A♥ When another's behavior is perceived as inconsistent with our value system, conflict can occur.

a personal attack. Conflicts over values are difficult to manage because people view values as nonnegotiable. Moreover, we often imagine that individuals who hold values different from our own are extremist and biased.

Strongly Held Beliefs. Beliefs are perceptions of what's true or untrue about someone or something. Where values are focused on what *should be*, beliefs concern what is. People are attached to their beliefs and often only look at things that are consistent with those beliefs. So when others challenge strongly held beliefs, individuals become emotional. It is almost perceived as a personal attack. The U.S.

© 2012 by CREATISTA. Used under license of Shutterstock, Inc.

believes that East Jerusalem settlements hurt the peace process. Thus, any announcement like the one delivered by the Israelis is filtered through that belief, and combined with the fact that it was a surprise, the announcement caused a great deal of emotion.

Relationship Differences. When individuals display a card style that implies a different definition of the relationship than was expected, conflict becomes emotional. For example, in the Sniper Game, the woman clearly was upset about something. The most common conflict in intimate relationships is the issue of commitment. One party is perceived to be more committed than the other. In this case, she may have been more committed than she perceived he was, causing her to snipe at him.

Relationships are personal because we give so much of ourselves. Interdependence intensifies as people become more involved socially and intimately. As a result, conflicts about relationships are emotional. There is so much at stake personally, socially, and even economically.

Opportunities Created by Conflict

It is difficult to grasp that conflict stirs up about as many **opportunities** as **dangers**. One of the classic books that focuses on how conflict creates opportunities is Professor Lewis Coser's (1956) book focusing on the functions of social conflict. He noted that most people can't see these opportunities because it requires them to look past conflict that is personally threatening. It takes courage and skill to see the opportunities instead of the conflicts. Let's look at several opportunities that the three conflict games offer the disputants.

Face Important Problems. Perhaps the most important opportunity created by conflict is that it can force individuals to **become aware of their problems** and respond to them. It is a force for change. Just as pain makes us aware that we need to take care of our bodies, conflict signals that something is wrong in our social world. It alerts us to take action before things worsen.

Can you hear the pain the woman is expressing in playing the Sniper Game? Her style is negative and forceful. The opportunities she presents include redefining their intimate relationship and perhaps strengthening it. Her partner may or may not choose to play the game, and take advantage of her caustically stated insult. If he plays his Boyfriend Card in return and asks her about the problem using a positive, low-power style, he keeps the issue focused on the material interests and less on face needs.

Provide a Tension Release. Second, conflict can serve as **a release of tension**. The sniper releases tension by playing the Sniping Game. The issue she was facing was probably causing her emotional distress. Getting it out in the open relieves her tension, while giving her an opportunity to face the issue directly rather than stew about it.

Expose Problem-Solving Alternatives. Third, conflict can make us aware of **alternative ways to do things**. The Diplomatic Slight Game provides an opportunity for the major parties in the Palestinian-Israeli dispute to address the settlements issue. Since this is such a key material issue in building peace, the perceived slight presents an opportunity to take on this issue directly. The parties may consider options to manage the settlement issue while working toward building a Palestinian homeland, a goal articulated by all sides in the conflict. Expressing diverse and often conflicting viewpoints is a necessary ingredient for effective decision making.

Strengthen Relationships. Finally, conflict has the **potential to strengthen relationships**. The willingness to confront a problem signals a commitment to the relationship. The Job Review Game played by the boss could certainly freak out the employee. Being confronted in that manner violates a number of social identity needs for respect and threatens both positive and negative face. Yet the opportunity she presents is a commitment to address vital material interests related to the business. The boss could have avoided the talk, but she cared enough about the employee and the relationship to try, even though the attempt was clumsy and potentially demotivating.

This is an important point. People who don't care about a relationship are unwilling to expend the energy necessary to solve a problem. They would rather avoid the issue until a better alternative comes along. Such neglectful behavior can be the prelude to the end of a relationship. In the Job Review Game, the employee needs the courage to face his boss and say he didn't appreciate her accusatory tone, but that he did want to know what she was talking about. That's a constructive beginning to a dialogue that will deal with the base issues.

Capitalizing on opportunities presented by conflict involves taking advantage of the energy and commitment people have invested in the situation. Realize that confronting a conflict often involves three steps:

1. Manage the conflict.
2. Resolve the conflict.
3. Transform the conflict.

Let's look closely at these three forms of conflict outcomes.

Three Forms of Conflict Outcomes

Conflict Management. My book (Donohue & Kolt, 1992) on managing interpersonal conflict begins with the assumption that disputes are rarely resolved. Resolution implies the issue is no longer meaningful or relevant to the parties. In reality, many conflicts do not conclude neatly. Frequently, the result is a standoff. People get tired and stop fighting. Or, the conflict is too complex, and people agree to confront it later.

In effect, **conflict management** focuses on the ways by which individuals control their disputes—to keep them from worsening or holding them off until another time. The Diplomatic Slight Game was never resolved. The parties only acknowledged their frustrations and concerns about the settlements issue, but there was no attempt to formally address it.

Conflict Resolution. On other hand, when parties are ready and motivated to address issues, they enter a discussion that focuses on the dispute with the intention of resolving the issues. The process might involve a mediator or someone to help define the issues and develop strategies for dealing with them. This is the point at which **conflict resolution** begins. Both parties have taken ownership of the conflict, and have agreed to develop a plan address it.

© 2012 by Kzenon. Used under license of Shutterstock, Inc.

When the boss played her Boss Card in the Job Review Game, she expressed her frustration. If the employee walked away, he would have avoided potentially escalating the conflict. This would have **managed** the conflict for him. If he stayed, played his Employee Card, and talked about the material interests with the intention of identifying and dealing with her concerns, then he would be engaging in conflict resolution.

Conflict Transformation. Disputants might be satisfied with resolving the issues and walking away from a dispute with some specific agreements for doing things differently. For example, the employee might agree to change his approach to the job, and the boss might agree to change her communication style and her task demands on the employee. Those actions would resolve the conflict. However, they would not have **transformed** their attitudes toward one another or used the conflict to restructure the workplace to enhance its productivity. When people use the conflict to take advantage of the opportunities it presents, the conflict can be **transformative**. The parties can confront both their social identity and material-based issues to create a better outcome for everyone.

Of course, this is difficult to achieve. During much of its post-colonial history, the Union of South Africa lived under a system of apartheid, or legal segregation, in which the white Afrikaner National Party government forced blacks (people of sub-Saharan Africa or of Indian descent) to live separately from whites in extreme poverty. During this period there were horrific crimes against the people of color. When apartheid ended in 1994, the new National Unity government had to decide whether to prosecute those who committed crimes against the blacks and Indians.

Nelson Mandela, the newly elected president, decided not to prosecute the crimes of apartheid because the country would have been bogged down for decades focusing on the past. Instead of having his country suffer under the burden of **conflict resolution**, Nelson Mandela and Archbishop Desmond Tutu decided to create the Truth and Reconciliation Commission and work toward **conflict transformation**. The Commission allowed people to go free if they openly confessed their crimes in public and asked for forgiveness.

© 2012 by Neftali. Used under license of Shutterstock, Inc.

The effect of the Commission was to **transform** South African society because it confronted the past head-on and built new relationships among citizens that would allow the country to grow and prosper. For their work in ending apartheid, both won Nobel Peace Prizes, Dr. Tutu in 1984 and President Mandela in 1993. You can read Dr. Tutu's amazing story in his book, *No Future Without Forgiveness* (Tutu, 1999).

Constructive vs. Destructive Conflict

This discussion about the dangers and opportunities of conflict and the possibility of transformation suggests that conflict is not necessarily something to be avoided. It is something to be embraced and channeled into a constructive opportunity. When is conflict constructive and when is it destructive?

Destructive Conflict. Conflict is more likely to be destructive to the disputants' relationships and their ability to resolve or even manage it when the parties approach a dispute using a **negative frame of reference**. A negative frame of reference is an attitude that says, "I want to protect what I have at all costs; I want to do what it takes to win the conflict and prove that I am right and can't be pushed around."

A **destructive conflict** is not about standing up for your rights, which is appropriate; it's about trying to defeat the other person as a way to save face or look tough. Sniping with no intention of follow-up, is a destructive conflict aimed at making the other person look bad. It is an attempt to get even and restore **positive face** by standing up to the other person.

A **positive frame** of reference takes a different approach. Whereas a negative frame focuses on conflict dangers and tries to minimize them by striking back at the other person, a positive frame focuses on opportunities. It says, "Hey, I might as well focus on what I can gain from the situation and look ahead to a better future, rather than trying to protect the past." As we see later, this is the foundation of constructive conflict.

Now that you know about what drives destructive conflict, what does it look like? Sniping is one of the best examples of destructive conflict brought on by a negative frame. It is one of several negative conflict management games that can trap people into a negative downward spiral. In addition to sniping, here are several other cycles that research tells us negatively impact a relationship:

Israeli Prime Minister Benjamin Netanyahu and Mayor of Jerusalem.

- **Skirting** is avoiding controversial topics. Avoiders and accommodators often ignore or try to get around tough issues by changing the topic or blowing off a comment with humor. It's possible that when President Obama met with Israeli Prime Minister Netanyahu after the diplomatic slight that both men skirted the real issues that led up to the slight.
- **Personalizing** involves accusing the other person of causing the conflict with some negative personality trait, such as being inconsiderate, insensitive, or uncaring. This is destructive because it assumes the person can't change and shoves 100 percent of the blame in his or her direction. When we call someone a name, it's like saying, "You can't change! You'll always be a loser!"
- **Complaining** involves repeating old problems again and again with no attempt to get to the underlying issues and resolve the problem. It is like sniping, but at least it brings up some specific concern, whereas sniping is simply throwing insults to cause emotional pain.

- **Aggressing** means attacking the other person either physically or psychologically so the aggressor can bolster his or her positive face or even repair negative face. Attacking someone usually involves accusing them of lying, cheating, or possessing some character flaws.

Constructive Conflict. I recently edited a book with two other professors that focused on how conflicts can be constructive (Donohue, Rogan, & Kaufman, 2011). Several chapters in the book made the point that constructive conflict focuses on at least **resolving** the conflict, and possibly using it to **transform** the relationship or some other important outcome associated with the parties' interdependence. It begins with a **positive frame**, or an attitude that looks at conflict opportunities as a potential force for change.

One of the most influential books on conflict resolution contended that substantive issues in conflicts are best resolved when parties first learn to transform their relationship (Bush & Folger, 1994). There are two major elements associated with achieving this transformation into more constructive conflict. The first is **recognition**. For conflict to be constructive it begins by **recognizing the impact** the conflict has had on the other person materially and emotionally. Recognition pulls the focus away from the individual and his or her wants and fears, and instead looks at the other person and what he or she is going through.

This recognition sets up the ability to collaborate. The process of **collaboration** involves each person recognizing the other's goals in the conflict and working toward achieving them. It means building creative solutions that can get both parties what they need from the conflict and transform the conflict into satisfying outcomes for both. Collaboration begins by not only committing to learn from the other person, but understanding the important problem driving the conflict that must be solved to transform it.

As you look at the Job Review Game, what is the boss' problem? Perhaps she is frustrated with the lack of progress in the business and she's taking it out on the employee. The boss might feel disrespected on some issue. The employee's job is to figure out what is really troubling her and address that issue. Notice how much that involves **recognizing** the conflict from the boss' perspective.

Put yourself in this situation. It's not easy to probe an issue like that with a boss. Most people would take the scolding and keep quiet. Plus, because the boss was emotional, perhaps she was not ready to talk about what's really on her mind. In that situation it would probably be best to take up the issue later when she is more composed and able to have a constructive conversation.

The second element of constructive conflict is **empowerment**. When we are empowered we have the skill and courage to take on the conflict. A person can talk about his or her issues and stick with the discussion to resolve and possibly transform the conflict. Four communication skills necessary for effective card talk games are:

1. **Listening** to the other's position;
2. **Speaking respectfully** by talking about your views on issues and avoiding personal attacks;
3. **Generating creative solutions** to both parties' problems; and
4. Working through **a specific process** to structure the discussion so it does not get off track.

© 2012 by Igor S. Srdanovic. Used under license of Shutterstock, Inc.

Generally when people begin a conflict talk card game like the Sniper Game or the Job Review Game, they begin by identifying their differences. They talk about how they see things differently and what they want to be changed. That's constructive. Parties need to understand their differences. Once those discussions take place, they can begin to address the future and what brings them together.

This **process of integration**, or coming together, is about identifying issues and generating options to address them. Don't be concerned if you are beginning a conflict and focusing on differences. That's to be expected. But once those differences have emerged, then the issue is: How can you integrate your interests and develop creative solutions to build value that both of you can use to create positive change?

Constructive conflict is all about building value. Value is your perception of two elements: (1) how well was I able to solve my problem and (2) what is the cost of the solution? If both parties were happy with how they jointly solved a problem and perceived costs were minimal, then they created value. Building value takes a commitment to spend the time necessary to create these win-win solutions.

Conflict Communication Style

This discussion lays out a path toward dealing with conflicts constructively. To take advantage of conflicts, you must first be willing to (a) confront the conflict and (b) use a communication style that allows you to listen attentively and work through the issues. These are the key elements of empowerment.

Directions: Below is a short survey of your conflict communication style. For each question give yourself a score of 1–5 using the scale provided: 1 = Strongly Disagree; 2 = Disagree; 3 = No Opinion; 4 = Agree; 5 = Strongly Agree.

CONFLICT COMMUNICATION STYLE QUESTIONS	SCORE 1–5
1. I try to act in a friendly manner when confronted by a conflict.	
2. When in a conflict I try to repeat the key points the other person says.	
3. I seldom interrupt the other person during a conflict.	
4. I pay attention to the other person's ideas.	
5. I am an open communicator when communicating during conflict.	
6. I make sure to be well prepared on the issues before I discuss them.	
7. In most conflict situations I explore the full range of issues.	
8. I usually give many good reasons why the other person should accept my ideas for dealing with the conflict.	
9. I try not to rush to a conclusion before the issues have been explored.	
10. I make a conscious effort to understand the other party's most important problems and issues.	

Total Score: _____

Results:

If you scored under 20, you are not confident in your communication style in handling conflict. If you scored above 40, you are confident. If you scored 20–40 you are unsure about your conflict communication style.

These 10 items assessed your ability to manage relational and material issues in conflict. The first 5 items focused on building relationships by being friendly, attentive, and open as a communicator. If you can achieve these objectives, you're more likely to create a collaborative climate in which to deal with the conflict. It also means you're probably able to manage your emotions and concentrate on the material issues.

The second five items addressed your ability to understand the issues in the context of the other's most important problem. Are you generally prepared when entering a conflict? Can you explore the full range of issues, develop them, and creatively ensure they solve both parties' main concerns?

If you scored well on this survey, then you are probably capable of confronting constructively. The first step in achieving this goal is being able to move through the stages of conflict constructively. Let's review these stages and see what the process looks like.

A ♥ It turns out that conflict card talk games often take a predictable path from a triggering event to the outcome. ♠ A

♣ Stages of Conflict

Another book that has made significant contributions to our understanding of conflict is from Folger, Poole, and Stutman (2008). I have known Drs. Joe Folger and Scott Poole for some time, and I've always been impressed with their insights about how conflicts progress. One of the more interesting parts of their book focuses on how conflicts evolve. It turns out that conflict card talk games often take a predictable path from a triggering event to the outcome.

Stage 1: Pre-Confrontation. The pre-confrontation stage constitutes the time between discovering an event that might have triggered the conflict and initially confronting the other person about it. In some cases, this stage is short. You see a person do something and you immediately tell him or her about it. A quick response often occurs when you are in charge of someone else's behavior. A parent might play a Dad Card when he sees his child doing something wrong or dangerous. "Hey, Samantha, don't play on the man-eating tiger. It's dangerous."

Impulsiveness may cause a person to react quickly. Sometimes another person makes you so frightened, angry, or irritated that you play a talk card without hesitation or thought. When the boss played her Boss Card and shouted at her employee in the Job Review Game, she may have done so impulsively.

If you can, it is best to delay confronting a conflict to give yourself a chance to plan. This lets you prepare and makes you feel empowered. What do you need to know to decide how to confront a conflict? What do you plan for? Use this checklist to develop the conflict most constructively.

Checklist for Confronting Conflict

- **What are your goals for the conflict materially and relationally?** When it's over what would you like to get from it? Prioritize your goals from most to least important, and concentrate on three or four of your most important goals.
- **What are the main issues in the dispute?** What are the issues you are most concerned about related to your material and relational needs? In the Job Review Game, the boss is concerned about the employee's performance and, more specifically, about the quality of the information she is receiving. She also seems to have an issue with trust and perhaps respect. The employee also has issues.
- **What data can be gathered about the issues?** What do we know about each issue to better assess the problems that need to be resolved? Have these issues been a problem in the past? To what extent have prior solutions worked?
- **How should you work through the issues?** Generally it's best to start with the easy issues and progress to the more difficult ones. The key is not to mix them up. Work through one at a time. It's important to show some progress and show the parties can work as a team to get something done. That is the key to building value.
- **What are some options for addressing each issue?** For each issue it's important to create options and determine which are most likely to be effective. Disputants should be ready to develop criteria about which options would be more useful than others. Otherwise, all options look the same. Why are some options better than others?
- **What is the best time to deal with these issues?** Determine when to talk about the issues and pick an occasion that allows sufficient time to talk about them and negotiate outcomes. It is also useful to have an agenda so you can provide structure to the problem-solving discussion. Some conflicts must be handled on the spot; others benefit by picking a date in the future.

© 2012 by e. Used under license of Shutterstock, Inc.

Stage 2: Confrontation. A confrontation is the initial statement by a person that something is wrong, or there's an issue to address. It might be the statement that kicks off the discussion and defines the card game as a conflict episode. In the Job Review Game the employee came in and got blasted by his boss! This is a typical confrontation. Most are brief and end in a matter of minutes.

In many cases, a person says something, the other responds, and it's over. This brief encounter might manage the conflict without resolving it. Planning might prolong the episode so the conflict can be moved from managed to resolved.

Although it is usually brief, a confrontation is a sequence that moves from an opening statement through extended responses to a closing statement. The opening of a confrontation typically involves a statement about what you wish the other would do or stop doing. Phrasing the opening statement is critical because it sets the tone for the rest of the confrontation. Starting a confrontation with an insult, command, or accusation attacks the positive image that most people have of themselves and prompts defensiveness.

The boss' outburst in the Job Review Game is a good example. Rather than start with this destructive approach, she should have used a friendlier opener to put the employee at ease and solicit his help in solving the main material interests. Part of the planning process should involve thinking about the confrontation's opening statement.

Stage 3: Reaction. Once the differences have been expressed, both parties react to one another's statements. In some cases, an explanation is provided for the negative behavior. In effect, the person has an opportunity to explain his or her side of the story. However, there may be defensive reactions. A person may respond to the opening statement by denying that anything happened, stating that he or she was not responsible for anything that might have happened, or by blaming the confronter.

Even more destructive, the accused person may countercomplain by stating the confronter has engaged in other actions that are equally bad. In effect, the tables are turned on the confronter. Equally upsetting, the accused person may ignore the confronter's complaint. Generally, confrontations are more productive when individuals acknowledge rather than ignore complaints and when they provide information about the problem, rather than trade accusations.

A
♥

Part of the planning process should involve thinking about the confrontation's opening statement.

♠
A

Stage 4: Resolution. At some point, people in a confrontation must bring it to a close. One or both parties may admit some degree of guilt and apologize, promising never to repeat the action. In other cases, the two may agree to drop the topic until some other time, or may even agree to never talk about it again. They may agree to disagree and leave it at that. Often, parties stop talking and leave the interaction feeling hurt, confused, or angry. Just because the initial confrontation has ended does not mean the conflict is over. The goal in achieving conflict resolution or transformation is to extend the resolution stage long enough to work through the issues and the options for solving the problems.

Stage 5: Post-Resolution. Even though a confrontation may be short, the effects can be long lasting. Individuals carry with them memories of what was said that they replay later. They can dwell on perceived insults and become angry. They can think of things they should have said or done and plan their attacks for the next confrontation. Furthermore, conflict may cause individuals to actively question the viability of their relationship. When the confrontation goes badly, this mulling makes matters worse.

If, however, the confrontation ended with the possibility of a resolution, the postconfrontation stage can be positive and even transformative. If you played out the Job Review Game over time, there are two possible resolutions. The employee might return an insult or he might try to constructively work through the issues. Of course, he would not have had time to plan, but he could try to work through the issues on the spot. Since the boss created some relationship problems by insulting the employee, they would need to repair their damaged relationship and work to prevent future blow-ups. Or, they may quit thinking about it and consider the issue resolved.

Chapter Summary

- **Conflict is a struggle about social identity needs and material interests.** The key to achieving positive outcomes in conflict is to focus the discussion on material interests, while granting each other's needs for inclusion, control, and affection.
- **Conflict is about danger and opportunity.** Each conflict presents both dangers and opportunities to disputants. If they look at a conflict with a negative frame and focus only on what they can lose, they will focus on dangers. If they approach the conflict with a positive frame and focus on what they can gain, they will see the opportunities.
- **Conflicts are stressful.** The stress can be relieved by not attacking each other's social identity. Such attacks only cause parties to lash out in an effort to restore positive and negative face.
- **Conflict presents many opportunities.** These opportunities include facing important problems, tension release, exploring creative solutions to problems, and strengthening relationships.
- **Conflict outcomes range from avoidance to transformation.** Disputants can give in to the danger approach and avoid conflicts to manage their own stress. Or they can work to resolve the conflict and create specific solutions to address their main problems. They can transform the conflict into an effective and enduring solution.
- **Destructive conflict is relationship focused** whereas constructive conflict focuses on resolving material interests. Avoiding destructive conflicts involves not getting stupid. Getting stupid means becoming overly emotional and resorting to attacks in the form of skirting, personalizing, complaining, and sniping.
- **Constructive conflict is about recognition and empowerment.** Recognition involves understanding the conflict from each party's perspective. Empowerment means that each party possesses the skills and abilities to work through the conflict constructively.
- **Your conflict communication style is a key element in empowerment.** If you are confident in your style, then you are better able to work through the issues that are vital for taking advantage of the opportunities the conflict presents.
- **Conflict evolves in stages.** The more we try to follow this structure, the more likely it is that we will work through the conflict constructively.

Lessons Learned

Here are the key lessons we learned about conflict and card talk games:

- **Plan your conflict approach carefully, when you can.** If you know you will have a conflict or negotiation over some issue, like buying a computer from someone or having a relational discussion with a friend, planning is useful. Most of us don't like doing it, but research tells us that planning makes conflict discussions go more smoothly.
- **Communicate in a way that is sufficiently direct that your concern is clear, but not so direct that it is offensive.** When you play your card, use polite language *(Please turn down the video game.).* Include reasons for your request *(I have to study tomorrow and the noise from the game is making it hard for me to concentrate.).* Include pre-apologies when possible to show respect for the other's face *(I'm sorry to bother you, but the video game you're playing is too loud.).* If those fail, move to more direct language, but avoid offensive language *(You suck!).* Offensive language inflames people, as you probably know.

- **Try to understand the other's perspective about the dispute.** Remember the issue of recognition. Recognition helps each party see the dispute from the other's perspective. That helps the parties be more integrative in their approach to the issues and solutions. Ask, "Why does he think I'm wrong?" In doing so, you may discover your perceptions are wrong. Even if you conclude your initial thoughts are right, you can at least anticipate what the other person may say and prepare how to best respond.
- **Be clear and committed to your goals** but remain flexible as to how to achieve them. Typically, there are several ways to meet your needs, and you should generate as many alternatives as you can. That way, you avoid becoming committed to a single but potentially losing course of action. Also, you might find one that is acceptable to the person with whom you are in conflict. As a result, everyone wins.
- **Be aware of issue linkages.** Work to remove links that create resistance, and add those that will facilitate agreement. Try to link your proposal to something that the other supports to help you reach an agreement. One technique for doing this is called log-rolling. When **log-rolling**, a person makes a concession on an issue that is less important in exchange for another person's concession on a more important issue.
- **Be sensitive to the need others have** to appear strong and capable, but be less sensitive to their attacks on you. This advice can be difficult to follow. It runs contrary to our nature. We must be respectful to individuals we don't like. When we have to communicate negative information to another, we must do so in a way that does not threaten their image. Negative feedback should be delivered so that it does not blame the person, is specific about the problem, and is considerate of their feelings.
- **Always acknowledge another person's complaints.** This does not mean you have to agree or comply with him or her. You can disagree or present your view of the matter; just don't ignore him or her.

References

Bush, R. A. B., & Folger, J. P. (1994). *The promise of mediation.* San Francisco: Jossey-Bass.

Coser, L. (1956). *The functions of social conflict.* New York: The Free Press.

Donohue, W. A., & Kolt, R. (1992). *Managing interpersonal conflict.* Thousand Oaks, CA: SAGE Publications, Inc.

Donohue, W. A., Rogan, R., & Kaufman, S. (2011). *Framing matters.* London: Peter Lang Publishers.

Felson, R. B., & Tedeschi, T. (1992). *Aggression and violence: Social interactionist perspectives.* Washington, DC: American Psychological Association.

Tutu, D. (1999). *No future without forgiveness.* New York: Doubleday.

PART Three

Group and Organizational Card Games

♠ Socialization Card Games

♦ Coordination Card Games

♣ Decision-Making Card Games

♥ Leadership Card Games

© 2012 by auremar. Used under license of Shutterstock, Inc.

Socialization Card Games

CHAPTER Eight

♣ Introduction

A big reason people leave their jobs or drop out of school is that they don't fit into the culture of the place. They fail to adapt to the new social system. The culture is moving one way, and the person is moving another. Learning what it takes to fit in and perform according to those rules can be more difficult than the job itself. Each organization develops a unique culture that requires adaptation. So much of the adjustment is acquiring the talk cards needed to play talk games that are valued in the new culture.

The goal of this chapter is to help you understand what it takes to fit in and describe some of the card games you are likely to face in pursuing your career.

♣ Talk Games That Socialize Members

To understand the challenge of becoming socialized into a new organizational culture, consider these talk games. Most of them should sound familiar since everyone belongs to multiple organizations such as family, living quarters, classes, and jobs. Of course, there are an infinite number of these games, but here are a few of the most common.

The Name Game. Groups and organizations communicate values to members by playing the Name Game. This game often surfaces when members are playing their organizational role cards. For example, let's say you are having a discussion at work with your supervisor about who is going to work on a new project. You are playing your Employee Card, and your supervisor is playing his or her Supervisor Card. Your Employee Card consists of many topics about how to do your work. The styles for communicating these topics are relatively friendly, informal, and low power.

Responding to the boss' request for names, you throw out a friend's name, and your supervisor responds, "We can't have him on the project. He just won't put in the time and pull in the right people to do the job. He's basically a lazy loner." In playing his Supervisor Card, he communicates his values about what counts as performance by **naming** some-one as a competent or incompetent group member. In other words, you get the message loud and clear about what it takes to be a member of the team. To play your Employee Card effectively, you know you must work extra hard and interact well with others.

The New Lingo Game. One of the more fun card games that people play in groups is to make up new words for stuff. When people use these unique words it shows solidar-ity for the culture of the group and a desire to continue being a member. For example, a student told me a story about his housemates and how they often made up words. He lived in a house of about 10 guys, and they were close friends. They regularly played beer pong on the front porch. This is a drinking game in which cups of beer and ping-pong balls are used. Beer became such a part of the house culture that they made up a word for anything good that happened to them as individuals. They called it beer-a-licious. Any time they wanted to label someone or something positively they used the beeralicious term. As the students each played their Roommate Cards, this new lingo game of making up words and spreading them reinforced the group's culture and the closeness of their relationships with each other.

© 2012 by Vibe Images. Used under license of Shutterstock, Inc.

The Funny Story Game. A common way to spread group cultural values is recalling funny or interesting stories about people in the group or organization. For example, our academic depart-ment places a high value on collegiality and the importance of faculty and graduate students work-ing together on research. So it is vital that the department establish activities that reinforce this value of student-faculty collaboration. One of the common group activities is touch football. Most Friday afternoons in the fall semester graduate stu-dents are invited (and expected) to play football with faculty for about an hour or so. These events always produce several funny stories about what happened during the games. When students and faculty retell those stories while playing their Fac-ulty and Graduate Student cards, they reinforce our value for collegiality. This has been going on for years, and stories have been passed down for decades, solidifying the value of collegiality in our department.

The Explanation Game. Research tells us that at work people expect their leaders to make sense out of the chaos there. In many cases things that happen around them don't make sense, and they need someone to help them understand what's happening so they can better perform their jobs. Effective leaders know the importance of playing the Explanation Game to keep employees focused and motivated.

For example, while playing his Supervisor Card, the individual might find himself in a conversation with a few employees who are playing their Employee Cards. Someone might make a comment about a rumor floating around about a new policy the boss is considering. At that point the supervisor might say, "Yeah, the boss isn't serious about that. It's all politics. She's just saying that to make the board of directors happy. Nothing is going to change." This socializes members by indicating who is in charge and how change really happens in the organization. It also helps everyone know which card to play next on this topic, and with how much style.

The Discipline Game. Supervisors also discipline members. They drop hints or tell people what behaviors are acceptable and not acceptable. How much freedom do people have to do their own thing in the workplace, or how much do they need to conform? One topic that supervisors must have on their cards is disciplining employees who step out of line and do the wrong thing. Other employees see that and learn by example.

For example, a supervisor might say to an employee, "That's not how we handle clients in this business. We don't send them emails when we need to deliver bad news. We call them right away and problem solve. Respect for clients is Job #1!" Sometimes the supervisor uses the situation as a teaching moment for the entire staff, to get everyone quickly on the same page. The supervisor's goal is to communicate the organization's values and create an effective working culture.

♣ Learning the Group Culture

My colleague at Michigan State University, Dr. Vernon Miller, and his co-author, Dr. Fred Jablin (1991) wrote an important article about how newcomers in organizations adjust to their surroundings. In an updated article about those findings (Bauer, Bodner, Erdogan, Truxillo, & Tucker, 2007), the authors found newcomers must quickly learn five key elements of the new culture:

1. Basic goals of the organization or group the person has just joined;
2. Preferred means members should use to achieve these goals;
3. Basic responsibilities of members in the role that is being granted to him or her by the organization;
4. Behavior patterns required for effective performance in the role; and
5. A set of rules or principles that pertain to maintenance of the identity and integrity of the organization.

© 2012 by Lori Sparkia. Used under license of Shutterstock, Inc.

How does this work in the real world? Most students have been an employee at some point before or during college. When you decided to become an employee, here's how you may have run down this list:

Basic Goals. The basic goal of being an effective employee is to do your job, get paid, and develop in ways that will help you personally and professionally. I hope you also want to develop a strong network of friends and have some fun in the process. As a result, your self-presentation goals are to look and act like a competent employee in a way that is consistent with your ethnicity, cultural heritage, and gender. Your relational goals at work are to impress customers, and get to know your boss and the other employees. But your achievement goals are performing well and getting paid. The job is secondary (or certainly should be) to getting a diploma while in school. Nevertheless, college jobs are excellent professional training.

In general, the talk cards you create and the games you choose to play in college hinge on these goal priorities. If academics are primary, then you join groups that expose you to your major and have you interacting with people who have a similar focus. If athletics are your focus, you hang out with other athletes and develop talk cards that socialize you into that arena. If your job is most important, your talk cards align with work priorities.

Preferred Means of Attaining Goals. An employee quickly learns there are both formal and informal means of attaining goals. The company tells you how to do your job, what duties are required, what to wear, and how to follow other important rules. Informally, employees learn how to game the system. They learn that some jobs are more important to do than others, that some supervisors are more lenient than others, and that some customers are more important than others. The point is that most people balance their formal job requirements with the informal expectations to accomplish their goals.

In addition to business goals, employees must accomplish their social goals. The primary goal is to fit in both with other employees and management so everyone can work as a team to serve customers. Sometimes this is a difficult task because people may not take the time to get to know one another socially. Some employers create community outreach projects for employees, like delivering holiday baskets to needy families, as a way to pull together as a team. Athletes are expected to hang out with each other and show that they are good teammates. In general, an organizational culture should create an environment in which people enjoy working together and sharing ideas.

Sometimes other factors intervene in working toward these social goals. Student employees are busy, so there might not be extra time to hang out with other employees. Maybe the job is unpleasant and the last thing you want to do is spend more time with others talking about it. Or you might not have much in common with the others who work at the company, making it more difficult to connect with them socially. You may be shy and like to keep to yourself. Some may feel they do not hold the talk cards needed to compete in the social scene.

If any of these apply to you, then you are limiting your ability to become more involved in your employment experience. Everyone has limits, but those who recognize them and learn to overcome them by taking charge of their experiences are most likely to succeed. *Jump in and grow!*

Basic Responsibilities of Being an Employee. The basic responsibilities of being a productive employee are usually straightforward. Show up on time, look good, have a good attitude, and be ready to put 100 percent into the job. The best employees think about creative ways to serve clients and take those ideas to their boss for potential implementation. If the organization's culture is effective, it encourages people to bring new ideas to management for consideration. That's how innovation happens in many cases.

Of course, there are also important social responsibilities employees are expected to fulfill. In addition to getting along, there are other key markers of a socially competent employee. Most workers are quickly advised on what language to use, how to dress a particular way, when to hang out with a certain group of people, and how to bring up certain topics on their Employee Card. Have you ever advised someone on these issues?

Behavior Patterns Required for Effective Employee Performance. The behavior patterns required for effective performance in your employee role are many. Think of the job requirements. You must learn the job skills and be able to perform them consistently and professionally. It's important to come to work on time and do whatever is necessary to advance the organization's goals.

If you are a supervisor, then communication skills are a top priority. Let's focus for a moment on your Supervisor Talk Card. All supervisors are expected to listen to employees about their concerns, provide information about the job, and direct decision making. Each of these topics requires a unique combination of style choices depending on the person and the situation. Over time the Supervisor Talk Card grows and becomes more complex but also more effective. You adapt to more situations so you feel more efficient and better able to get more work done.

Rules Needed to Maintain the Identity and Integrity of the Organization. What does it mean to be a good employee? Each student employee on campus or off campus is viewed as representing his or her school. If you work for a restaurant off campus you represent both your school and the company you work for. Acting responsibly and ethically reflects well on the school and the company.

Many times employers try to teach people rules and create a culture through the use of metaphors. Another friend and colleague who has written extensively about this issue is Dr. Katherine Miller (2012). She points out that companies are often organized around some kind of metaphor that is used to communicate informal rules. For example, the

© 2012 by Alistair Cotton. Used under license of Shutterstock, Inc.

boss might say, "Let's pull the troops together for a meeting." This is a military metaphor and suggests a rigid, top-down decision-making structure.

If the company revolves around a family metaphor, then the expectation is that people should provide social support to one another. These cultural metaphors also guide the card talk. If the company supports a family metaphor then employees are expected to have a big Friend Card to play in communicating with other employees. If a military metaphor guides the culture, then playing a Friend Card might be out of place.

This framework for thinking about becoming socialized helps us understand the role it plays in being successful communicators. Let's look at a definition of socialization and explore how it impacts our ability to create talk cards and play talk games.

Socialization Defined. Based on these five elements listed earlier from the Bauer et al. (2007) article focusing on how newcomers orient to new cultures, here is a definition of **socialization**: You are socialized into an organization when you (a) have acquired the skills, knowledge, values, motives, and role requirements (b) that are appropriate to your position in the group (c) that allows you to fit into the group (d) while perpetuating the group, building its cultural values and (e) forming your individual social identity.

In other words, people fit in when they know what the group needs them to do, when they are motivated to fit in, and when they are able to perform up to everyone's expectations. There is a **cultural fit**, in essence. The newcomer understands the group's culture, and it seems attractive and attainable. When this fit occurs, it reinforces and strengthens the culture's value for the group. Buy-in from more people means the culture grows and becomes stronger.

A ♥

People fit in when they know what the group needs them to do, when they are motivated to fit in, and when they are able to perform up to everyone's expectations.

A ♠

When this buy-in occurs, the group becomes a significant source of influence for that individual. It begins to shape his or her behavior in important ways. The individual's talk cards change rapidly to strengthen his or her ability to participate. Think of someone new to a school. New students quickly learn to build the talk cards they need to make friends and fit into that new school.

Socialization and Communication

That brings us to the issue of socialization and communication. When we play talk games in organizations like the Discipline Game or the New Lingo Game, they serve important functions for these organizations. Here are some of the more important functions.

Messages Transfer Values from One Generation to the Next. Each group develops unique talk cards, just as individuals create their own cards. In other words, group members often discuss the same topics, repeatedly using similar styles related to the job the group has to do. I'll bet your family shares many common topics, like food, family activities, maybe even politics. Family members use similar styles for these topics.

We talked a lot about sports growing up in my family and played the New Lingo Game by making up words about sports. In our family the word dogger meant someone who slacked off and didn't care. The style we used playing these games was informal, but often confrontational (high power) as everyone tried to assert different opinions. The message my brother and I learned was that to be successful in sports (and in life), it's important to be committed, dedicated, and disciplined. There was no being a dogger at our house!

These are value lessons, transferred through the cards we play and how we play them. Over time, this card play becomes important to sustaining the family culture. Our sports discussions communicated the value of hard work, discipline, learning, and commitment. When you have these discussions repeatedly, they create a set of values that guide the group's culture that gets passed down from member to member over generations. Later, we describe some family talk games to which you might relate.

© 2012 by Yuri Arcurs. Used under license of Shutterstock, Inc.

Messages Shape Our Identities. Listening to these recurring value discussions, we quickly learn the right and wrong way to behave in the group. The right way refers to how the group wants us to act, whether or not it is right in any moral or appropriate way. The wrong way refers to how the group does not want us to act. Many times we conform to group requirements even though we know it's inappropriate or not good for us. These value discussions shape our identities because we create an image of ourselves that is both consistent with these values, while also living them.

For example, the Funny Story Game becomes a tool to shape graduate student identities in our Communication Department. The funny stories that we share over the years about Friday afternoon football shape an identity of collegiality between faculty and graduate students. When the stories are retold the message is, We work together and we play together and we respect each other. Our department's goal is to infuse the collegiality ethic into a student's academic identity.

Messages Shape Our Role Expectations. One of the key requirements for finding out how to fit into the group is discovering others' expectations of our role. The Name Game aims to achieve this goal. When we hear labels being applied to people as either performers or slackers, we gain a sense of what expectations others have of how we should behave. Does the organization expect a lot from me or not very much? When people take the time to label others based on how hard they work, that sends a clear message about how we're expected to perform.

Socialization and Group Climate

According to a paper by Drs. Duane Ireland, Philip Van Auken, and Phillip Lewis (1978), we constantly search for clues about group climate when playing talk card games. The climate metaphor, taken from the weather people, refers to our feelings about the group, just like climate refers to how we feel about the weather when we go outside.

Recall that the last dimension of becoming socialized is learning the rules for fitting in. The climate feelings refer to whether we like the rules for how the group does its business. There are **four climate elements** we pay close attention to when trying to decide if we want to fit into a group:

1. **Autonomy.** How much individual freedom and flexibility do I have? If I want to wear something weird or tell the kind of jokes I want or play a card that I feel is necessary, will anyone care? If not, then the rules are flexible and the climate gives me a lot of autonomy. If rules are rigid and the slightest deviation from the norm is unacceptable, then my autonomy is low.

2. **Structure.** Who is in charge and how do decisions get made? A second climate assessment that we make is deciding who runs the show. Does one person make all the decisions or are they shared? Do people have specific roles to play or do they cross boundaries depending on the task? If there is a lot of structure, then people are concerned about following a specific chain of command to get anything accomplished.

3. **Rewards.** What behaviors are supported or rejected? What does the group reward and what does it punish? This climate element focuses on values. Does the group value hard work? Does it value honesty and commitment or even loyalty? Effective groups usually make their values clear. If people don't like the values they see, then they are likely to claim that the climate is not right for them.

4. **Support.** How emotionally supportive is the climate? If people are nice and willing to help, we feel the climate is warm. If no one pays attention to anyone else, then the climate feels chilly.

How does playing talk games inform us about the social climate? Consider the Name Game for example. If your supervisor calls someone a lazy loner, the supervisor is telling you what the organization values (**rewards**), that the supervisor is in charge of making decisions (**structure**), and the act of calling someone a lazy loner is not warm and fuzzy (**support**). Playing the Funny Story Game also tells members what the group values while the Explanation Game reveals a lot about the organization's structure.

The point is that when we play card talk games, we scan them for climate information to help us understand what's necessary to plug into the group. What are the rules, what's my role, and what should I do next to win my membership card?

> A ♥
>
> When we play card talk games, we scan them for climate information to help us understand what's necessary to plug into the group.
>
> A ♠

© 2012 by.iofoto. Used under license of Shutterstock, Inc.

Learning Socialization Games

The first card talk games we play are with our **family** members. Moms, dads, brothers, and sisters play their cards as you listen and watch. I watched intently as my parents played the Discipline Game with my brother. He was always getting into trouble, so as I watched I certainly learned what not to do, how to act around my parents to get rewards, and avoid trouble. They also taught me how to properly name people and events, and shaped the role I would play in the family.

As you mature into your teen years, **peers** play a dominant role in providing socialization information and helping you fill in topics and styles for your Friend Card. As you play talk games with peers, you develop your Friend Card and learn a great deal about your gender, identity, ethnicity, and group membership.

For example, if you were a girl who hung out with a lot of boys growing up, you probably learned to talk about many boy topics. As a result your Friend Card consists of many of those topics. If you did not hang out with girls, then you didn't learn much about those topics, suggesting your identity is probably shaped more by the boys, since that's how you talk.

Schools play an important part in socialization. Teachers play many talk games and teach us more about structure, authority, rewards, and support. Schools are the second real socialization challenge we have because we go from one group governed by one set of rules (our family) to another group with a whole new set of rules (school). This change forces us to become socialized into a new system that probably is not much like our family structure. School might be more like a job than a family. In fact, one of the main functions of education is to prepare us to enter the workplace by teaching us how to get along with strangers and work in teams.

We also look to various electronic **media** for information about how to fit in. The talk games of celebrities on TV shows seem different than our everyday lives. They wear different clothes, talk differently, and live the good life. Media card talk games are meant to provide simple images of characters so we can learn about them quickly, sometimes too quickly. This oversimplification can lead to stereotyping, which we talk more about when we get to the media chapter. Media gives us new lingo, transmits values, and tells us what's cool (rewarding) and not cool to believe.

What group exerts the most influence over you? Is it your family, work, or peer group? What talk card games do they play? What cards do they ask you to play? Can you play the cards well and win games effortlessly? Do you think the cards you develop and the games you play are good for you or hinder you in some way? If your family dominates your cards and games and they don't transfer well to work, you have a problem. As I said before, we argued a lot in our house, so I was used to playing games that way. I quickly learned once I got to school that my teachers and new friends did not appreciate the cards or the games I played. I had to calm down.

Socialization Trouble

My initial challenge of fitting in at school is a good example of socialization trouble. What are some of the main causes of being unable to fit in? The quick answer is a lack of the relevant talk cards needed to play the important talk games the group wants to play. Why might people lack the talk cards needed to fit in? There are several reasons.

Communication Apprehension. The communication field has a long tradition of helping people overcome their fear of communicating with others in various situations. For many years Dr. James McCroskey and his colleagues (McCroskey, Beatty, Kearney, & Plax, 1985) have used a survey to measure how apprehensive people are in communicating across various contexts. Clearly, the more apprehensive you are, the more trouble you are likely to experience fitting in with others.

Results:

If your score is over 30 on either of these scales you are probably apprehensive about communicating in interpersonal or group situations. A high score translates into difficulty stepping into new situations and being willing to risk talking to people. A willingness to risk new communication situations means you would have a better chance of fitting in and making friends.

Poor Orientation. If you are willing to jump into new situations, then you would naturally want to find out what those situations are like. Most people search for information from people they trust, like friends and relatives. Then they might search for official information from an online source or from official representatives of the group or organization. If you rely only on unofficial information from friends and relatives, you risk getting only part of the picture about what it's like to be a new member of that group.

Poor orientation results in not knowing which topics to discuss, when to discuss them, or what styles to use in raising the topics. Most groups and organizations present many faces to a new member and the more information the member can get about these differences the better.

Poor Communication Competence. Even if the individual receives excellent orientation from multiple reliable sources, he or she can still experience difficulty adjusting. Drs. Brian Spitzberg and William Cupach (1985) wrote an excellent book about the concept of communication competence. They indicated that people are **communicatively competent** when they can (a) accurately interpret messages from the specific group's perspective and (b) create messages that are consistent and appropriate for their role in the group. Regarding the message interpretation challenge, recall that earlier in this chapter I talked about all the up-front investigative work needed to be accepted into a group. We search for information about what the organization is trying to do and how it should be done.

A key part of that search is examining the talk cards and card games that people are playing as they work in the group context. **Communication competence** suggests that when people pay attention to the cards and card games, they learn the rules and expectations of the group and how to interpret messages. Having greater self-monitoring skills certainly helps this learning process, but being able to interpret the meaning and significance of group-generated messages is the first step toward competence.

The result of accurate interpretation is being able to play a card and win a talk game with group members. The more games someone succeeds at, the more likely that person is to be accepted into the group. Each message from that person sounds appropriate to and consistent with group expectations. In other words, the person seems **communicatively competent**. When these stars don't align and the person can't accurately interpret what's going on and can't participate in the interaction, he or she will have trouble fitting in and thriving in the new situation.

For example, have you ever heard someone tell a crude joke that seemed totally inappropriate and made everyone uncomfortable? What made that person think that joke

The more games someone succeeds at, the more likely that person is to be accepted into the group.

© 2012 by mikeledray. Used under license of Shutterstock, Inc.

was appropriate? Did the person get bad information about what the group is like? Is the person incapable of reading the cards others are playing and thought the joke would go over well? Inappropriate humor is a good example of being communicatively incompetent. It's not that the joke is bad as much as it doesn't fit the situation or the group.

♣ The Process of Becoming Socialized

In a classic and widely cited paper on the subject of socialization, Drs. John Levine and Richard Moreland (1990) wrote about how individuals become socialized into groups. They discovered that trouble fitting in generally surfaces quickly as people try to enter the group. If they stick it out, most people start to catch on, as they gather information about the climate and play simple talk card games on a limited basis to gradually fit in.

As the individuals become more comfortable, the old-timers might even design tests to see how new members react under pressure. The Name Game is one such test. The experienced members check to see how new members label outsiders. If the labels are "correct," then the experienced members start to feel as if the new folks are part of the group. It is a process that can take weeks, months, or even years to complete. Let's see what research tells us about the phases of socialization.

Anticipation. In this first phase, sometimes known as **getting in**, both the group and the potential new member develop expectations of the other. When you thought about the benefits of going to college, you probably also thought about how you might fit in with the other students on campus. You wondered about the climate at the school. What kind of freedoms might you have? How friendly would people be?

On the flip side, faculty and staff develop expectations about the ease or difficulty of working with new students. Greater familiarity by both parties generally results in a smoother transition for recruits from outsider to insider. A good orientation program clearly communicates job requirements, formal and informal rules needed to do the job well, and information about the social climate that makes it easy to fit in.

Accommodation. After learning about one another, the new member finally enters the scene and joins the group. This is the **breaking in** phase in which the individual starts quickly gathering climate information to begin the new job. For you, is the job of being a student what you expected? Is it more or less difficult? Is the life of being a student like you expected or is it vastly different? Your answers to these questions reveal how many accommodations you need to make to continue to be a student. Maybe you study more than you did in high school. Maybe you play fewer video games than before. Perhaps you interact with many more kinds of people than you imagined you would. The point is, you learn what talk cards are needed, when and how to play them, and how to change to be a more effective communicator. People who resist the accommodation phase generally decide to leave the group because the process is too difficult.

Role Management. Once the decision is made to continue participating in the group or organization, the individual starts **settling in** the new role. The person has made the necessary accommodations and is building new cards and playing new and different games. This settling-in process can be a little bumpy. Creating a smooth path requires that new members resolve two types of conflicts:

© 2012 by Monkey Business Images. Used under license of Shutterstock, Inc.

(1) work-life and social-life conflicts (e.g., attending after-work meetings instead of visiting with friends and family) and (2) conflicts in the workplace itself (e.g., getting along with coworkers and bosses). After the fun and newness wear off, the realities of work-life and time demands must be managed.

How successful was the transition to your new role as college student? If you took the time to get good information about campus life, scoped out your new friends on Facebook, and maybe read some of the material for your new classes, it probably went fairly well. For some, the conflict between work life and social life might cause problems. If you didn't like your roommate, then school might have been more stressful. Regarding classes, if you got into groups that were unproductive or had professors who were difficult to understand, then the socialization process was more difficult. At the end of the day, taking charge of role management and life transitions is what matters most. Find out what's best for you and make it happen!

> A♥
>
> At the end of the day, taking charge of role management and life transitions is what matters most.
>
> ♠A

Outcomes of Socialization

I'm sure you have gone in and out of many groups or organizations on your way to college. The decision to stay or go generally hinges on one or more of four outcomes that we use to judge the success of our socialization.

1. **Satisfaction.** Satisfaction refers to how emotionally attached to the new group you become. Do you like it and feel good in it? Do you have a positive attitude about membership? Do you feel as if you are being productive and effective in your job, and able to resolve conflicts you face in settling into the new role?

2. **Identification.** Another socialization marker is identification or the extent to which the group has shaped your identity. If the group values showing pride in your school, do you share that value? Do you wear clothes showing your school name? Is your identity now permanently linked to your school? Playing the New Lingo Talk Game, which involves making up words, is a concrete demonstration of identifying with the new group. Group members formally declare their membership by frequently using the new words on their talk cards.

3. **Integration.** If you belong to the group you see yourself as having extensive contacts with other members. People hang out together, share information, and work more as a team. Being integrated into a major field of study is an important achievement for a student. By the time you are ready to graduate you ought to know other students in your classes, key faculty members, and perhaps even corporate sponsors that want to hire people from your field. I always advise students to join student organizations related to their major to take advantage of these integration opportunities.

4. **Communication Competence.** A final socialization marker is being communicatively competent. Members who are settled into the group know how to interpret a wide range of situations and can carefully craft their messages to adapt to these situations. You can see how much people grow into their roles by witnessing whether the cards they play and the topics they discuss look like those with whom they associate.

I teach a course in sales communication, and it is fun to see students' progress from the beginning to the end of the course. They learn to develop a professional sales voice, or style, that enables them to clearly and confidently articulate their positions. In essence, it is the ultimate achievement: the development of the talk cards needed for success and the ability to play those cards to perfection. It is a beautiful thing to watch.

Chapter Summary

- **New members seeking group membership** must become socialized into the group's culture. Understanding a group's culture is learned by observing and participating in the card talk games that members play as they interact with one another. Decoding these games reveals information about the organization's goals and how to perform effectively. When someone is socialized into a group, that person has acquired the skills, knowledge, values, motives, and role requirements needed to fit in and perform well.

- **When new members want to integrate** into the group, they look around. They examine the messages that come from leadership and coworkers to learn about the organization's values, such as hard work, professionalism, or continuous learning. As individuals accept these values and incorporate them into their lives, the messages shape their personal and professional identities. Once this identification process is complete, members strengthen the culture of their group or organization—they've bought into the process and then they pass it on to other new members.

- **Social climate is another key focus** of new member integration. Individuals constantly analyze the social interaction of a new place to determine how much individual freedom they have to act as they wish, how decisions are made, what behaviors are rewarded, and how emotionally supportive the environment is. As these climate parameters become increasingly stable, they start to form the organization's culture.

- **We learn socialization games from many sources.** Family, schools, media, and the workplace are some of the most common sources. Each represents a new group that members must learn to adapt to by learning the card talk games that the members play. Members fit in when they have constructed the cards necessary to participate in these games.

- **Trouble integrating into a group** comes from many sources. People who struggle to fit in are typically apprehensive about interacting with people, receive poor orientation, or are unable to develop the cards necessary to play the games needed for success in that organization. The idea of communication competence is that people are competent when they can understand the games being played and learn to play them well. Your goal as a communicator is to become communicatively competent. Learn to form more accurate interpretations of social events and how to play cards to succeed in the groups.

- **Success is about being happy as a group member.** Are you integrated, satisfied, connected, and having fun? Are you performing well and emotionally supported? As you investigate membership in more diverse groups you will create diverse cards and greatly bolster your communicative competence.

Lessons Learned

When facing a major life transition, whether it's a new school, a new job, a move abroad, or even a new relationship, consider what's required to be successful in those transitions. Developing these card talk features will ease the transition.

- **First, be clear about your goals in entering a new group or organization.** What are you trying to achieve, and is this group the best place to achieve it? The more information you can gather about the new groups you are about to enter, including their goals, rules, and other factors, the more successful you'll be at building talk cards and playing talk games.
- **When you make the transition into the new group, assess the fit.** Are you culturally compatible with the other group members? Can you effectively perform the roles assigned to you? It might take some time, but this fit is important, and it's essential that you be honest with yourself about the fit.
- **Pay attention to the talk games.** Each conversation in a new group represents a new card talk game. Even when you are receiving a formal orientation or interacting casually with folks around the latte machine, people are playing talk games. Each of these games, like the Name Game, displays valuable information about how to become successfully socialized into the group. So pay attention!
- **Assess the group's social climate.** Can you grow within this climate? Can you learn, mature, and profit within this new structure? I like to throw myself into some high-risk groups just to see if I can integrate. Sometimes I am successful and it's energizing. I have failed on several occasions, but that's OK. I am happy with the effort.
- **Grow beyond a single influence in talk games.** As you make personal and professional transitions, examine the talk games that take you through these times. As you learn how to shape your games, you will become more flexible communicatively and, therefore, more communicatively competent. Remember, you're learning about talk games so you can make more deliberate and productive transitions. Don't only react to the games others want to play; initiate your own games to test the group's climate. Play and learn!

References

Bauer, T. N., Bodner, T., Erdogan, B., Truxillo, D., & Tucker, J. S. (2007). Newcomer adjustment during organizational socialization: A meta-analytic review of antecedents, outcomes, and methods. *Journal of Applied Psychology, 92,* 707–721.

Ireland, R. D., Van Auken, P. M., & Lewis, P. V. (1978). An investigation of the relationship between organizational climate and communication climate. *Journal of Business Communication, 16,* 3–10.

Levine, J. M., & Moreland, R. L. (1990). Progress in small group research. *Annual Review of Psychology, 41,* 585–634.

McCroskey, J. C., Beatty, M. J., Kearney, P., & Plax, T. G. (1985). The content validity of the PRCA-24 as a measure of communication apprehension across communication contexts. *Communication Quarterly, 33,* 165–173.

Miller, K. I. (2012). *Organizational communication: Approaches and processes.* Boston: Wadsworth.

Miller, V. D., & Jablin, F. M. (1991). Information seeking during organizational entry: Influences, tactics, and a model of the process. *Academy of Management Review, 16,* 92–120.

Spitzberg, B. H., & Cupach, W. R. (1985). *Interpersonal communication competence.* Beverly Hills: SAGE Publications, Inc.

Coordination Card Games

♣ Introduction

The April 9, 2010 edition of *The New York Times* reported that two days earlier, a 27-year-old diplomat from Qatar, Mohammed al-Madadi, went to the lavatory of the plane he was taking from New York to Denver and briefly smoked his pipe. He left the remaining tobacco in the trash container and returned to his seat. Smelling smoke, the flight attendant confronted al-Madadi about illegally smoking in the restroom, which he denied.

The flight attendant alerted a federal air marshal on board who confronted al-Madadi about the smoking. Again, he denied it, but admitted he had a pipe. Al-Madidi then made a joking reference to trying to set his shoes on fire.

Authorities feared a repeat of the December 25, 2009 attempted bombing of a Detroit-bound airliner by a Nigerian passenger who tried to explode a bomb hidden in his underwear. This Nigerian man later said he had been trained by the al-Qaeda affiliate in Yemen.

Within a few minutes after confronting al-Madidi, top Transportation Security officials were on a conference call, the Federal Aviation Administration alerted the pilots of the thousands of flights then in the air about a possible terrorist threat, an FBI team assembled in Denver, and airport authorities positioned fire and safety equipment for the 6:45 p.m. landing.

NORAD (North American Aerospace Defense Command) scrambled fighter jets to accompany the plane for the final segment of its route. While the plane was still in the air, intelligence agency personnel checked records not only for al-Madadi but for all the other passengers as well. They checked for the possibility that a team of terrorists might be on the flight.

This is an amazing example of a how a highly coordinated system of agencies and individuals functions to prevent terrorist attacks. Before September 11, 2001 there was no system that enabled agencies, pilots, NORAD, and others to take actions that might prevent a coordinated terrorist attack. As a result, the United States was more vulnerable to attack because there was no plan to coordinate information resources to make effective decisions and take quick action. Now that system exists and apparently it works.

What does coordination have to do with card talk? Chapter 8 introduced you to the challenge of communicating in groups. This chapter expands our vision beyond small groups to interacting with others in different networks. Anytime people send a message, they play a card. Imagine lots of people playing cards within the context of a large organization or social network, as the example above illustrates. Not only did the people in the al-Madadi incident play their professional cards, they chose to interconnect their messages to form a network. That's what we talk about in this chapter—the process of building communication networks.

♣ Coordination Card Games

Before we define coordination and talk about its elements, let's describe some typical talk card games that are played out in the context of people sharing information.

The Blogging Game. In 2009 Jeff Jarvis wrote a book called *What Would Google Do?* I recommend it to anyone trying to understand the revolution in information sharing that has dramatically altered the way every organization does business. The book lays out how Google learned to exploit the power of the Internet by providing users with free content and services, who then form vast networks engaged in common enterprises.

For example, Google owns YouTube in which people form networks to share videos and other entertainment. Using information about whom you connect with and what you search for, Google tailors advertisements specifically for you. It is a powerful marketing scheme, perhaps the best ever developed.

Jarvis became interested in blogging when he got frustrated with the service he received from Dell on his broken computer. He created a blog that ranted about his experience. In just a few short days, thousands of other unhappy Dell customers read Jarvis's blog and shared their negative service stories. Google enabled this sharing. Facebook is another platform that allows users to share personal information. By playing his Customer Card in a blog, Jarvis created a powerful angry-customer network that ultimately resulted in Dell changing its service policies.

The Decision-Making Game. In 1986, the Challenger Space Shuttle exploded about 70 seconds into its flight, killing all eight astronauts aboard. I still remember the day it happened, watching the video over and over. Perhaps you've seen it on YouTube.

Challenger exploded because the O-rings connecting sections of the booster rocket failed, allowing fuel to escape its tank during takeoff, which ignited and destroyed the rocket. The O-rings failed because the freezing nighttime weather caused the rubber to contract, leaving gaps through which the fuel escaped.

Building and launching the Space Shuttle involved many organizations spread over many states. The rockets were built in California and other states, the Shuttle was launched in Florida, and controlled from a base in Texas. The NASA (National Aeronautics and Space Administration) office in charge of the Shuttle program is in Washington, D.C. In several meetings before the launch, engineers in California and Washington state warned their superiors against launching in cold weather. None of that information was received by the decision makers at NASA in Washington, D.C., Florida, or Texas. As a result, the decision makers decided to launch the Shuttle.

The Prize Bull Game. Robert Putnam and Richard Feldman (2003) wrote a book about how communities have created networks of people to complete important community improvement projects. One of my favorite stories in the book is about a group of merchants in Tupelo, Mississippi (the birthplace of Elvis Presley, by the way) in the late 1940s who desperately wanted to build their economy. Each of these individuals played their Business Leader Cards and held several meetings over the course of many months. By pulling together and discussing their options, they decided to purchase a prize bull and begin a dairy farm. The farm was successful, which led to many other enterprises coming to Tupelo. To this day, Tupelo is the economic engine of Mississippi.

What Is Coordination?

Each of these examples provides insights into what happens when individuals play certain talk cards in the context of large networks of individuals. That is, when people in organizations coordinate to perform some task, they form a network. According to my good friends and colleagues Drs. Peter Monge and Noshir Contractor (2003), **networks** are the patterns of contact that emerge when people exchange messages over space and time. People use these networks with varying levels of success to **coordinate** their thoughts and take some action.

To understand why some coordination games are successful while others fail, let's first understand the nature of coordination itself and what makes it work or fail to work.

Coordination is the process of creating **interdependence**. As people evolve into a team or need each other to perform some task, they form a network or large organization to coordinate with one another for some purpose. Using these networks, people exchange both **tangible resources**, such as information, ideas, and money, and **sentiment**, or the desire and motivation to work together. The point of this chapter is that achieving quality outcomes requires creating the right kind of coordination network to avoid outcomes like the Shuttle disaster.

When people in organizations coordinate to perform some task they form a network.

Types of Coordination. According to an influential paper by Drs. Andrew Van De Ven, Andre Delbecq, and Richard Koenig (1976), there are actually three ways to coordinate. **Pooled coordination** involves assembling resources into a central location for later use. If a team of five students was charged with writing a group paper, and each person wrote two pages and stapled them all together, that would be a pooled coordination effort. This approach is useful when people don't need to rely on one another's opinions about the task; they assemble what they have into some common location. The Blogging Game is a good example of pooled interdependence. To complain about their computers, people were piling their gripes into a website. The bloggers group complaining about Dell didn't really have any task to perform other than building a collective awareness of frustrations with their Dell computers.

The second way to create interdependence is called **sequential coordination**. This method of working together involves passing resources from station to station over time. Think of an assembly line. In the group paper writing example, if the first person wrote two pages, then passed them to the second person who built on these ideas by adding a few additional pages, and passed the four pages to the third person who added more material and so on, they would be using sequential coordination.

The Decision-Making Game was played using sequential coordination. People at lower levels of decision making had some thoughts and passed them up through successive layers of management who filtered the messages or just didn't pass them

© 2012 by Golden Pixels LLC. Used under license of Shutterstock, Inc.

along. The results were disastrous for the Shuttle crew and NASA.

The third way to create interdependence is **reciprocal coordination**. In this approach, all five people writing the paper would sit in a room together or use some online chat tool to share thoughts with one another and decide how to write the paper. Everyone is free to connect with one another to generate ideas in real time reciprocally. The key advantage of this approach is that everyone has immediate access to everyone else's thoughts, which is useful in adapting to changing situations. In a real-life interdependent work environment, a quick meeting can be called and people can decide what to do in response.

Adaptability. The Prize Bull Game worked well because people got together in Tupelo and created a plan. That planning would have been impossible using only a pooled or even a sequential approach. The decision to launch the Challenger Shuttle should have been done in a reciprocal manner, with everyone having information about the changing weather conditions in the same room making the decision. Using a sequential approach does not allow people to change rapidly.

Sentiment and Resources. Regardless of what kind of coordination strategy a team uses, its success hinges on the ability to effectively exchange resources and sentiment. Let's look at these two needs. **Resource exchange** involves sharing information and other, more tangible resources such as personnel, money, and inventory. When people give these items to one another, it demonstrates they are serious about working together. Oddly enough, information is *not* often perceived as adequate for building interdependence. Perhaps members believe that *information is cheap* and intangible. The common perception is that if others are serious, they will contribute money, personnel, or other tangibles to the task. Information is not enough.

Sentiment exchange is the desire or motivation to coordinate. For example, in the Prize Bull Game the merchants of Tupelo made a structural shift in their community by deciding to work together reciprocally to grow their regional economy. Developing that kind of coordination was not easy. It took a few persistent people to go door to door, visit each merchant, and persuade them to join the group. In other words, those people had to develop an interest among other merchants to team up. Perhaps out of desperation the merchants developed a **sentiment** toward coordination; they knew they needed to coordinate to grow. Building motivation began by sharing information, money, and other resources and by focusing on the tangible benefits of building a dairy industry. If the merchants had not made the case for the potential rewards, then the sentiment toward coordination would have been lost.

Two other elements in building sentiment are also key. The first is **open communication**. Individuals working in groups must be open with one another and willing to share information that might be relevant to the task. Second, that openness builds **trust** and encourages more openness. Trust is the perception that the other party is working in your best interests and will always be a reliable helper. We learn later that a **lack of openness** causes people to make poor decisions and mistrust one another.

> **A♥**
> If others are serious, they will contribute money, personnel, or other tangibles to the task. Information is not enough.
> **A♠**

How Coordination Works

Creating the Network. To perform some task like deciding to ignite a rocket or creating a dairy farm, people will form a network. These are examples of **task networks** in which the goal is to accomplish something specific. I receive several Facebook requests weekly to join a group to protest something or contribute to a cause. However, most Facebook requests are simply aimed at building **social networks**, the purpose of which is to make social connections that keep people up to date on one another's personal events. Sometimes these networks form quickly, while others take forever to gel.

Developing a Coordination Strategy. Once the network is created, the group must decide on a **coordination strategy** to accomplish its goals. What's best: a pooled, sequential, or reciprocal approach? It would have been great if the NASA people had asked this question prior to deciding to launch the Shuttle. Unfortunately, they used the **sequential** approach in which a lot of information was lost as it passed from one station to the next. They needed a **reciprocal** approach in which everyone with key information had an opportunity to share it.

Developing Links. Once the network is in motion and people are playing their cards and exchanging information, they develop **communication links**. A link is a two-way channel of communication—a pipeline that connects at least two individuals. Links have three important properties. First, how **strong** is the link? A strong link is one in which the individuals use it frequently to exchange information. That frequency is relative to the purpose of the network. If the network is social, perhaps a daily exchange of information is frequent, whereas a weekly exchange would be infrequent.

What is the **content** of the information exchanged through the link? The content might be **task-related** in which people are making a decision about launching the Shuttle or creating a dairy farm. Or the link might be **social** in which people are updating one another on personal information. The link could also be used to share ideas about improving **innovation** within the team. These three kinds of links (content, task, innovation) form different-looking networks.

Task and innovation links tend to form networks around people's roles in the groups. Managers talk to other managers; employees talk with other employees. Communication is horizontal. Social networks are more fluid. People share information up and down the organizational hierarchy depending on who their friends are and what information they have to share.

What **channels** are used to create different networks? Since the NASA people were spread out, they used the phone to communicate across their various sites because the Internet and email had not yet been invented. For creating the dairy farm,

the Tupelo merchants used face-to-face communication for their networks. If you examine the networks in which you participate, you will notice great differences in channel use. You may use face-to-face for your task networks and electronic communication for your social interactions, for example.

♣ Network Descriptors

Now you have a picture of the three kinds of networks that form when groups of people communicate (task, social, innovation) and an understanding of the three kinds of coordination they use within that network (pooled, sequential, reciprocal). We've learned that the Shuttle disaster might have been prevented if NASA had used a reciprocal approach rather than a sequential approach in sharing task information. We also understand that the Tupelo merchants were successful because they used reciprocal face-to-face networks to build sentiment to create a dairy farm, thereby building their community and its economic clout.

People fit in when they know what the group needs them to do, when they are motivated to fit in, and when they are able to perform up to everyone's expectations.

If you think about what these networks might have looked like as they evolved, they had different appearances. Imagine the NASA network in which people inside the different contractors communicated frequently *within their own companies*, but there was little communication *among* contractors. The people in California talked to each other but they didn't interact frequently with people in Florida, Texas, or Washington, D.C. That network would look like a series of unconnected balls of activity.

Now imagine the Tupelo network. If you plotted the connections among merchants as they planned the dairy farm, the network would look busy with lots of frequent connections among people on all three levels. These people shared information about the task, about innovative ideas, and about social news, since they all knew one another in this small town.

We can use three terms to describe these network differences: **integrativeness, reachability,** and **dominance**. A thoroughly **integrated** network is one like the Tupelo model in which everyone shared information reciprocally. It contrasts to the sparsely integrated NASA network in which few groups talked outside their own companies in their own states. **Reachability** refers to how easy it is to reach any one person in the network.

In a thoroughly integrated network like the Tupelo merchants, each person was immediately reachable by any other person in the group. They used reciprocal coordination, and all worked hard to build the dairy. In the sequentially organized NASA network, people were widely separated. If a person in California wanted to reach someone in Florida, he (they were mostly men) would need to go through people in Texas and then in Washington, D.C. In this case, reachability was low.

Dominance refers to how much the links are controlled from a central location. In a completely integrated network each person is immediately reachable by any other person. In that case, no one individual dominates the network. Everyone has the same number of links. Imagine a network in which one person connects with everyone else in the group, but the other members of the group only talk individually with that one person and no one else. The person with multiple links would **dominate** the network since that person has a disproportionately large number of links—and more information—compared with everyone else. Perhaps you know someone who is in touch with every-

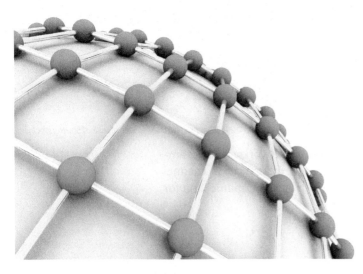

one else, but the other members of the group don't talk much with each other. Does that person dominate the network?

Are social networks more or less integrated than task networks? Are task networks typically dominated by fewer people than are social networks? The answer is yes to both questions. Social networks tend to be more open. Everyone talks with everyone. There are few restrictions and few rules. In contrast, task networks are more regulated. People who are knowledgeable or have leadership roles tend to dominate the network, giving it a different structure.

Because social networks are more integrated, people are more directly reachable and there is less domination. Wise managers nurture these social networks and help them grow. Some businesses create opportunities for employees to volunteer for community projects on company time in order to build social networks among the volunteers. My son is a computer engineer, and his workplace has set aside rooms with board and video games to encourage sharing. These networks open up communication in general and create trust among members. When it is time to coordinate, managers can take advantage of these social bonds because people know and trust one another and want to work as a team.

A ♥
Wise managers nurture these social networks and help them grow.
♠ A

♣ Communication Roles

One of the best resources for understanding roles in networks is the Monge and Contractor (2003) book. They said that individuals can be categorized into three types of communication roles in any given network. The first group of individuals, labeled **non-participants**, has relatively few communication contacts with others. They are formally members of the organization but they don't noticeably contribute. Another word for these people is **isolates**. They are isolated from others, basically doing their jobs but infrequently connecting to the action.

The second group, labeled **participants**, communicates frequently with others in the group. These within-group communicators form intense interaction patterns that label them as an active group. They grow accustomed to playing consistent card talk games with a limited number of talk cards. These individuals stay within their groups and don't venture out often or connect with people from other groups.

The most important communication role in a network is the **liaison**. These individuals link two or more communication groups, while not being a member of any one group. Serving as **linking pins**, liaisons ensure that groups communicate with one another when needed to improve coordination. They bridge relations among units within an organization. As a result, they play a broader number of card talk games and a more diverse set of cards.

A good example of a liaison is an advertising agency account executive. That person directs all the agency's efforts to serve the client. He or she links the different units in the ad agency with units in the client's company. Account execs are generally skilled communicators who are perceived as friendly and attentive. These liaisons (the account execs) generally promote a positive working climate and are often responsible for the successful coordination of organizational functions. They also tend to dominate networks since they like to communicate and they're good at it.

Liaisons are important as organizations grow and break into more subgroups. A critical job is pulling these groups together so organizational members better adapt to

© 2012 by Stephen Aaron Rees. Used under license of Shutterstock, Inc.

© 2012 by JustASC. Used under license of Shutterstock, Inc.

change. Without the liaisons, the organization would be a loose collection of groups, each going off in its own direction. Typically, liaisons are the most efficient personal integrating mechanism because of their strategic positioning. Due to their centrality and their direct linkages with others, liaisons reduce the probability of message **distortion**, reduce information **load**, and increase the **timeliness** of communication.

Before its shift toward greater collaboration, the Tupelo community had few liaisons who could successfully bridge the disparate local business groups. It wasn't until a few key merchants stepped up and started talking to people in these groups that progress accelerated. Soon there were many liaisons who bridged key community groups, resulting in more merchants supporting the dairy farm project. These connectors kept communication flowing among community groups and created a whole new communication culture of collaboration.

Why do some people in organizations emerge as liaisons and others do not? Since liaisons are natural communicators, they tend to develop open communication relationships with others. And people like to talk to them. Liaisons initiate more conversations, opening up communication among diverse groups. Liaisons can quickly and creatively process information. In fact, many of a liaison's characteristics (openness, trust, sensitivity to others, getting a wide array of input) have also been used to specify the characteristics of more effective managers and, more generally, of open communication climates.

The point is that when more managers become liaisons, the organization is better equipped to adopt coordination strategies that better fit the tasks at hand. They connect more groups and can better detect the need for change. Organizations need linkers. If NASA had had more of them, the Challenger Shuttle mission might have turned out differently.

As networks evolve in communities like Tupelo and in organizations like NASA, they develop a communication structure. These structures can either help or hinder an organization's ability to do its job successfully. Sometimes leaders can't see or don't think about the structure they're creating, so they can't control it. At this point in our discussion, it's useful to introduce this concept of **networks** and talk about how best to manage the structure to strengthen the organization.

Results:

Look at the patterns and consider these questions:

- Do you play a consistent role in these groups? Perhaps you are a liaison in your extended family, at your job, or in a class project.
- Are most of the networks highly integrated or not very integrated? If you are generally an isolate in a highly integrated network, why don't you participate?
- If the coordination is mostly reciprocal and the networks are not highly integrated, why not? What prevents people from talking with one another?

♣ Network Communication Structures

Over time, network communication patterns **stabilize**. People become accustomed to playing similar talk cards and talk games in family gatherings, at work, in their communities, and in other settings. In other words, people find a role they like to play in their communication networks and stay there. **Liaisons** keep connecting; nonparticipants remain isolated and avoid interacting with others. Traditionally, researchers have focused on network patterns of information exchange and the manner in which those patterns shape relationships.

For example, the Internet and smartphones let managers and team members communicate directly with one another routinely in real time. This **direct communication** changes the relationship between the parties so that everyone has nearly equal status. Before web applications and email, employees were often forbidden to speak with managers several layers above them. They had to go through supervisors and others to communicate. Customers had the same problem. The information explosion has changed those rules as Jeff Jarvis' Blogging Game illustrates. We now live in a world of **instant access**; anyone can interact with anyone else based on his or her needs without the constraints of superficial communication rules or business protocols. That's what employees and customers expect.

A ♥ Anyone can interact with anyone else based on his or her needs without the constraints of superficial communication rules or business protocols. ♠ A

Downward Communication. When the communication network is structured so that people in upper management levels push information down to lower levels, this is called **downward communication**. This type of communication is intended to control the organization and personnel operations. Typically, downward communication messages, since they are official, are usually formal and in writing. The most common form of downward communication content deals with job instructions, usually direct messages that instruct an employee to perform a specific operation at a particular place and time. Other types of downward communication might include messages to orient individuals to the goals of the organization.

According to my friend and colleague Dr. Vernon Miller (1996), one the biggest failures in downward communication lies in feedback about job performance. Organizations often fail to adopt systematic means of providing members with feedback, such as appraisal interviews about job performance. Employees want to know how well they are doing and where they need to improve, but many organizations operate under the belief that no news is good news. To gain information about the organization's expectations, most employees play a variety of card talk communication games such as the Testing Game. They annoy someone or break a communication rule to get a reaction.

According to Dr. Miller's research, excellent companies believe that positive employee recognition is the best motivator. We know from many studies that feedback is essential to improve performance and commitment to the organization. If people have no idea how well they are progressing, they lose interest in the organization, and become isolated in their own interests.

© 2012 by Kathy Burns-Millyard/Shutterstock.com.

Upward Communication. The opposite of downward communication is **upward communication** (communication from workers to bosses). Upward communication in command-and-control organizations like the military tends to be formal and written and flows along the formal chain of command. Without adequate upward communication from workers, management cannot react quickly enough to prevent minor problems from developing into major problems for the organization.

Upward communication is often difficult in formal command-and-control organizations because there are many layers of management between people at the bottom and people at the top. Also, these layers cause status problems. People at the top may think they don't have to listen to people at the bottom; so upward communication is often undervalued.

By contrast, in team-based organizations, upward communication is essential. These organizations have only a few layers of hierarchy and people respect others' opinions, so information flows more freely. One of the most important changes that NASA experienced after the Challenger disaster was to significantly increase upward communication. Suddenly, people were talking to each other so they could avoid the kind of communication breakdowns that led to the explosion.

Horizontal Communication. The third pattern is termed **horizontal communication**. It occurs at the same level, or sideways, along the organizational chart. This type of communication is informal, face-to-face, and personal. Since it is faster and better attuned to communicators' personal needs, horizontal communication tends to be used to coordinate activities.

For example, the networks that sprang up in Tupelo were essentially **horizontal networks**. Merchants and community members started talking to one another about how to tackle a particular problem, what tasks each would perform, when the tasks would be performed, and how to keep each other updated on problems and progress. This type of communication is the usual style in a team-based business. Individuals figure out whom they need to talk to and simply contact those individuals.

What's exciting about the communication technologies revolution is that it has significantly flattened organizational structures by increasing horizontal communication. Most companies have only one or two layers of management, and make it clear that a strong, robust information flow is important to the organization's health and its ability to respond quickly to customer needs. In the Blogging Game, networks formed rapidly around customer complaints and became powerful. People from all walks of life contributed and made a noise loud enough that Dell could not ignore them.

Communication Culture

In chapter 3 we explored how culture impacts communication. We talked about culture mostly from personal and national identity standpoints. People from diverse countries display different communication preferences that are important to know when interacting cross-culturally. This concept of culture relates to people in organizations. Over time, as their networks stabilize, people develop organizational cultures. Consistent with the discussion in chapter 3, we define **organizational culture** as the framework of beliefs, values, and patterned behaviors that members use to create, maintain, and modify their communicative interactions.

Communication culture serves two key functions: **understanding** and **regulation**. First, culture helps coworkers **understand** their work environment, especially the attitudinal and behavioral expectancies. If downward communication is the norm, then the culture probably places more value on complying with authority than on creating ideas and sending them upward to management.

We might say that this kind of organization has created a compliance culture rather than an innovation culture. Downward communication in this organization is understood as more appropriate, and upward communication is viewed as inappropriate and maybe even disrespectful.

The second function of communication culture is to **regulate behavior**. If upward communication is interpreted as disrespectful, then the organization probably has rules or unwritten codes about who can talk to whom. In these organizations, people are only allowed to speak with their immediate supervisor and no one above the supervisor. The network paths are carefully regulated.

Government agencies like NASA typically create highly regulated cultures that permit only downward communication. To understand the role this

© 2012 by Edwin Verin/Shutterstock.com. Used under license of Shutterstock, Inc.

highly regulated culture played at NASA, it's important to talk a bit about its history. NASA began after World War II when scientists in Alabama were given the green light to experiment with rockets. These Alabama scientists were viewed as the brains of NASA. Because they thought they were smarter than others, they often shunned interaction with other NASA groups.

This culture of devaluing input from other NASA work groups doomed the organization to a series of isolated units incapable of **reciprocal coordination** and adapting to change. This culture lasted for several decades, from the early 1950s until the Challenger tragedy.

In NASA's defense, culture is a difficult element to change because people become comfortable within a culture and resist change. However, after the Challenger disaster NASA was ready for a change. Directors wanted to open up the organization and create a more highly integrated agency capable of building a more responsive program. That could not have happened without a significant cultural change.

Chapter Summary

Here are the key points of this chapter:

- **The best coordination approach depends on the work to be done.** When people only want to collect opinions for later use, pooled coordination works best. When the task requires creative adaptation to change, reciprocal coordination works best. Reciprocal coordination is more expensive because it takes more time and resources to implement.
- **Coordination forms networks.** Networks build links among members. Links can be strong or weak; they focus on task, social, or innovation topics; and can be formed and maintained through multiple channels. Social networks tend to be integrated horizontally, whereas task networks tend to be vertically integrated, going up and down the organization as people need to get their work done.
- **Networks vary in integrativeness, reachability, and dominance.** When an organization is dominated by liaisons working to connect employee groups, then that organization is likely to be more highly integrated and people are more reachable. Liaisons play an important organizational role.
- **Reciprocal coordination** produces highly integrated and reachable networks with low dominance. Sequential coordination is poor at integrating people and making them quickly reachable. Reciprocal coordination is better for adapting to change.
- **Networks form communication structures** that cause information to flow downward, upward, or horizontally. Often organizations get stuck in these patterns, and when challenged by a new job that requires new communication patterns, change is difficult for them.
- **Organizational culture is a key element** in performance. Communication flows create cultures that help members understand how to interpret behaviors and how to regulate their own behavior. These cultures can either help or hinder the organization in accomplishing its task.
- **Cultural issues played a role in the Challenger tragedy.** Since a noncooperating culture had emerged among NASA units, the impetus to coordinate was lacking. That lack of impetus created a bottleneck in upward information flow and a disincentive for individuals to play a different talk card to break away from this tradition.

Lessons Learned

- **The coordination model must match the task.** When the task calls for a reciprocal model, then to be effective, the network must build that model. That change requires someone to play a Leadership Card and help the team move in that direction.
- **Don't let bad habits dictate the coordination model.** Teams or organizations often take on new tasks using the same kind of coordination model they've used in the past. In essence they make the task fit the coordination model, and not the other way around.
- **Keep information flowing freely and smoothly.** It is probably best to err on the side of maintaining a smooth information flow. Information is the raw material of creativity. A smooth information flow stimulates creativity. That means constantly monitoring the culture to ensure people coordinate and share.

- **Nurture the liaison role.** Many studies indicate that when organizations encourage a few natural linkers to span organizational boundaries and get to know people from multiple units, the organization is better positioned to coordinate effectively. Helping people create a Liaison Card is productive.
- **Create communication policies that prevent information overload.** The danger of too much information is that it can bury people. When they must manage hundreds of emails a day or labor under constant meetings, they have little time to look forward at the big-picture issues. It's important to play the Leadership Card and establish policies about how the network can best function to achieve its organizational goals.
- **Make innovation talk and upward communication a priority.** Adapting to change requires creativity. People won't offer new ideas unless they're asked several times to do so and they see their ideas are used and valued. The process of stimulating ideas creates a culture of exchange and a sentiment to grow.
- **Information is the currency of the knowledge organization.** This currency should be carefully audited and monitored, just as money is watched. Mismanaged information is at best squandered, and at worst, crippling to an organization's ability to function effectively.

References

Putnam, R. D., & Feldman, R. D. (2003). *Better together: Restoring the American community.* New York: Simon & Schuster.

Jarvis, J. (2009). *What would Google do?* New York: Harper Collins.

Miller, V. D. (1996). An experimental study of newcomers' information seeking behaviors during organizational entry. *Communication Studies, 47,* 1–24.

Monge, P. R., & Contractor, N. S. (2003). *Theories of communication networks.* New York: Oxford University Press.

Van De Ven, A. H., Delbecq, A. L., & Koenig, R. (1976). Determinants of coordination modes within organizations. *American Sociological Review, 41,* 322–338.

Decision-Making Card Games

♣ Introduction

Chapter 9 made the point that effective coordination is essential for making great decisions. The Prize Bull Game from that chapter illustrated the point that once the Tupelo, Mississippi merchants started to communicate like a team, they were able to make good decisions to pull them out of their poor economic condition. They decided to exchange the information needed to understand the problem, weigh the options, and select the best choice.

What we skipped in that discussion was an in-depth analysis of the group decision-making process. Once people start talking, there is a dynamic that emerges in terms of how the group forms, exchanges information, develops leadership, manages conflict, and makes a decision. The key for you is to learn how to manage this process to create productive teams and groups.

When groups get lazy about their communication policies, the outcomes can be disastrous, as we saw from the Challenger explosion in the last chapter. The whole system collapsed, and people lost their lives as a result. The purpose of this chapter is to look at how groups communicate and make decisions.

Let's look at some typical decision-making games that many college students play as they move through their college careers.

♣ Decision-Making Games

The College Selection Game. One of the first games you play in your pursuit of higher education is the College Selection Game. Once you decide to attend college, the question becomes, Where do I go? That decision is complex because there are many factors to consider. Among the most

A♥
The key is to learn how to control this process to create productive teams and groups.
♠A

common questions are: Which schools fit your interests best? What is the campus atmosphere like? What are the costs and opportunities for employment after graduation?

Maybe your parents or friends took you on a college road trip to visit campuses and talk with recruiters. After these trips you probably sat down with your parents and friends to decide whether to apply to or attend the schools you visited. Did your parents and friends lead this discussion while playing their respective cards? Or, did you play a College Student Card and lead the discussion by laying out the pros and cons of each school?

The Academic Major Selection Game

Many new college students have difficulty selecting a major area of study. It's a lot to ask a young student to make such an important decision so early in his or her life. The best way to select a major is to look deep inside for some kind of passion that makes the major fun and exciting. Many people are interested in several areas—like my youngest son, who really likes history, politics, and art. When he goes to college, how will he select his major? He might play a Friend Card and get advice from friends. He might play a Student Card and ask an advisor to provide some insights. I hope he also plays a Son Card and asks his parents about a major that would be best for him.

Typically, for these kinds of difficult situations, students turn to many people and play several cards, seeking as much input as possible to make the best decision.

The Class Project Game

Many classes require students to complete team projects, such as a paper or big presentation. These teams are often three to five students in size. Instructors typically do not assign roles in these teams, so students must decide themselves how to manage the team's affairs. The typical team struggles with how to proceed, and often no one wants to step up and take a leadership role. Students try to play this game with their Friend Cards and get by with casual conversation.

At some point, someone needs to step up and organize the group to bring the team together. That job requires a Leadership Card to facilitate the meetings and keep the team on task and working effectively. Students sometimes criticize these assignments because they feel uncomfortable playing a Leadership Card. As a result, the group fails to gel, resulting in a few students doing most of the work. But you could consider team projects an opportunity to build leadership experience.

To build a Leadership Card that is effective in group decision making with parents, intimate partners, or classmates, it is important to know:

- What does effective decision making look like?
- How do groups function effectively?
- What are some typical barriers to effective group communication?

♣ What Is Group Decision Making?

My good friends and colleagues Drs. Marshall Scott Poole and Andrea Hollingshead edited one of the best books available on group decision making (Poole & Hollingshead, 2005). The general consensus from these authors is that **decision making** is a communication game consisting of two or more people picking a solution to a problem from a set of alternatives. The question is, Why do some groups make better decisions than others? While there are many answers to this question, the Functional Perspective outlined in the Poole and Hollingshead book finds groups that are effective in making decisions perform the following communication functions:

1. **They thoroughly and accurately understand all important aspects of the problem.** What are the important aspects of the problem in playing the College Selection and Major Selection Games? For both games the challenge is to look at all elements necessary to be successful in a college. What about the ability to get a good job after school, the social atmosphere on campus, the school's reputation, financial considerations, location, transportation issues, expenses, and so forth? When preparing to make a major decision, it is important to break down all relevant aspects of the problem and get good information about all these aspects so their impact on the decision can be assessed.

2. **The team develops criteria for making an acceptable choice to solve the problem.** Once the group reviews the important aspects of the problem, it's important to determine how they compare with one another. For you, what's more important—the kind of job you could get upon graduation or the campus social life? Is the school's reputation more important than the financial costs? At the end of this process, it's best to have a few key criteria that are most important in selecting an option to solve the problem.

3. **The team develops a range of realistic and acceptable alternatives that meet these criteria.** Once the criteria are set, it's best to identify several choices that meet these criteria. For example, if the order of your criteria for selecting a college is: job placement, social life, close to home, and financially feasible, then you should find three or four colleges that meet these criteria. The colleges probably won't be equally desirable, but if all are acceptable, then you can visit them and see which one feels right for you.

4. **The team assesses the positive and negative consequences of the alternatives.** After selecting a range of options, it's important to identify the likely positive and negative consequences of each option. What will life be like at each school? What are the positives and negatives? Research cited in the Poole and Hollingshead book reveals that people weigh the negative factors more heavily in making a final choice. In other words, people are often determined to avoid an option with even one negative consequence even if the other options have only weak positive consequences.

5. **The team selects the best alternative and commits to implementing it.** After weighing all the positive and negative consequences, people select an option (**probably the one with the fewest negative consequences**) and commit to it by agreeing to follow through. You did that when you selected a college to attend. If you look back on the process, how would you grade your decision-making process? Did you walk through each of the first four steps before making your choice? Certainly you would want to do that for important decisions in the future.

Walking through these five steps defines a **group decision-making context**. But are groups always best for making decisions? Many students don't like to work in groups, as I mentioned previously. Groups take more time to make a decision than an individual, and students are uncomfortable playing a Leadership Card to move the decision-making process along. However, research is clear that *groups typically make better decisions than individuals working alone* (Michaelsen, Watson, & Black, 1989). Real-world groups performing typical work-related tasks almost always perform better than the best-performing individual in the group. So instead of avoiding groups for important decisions, we should embrace them.

If groups generally produce better results than individuals working alone, what factors are important in making groups productive? Let's answer this question by reviewing some chapters in the Poole and Hollingshead (2005) book.

A ♥

Research is clear that groups typically make better decisions than individuals working alone.

A ♥

What Makes Groups Productive?

We've already talked about the Class Project Game and how most students prefer to work alone. Yet we know that groups are generally better when they perform well. Here are a dozen key factors derived from research that boost group performance.

1. **An Effective Size.** When groups grow too large for the task at hand, they are ineffective. Groups of three to eight people are optimal for most tasks. Groups of this size allow for more open communication and a freer information flow. Plus, it's easier to schedule a smaller number of people to get together and discuss the problem.

2. **Clear Group Goals.** High-performing groups have clear goals. But groups consist of many members, each of whom might have a different goal. To deal with this challenge the group must develop clear, achievable, and measurable goals early on, and be rewarded for achieving these goals. This task typically falls to the group leader.

© 2012 by Wayne0216. Used under license of Shutterstock, Inc.

The Class Project Game is a good example. Students must select a project that will receive a good grade. That's a clear, achievable, and measurable goal. It also has a specific reward associated with it: a good grade. It would be easier for one student to take charge of the project and decide the project's goals without group input, but would it produce a better result? Research says no! The result will likely be worse. When the other students drop out of the group and let one student take over, the final product suffers.

To prevent this kind of collapse, one of the first tasks the group should tackle when playing the Class Project Game is defining goals. What does the group really want to accomplish and by when? If the group has a **designated leader,** then that person should facilitate the discussion and move it along in a focused, productive way.

3. **Coordination of Effort.** A third factor that can make or break a group's effectiveness is **coordination of effort.** To understand this phenomenon, we turn to researcher Dr. Max Ringelmann, who published an article in 1913 in which he sought to determine if individual efforts can be summed up to yield group outputs (Kravitz & Martin, 1986). He wondered if during games such as tug-of-war every individual on a five-member team could maximally exert 50 pounds of "pull" on the rope, whether all members pulling together would be able to exert 250 pounds of pull.

What Ringelmann found was that as more members were added to the team, **individual effort declined**. While one member was able to pull 50 pounds, adding another member did not guarantee that both could pull 100 pounds together. Indeed, the number is less than that. One person might consistently pull, when all other members are concentrating more on getting a firm foothold or a better grip on the rope. Thus, all members are not exerting maximum effort at the same time; they are not coordinating their efforts in the best possible way. Some people are working at cross purposes from others.

The College Selection Game provides a good example. Perhaps when you started the process, you were not too excited about looking at several colleges. Maybe you only wanted to apply to one college. But your parents wanted you to add a few more schools to the list for comparison purposes. They were playing their Mom and Dad Cards, while you were playing your Son or Daughter Card with passive interest. Then later in the process, perhaps it became more interesting and your participation picked up. You started playing a Leader Card and gathered information and evaluated schools. The point is that individuals don't all participate at the same level all the time. The key is coordinating the effort to reach the team's goal.

The point is that individuals don't all participate at the same level all the time.

4. **A Motivation to Perform.** As you can see from this last example, a fourth reason why groups underperform is motivation. Ringelmann claimed that in cases where individuals are given the opportunity to slough off work on someone else, they probably will. In other words, members may not work as hard on their part of the group assignment if they perceive that others in the group will cover for them.

   If there is **no sentiment to coordinate** or no team spirit focused on achieving the goal as we learned from chapter 9, the group often falls apart. If there are no **consequences** for failing to meet one's responsibilities, the group is likely to underperform. **Sentiment** and **consequences** are keys in getting people to perform their duties.

5. **Open Communication.** When people feel free to bounce ideas off one another in an open, accepting fashion, the final group product improves. Of course, members must feel as if the group climate is such that they want to contribute. If the climate is punishing when people speak up, they won't contribute. In other words, sometimes members are rewarded for speaking up and contributing, and other times they are punished.

   That kind of climate can happen in the Academic Major Selection Game. What if the student's friends make fun of the majors that the student liked and called them stupid or nerdy? Would the student continue to explain why those majors would be good, or would the friends' comments close down the Academic Major Selection Game? In most cases it would close down this conversation because the climate was no longer about open communication. It was about making fun of the student's choices. This hostile climate compromises the decision-making process and puts the student at risk for making a bad decision about a potentially life-changing choice.

6. **Clear Role Development.** Groups produce better outcomes when everyone is clear about his or her role. Two important group roles are task and social leadership. (We talk about effective leadership in the next chapter.)

© 2012 by Monkey Business Images. Used under license of Shutterstock, Inc.

Task leaders develop the agenda, keep everyone on track, keep information flowing, and ensure everyone is involved. **Social leaders** ensure that everyone in the group feels comfortable and respected. They keep things light, ask people if they're happy with how things are progressing, and keep people connected. Task leaders are the liaisons we talked about in the last chapter on coordination. They link people with their own good nature and interest in talking about others' lives. When groups have people who can play both Task and Social Leader Cards, they are more effective.

7. **A Conflict Resolution Plan.** What happens if group members disagree? This is an important question that should be discussed shortly after the group forms. For those of you who pursue student leadership opportunities, your Leadership Card should include topics related to creating a plan for member disagreement. The plan might include taking an **issues time out** to explore the source of the conflict, working through it, voting on key issues, or asking an outside advisor to mediate the dispute. If the group has someone who plays a Social Leader Card, that person needs to be watchful for anything that might upset group progress.

8. **A Willingness to Disagree.** A significant threat to group decision making is mindless conformance. In an often-cited book Dr. Irving Janis (1982) coined the term **groupthink** to describe the dangers of going along with the crowd. He found that group members tend to conform to the decisions of others. People don't like to stick out their necks and be different from the group. Over time, this desire to conform closes down discussion and prevents new information from entering the group. You can easily see this might not lead to the best decisions.

9. **Not Too Much Disagreement!** I conducted a study several years ago about the optimum level of disagreement in a group for it to function effectively (Donohue, Hawes, & Mabee, 1981). The research found that at least 10 percent of the interaction should show some kind of disagreement for the group to be productive. With more than 30 percent disagreement, the group risks disintegrating. That's too much conflict. Did you feel comfortable disagreeing with your parents during the College Selection Game? It is difficult to disagree with others in general, but particularly difficult when talking with parents.

10. **Sufficient Time to Deliberate.** Information is the lifeblood of group decision making. If the group cuts short the process, there is little time for members to share what they know about the problem or to analyze it carefully. Less information means lower-quality decisions. Rushing the process also limits the number of options the group is willing to consider. For any group decision, there should be *at least three options* that are viable and well understood by everyone. Sometimes groups are dominated by one person who favors a particular approach and cuts off discussion of other options. The task leader must prevent this kind of domination since it restricts information flow.

11. **A Culture of Trust and Respect.** The group's culture, as we learned from the last chapter, has a dramatic impact on member willingness to participate. Establishing trust, or the perception that others are acting in one another's best interests, enables everyone to contribute freely and openly. Imagine trying to play the Class Project Game if members created a coalition to gang up on the leader. **Coalitions** are small subgroups of members who have a separate agenda that they want to accomplish. Sometimes coalitions cause culture problems in groups when people are afraid to open up or trust one another to problem solve effectively. The point is to watch out for coalition development so that trust and respect are not compromised.

12. **A Practice of Celebrating Success.** It is important to celebrate success as a way to build sentiment or team spirit. If you celebrated your admission to the college of your choice, that was a good idea. If you went out for pizza after the big class presentation with your group, you probably felt better about your group experience. These are important milestones to celebrate. Leaders should take the initiative to acknowledge members' hard work in accomplishing group goals.

Leaders should take the initiative to acknowledge members' hard work in accomplishing group goals.

© 2012 by mangostock. Used under license of Shutterstock, Inc.

Results:

Do you have more check marks for the successful group? In theory the groups should be different based on the research findings cited earlier. If the groups are about the same, then you might want to rethink the criteria you used to define success. For example, maybe you thought a group was successful if you had fun or if you liked the outcome looking back on it. Generally, groups that pay more attention to the process of group communication perform better.

♣ Group Decision-Making Lifecycle Stages

For the most part, groups do not play these communication games randomly or haphazardly. While it may seem that way at times, groups experience a predictable lifecycle as they form, work toward a goal, and then fall apart. This lifecycle consists of a series of stages, according to a chapter by Arrow, Henry, Poole, Wheelan, and Moreland (2005) in the Poole and Hollingshead (2005) book. This chapter provides an excellent review of how groups change over time as they communicate. Let's look at a typical lifecycle model of change to see how student groups evolve and how transitions play out in the context of the Class Project Game.

The Orientation Stage. In many class projects the instructor either assigns individuals to groups or people randomly join a project. I teach a class in Sales Communication, and we assign students to groups of about five to give a final sales presentation to a mock client. The first task these students face is orientation. What is the task? When is the assignment due? Who is the client?

In this orientation stage students swing back and forth between task and social considerations. They might play Student Cards to figure out the assignment and Friend or Acquaintance Cards to express their feelings about the task, the class, their social life, or their professional prospects. Topics include exploring the assignment requirements, who has what skills and resources, and who is willing to do which roles. Generally, people participate with all the best intentions. But students are busy and each has his or her own motivation for completing the assignment, with some more eager for good grades than others.

The Discontent Stage. After this initial orientation effort, members often enter a stage of discontent with the task and perhaps other group members. Schedules and other course requirements often interfere with playing the Class Project Game well. Students in my Sales Communication class start to feel the pinch as the semester comes to a close and other class assignments compete for their time. This discontent also arises because the group may not be a significant part of members' identities. Members might already have a job and want the semester to end, get their degrees, and start their lives. They can feel alienated; they may want to check out and avoid participating in meetings.

The Group Identification Stage. If the group does not respond to its discontent with a greater commitment to the task and stronger group identification, then it fails to perform and breaks up. What often triggers a greater commitment to the task is some **precipitating event** that sparks members into focusing on the task and helps them rediscover and renew their commitment to the group. In the Class Project Game, the precipitating event might be the instructor clamping down on the group and threatening them with failure if they don't shape up. Sometimes this "wake-up call" is sufficient to motivate students to change. I have had this conversation with many student groups. Generally, they decide to get serious about the assignment, restructure their roles, and increase their efforts.

© 2012 by Junker. Used under license of Shutterstock, Inc.

This newly invested activity bolsters each member's group identification. The result is that communication rules and boundaries about what's acceptable and unacceptable change. No longer is it acceptable to play a Comedian Card and joke around all the time or give excuses for not attending meetings. When people get together it's time to change talk cards, get to work, and perform well. The net result of these stronger communication rules is a renewed vision of what the group can do. The group is now viewed as an important part of each student's life and college success.

The Group Productivity Stage. When a group commits to a new vision and increases its dedication to the task, it enters a **productivity stage** marked by energetic collective work. I have been impressed with how groups in my classes kick into gear at the semester end and deliver a spectacular performance for their final projects. In many cases I would have never predicted that they would kick their effort into a higher gear and succeed. But after a stern talk and a commitment to group goals, they get serious and get to work. Some groups meet 20 times to rehearse for their final presentations!

The Individuation Stage. As groups perform well in pursuing a specific goal, like a final class presentation, members come to expect recognition for their success. They want others to notice their achievements. At this point, members are still attracted to the group, but they turn more toward satisfying their individual needs. If another project does not emerge to keep the group's attention focused on a new goal, they generally attend to their personal goals. If this pattern continues long-term, group commitment may decay as members' needs eclipse group needs. The collective identity dissolves, resulting in members becoming alienated from the group. They look for ways to avoid participating in the group, which returns them to the **Discontent Stage** and the cycle starts again.

Business groups experience this lifecycle. For example, a group might be formed to serve a client and take great pride in performing well. After this task is complete, the group risks falling apart unless another challenge emerges. The key is keep the group engaged and play a variety of Talk Card Games so the members maintain their group identity.

Theories of Group Decision Making

So far, we've talked about what makes groups perform well and the lifecycle stages they experience as they grow and change. Now let's take a broader look at why groups perform as they do by describing some important theories of group communication behavior.

Structuration Theory. In chapter 1, we described how talk games are governed by **constitutive** and **regulative rules**. Because people play certain talk games over and over, they know how to create (or constitute) rules and how to keep (or regulate) people from playing them inappropriately. The Course Project Game is a good example. Students play this game many times throughout their college careers, so they know the rules of the game—both what constitutes the game and how to play it appropriately. I have seen students organize into a group so they know what to do (creating constitutive rules) and reprimand group members for not following through with their commitments (enforcing regulative rules).

Structuration theory, outlined in the Poole and Hollingshead (2005) book, tells us how groups use these rule structures to guide their card play. The theory says that we select topics and styles to "cook up" a talk card game in the same way as a chef creates a dish using a recipe. Once we define a group conversation as a particular kind of card game (the constitutive rules), we follow a recipe for how that game should be played. We mix in Topics A, B, and C with Styles X, Y, and Z, and people recognize it as the Course Project Game and not the Academic Major Selection Game, for example. After playing this card talk game repeatedly, the rules become better known and exert more influence over what topics and styles are seen as appropriate (the regulative rules).

Thus, there are **dual structures** that emerge in every interaction: (1) knowing what game we're playing and (2) knowing how to play the game appropriately and effectively. This **duality** idea is important because when we play a talk game, we must be aware of *both* how we play it and the impact it has on the other people and the group. If all parties are not playing the same game or playing it poorly using inappropriate cards, they will fail to have a productive discussion.

This duality idea explains why sometimes groups fail to move beyond the Discontent Stage. Members can't focus on one game and play the talk cards needed to be effective. One member might play the Excuse Game and make up reasons to leave the group, while another member plays the Random Topic Game and constantly brings up topics irrelevant to the task. In the next chapter we talk about how leaders can better structure group discussions to get everyone on the same page and working together.

© 2012 by Yuri Arcurs. Used under license of Shutterstock, Inc.

Structuration theory also says that there are various factors, or **contingencies**, that can throw off group communication structures. These contingencies may cause individual group members to play different talk card games when they should be playing the same game as a group. These contingencies include:

- **The nature of the task.** When talk games focus on controversial or emotional topics, like values, or when games are ambiguous in that the need for a specific decision disappears, it is more difficult for group members to focus on one game that will help them coordinate their communication structure productively. Only when the group's task is specific or factual and everyone is clear on what is needed does the group develop a consensus around a specific game.
- **The quality of the leadership.** If the group leader does not participate in the interaction and lets the group do what it wants, it is less likely to keep on track and follow any given sequence of steps. Leaders with an agenda who encourage open communication are more likely to see the group form their communication around a specific game.
- **Whether the task is novel.** If group members have little experience with the task, they might not have a recipe for how to play the talk card games needed to be productive. They are forced to make up the rules as they go, which can be challenging. With strong leadership the group may find its way, but novel decision-making tasks are difficult for groups to process.

- **Group sentiment.** When group members like, trust, and respect each other, they are more likely to play their Friend Cards occasionally. If they are played at appropriate moments when everyone wants to take a break and play a social game, then group sentiment grows and people feel better about being part of the group. If the leader allows too much time for socializing, the group starts to play too many games at once and has difficulty completing the task.
- **Group size.** Larger groups with assigned leaders are more likely to use a specific path than smaller groups. When groups are smaller the leader must be careful to keep the group focused on a productive game in the event that one member wants to hijack control and distract the group.
- **Cultural norms.** As we have seen in previous chapters, some group cultures dislike conflict. As a result, they are more likely to avoid open conflict, which is needed for the groups to sort out their differences and find a productive path. If the group faces being in a Discontent Stage but people are unwilling to confront this challenge, then the group risks dissolving.

Hidden Profiles Theory. A second theoretical perspective explains why some groups are better at making higher-quality decisions than others (Stasser & Titus, 2003). Aside from being able to manage the structures that groups create as they interact, this theory focuses specifically on what happens when people fail to share information properly.

The theory makes a distinction between the kinds of information people use when making decisions. When members interact, they use both **common** and **unique information**. **Common information** includes facts that everyone knows. If you're playing the Class Project Game and trying to decide which topic to select for the project, then all members are likely to have some information available about the facts of the situation from the course syllabus. The syllabus says that the topic should conform to certain criteria, and the paper should be a specific length and include a PowerPoint presentation. Everyone knows these facts.

Unique information includes facts and perceptions that only each individual group member has. The totality of this unique information is called the **hidden profile**. For example, in the Class Project Game, each member is likely to have an opinion about the class, the project, and the professor. Since most people have many opinions and perceptions of the situation, each person typically has an abundance of both common and unique information. The question is, Which type of information are they most likely to share while playing the Class Project Game?

Research indicates that people are more likely to emphasize **common information** and not share their unique information. The reason is that they may not want to share their unique opinions because of a risk of getting criticized or being made to look foolish or incompetent. They may not want to challenge the group leader's opinions. Or group members might be reluctant to disappoint anyone in the group by stating a different point of view. There are lots of reasons why people are reluctant to share, as we know from the last chapter on coordination when we talked about the dangers of **groupthink**.

Groups that are reluctant to share unique information tend to make poor-quality decisions. The hidden profile is not revealed so the group can't get access to the information it needs to be successful. The group lacks a complete picture of the situation, hindering its ability to develop options for addressing their problem.

Sometimes group members prefer to share unique information. When there is a right answer to the task, like figuring out a math problem in a group setting, people are more willing to share unique information. In this case people probably feel their opinions will not be judged harshly because they are simply trying to solve a puzzle. But when the decision involves a judgment about the best thing to do, as in the Class Project Game, people are generally only willing to discuss common information.

Finally, the theory indicates that people's initial preferences often dominate the discussions and determine if people are willing to share their hidden information. When a leader has a strong preference, he or she may try to push it on the group. If the leader is forceful, others often give up and side with this person even if they have unique information that contradicts the leader's preference. The leader might have high status or be popular, and members want to defer to that person. This tendency often limits discussion to common information, thereby compromising decision quality.

Communication Process Theory. A final theory of interest in understanding how groups play and win (or lose) card talk games focuses on the communication process. What are the important communication processes associated with effective and ineffective group decision making? In general, research concludes that effective decision making is characterized by four recurring themes of communicative activity.

© 2012 by EDHAR. Used under license of Shutterstock, Inc.

1. **Rigorously evaluating the validity of opinions and assumptions.** When the information and opinions of group members are closely scrutinized, as opposed to receiving only cursory examination, the group is more likely to be effective. Not checking facts or letting people make grand leaps in logic without asking for documentation often results in poor decision making because the information is of lower quality.

2. **Rigorously evaluating suggested courses of action using pre-established criteria.** When groups develop criteria for determining whether an option is good or bad and each option is evaluated using those criteria, the decision is more likely be successful. Playing the College Selection Game is a good example. If no one develops a thorough analysis for the colleges, then they all look alike—there's no way to tell which one is better.

3. **Making the final choice based on facts, assumptions, and inferences that are reasonable and accurate.** If an outside observer can see that the assumptions and inferences made by the group are reasonable, then the decision is likely to work well. If the group lets members make assumptions based on invalid and incorrect inferences, then group decision making suffers. An objective third party should be able to tell if this process was effective.

4. **Having influential members ask questions, point out important information, challenge unwarranted assumptions, and keep the group from digressing to irrelevant topics.** This is the leader's job description. When a group lacks that kind of leader, it is more likely to lose its way. Effective task leaders ask questions, they know what important information to continuously bring back to the group, and they keep the group on task.

These four elements define how an effective leader interacts with the group. Chapter 11 focuses on leadership from a communication standpoint.

Chapter Summary

- **Group decision making is about making good choices.** The more choices the group has for solving its problem and the more it is committed to implementing the best choice, the better the decision looks in the long term.
- **Groups are most likely to make better decisions when they pay attention to the process.** Members should take time to establish clear goals, select a coordination strategy for the task they must perform, be clear about what counts as quality performance, promote open communication, develop both task and social leadership roles, foster a clear problem analysis, and be willing and able to have productive conflict. These elements create a culture of trust, respect, and success.
- **Groups move through specific stages as they deliberate.** They begin by orienting to the task and getting to know one another. As members pursue the task, they might express a discontent that is often turned around by some precipitating event—including a competition for leadership—as ideas are tossed around. As members line up with one set of ideas, that person assumes leadership and a decision emerges. The group reflects on that decision to decide if the group is effective.
- **The theories of group decision making focus mostly on how members exchange information.** Structuration Theory tells us that knowing the constitutive and regulative rules of the discussion are important. Hidden Profiles Theory reveals the importance of exchanging both common and unique information. Communication Process Theory asks members to reflect on how well they process the information necessary to make a good decision.

Lessons Learned

I hope you picked up some recurring themes about how to play effective group decision-making talk games. Here are the key lessons that will help you craft more effective talk game strategies:

- **Groups need to enter the decision-making arena with the right focus.** They should enter with an open mind to explore alternatives and be willing to commit to the group's decisions.
- **Effective group decision making requires structure.** Groups need to commit to developing clear goals and clear roles for its members, a team spirit, open communication, a willingness to share private thoughts, and time to build a culture of trust and respect.
- **Groups should not shortcut the decision-making process.** Groups should work through the decision-making phases deliberately, taking their time. They should select a coordination strategy that works for the task they are asked to perform.
- **Group members should define and determine the extent of the problem situation.** Proper problem analysis and definition helps the group decide whether a given alternative will successfully deal with the problem.
- **Alternative options should be considered in light of negative and positive consequences.** Group members should determine for each alternative the possible benefits as well as the possible disadvantages.
- **Avoid glossing over disagreements.** Members should adopt a constructive approach to managing differences. Emphasis should be placed on resolution through critical examination, rather than consensus through superficial appeal.

- **Everyone should be encouraged to participate and communicate.** Members who remain silent almost always have something to say, but for some reason or another, decline to say it. All members should be asked for input and be assured that the group is interested in hearing what they have to say.
- **Groups ought to be kept relatively small.** As group size increases, especially under time constraints, the opportunities that group members have to communicate with one another diminish. Smaller groups are better at soliciting and including member input.

References

Arrow, H., Henry, K. B., Poole, M. S., Wheelan, S., & Moreland, R. (2005). Traces, trajectories, and timing. In M. S. Poole & A. B. Hollingshead (Eds.), *Theories of small groups: Interdisciplinary perspectives* (pp. 313–367). Thousand Oaks, CA: SAGE Publications, Inc.

Donohue, W. A., Hawes, L. C., & Mabee, T. (1981). Testing a structural functional model of group decision making using Markov analysis. *Human Communication Research, 7,* 133–146.

Janis, I. L. (1982). *Groupthink: Psychological studies of policy decisions and fiascoes.* Boston: Houghton Mifflin.

Kravitz, D. A., & Martin, B. (1986). Ringelmann rediscovered: The original article. *Journal of Personality and Social Psychology, 50,* 936–941.

Michaelsen, L. K., Watson, W. E., & Black, R. H. (1989). A realistic test of individual versus group consensus decision making. *Journal of Applied Psychology, 74,* 834–839.

Poole, M. S. & Hollingshead, A. B. (2005). *Theories of small groups: Interdisciplinary perspectives.* Thousand Oaks, CA: SAGE Publications, Inc.

Stasser, G., & Titus, W. (2003). Hidden profiles: A brief history. *Psychological Inquiry, 14,* 304–313.

© 2012 by Salim October. Used under license of Shutterstock, Inc.

Leadership Card Games

♣ Introduction

Do you consider yourself a leader? Have you ever performed that role in school, at work, or even in your home? As we learned from chapter 10 on Group Decision Making, winning those games by making high-quality decisions requires effective leadership. Leaders emerge by proposing ideas on how to define and solve a problem while receiving support from group members. Even appointed leaders must earn their leadership status by helping to define clear goals and developing a process to achieve those goals.

We also learned from the last chapter that leadership is earned through effective card talk play. Another way to frame this idea is to say that communication is vital to leadership. Leaders who connect well with group members, provide good ideas for solving problems, and promote a thoughtful and interesting process stand a good chance of playing successful talk games. To better understand the role of communication in building an effective leadership strategy, consider these leadership talk card games.

A ♥

Even appointed leaders must earn their leadership status by helping to define clear goals and developing a process to achieve those goals.

♠ A

♣ Leadership Talk Games

The Vision Game. On May 25, 1961 President John F. Kennedy addressed a joint session of Congress. In his opinion, and in the opinion of many others, the United States faced a crisis because the Soviet Union (now Russia) had put a man into space before the United States. To address this crisis President Kennedy made the following remarks:

> *If we are to win the battle that is now going on around the world between freedom and tyranny, the dramatic achievements in space which occurred in recent weeks should have made it clear to us all, as did the Sputnik in 1957, the impact of this adventure on the minds of men everywhere. I believe this nation should commit itself to achieving the goal, before this decade is out, of landing a man on the moon and returning him safely to Earth. No single space project in this period will be more impressive to mankind.*

Kennedy then asked Congress for a multibillion-dollar increase in funding for space travel, which was granted. His vision not only inspired a nation but resulted in the United States landing a man on the moon in July 1969, as President Kennedy promised. I saw that landing as it happened and it was certainly a moving experience.

The Defiance Game. On Sunday, March 7, 1965 about 600 people began a 54-mile march from Selma, Alabama to the state capitol in Montgomery to commemorate the death of Jimmie Lee Jackson, shot three weeks earlier by a state trooper while Jackson was trying to protect his mother at a civil rights demonstration. On the outskirts of Selma, after crossing the Edmund Pettus Bridge, the marchers, in plain sight of photographers and journalists, were brutally assaulted by heavily armed state troopers and deputies. I recall watching the brutality on TV and wondered how the nation might hold together.

While this march was led by John Lewis, who serves today as a congressional representative from Georgia, Dr. Martin Luther King Jr. led a group of marchers two days

later on the same route to again fight for the civil rights of African Americans. These marches set the stage for the Voting Rights Act of 1965 which dramatically increased African American voter registration in the South and around the nation.

Lewis and King realized that oppression is sustained only when oppressed people give their permission to be oppressed. They understood that this permission had to be explicitly withdrawn, even though the price for challenging the entrenched powers would be high. Their courage helped build a national consensus for civil rights that has expanded to include rights related to women, Hispanics, and others. King and Lewis played the Defiance Game with courage and conviction, and we owe them a huge debt of gratitude for playing it well.

The Showtime Game. My home school, Michigan State University (MSU), has had some great basketball players over the years. Perhaps the most recognizable leader of Spartan basketball is Earvin "Magic" Johnson. When Johnson was in his sophomore year at MSU, the team was not performing well early in the Big Ten season. Coach Jud Heathcote liked to play a slow, half-court game that emphasized executing plays and relentless defense.

After a tough loss, Johnson went to Coach Heathcote and asked if the team could run more, taking advantage of Johnson's passing and running skills. Exasperated and needing some success, Heathcote agreed. The next game, the team ran an offense, called Showtime, in which the team ran up and down the court with fancy passing and lots of dunks. If Johnson had not stepped up as team captain and played the Showtime Game, the team might not have gone on to win the 1979 NCAA (National Collegiate Athletic Association) championship.

Defining Leadership

These talk games illustrate how stepping up and showing a Leadership Card can build a consensus for change. Perhaps the best definition of leadership that captures what's involved in creating and playing this card is from a book called *The Leadership Challenge* by James Kouzes and Barry Posner. They contend that **leadership** is "the art of mobilizing others to want to struggle for shared aspirations." Another way to think about this is that a **leader** is the person asked by followers to speak for them. After all, they are struggling together to achieve some vision of a better future and they believe that their selected person will provide the right strategy to achieve that better future.

Each of the games played by the leaders in this chapter illustrates this relationship between leaders and followers. The American people asked Kennedy to help solve the problem of Soviet dominance in space. Americans could not conceive of the Soviet empire controlling space, so Kennedy needed a bold vision to establish American dominance in space. Lewis and King were asked by their long-suffering people to lead them into equal citizenship as fully free Americans. Johnson's teammates sent a clear signal to him as the team captain that something needed to change, prompting Johnson to talk to the coach about playing Showtime basketball to start winning. Followers demanded that these people play their Leadership Cards to win these important talk games. Based on Kouzes and Posner's perspective, a Leadership Card should:

- **Communicate a clear vision of the future.** Like President Kennedy, we want our leaders to present us with a clear picture of a better future—one we as followers want. Lewis, King, and Johnson painted clear and compelling visions with emotion and conviction.
- **Model appropriate behavior.** We want our leaders to practice what they preach. When Lewis and King asked their followers to march, these leaders were at the front of the crowd marching arm-in-arm for justice.
- **Inspire us to act.** In the situations described in the three talk games, leaders faced life-changing challenges—defending a country, fighting for civil rights, pursuing a championship. These situations required a strong person to step up to meet the challenge, and in each situation they did. They inspired with rhetoric, determination, and powerful deeds. They showed the way, and people enthusiastically followed and became better than they thought they could be.
- **Remain sociable and friendly.** Because these leaders stepped up to the challenges they faced, they became famous. However, they never lost sight of their need to connect personally with followers. They appeared approachable, friendly, part of the group, and always available to listen.
- **Challenge the process.** We expect a leader to recognize when the process isn't working, when a crisis is approaching, or when a change is needed. Then we want them to forge a new direction because the old process is broken. "Fix it!" the people entreat, and the great ones will take it on and succeed.

These are difficult expectations for leaders to fulfill for followers. The Leadership Card is tough to create and sustain. Sometimes leaders are inspiring, but don't act appropriately or are unfriendly. Other times leaders are inspiring, but they don't present a clear vision of the future. When individuals can pull all these leadership elements together,

© 2012 thatsmymop/Shutterstock.com

as they did in reaching the moon, rejecting oppression, or being the best college basketball team, we hold them up as examples of exceptional individuals.

The Leaders' Questions. Leadership is earned; it is not given. Even if someone is elected president of the United States, he does not become a leader until followers agree to march in the direction advocated by the leader. The moment in which followers proceed down the path behind an individual is the point at which that person becomes a leader. As more people join this parade, the leadership becomes stronger. Building a Leadership Card begins by asking three critical questions:

1. **What needs to be done to make this situation better?** The first question is the most important: What needs to be done? The team is here to win, the nation must be free, man must walk on the moon! How can these goals be achieved? The first job of a leader is to *listen* to others. What are the people's aspirations? Lewis and King could not have led a march for freedom if people were not ready to fight for it. Those two men listened intently to the stories of oppression and segregation and heard yearnings for a better life and a future that breathed justice. They knew the people were ready and the time was right after many sessions listening to these stories. Their own experiences added further confirmation to those stories.

2. **What can and should I do to make a difference?** After listening and connecting with others, Lewis and King decided that what needed to be done was to stop giving permission to be oppressed and to demand change. They decided they could make a difference by publicly demanding change through speeches, boycotts, and marches. They looked at their own skills and resources and decided they had the ability to do these things and the courage and motivation to do them. They never would have been successful if they did not look at themselves as individuals and ask what they could do to make a difference.

3. **What should I say to keep the struggle visible and the path to success clear?** Leaders are communicators. They must continuously listen to others and talk to others. They must remain constantly visible to the followers to keep the vision real, maintain enthusiasm for the cause, and most important, to inspire. This is the key challenge in playing leadership games in organizations. Leaders have been granted the privilege of leading. As a result, they must constantly be out front in plain view of followers, encouraging them to move forward with the vision.

Communication Strategies of Effective Leaders. Besides asking these questions, what else should be on the Leadership Card? Followers expect leaders to use a variety of communication behaviors to mobilize others. Here is a list of behaviors that research tells us are common on Leadership Cards. Let's review the list and explore how they promote leadership.

- **Problem identification.** Leaders do a better job of examining the nature of the problem that needs to be solved and keeping people on task to explore it from many different perspectives.
- **Proposing solutions.** They also have good suggestions for how to solve these problems, and they are seen as more creative and effective.

- **Seeking information.** Remember that leaders are good at listening. They ask questions and listen to the answers. They don't change the topic to something they want to talk about. They let followers teach them how to lead. Shared aspirations drive leadership behaviors, so learning the followers' aspirations from every angle is key.
- **Giving information.** People want leaders to be smart and that usually means providing unique information about the challenges the group faces. Leaders' unique perspectives are valued.
- **Structuring the process of decision making.** Leaders should challenge the process, but more important, build a new

© 2012 by StockLite. Used under license of Shutterstock, Inc.

and better process for moving forward. If followers want new leadership, it's generally because the old leaders were stuck in a dysfunctional process.
- **Leaders are active, but not pushy.** Leaders communicate and facilitate. They don't force people into compliance. Leaders who push are generally ineffective. Leaders who listen are more effective.

Results:

If you said Yes to six or more behaviors, then you appear to have some confidence in your leadership communication behaviors. But what about style choices? Remember, leaders are expected to be:

- Friendly to most everyone to make them feel at ease when communicating;
- Informal in social gatherings and formal during meetings when the group needs direction;
- Powerful and directive to keep things moving forward but deferential (able to give power) to others' opinions when exploring solutions to problems.

If we review this list of communication behaviors in light of the Vision Game at the beginning of the chapter, you can see how effectively President Kennedy used them when laying out his moon vision. He asked people to take on responsibilities, he proposed solutions to problems, and he made a powerful challenge to all Americans to embrace the idea of putting a man on the moon by the end of the 1960s.

Author Warren Bennis (2009) says that leaders must also be managers occasionally. Using a seafaring metaphor, Bennis says that where leaders chart the ship's course, managers steer the ship in the direction desired by the leader. I am sure Bennis would agree that in addition to playing his Leader Card, President Kennedy could also play his Manager Card when necessary. American presidents work hard to get legislation passed through Congress and are responsible for directing cabinet secretaries to implement important policies. Many managers are promoted to leadership positions but fail because they have difficulty letting go of their management role. They want to steer the ship instead of charting its course. If all people do is steer, they soon get lost.

© 2012 by Rambleon. Used under license of Shutterstock, Inc.

Leadership Emergence

In his book on leadership Dr. Peter Northouse (2013) provides a compelling set of explanations for how individuals emerge and sustain a leadership position in a group. Many wonder whether some people are born to be leaders and others might feel that leaders are made by followers. How might one predict who, from among a set of group members, will emerge as the leader? Northouse helps us answer this important question.

The Trait Approach. One school of thought is that certain individuals are born with certain traits that predispose them to become leaders. Traits associated with leadership emergence include intelligence, sociability, and dominance. A leader tends to be more intelligent than the average group member. He or she tends to be more sociable by being highly integrated into social networks and possessing effective communication skills. A leader tends to have a stronger need to dominate than do most group members.

However, these traits are limited in their ability to help us understand leadership emergence. Consider the office of U.S. President. Presidents both high and low on intelligence, dominance, sociability, and other traits are common. For instance, Jefferson was highly intelligent; Harding was not. Theodore Roosevelt and Lyndon Johnson were dominant chief executives; Grant was low on this trait. Eisenhower ranks as a sociable president; Polk was unfriendly. Yet, each of these men emerged as an important leader in the United States.

The Situational Demands Approach. A second way to view leadership is that certain situational demands may favor one type of leader with a specific profile of traits **at one time,** and a leader with a completely different profile at another time. At the beginning of World War II, England needed a wartime leader who could be tough and inspirational. The British people turned to Winston Churchill to serve as prime minister from 1940 until July of 1945. After the defeat of Nazi Germany, the British people needed a leader who could turn inward and rebuild the nation. While Churchill was an inspirational leader, he had little interest managing and sorting through the details of rebuilding. Instead, the people turned to Clement Attlee of the Labour Party as prime minister in July 1945, a different type of person who asked how and when rather than what and why.

Individual Difference Approach. Aside from analyzing leadership on a case-by-case basis, is there anything of a more general nature that can be said about the manner in which traits and situational characteristics combine to determine leadership emergence? One psychologist, Dr. Fred Fiedler, argued that people differ in an important personality trait that might predispose them to emerge in some situations as leaders. He refers to this individual difference as the **assumed similarity of opposites** (ASO). People are high on this dimension to the extent that they see opposites as being alike, or they are low on this dimension to the extent that they perceive opposites to be different from each other. If you worked in a company and rated your most preferred and least preferred coworker in much the same manner, then you would be a high ASO individual. Someone low in ASO would rate these two people differently.

Why is this individual personality trait important? Remember from our discussion in chapter 10 that some people emerge as task leaders and others as social leaders in groups? The task leader focuses on effective completion of the work that the group must handle. This type of leader is seen as providing suggestions, opinions, and information to fellow group members and, perhaps, showing antagonism if they reject them. In contrast, the social leader focuses on the relationships among group members. This type of leader is more likely identified by behavior that displays solidarity.

In his research Fiedler found that **low ASO people** are likely to become task leaders. They focus on and see differences among the group members. For example, they have the skills necessary to make personnel and task assignment decisions—skills required of a task leader. On the other hand, those **high in ASO** are likely to become social leaders. High ASOs focus on and see similarities in people. For instance, when conflict occurs, they are able to manage it by emphasizing to the participants that the ways in which they agree are more pronounced and important than the ways in which they disagree—skills required of a social leader.

Leadership as a Combination of Traits and Situational Demands. Rather than relying on either a trait or a situational explanation, it is probable that the combination of these two elements provides the best understanding of why some leaders emerge and others don't. Common sense tells us that many people are presented with situations that demand leadership but few are willing and capable of stepping up.

© 2012 by Celso Diniz. Used under license of Shutterstock, Inc.

The need for a leader was apparent when MSU's basketball team was dramatically underperforming, as in the Showtime Game. The need for leadership to fight for civil rights was apparent when Jimmy Lee Jackson was shot, as described in the Defiance Game. America needed a leader to fight for a vision when the Soviet Union grabbed first place in the space race. Only a few stepped up and seized the opportunity.

What are the key elements that help us understand when certain people will step up to lead? Fiedler (1996) asserts that there are three characteristics of situations that are crucial to leadership.

1. **Leader/Follower Chemistry.** In many ways followers anoint leaders. In chapter 10 we talked about how individuals propose ideas and then others in the group start to support those ideas. Ultimately, a chemistry or special relationship develops between leaders and followers where the followers become more confident in one person's vision of how to lead the group. Over time, members develop a loyalty to their leader as successes build and members see more traits they believe will address the situation at hand. I am sure that the character, determination, and courage that King and Lewis showed in marching through Alabama solidified every follower's confidence in their leadership. In fact, these men inspired generations of individuals to go on and fight for civil rights not only in the U.S., but around the world.

2. **Task Structure.** The second element that contributes to some individuals being better able than others to step up in certain situations is the nature of the task. Some people have the traits necessary to perform the tasks that members are looking for. These leaders have the skills and the personalities that suit them for the vision that group members highly prize. One of the key skills that President Kennedy needed was the rhetorical skill to articulate the vision and put the pieces in place to carry out the vision. Those were important traits needed for that specific task.

3. **The Use of Social Power.** In the next section of this chapter we describe ways in which individuals can build social power with group members. Power is all about influence. The leader's goal is to use a form of influence that binds group members together and inspires them to work collectively toward accomplishing their shared vision. That influence may be a tough kind of influence, such as a coach might use when training athletes. Or it may be centered on respect and admiration, as in leaders fighting for a social cause. But the combination of the right kind of power in the right situation is a strong predictor of leadership emergence.

Combining these three situational characteristics, Fiedler (1996) claims that the situation is **favorable for leadership** when followers support the leader, the task is highly structured, and the leader's power is strong. Conversely, the situation is said to be **unfavorable for leadership** when followers do not support the leader, the task is unstructured, and the leader's power is weak.

The key lesson here is that if you're participating in a group and you have been appointed leader but your traits do not mesh with the situational requirements, then your power is likely to be weak and your leadership ineffective. It's best to seek leadership when the group wants a leader and the task is ready-made for you to step up. Putting this advice into action in effectively creating and playing a Leader Card means understanding how social power works in a leadership context.

It's best to seek leadership when the group wants a leader and the task is ready-made for you to step up.

Leadership and Power

Power Defined. A leader's **social power** is defined as the extent to which followers perceive that the leader has the ability and willingness to control group outcomes. Let's break down these two perceptions of ability and willingness because often they are two different judgments. If members believe that the leader is able to help them achieve their goals, then the question in the minds of followers is whether the leader has the willingness to step up and use that ability. Magic Johnson certainly had the ability to lead, but stepping up to play the Showtime Game proved he had the willingness as well.

There are **two forms of social power:** (1) Forcibly driving change through coercion and (2) encouraging change through persuasion and modeling. Sometimes a coach has to forcibly push a player in a specific direction that the player doesn't want to go to help that player improve. The player certainly doesn't want to change, but it's the coach's job to find the right kind of power to help the player improve so the team can win. At other times, the coach may use persuasion and modeling to convince the player to change and show the athlete how best to perform.

Power Is in Relationships. Power is all about how individuals become interdependent through the roles they play with one another. Professors have no power without students; mothers have no power without children; players have no power without other players and coaches. The key is that *the more interdependent individuals are with one another, the more they can influence or exert power over one another.* If you had to list the person who has the most power or influence over you right now, your answer would probably be the person you are closest to relationally, say a parent, sibling, or spouse. Sorting out power requires sorting out the nature of the interdependencies that role partners have with one another.

It's important to note that **power** is a highly subjective judgment based on your perception of how much someone can influence you or you can influence them. Some people use that subjectivity to their advantage by threatening violence, for example, but never following through with the violence. Over time the perception of a leader's power may grow either because the people's dependence on the leader increases or their fear of the leader escalates.

Forms of Social Power. Individuals can use a combination of strategies in trying to influence one another. Here are the six strategies that can be used individually or in combination:

1. **Coercive Power.** Forcing individuals through punishments or threatening to withhold rewards.
2. **Reward Power.** Consistently providing something of value to the other person that they find pleasant or useful in some way.
3. **Legitimate Power.** Compliance based on one's position. "Do it because I'm the boss."
4. **Referent Power.** Gaining influence through respect.
5. **Expert Power.** Gaining influence by demonstrating competence in performing skills that the other person values.
6. **Information Power.** Providing data or information the other values.

Leaders typically combine these strategies as they play their cards. For example, leaders may begin by using coercive power and interrupting the other's talk, changing the topic, using loud and intimidating speech, or directing people about what they should do (a power-oriented style). Then they may switch and use referent power by listening attentively, following up on others' topics, and speaking sincerely while giving emotional support (a high affiliation style).

These are communicative extremes but a leader who is **situationally competent** can switch their card play depending on what needs to be done to complete the task. Regardless of which strategies the leader uses, the more followers comply with the leader's requests, the more they build their dependency on the leader and submit to the leader's influence.

Leader Longevity

Longevity Varies. In many areas, such as business or sports, the leader's duration can be brief. Unless they die in office, are impeached, or resign, presidents of the United States serve at least four years. Since Franklin D. Roosevelt, however, no president has served for more than eight years because the **Constitution** now prohibits it. The chief executive officer of a major corporation may not last as long. Presidents of major universities in the United States serve, on average, approximately seven years.

Throughout human history some kings and queens, czars, chiefs, emperors, emirs, and sundry other monarchs have ruled for lengthy periods. Catherine II reigned as Empress of Russia for 34 years. Henry VIII was King

© 2012 by Bikeworldtravel/Shutterstock.com. Used under license of Shutterstock, Inc.

of England for approximately 38 years. Louis XIV was King of France for more than 70 years. Of course, these leaders had the force of the state as a means of preserving their longevity!

In some instances departing the leadership role is a matter of choice; in other cases it is forced on the occupant of this position. For example, sports coaches are fired all the time for failing to win. Czar Nicholas II of Russia was forced to abdicate and was executed. President Richard M. Nixon resigned his office to avoid impeachment. Regardless of the method of departing the role, it is clear that maintaining a position of leadership is as challenging, if not more so, than obtaining the position.

Time Challenges. Specifically, leaders face two important problems relating to time. The first is **time management**. In many leadership contexts, the leader's time is the most important commodity for the followers. For example, in modern corporate life employees measure their success by how much "face time" they are allowed to spend with the **chief executive officer**. Obtaining additional time is a major reward, and having one's time reduced or eliminated indicates major career failure. Because time is a finite commodity and there are typically so many time demands, leaders have little discretionary time. Moreover, what they have of it they tend to guard carefully.

Second, visions generally have a **time span**. Some visions are premature, or ahead of their time, such as the group of people who predicted the financial collapse of 2008–2009. Many people raised red flags about the economy and proposed remedies, but government leaders chose to ignore them or simply didn't believe it could happen. Sometimes visions become outdated. For instance, President Kennedy created the vision of putting a man on the moon before the end of the 1960s and the United States achieved that vision. Following a few more trips to the moon, a new space vision was created that included the Space Shuttle, which carried objects into space for research purposes. Changing outdated visions are not unique to American politics. Many companies shift their visions often in response to changes in the economic or political environment.

The problem for the leader whose vision becomes dated appears to have a straight-forward solution—generate a new vision. Unfortunately, inspirational new ideas do not come to mind easily for most of us. Moreover, it is especially difficult for leaders to generate these new visions because their followers often prevent it. The followers may not want the burden of change that new visions bring. Also, leaders may have difficulty being exposed to the sorts of new ideas that would allow them to update, or radically alter, their visions. As a result, a leader's job tenure is likely to end when the original vision becomes dated or has been fulfilled.

Focusing Energy. A central problem of leadership maintenance becomes finding ways to avoid the stale-vision trap. Research shows that successful leaders are careful to **restrict their agenda** so that they pursue only one or two goals at a time. In this way they avoid micromanaging, spreading their time thinly across many issues, several of which are likely to be relatively minor. Moreover, they tend to attack only those problems they believe can be solved.

This focusing tactic is interesting for at least two reasons. First, it implies that these leaders believe that some of their organization's problems are unsolvable or not worth the effort. Restated, even successful leaders are aware that they cannot succeed in eliminating every problem. Focus is critical.

Second, the idea of focus reinforces the view of leadership as a visionary process aimed at addressing a limited number of critical issues that will move the organization forward. Managers, on the other hand, try to do everything by managing or even micromanaging staff. When leaders develop a Leader Card it must include topics related to creating and discussing these vision opportunities.

Finally, successful leaders take time to sharpen their intellectual skills. Many spend considerable time reading, and their reading is often done in diverse fields. One reason that activity of this sort enhances their success is that it improves their ability to form new visions.

Leader Card Inventory Survey

Now it's time to focus on your own Leader Card. Think of a situation in which you served in a leadership role—work, sports, school, or another area. Score yourself on the extent to which you demonstrate these behaviors in that role.

Directions: Circle the number that best represents how often you performed these behaviors using this scale: 1 = Never; 2 = Seldom; 3 = Sometimes; 4 = Often.

CHALLENGING THE PROCESS: HOW OFTEN DID YOU ...	SCORE 1–4
1. question assumptions underlying how the group worked?	
2. offer solutions to problems the group faced?	
3. share information across different groups in the organization?	
4. have in-depth knowledge of how to accomplish the task?	

Total: _____

INSPIRING A SHARED VISION: HOW OFTEN DID YOU ...	SCORE 1–4
5. incorporate diverse ideas into the decision-making?	
6. seek the commitment of others to common goals?	
7. run meetings and make presentations effectively?	
8. communicate with outsiders to learn what they thought?	

Total: _____

ENABLING OTHERS TO ACT: HOW OFTEN DID YOU ...	SCORE 1–4
9. articulate a clear vision of the road ahead?	
10. generate creative solutions to complex problems?	
11. show honesty and forthrightness in dealings with others?	
12. demonstrate a caring attitude toward others?	

Total: _____

MODELING THE WAY: HOW OFTEN DID YOU ...	SCORE 1–4
13. work to include all cultural and ethnic groups in the task?	
14. generate new resources to serve organizational goals?	
15. seek input from experts when necessary?	
16. xhibit a sense of humor?	

Total: _____

ENCOURAGING THE HEART: HOW OFTEN DID YOU ...	SCORE 1–4
17. demonstrate flexibility in responding to tough issues?	
18. consistently build on others' ideas in problem-solving discussions?	
19. step in and redirect destructive conflict?	
20. promote recognition of others' contributions?	

Total: _____

Add your scores using the following table.

Total for items 1–4 Challenging the Process =
Total for Items 5–8 Inspiring a Shared Vision =
Total for Items 9–12 Enabling Others to Act =
Total for Items 13–16 Modeling the Way =
Total for Items 17–20 Encouraging the Heart =
Total of All 5 Categories =

_____

_____

_____

_____

Results:

Now add your scores for each of the five dimensions and total those five scores. If you scored 60–80 points, you have a great deal of confidence in your leadership skills. If you scored 20–40, you probably lack confidence. A score between 41–59 could indicate you are unsure about your skills.

Now look at your scores on each dimension. What was your highest and lowest score and what do these differences mean? For example, if you had low scores on Challenging the Process and high scores on Encouraging the Heart, you may think of yourself as more of a task leader than a social leader.

Chapter Summary

- **Leadership is earned, not given.** Members have to decide who will lead them. Leaders must listen first to members' desires for a better future and be willing to step up to the leadership challenges as their skills and abilities dictate.
- **Leadership is about vision and communicating it effectively.** So often leaders who come from a management background have difficulty forming a Leader Card and articulating a clear vision for their group. Leaders can manage, but they should spend most of their time defining and executing the vision. Leaders want to know what needs to be done to make the place better and what they can do to make a difference.
- **Leadership is about effective communication.** Leaders are expected to be effective at problem identification, proposing solutions, and listening to others while leading the process of decision making.
- **Leaders are not born, they are the people who step up when needed.** Leaders are not born in the sense that they can lead anywhere or anytime. Leaders have traits that match the situations in which they find themselves. They use these traits by stepping up when called.
- **Effective leadership is based on respect, not coercion.** Think of the leaders you most admire. I talked about four at the beginning of this chapter. Each of them led by respect. They forged a vision and had the courage to see it through. That earns trust and respect from group members.
- **Leadership is different than being a manager.** Leaders chart the course and managers steer the ship. Effective leaders can do both when necessary.
- **Leaders who keep the vision alive endure the longest.** Leaders must constantly build a rationale for their leadership. They must continue to be perceived by group members as the best option for implementing the vision, so the vision must be constantly updated to keep it fresh and important to group members.

Lessons Learned

Leaders emerge over time by proposing ideas that are supported by the followers. Since your Leader Card is probably still developing, here are some guidelines for making it stronger.

- **Assess Your Own Leadership Strengths and Weaknesses.** Are you willing to step up when needed or are you afraid to assert yourself? Developing a Leadership Card takes time. Each time you play the card, it grows and the process is easier.
- **Leadership Grows from Your Own Communication Skills.** Don't think that leadership is about being glib and slick; that's not the kind of communication needed. What's needed is someone willing to ask questions about what's happening and willing to help others think about what could happen.
- **Look for Leadership Opportunities.** One of the great advantages of being a college student is exposure to many leadership opportunities. There are hundreds of groups to join and many work-related groups that students commonly experience. Pick one or two and stretch yourself.
- **Leaders Like to Learn.** Leaders are constantly reading and listening to others. They want to know what successes and failures others are experiencing. They learn about new trends to discover opportunities for their own organization.
- **Start Small and Think Big.** Finally, think BIG. Start with modest opportunities and work your way up to a leadership position. Excellent leaders are rare, so start now and pursue it passionately.

References

Bennis, W. (2009). *On becoming a leader.* New York: Basic Books.

Fiedler, F. E. (1996). Research on leadership selection and training: One view of the future. *Administrative Science Quarterly, 41,* 241–250.

Kouzes, J., & Posner, B. (2007). *The leadership challenge.* New York: John Wiley & Sons.

Northouse, P. (2013). *Leadership: Theory and practice.* Thousand Oaks, CA: SAGE Publications, Inc.

PART four

New Media Card Games

♠ Social Media Card Games

♦ Diffusion of Innovation Card Games

♣ Media Learning and Entertainment Card Games

© 2012 by photomak. Used under license of Shutterstock, Inc.

Social Media Card Games

♣ Introduction

Chapters 12, 13, and 14 focus on the convergence of New and Old Media as an important card talk issue. We have moved beyond Media 1.0, which is an Old Media view of the world, into Media 2.0 that unites Old and New Media. Briefly, the idea of **New Media** refers to the use of personal and mobile computer devices that are Internet- or network-enabled with which individuals take an active role in shaping their media experience. People use electronic tablets and readers, smartphones, video game consoles, and computers of various configurations to actively post their pictures, blog their ideas, and create video channels. These active media behaviors and the devices that enable them have revolutionized the ways in which people connect with one another both personally and professionally.

People still spend a lot of time consuming **Old Media**, also called mass media, which involves centrally produced information and entertainment messages distributed to large audiences through separate channels. TV and radio networks create shows and send them out through many channels, including cable, over the air, and online. Newspapers, magazines, and other print vehicles would also be considered Old Media. Old Media are different than New Media. Old Media are passively consumed; we turn on the device and watch and/or listen.

But don't be fooled by the "old" label. These more traditional media continue to evolve, and still exert a tremendous influence on how individuals perceive one another and the world around them.

In his book *Convergence Culture*, Dr. Henry Jenkins (2006) provides a framework that explains how content flows across multiple media platforms, how media industries cooperate to create and deliver that content, and how audiences migrate across these media in search of satisfying experiences. Jenkins argues that in the Media 2.0 world of total convergence, "every important story gets told, every brand gets sold, and every consumer gets courted across multiple media platforms" (p. 3).

What's really different about Media 2.0 is that this convergence process marks a shift from assuming that audiences are passive recipients of information to viewing them as active consumers who shape media content to suit their needs. The Old Media continue to provide a broad set of information and entertainment messages that are culturally influential in many ways and set the stage for how we interpret our surroundings.

In contrast, New Media provide us with tools to create specialized and customizable media content for a few people (or even large number of people). In other words, we live in an electronic cloud in which we can find multiple media to shape whatever experience we want to encounter.

The following three chapters discuss this epic shift to Media 2.0. First, in Chapter 12 we explore social media and how they have changed the nature of our relationships. In chapter 13 we discuss how media combine with interpersonal communication to promote innovation. Finally, chapter 14 talks about how the Media 1.0 world informs and entertains us and is beginning to converge with New Media to form our Media 2.0 cloud. For now, let's begin by describing some interesting and popular social media talk card games.

The Pinterest Passion Game. One of the fastest-growing social media sites is Pinterest. As you may know, this site enables users to post photos of all the beautiful things that interest them online, around their home, or wherever. My wife uses Pinterest to post pictures of her gardens in which she takes great pride. I use it to post pictures of my special applesauce recipes. People then comment on these photos and videos and offer suggestions to improve them.

We go to their pin boards and see what impresses them. One student commented to me that the site is addictive because there are so many beautiful things to look at in this world. What's interesting about Pinterest—and it's similar to Facebook in this regard—is that people like to express themselves about all the things that are important to them, and make lots of friends doing it. After all, people like to play their Friend Cards as often as possible and have fun.

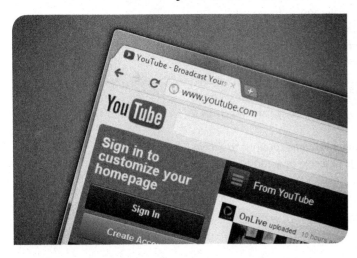

© 2012 by bloomua/Shutterstock.com.

The YouTube Channel Game. My teenage son is excited about video games. His current love is the game Battlefield. And he plays many of his games online with his friends, which is common. In his spare time he captures some of his missions and posts them to his own YouTube channel for others to see. He often checks how many viewers he attracts, and I am surprised at how many people (probably other teenage boys) actually watch them.

My son uses YouTube for most of his entertainment and spends virtually no time in front of a traditional TV watching network shows. He likes to control the content and participate more actively in his entertainment. This approach is classic Media 2.0. His media have totally converged. His games, music, news, and even school research are all pulled together in a cloud that he creates and shares with others, playing his Friend Card and his Audience Card almost interchangeably.

The Twitter Time Game. My Twitter name is @WADonohue. Follow me if you like. I tweet about many things on a fairly regular basis. Twittertime (I just made up that word) reflects a need to connect immediately with others about anything of interest. Social revolutionaries in the Arab world have used it to overturn governments as they form flash mobs to protest government policies. The Occupy movement has used Twitter to organize their activities.

What's significant about this site, and many others like it, is its raw democratic impact. It answers the question, what would happen if everybody could communicate instantly with everybody? Mass communication channels in the Old Media world were controlled by a small number of big players who owned radio, TV, and newspapers/magazines. They sent out a few people to learn what's going on in a community, then reported it back to people on a daily or weekly or hourly basis. With Media 2.0 everyone can connect with everyone, making communication marvelously democratic and infinitely powerful.

A ♥

With Media 2.0 everyone can connect with everyone, making communication marvelously democratic and infinitely powerful.

♠ A

♣ Social Media: What's the Big Deal?

Media 2.0 is all about community. Recall from the chapter focusing on social identity that we build our self-concept to satisfy our needs for inclusion, control, and affection. We want to be part of a community that accepts us for who we are, and we also want to have an impact on how that community grows and changes. We also want these folks to support us emotionally. Social media accomplishes all these goals by allowing us to build and participate in our own communities, whether through Facebook, Pinterest, Twitter, YouTube, or other options. That's why they are so popular. Here's a link that gives you a good sense of social media's impact: http://www.youtube.com/watch?v=0eUeL3n7fDs&feature=related.

We no longer need to be physically proximal to others to build this community. Members can be, and are, from anywhere. We can form and participate in multiple communities all at once. This is a huge shift from times when people had a few friends in their hometowns and hung out with them. Now people participate in multiple networks with some people they know personally and others they know only virtually. These networks shift all the time as people come in and out quickly and easily.

Dr. Jenkins (2006) makes the point that in the Media 2.0 world of convergence the trend is for Old Media giants like TV networks to build social media communities around their programming as much as possible. The CBS television network runs the show *Survivor*, which involves 16 people competing to see who will be the last one standing on some exotic island. A whole community of people has emerged around the show to "spoil" the outcome by predicting who will win the contest—information that CBS tightly controls. People pore over every detail of the show to figure out who is going to win and members of this spoiler community interact frequently over social media sites to work together in this effort.

Collective Intelligence. This "collective intelligence," as Jenkins calls it, reveals the true power of social media's impact. People use social media to build ideas and possibly a consensus about some kind of action. The action might be as dramatic as enabling individuals to protest and overthrow a government, or it might be as personal as helping a friend cope with a family loss. Collective intelligence comes quickly and thoroughly as individuals share their thoughts and feelings about specific issues of interest.

Recently, a friend in another state told me how social intelligence worked in his neighborhood in a potentially life-saving way. He heard a helicopter hovering over his neighborhood late on a weeknight. Thinking this was unusual, he immediately went on Facebook and Twitter and asked if anyone knew what was going on. Within seconds he got a post and a tweet from a friend (who was a member of the police department) that a local teenager had gone missing and was possibly a danger to herself. In fact, he received several posts about the situation from a dozen other people in the area.

Within minutes, neighbors and friends convened in the area and began an active search for the teen. As people were searching, they were tweeting their locations to better coordinate the search. A lot of ground was covered in a short time. Fortunately, the girl was found unharmed a few hours later. Perhaps because everyone was sharing what they knew about the situation and coordinating their efforts, police created a great deal of collective intelligence to achieve this happy ending.

Product Marketing. Social media have changed the way in which businesses market to consumers. Most marketing textbooks talk about the **traditional four Ps of marketing**:

- Product (identifying features that satisfy customer needs);
- Price (finding the right price point to ensure customer value);
- Place (locating the key spots to make the product available to the customer); and
- Promotion (advertising, branding, and selling the product).

These four elements in this order constituted how companies would structure their products to attract a specific group of customers. The product had to contain features that customers wanted. The price had to be in line with customer expectations. The product had to be placed in attractive locations so customers could find it. And the product needed a snazzy promotional campaign to bring it to the customers' attention.

This old 4-P approach to marketing is a "push" model. That is, it assumes that customers are passive recipients of information about products and services. They become aware of the product, generally through Old Media, evaluate its features and price, and make a decision about purchasing it. The company essentially pushes information out to potential customers to gain interest and hopefully a sale.

The New Media way of marketing products, according to blogger Paul Chaney (http://thesocialmediahandyman.com/), focuses on "pulling" people into the shopping and buying experience through participation in a social network. The **new four Ps of marketing** are:

- Personalization (mass customization of products and services to meet customers' needs);
- Participation (letting the customers decide what a brand should stand for and letting them build the product);
- Peer-to-Peer (building customer networks and communities to talk about the brand); and
- Pulling and not Pushing (attracting people into the company's story—the company's life).

In this approach a company might offer products and services that are configurable for or by each individual. Athletic shoe companies do this all the time by letting customers decide what their shoes should look and feel like. They build social media sites to create product buzz and encourage customers to discuss features they want to incorporate into the products. Again, this is collective intelligence at work. Let the hive mind decide what's important and what the brand stands for. This community will then talk up and tweet up these products as they evolve to serve more customers.

In 2010 journalist Jeff Jarvis wrote a book called *What Would Google Do?* The theme of the book is that Google takes a New Media approach to its business. It creates tools and then lets communities grow around and refine them to become more valuable over time. Jeff's inspiration for writing the book was his bad experience with a Dell computer. After purchasing the computer he had some problems with it and found that Dell's service did not meet his expectations. He blogged about his troubles and within hours he had a whole following of dissatisfied Dell customers sharing their tales of bad service. After collecting thousands of troubled users in his community Jarvis finally got Dell's attention and his computer got fixed.

Social media means people taking charge by collectively telling their stories and making their opinions and preferences known. Never underestimate the power of an angry (or happy) mob.

In a recent academic paper, Drs. Sitaram Asur and Bernardo Huberman (2010) wanted to know if understanding this mob mentality was commercially useful. They sought to learn whether the chatter from Twitter could be used to forecast box-office revenues for movies. They found that the rate at which tweets are created about particular topics can outperform other, more traditional predictors of box-office revenues. The Twitter traffic turned out to be like listening in on thousands of conversations at once about specific movies. The community was talking and its preferences were useful to market researchers.

Social Media Use

Teens and Social Media. Who uses social media to communicate? In a study commissioned by the Pew Internet & American Life Project, Dr. Amanda Lenhart (2009) found that Internet use by adults is currently about 73 percent and about 93 percent for teens. About 63 percent of connected teens go online daily, making use by this group fairly heavy, and increasing as smartphones grow in popularity.

The study also found that teens still use traditional ways to communicate as well. About 95 percent of teens spend time with friends face-to-face and 88 percent talk to their friends on a landline, with 67 percent using a cell phone. About 61 percent of teens send messages to friends through social networking sites and 58 percent text regularly. It is clear that, as always, teens like to connect electronically with one another.

Regarding social media, about 65 percent of teens have an online profile with girls (86 percent) more likely to have a profile than boys (69 percent). As teens get older they are more likely to have an online profile and visit it daily. Teens from higher economic family incomes are more likely to have profiles. For teens, the most common activity on social networking sites is adding comments to a friend's picture.

College Students and Social Media. Several of my colleagues at Michigan State University have conducted research on whether using social media can improve students' adjustment to college. Drs. David DeAndrea, Nicole Ellison, Robert LaRose, Charles Steinfield, and Andrew Fiore (2011) were interested in learning whether connecting into a larger online social media community would be a more powerful resource in helping students adjust to college than traditional face-to-face support interventions. Most colleges have about a 50–80 percent six-year graduation rate and they are eager to improve that rate and help students stay in school.

The study found that the more students used a student-centered, school-specific social media site, the more they came to believe that they would have a diverse social support network during their first semester at college. It was even more potent than face-to-face networking activities in driving their sense of social support among their networks. The authors indicated that participation in this networking site dramatically increased their social capital, or sense of integration into important social networks. The students connected with more people and felt more plugged into the college. They were able to quickly seek help and express their feelings and concerns more readily through social media.

Health Care and Social Media Use. One of the more rapidly evolving trends in health care is to integrate social media into the ways in which patients communicate with physicians. The idea is that more immediate connections can bring faster treatment and keep problems from becoming more severe.

In an interesting article outlining uses of social media in medicine, author Carleen Hawn (2009) reported on the ways in which physicians were using Twitter, Facebook, and other tools to connect with patients. She found that physicians are starting to realize that patients spend a lot more time on social media activities. They use instant messaging sites, send texts, and build large communities of friends and advisors through their social media activities.

As a result, physicians are starting to encourage patients to communicate using instant messaging tools or texting doctors when they experience health problems. Physicians are putting their profiles on Facebook so people can get to know them better and, in turn, feel more comfortable communicating with them. Other physicians write blogs and participate in electronic forums for people who have chronic disease issues. Specifically, Hawn reported that some physicians use sites such as ParentsLikeMe to share insights about medicine and specific trends related to childhood diseases. Many doctors tweet their patients about issues they see in the community to alert them of special and immediate concerns.

In essence, physicians are beginning to realize there is power in building communities, just like marketing experts and many others in our society. Imagine doctors playing the YouTube Game by creating their own video channels about the health concerns they are seeing. I think it would be helpful and interesting to follow my physicians online to learn new information. These tools are available for all to use, and it only takes imagination to figure out how best to use them.

Social Media Effects

Any time there is a massive change in the way in which people communicate, there are significant consequences for peoples' lives. Social media have changed the way teens, students, business owners, physicians, and others communicate, so what's the impact? To understand such effects let's look at how talk card play is different online than in face-to-face settings.

© 2012 by 1000 Words/Shutterstock.com.

Card Play Choices. We typically play different cards when communicating online than in face-to-face interactions. Face-to-face situations generally require us to play multiple cards to keep the interaction interesting. In a personal conversation we might switch back and forth among Friend, Comic, Expert, and Student Cards, depending on the topic and the communicators' goals. In an online situation each site offers different constraints about which cards are appropriate or available to be played. The Twitter Time Game is interesting because it's difficult to play more than one card with only 140 characters. This also limits style and topic choices in a single tweet. Of course you can post multiple tweets and change cards, topics, and styles as you like.

The point is that card choice requires everyone to adapt to whatever the setting might require. In an online setting when it's unclear who might be reading posts, people may choose safer topics or monitor their selections carefully to ensure they are not misinterpreted. Regarding style choices, some sites have strong expectations about what styles are appropriate. For example, when posting to Pinterest, an informal and friendly style is generally expected, since the site is all about sharing stuff that people like. Just remember that each social media site imposes different talk card playing rules and constraints. One strategy does not fit all situations or all sites.

Interpreting Card Play. When using social media we also have different information available to interpret one another's card play. Since posting to sites is largely text-based, we have little nonverbal information to get a thorough read on the other person's card play intentions. In contrast, when communicating face-to-face, we have the visual information needed to get an accurate understanding of the other's style choices. Eye contact, voice volume, and facial expressions give us great detail to determine how angry, friendly, flirtatious, or anxious the other person might be at that point. In other words, we need that information to get a more precise understanding of the other's feelings and emotions. And we need it to make better social judgments of how to respond to that individual.

Recently my wife wrote a message on my Facebook page about a blog she successfully posted to a prestigious site. She was excited about her accomplishment, but in reading the wall posting it was difficult to tell that she was excited. (Of course, if someone is excited in a post and it appears important to the reader, the Facebook convention is to come back immediately and "Like" the entry and congratulate the person.) After reading my wife's post, I did not make an immediate reply, which prompted her to call me about her accomplishment. I could hear the excitement in her voice, but that information was absent from her post.

Effects of Social Media on Emotional Intelligence. Dr. Clifford Nass (2012) from Stanford University wrote an interesting article about how overindulging in social media can negatively impact the development of emotional intelligence (www.psmag.com/culture/is-facebook-stunting-your-childs-growth-40577/). The idea of **emotional intelligence** is being able to both understand and ultimately control one's emotions in various communication situations.

People who lack emotional intelligence have trouble interpreting others' emotions and figuring out what card the other is asking the person to play in critical situations. If a teenager is unable to accurately read emotions being expressed in card play styles, then she will react inappropriately in many situations. We have just talked about how social media provide limited emotional information since it is largely text-based. Can too much social media play stunt one's emotional intelligence?

In his article Nass pointed out that for females, the most critical period of emotional development is between the ages of 8–12. If girls fail to establish a healthy emotional life by age 12, they tend to have much higher rates of depression and social trouble than girls who have better emotional connections. For boys, Nass indicated their emotional intelligence development is spread out over a longer period. In fact, boys might not be fully developed emotionally until well into their 20s.

In his research Professor Nass discovered that girls who spend more time doing Facebook, Twitter, email, videos, and reading were less emotionally intelligent than girls who spent more time in face-to-face interaction. His explanation was consistent with the idea that fewer emotional cues are available in the digital world than in the real world and that lack stunts growth.

According to a book by Daniel Coleman (2006) there are four steps to achieving emotional intelligence. As you read them, think about how well you demonstrate them.

1. **Self-Awareness:** The ability to accurately label feelings as emotions. This skill is important because we have many different feelings all the time, and being able to discriminate among them helps control them. Can you discriminate between, say, being scared and being afraid? Can you tell the difference between loving your parents and loving a spouse?
2. **Self-Management:** The ability to control emotions and impulses and to adapt to changing circumstances. Is the reasoning, front part of your brain able to tell the emotional back part of your brain to calm down or rethink an emotional condition? Are you able to judge if you're overreacting?
3. **Social Awareness:** The ability to sense, understand, and react to others' emotions. When the other person plays a card, do you understand the emotions that went into that play? Can you put yourself in the other's shoes and feel what that person is likely feeling?
4. **Relationship Management:** The ability to inspire, influence, and develop emotions that will help build constructive relationships. Can you use your emotions strategically to improve your communication so you can develop more productive relationships with others?

Of course, you have to want to become more emotionally intelligent as you communicate to make relational progress. This journey starts by gaining a sense of how emotionally intelligent you are now and how you might improve this capability.

Results:

If you scored 20 or below, you lack confidence in your ability to understand your own and others' emotions. Your EI is relatively low. However, if you scored 40 or above, you are confident in your emotional awareness and have a high EI. If your score is 21–39, you are unsure about your emotional intelligence. The goal is to increase your score as much as possible so that you can understand your emotions more clearly and effectively and understand how they impact your life.

Effects of Social Media on Interpersonal Relationships. Because social media impact EI, social media's extensive use most certainly impacts how people conduct interpersonal relationships. My good friend and colleague Dr. Joe Walther and his colleague, Dr. Lisa Tidwell, (2002) have conducted a number of studies exploring this important issue.

In one study Tidwell and Walther examined how interpersonal communication conducted online differed from using face-to-face channels as parties sought to get to know one another. I am sure you have been in the situation in which you initiated an interaction with someone online without getting to know them first in a face-to-face setting.

The results of this study indicate that when individuals communicate online they typically forego the trivial questions and answers that mark normal, superficial exchanges between people who first meet one another in face-to-face interactions. Rather, when people communicate online they are more direct. They use more questions and disclose more personal information.

When the medium trips out the nonverbal cues that might hold someone back, people become more intimate more quickly online.

In other words, when the electronic medium strips out the nonverbal cues that might hold someone back, people become more intimate more quickly online. This quick escalation in intimacy talk generally leads to perceptions of extraordinarily affectionate relations, or **hyperpersonal** states. People jump right in with more intimate topics, more powerful styles, and increased friendliness and informality. A word of caution: Sometimes people go too far too fast.

♣ Taking Charge of Social Media

Personal Implications. It seems clear that people will continue to play talk card games online using social media. The number of sites continues to expand rapidly and more people find them useful to meet others online and develop all kinds of interpersonal relationships. Yet social media present some notable challenges in managing relationships.

The first challenge is not to rely exclusively on these sites to form relationships. Perhaps you use them casually to learn about people or see the interesting things in their lives. But social media should not become the primary source of information about people. It is important to develop face-to-face skills that enable you to connect personally with people and play your hand of talk cards effectively.

The second challenge is to make sure your online presence is not personally inappropriate. I have seen many students post pictures of themselves in naughty poses or in states of intoxication. Employers see these pictures and can't help but use them as an indication of your character. Be careful about what and how you post!

The third challenge is to make sure you diversify your social media presence appropriately. Find a few sites that you like to use and cultivate your presence on those sites. If you are continuously setting up a profile on the latest sites, pretty soon you'll be on 10 or 20 sites, and all your interpersonal, face-to-face time will be lost. I have a profile on some

© 2012 by Elena Elisseeva. Used under license of Shutterstock, Inc.

of the most popular sites, but I wait for the others to shake out before I become too involved.

Professional Implications. I require students in my Sales Communication course to join LinkedIn. They create a profile and use it to find mentors, jobs, and personal advice. People often exchange email in this site and use it to conduct research when trying to figure out whom to call on as clients. Remember, you will probably have two or three jobs after college before you settle into something long term. Your professional value centers on your contact network and your ability to develop potent professional relationships. The site Klout.com is interesting because it measures your professional clout as a social media user. How much exposure and influence do you have in this world? You currently have a Klout score so go online and see what it is.

In addition to creating a professional presence online, a second challenge is to figure out ways to make social media work for you in your career. If you are in sales, you can find prospects for your products and services. Whatever your chosen profession, there are groups of people who can help you in any number of ways. Try to spend at least 30 minutes daily exploring these networks and see how they might help you. The section on product marketing earlier in this chapter lays out a path that shows how necessary it is to occasionally rethink business practices. How might a business be different if it were structured around social media?

Chapter Summary

- **Media 2.0 is all about convergence.** It combines Old Media's passive audience interested in only consuming the story with New Media's active audience interested in participating in the story. The line between Old and New is blurred and the media form a cloud of messages that surround us daily.
- **Social media build a collective intelligence.** We are constantly sharing what we know and think, as well as searching for more information. This is not only information; these are ideas and reflections and are the foundations of creative achievement.
- **Social media are used broadly for many purposes.** Marketing experts use social media to make people more aware of their products and services, physicians use them to help patients take more control over their medical issues, and students use these new media to build many communities that make school more interesting.
- **Social media impacts our card play.** When we communicate via social media, we're unsure who is consuming our messages. We typically cannot see the people with whom we're communicating (unless in some pictures posted to their site) which makes it difficult to predict how these dispersed others will respond to our messages. This limitation can restrict the kinds of cards we play, topics we introduce, and styles we emphasize in our card play.

- **Extensive social media use can stunt our emotional intelligence.** Particularly for young girls, the more addicted we are to social media the less capable we are of interpreting others' emotional messages. We're not used to looking for the additional information necessary to detect the subtle shifts individuals project in their mood swings. As a result, we might make the wrong interpretations.
- **Social media use impacts our ability to sustain satisfying interpersonal relationships.** Social media's online world strips away visual information and, thus, many inhibitions about becoming too personal too quickly. This tendency encourages people to become more intimate in online relationships than in face-to-face relationships.
- **We need to take charge of our social media use.** Rather than mindlessly participating in online and social media communities, people need to limit their exposure and learn to interact in face-to-face environments. We benefit both personally and professionally from limiting our virtual lives and managing our real lives.

Lessons Learned

Social media are changing the way people communicate, and they definitely require playing your talk cards differently. Here are some guidelines for improving your social media communication skills.

- **Learn the social media world.** People should stick to only a few sites. That's useful for creating profiles, but this world is expanding rapidly and everyone needs to keep learning what new sites are popping up and whether they can be useful personally or professionally.
- **Learn to control your presence in the social media world.** One of the biggest challenges for most businesses and organizations is learning how to take advantage of these vast and powerful communication tools. How can they build communities around their missions and then allow these communities to shape their missions? People want to participate in the change process and companies must adapt to this new environment.
- **Don't let the social media world control you.** The more time you spend on these sites, the more you come to see the world through these lenses. This limits you interpersonally, and your emotional intelligence can suffer with too much media time.
- **Don't neglect your emotional intelligence.** Most people understand the importance of being able to read others effectively. People often try to hide their true feelings, and if we spend too much time online, we miss the subtle cues that people let escape that reveal their true feelings. Tuning into them is important in knowing which cards to play to build a winning conversation.

References

Asur, S. & Huberman, B. A. (2010). Predicting the future with social media. *Computers and Society.* arXiv:1003.5699v1 [cs.CY].

Coleman, D. (2006). *Emotional intelligence.* New York: Bantam Dell.

DeAndrea, D. C., Ellison, N. B., LaRose, R., Steinfield, C., & Fiore, A. (2011). Serious social media: On the use of social media for improving students' adjustment to College. *Internet and Higher Education.* doi:10.1016/j.iheduc.2011.05.009

Hawn, C. (2009). Take two aspirin and tweet me in the morning: How Twitter, Facebook, and other social media are reshaping health care. *Health Affairs, 28,* 361–368.

Jenkins, H. (2006). *Convergence culture: Where old and new media collide.* New York: New York University Press.

Nass, C. (2012). Is Facebook stunting your child's growth? *Pacific Standard,* May–June.

Tidwell, L. C. & Walther, J. B. (2002). Computer-mediated communication effects on disclosure, impressions, and interpersonal evaluations: Getting to know one another a bit at a time. *Human Communication Research, 28,* 317–348.

© 2012 by bloomua/Shutterstock.com.

CHAPTER Thirteen

Diffusion of Innovation Card Games

♣ Introduction

Many students are obsessed with technology. When you see a new cell phone, new computer, or cool electronic reader, are you immediately attracted to it? The marketing folks at the tech companies that sell these devices spend a lot of time trying to get you excited about their electronic tools.

The purpose of this chapter is to talk about tech companies and anyone else with new ideas or products, and how they go about diffusing innovations or promoting changes through society or some organization.

How can we promote change to help people adopt the new concept most quickly? It is an important question for companies promoting products or any organization facing the challenge of changing what people do or how they think. Let's look at some typical innovation games aimed at promoting change.

> **A ♥**
> How can we promote change to help people adopt the new concept most quickly?

♣ Innovation Card Games

The Buzz Game. One of the most experienced companies at promoting technology is Apple. The late Steve Jobs, founder of Apple Computers, was a master of manipulating **buzz**, that is, lots of communication about the latest and greatest. Jobs and Apple certainly got everyone excited about the iPod®, iPhone®, and iTouch® when they were introduced to the marketplace. Most recently Apple created lots of buzz about the iPad®, a multimedia computing device that can be used for reading newspapers, watching videos, and more.

Apple's promotional strategy is to first let rumors leak out about whatever game-changer technologies it wants to produce. The goal is to get technology leaders blogging about what these devices might be like, months in advance of a new product release. Apple then dribbles out product features bit by bit to keep feeding this blogging frenzy.

Ultimately, Old Media, like TV, newspapers, and radio pick up on the new Apple device and start running features about what it does. This is the point at which Old Media and New Media converge into Media 2.0, discussed in Chapter 12. As more Old Media stories emerge, activity on social media sites intensifies. Then a couple of weeks before the item is scheduled to be released, Jobs would play his Technology Guru Card and create a multimedia extravaganza about the new device. By the time the iPad was released, everybody wanted one because the buzz had been so intense.

The New Policy Communication Game. Diffusion of innovation is really about the broader issue of promoting change. This is a difficult challenge for leaders in large organizations. Often the leaders must change policies that directly impact workers. The problem is to figure out how best to **communicate** that change. When playing his Boss Card, should the boss directly communicate to all employees at once or talk only to direct supervisors who then tell the employees the message about the change?

Research by Dr. T. J. Larkin, a good friend and colleague (Larkin & Larkin, 1994), indicates the second strategy is preferable. Working through the supervisor bolsters the supervisor's credibility in looking like an expert and in having a special relationship with the boss. By going around supervisors to deliver a message, the boss undercuts the supervisor's role and diminishes his or her credibility with direct reports. Many organizations now use social networking sites, discussed in the last chapter, to promote change. They identify people who have many contacts with colleagues and work with them to promote the idea.

The Beer Promotion Game. In the late 1950s diet soda was becoming the rage. Women loved Diet Coke®, Diet Pepsi®, and Diet-Rite Cola® because they had no calories. Miller Brewing Company decided to come out with a product called Diet Beer. It actually had that name on the can, if you can believe it. It offered one-third fewer calories than regular beer with the same great taste. It failed miserably because mainly women drink diet soda and mostly men drink beer. A man holding a can that says Diet Beer is basically saying, "I want to be perceived as a woman."

In another five years, Miller decided to take the same product and call it Lite Beer. Miller marketed it by showing commercials with manly men fighting about whether the best part of the beer was its taste or that it was less filling. The product became so successful that every beer manufacturer quickly marketed a lite beer; but it's really 1950s Diet Beer with a different name.

The Cereal City Game. One of Michigan's most famous industries is dried, ready-to-eat breakfast cereal. Prior to the early 1900s, millions of Americans ate breakfasts of meat, eggs, potatoes fried in lard, and homemade bread

Diet Beer

topped with bacon. John Harvey Kellogg from Battle Creek, Michigan noticed that hundreds of patients were suffering from colon cancer, which he believed was caused by an unhealthy diet high in fat and low in fiber. In 1894, Dr. Kellogg first produced toasted cereal flakes as a breakfast food substitute for his patients. With his older brother, William, John established the Battle Creek Toasted Corn Flake Company in 1906, and made Kellogg's Corn Flakes® an instant hit. By 1912, more than 100 companies were producing cereal in Battle Creek, making it the Cereal City!

To promote corn flakes, Kellogg used mass media advertising to garner public attention offering a free year's supply of the toasted corn cereal to housewives who would show it to their friends. Without knowing it, William Kellogg was using a key diffusion strategy of achieving high source credibility through the use of **homophilous change agents**, or people of similar interests who were able to change the minds of others.

Kellogg gave away tens of thousands of boxes of cereal to convince consumers of the product's advantages. But the message was also key. Kellogg shrewdly associated Toasted Corn Flakes with being the breakfast of industry and modernization in America. In effect, consumers were told that eating ready-to-eat cereal was key to being a modern American. Hot breakfasts were portrayed as a thing of the past.

The Mommy Blogger Game. Fast-forward 100 years, and we find that diffusion through well-connected, outspoken women is still important. The mommy blogs, which surged in the last five years, are the personal writings of that key consumer demographic, mothers, to sometimes surprisingly large groups of followers. Mommy bloggers have become a force to be harnessed for marketing, political movements and candidates, and social issues.

Consider Bettina Elias Siegel, the mommy blogger credited with the "pink slime" debacle. This mommy blogger wrote on her blog, The Lunch Tray, that readers should "put a stop to pink slime" used in school lunch programs. This product is essentially lean, finely processed beef and has been used for years in various hamburger products, but Siegel thought it was gross. Eight days after she blogged about it, over 200,000 people signed her online petition to get it off the market. Weeks later the product was almost forced off the market. The article about this event was printed in the *Washington Post* on April 20, 2012.

Defining Diffusion of Innovation

The person most often viewed as the founder of innovation research is another good friend, Dr. Everett Rogers (1983). He traveled broadly around the world, exploring how people adopted changes in their societies. He defined **diffusion** as the process by which an innovation or new idea is communicated through certain channels over time among the members of a social system, and then ultimately adopted for use by those members. When a new Apple computer device, a new hairstyle, or a type of cereal becomes popular, that's diffusion at work.

Diffusion consists of four main elements:

1. **The innovation,** an idea, practice, or object perceived as new by an individual, company, or society;
2. **Communication channels,** the means by which messages about the innovation are exchanged;
3. **Time,** or the process by which the adoption is promoted; and
4. **A social system,** the structure and function of relations among a set of individuals or other units, such as networks or organizations.

The Innovation. Let's look at each of these four elements to understand how they fit together. First, **innovation** is any change that is *perceived* as new to the target audience. It doesn't necessarily have to be new, but it does have to be *perceived* that way by the target audience. Lite Beer was really plain old Diet Beer with a new label. It was perceived as new. Is the iPad® really a regular laptop computer without a keyboard? If so, is it really a new product? Apple wants you to think it is new so Apple can sell more of them. I visited the Apple Store in New York City recently and can attest that everyone wanted to play with the iPad®. Corn flakes is a true innovation in the sense that Kellogg invented them and then used sophisticated strategies to promote them.

Communication Channels. Notice in Buzz Game that Steve Jobs was fond of playing, there are three channels he used to create change: **mass media, social media,** and **face-to-face communication**. Apple's approach to a new product rollout is an excellent example of the convergence idea from the last chapter. As indicated in the Buzz Game, Apple takes a Media 2.0 approach to promotion. Apple uses Old and New Media to hype its products. It also constructed attractive retail outlets to let everyone try the new product and tell their friends about it. Kellogg used an old-school convergence strategy to promote Corn Flakes by advertising in newspapers and billboards and then giving Corn Flakes away to families to try them and spread the news through word-of-mouth.

The general strategy is that marketers try to make people aware of the products through electronic channels, including a Media 2.0 convergence strategy (from chapter 12), and then use **interpersonal** channels to give people hands-on experience with the new ideas. Kellogg's gift of a year's worth of cereal to highly connected housewives was brilliant! They quickly spread the word about the cereal across America. Apple's traditional brick-and-mortar stores give people a chance to touch its products. Beer manufacturers like to have taste tests at football tailgates and other events so people can try their different brews.

Interpersonal channels are important for companies that need to explain new policies to employees. Companies that want to do it right empower supervisors to explain new policies to increase trust between employees and supervisors. Interpersonal channels are most important when the innovation is really different, complex, or difficult to understand.

Time. The critical factor that determines whether a new idea or product is adopted is taking the time to work through the adoption process. There are five stages to the adoption process that are important to work through for the adoption to be successful. Rushing the process generally results in failure. The five stages from Rogers (1983) include:

1. **The Knowledge Stage.** In this stage people learn about the idea and get some sense that this is different than other ideas or products, maybe even that it's brand new. Apple uses a Media 2.0 approach that integrates social and mass media channels to raise awareness that a new product is coming. Kellogg used newspaper advertising, which was effective at the turn of the 19th century.

2. **The Persuasion Stage.** Once people become aware of the new idea or product, they must be given a chance to express an interest in it and possibly seek additional information. The Internet is a great resource for that persuasion process to begin. People can learn about the new Apple device or the new company policy if they like. At this stage a **change agent** is important for the persuasion to be effective. A change agent is someone who is invested in the idea and decides to champion it to others. That person can be a personal friend, a Facebook friend, or a technology blogger. Or it can be someone who has the new iPad® and is willing to let others try it. In a company it could be the supervisor explaining a new policy. For Kellogg, it was housewives. For many companies today, it's mommy bloggers.

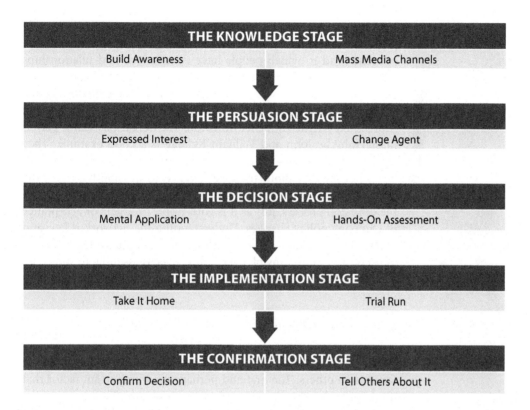

THE KNOWLEDGE STAGE	
Build Awareness	Mass Media Channels

THE PERSUASION STAGE	
Expressed Interest	Change Agent

THE DECISION STAGE	
Mental Application	Hands-On Assessment

THE IMPLEMENTATION STAGE	
Take It Home	Trial Run

THE CONFIRMATION STAGE	
Confirm Decision	Tell Others About It

3. **The Decision Stage.** Once people express an interest in the new idea or policy, they make a decision about adopting the innovation. This process involves them mentally applying it to their lives. They might decide to try out the new iPad® at the Apple Store, taste the new cereal at a trusted friend's home, or try a free sample of the new product. This is the **hands-on stage**, the goal of which is to help people decide how the innovation would fit into their lives.

4. **The Implementation Stage.** After people decide to try the new product or idea, they may take it home and see if it is effective. Most companies have a return policy, so if the new product doesn't work it can be returned easily. For organizations trying to implement a new policy, the goal is to give people materials so they can discuss it with their families, coworkers, or other peer groups and figure out how to best integrate the policy into their lives. This is the **trial-run stage** in which people try to make the new idea work for them. Once the trial run is over, people often decide to adopt the policy idea or purchase the product.

5. **The Confirmation Stage.** Once people have adopted the idea or purchased the product, they seek additional information to confirm their decision. Apple does a great job of constantly making new applications available for their devices. One result of this continuous development is that it creates more value for Apple products and helps people justify their decisions to buy the products. After Kellogg's success with toasted corn flakes, Kellogg added Frosted Flakes®, which are corn flakes with sugar on them, to keep the cold cereal concept fresh. They also introduced several more breakfast cereals to move the market toward children, which was effective. This is the **satisfaction stage** during which people build their sense of value associated with the new idea.

> A change agent is someone who is invested in the idea and decides to champion it to others.

A Social System. Finally, discussion or adoption of every new product or idea ultimately takes place in a social system or network of some kind in which people have connections and relationships with one another. This is how word of mouth spreads through interpersonal and social media channels. Someone likes or doesn't like a new product or idea and those opinions from trusted, credible sources like friends influence diffusion. The Cereal City Game played masterfully by John and William Kellogg is a good example. They used trusted housewives as credible sources who would talk with other housewives about the cereal. As word of mouth spread, the cereal grew in popularity. The social system was an important part of the diffusion process, just as it is with Apple products or acceptance of company policy changes. Understanding the network is key, and identifying the change agents who are the big opinion leaders, such as housewives, mommy bloggers, or techies, is essential to spread an innovation successfully into the culture.

Diffusion Speed

Innovation Features. Some new ideas, products, or services are adopted more quickly and are diffused throughout a social system faster than others. The first and perhaps most important factor that determines speed is the innovation's features. Are the features of the new thing better than the features of the old thing? If we break this down further, we find that there are three issues that drive the perception of whether something is better:

- **Relative Advantage.** The new idea or product must be cheaper and work better than the old one. The new iPad® must be better than other computer readers from competition like Amazon's Kindle®, and do a better job of presenting information. If people are going to compare it to an Apple laptop of some kind, then maybe it's cheaper. But is it better? Is it lighter, faster, and more hip than the other options? Corn flakes were promoted as being cheaper, healthier, and better tasting, in addition to being modern.

- **Compatibility.** The new idea or product must be compatible with or fit into the person's lifestyle. It must be sufficiently familiar that it doesn't freak out anyone, but it also must be perceived as new and have several advantages over the old ideas. The iPad® works like a larger iPhone®, so it's somewhat familiar. Anyone who has worked one of these Apple products will find the iPad® familiar, and that's intentional. If it's too weird, it won't become popular.

- **Complexity.** It must be easy to use. If the new idea or product is more complex than the old one, people are less motivated to change, unless the relative advantages are really high. If the advantages are stronger, people might be willing to deal with the complexity. Most people want it both ways— better and easier. The switch to corn flakes met these two criteria. Pouring a bowl of corn flakes was not only healthier; it was much easier than cooking a large breakfast. This powerful combination helped change people's eating habits, which is no small feat.

A♥ Three issues drive adoption: (1) It must be cheaper and work better; (2) It must fit lifestyle; and (3) It must be easy to use. ♠A

The Message. The second factor determining the speed with which new ideas are adopted involves the informative and persuasive powers of the messages that announce and promote the innovation. Since innovations are *adopted in stages*, the message must change to accommodate the shift in audience information needs. In the initial stages it is important to ensure that the mass media messages get through all the clutter to create some kind of buzz. That's the first goal.

Second, once through the clutter, it's important that the message is informative while also touching a nerve. It must be relevant and resonate with the audience. Third, once the audience decides to try the new idea, the message must change again to talk specifically about benefits and issues like relative advantage, compatibility, and complexity. Finally, when interpersonal channels are involved, what persuasive strategies do companies use to encourage potential adopters to try the new idea?

© 2012 by RetroClipArt. Used under license of Shutterstock, Inc.

The Beer Promotion and Cereal City Games are case studies in how important it is to get the message right so the target customers are informed and emotionally engaged. The initial diet beer campaign failed because the diet message was all wrong for the male audience. Few guys wanted to hold an unmanly can of diet beer. Once Miller changed the name to lite beer and started an expensive advertising campaign with sports figures arguing whether Miller Lite® "Tastes Great" or is "Less Filling," they broke through the clutter and engaged the target audience emotionally though the competition theme.

The Kellogg brothers focused their message on being modern, which was important to the targeted housewife as the industrial revolution was in full swing. People wanted to be modern and show a significant break from the old ways.

The Channels. As indicated above, mass communication, social media, and interpersonal channels should be integrated for an innovation's successful diffusion. For example, the New Policy Communication Game works best if it begins with the boss talking to the supervisors and empowering them to talk directly with their employees. After that interaction has occurred, then the boss can follow-up with an email, blog, or social media post praising the supervisors and reinforcing the message. Over time, it would be useful for the boss to continuously update the supervisors and ask them to update their staff members to further enhance the relationship between supervisors and staff members.

Amount of Time. Time is an important issue in determining the speed with which the innovation is adopted by the target audience. If the time is too short and companies try to rush the process, the diffusion can fail. For example, if Steve Jobs had just come out with the iPad® one day with no hype and no people to try it, the launch would not have been as successful as it was. On the other hand, if *too much time* elapses between introduction of the idea and the target audience's ability to try the product, then the product or idea might appear stale. The key is that it must appear new and fresh, but there must be plenty of time devoted to setting up the hype.

It's important to understand how audiences react in terms of time when innovations are launched. Audiences don't necessarily adopt an innovation in a linear fashion. They are slow at first to pay attention or become interested in the innovation. Apple speeds that up because it already has a bunch of products on the market, and consumers are always waiting for the next new electronic toy.

For new ideas with no history, audiences are slow to shift to something new until the change reaches a **tipping point** (Gladwell, 2005). That is, when a certain number of adopters finally pick up on the idea it reaches a critical mass, making the idea suddenly "popular." At that point, adoption often skyrockets with fast approval and acceptance.

This is what happened with lite beer. It was slow to catch on, then all at once after a certain critical mass accepted it, lite beer took off. The "pink slime" mommy blogger incident accelerated very quickly and resulted in the quick demise of that beef product.

The Context. In a recent article, Drs. Jason MacVaugh and Francesco Schiavone (2010) made the point that the context in which the innovation is presented is crucial. Some contexts are more supportive of innovation than others. These authors talk about three contextual domains that are important to consider. In the **market domain**, or the general public sphere, people may or may not have access to broad communication channels. For example, students at universities generally watch little traditional TV, so they miss new products or services advertised in this domain.

The second contextual domain is the **community of users** or social system in which the potential users communicate with one another. Some businesses, neighborhoods, or other groups are more open to change than others. For example, if you worked in a company that did not like to discuss new ideas or policies, then introducing a policy into this environment would be met with resistance. If the company liked and nurtured new ideas, then it would be more open to change.

The third contextual domain is the **individual or single adopter** of an innovation. We talk later in this chapter about how some individuals are more open to change than others. In fact, there are many kinds of individual adopters, but if change is introduced to a group of people who personally don't like change, then it is difficult to successfully introduce that change.

How Do People React to Innovations?

Uncertainty Reduction. Any time people are confronted with change, including new products or ideas, they tend to feel personally uncertain about the change. **Uncertainty** is the degree to which people can predict how effective or useful the change will be for them personally. If people are highly uncertain, they are reluctant to change unless the uncertainty is reduced.

Kellogg knew that switching from a cooked breakfast to a ready-to-eat breakfast was a big change. After all, cooking was an integral part of a housewife's identity at the turn of the 19th century. To reduce that uncertainty, Kellogg enlisted the help of the housewives to promote his product by giving away the cereal and letting thousands try it at no risk. Combined with the newspaper advertising promoting Kellogg's Corn Flakes® as modern, people were able to reduce the uncertainty, try the product, and make the switch.

My good friend and colleague Dr. Malcolm Parks and his colleague Dr. Mara Adelman wrote an interesting article about uncertainty reduction in romantic relationships (Parks & Adelman, 1983). They found that the ability to reduce uncertainty was important in enabling couples to stay together longer. Specifically, they learned that couples who were more certain about each other received greater support for their relationship from family and friends. They also communicated more often with their partners' family and friends, and they were less likely to break up. In other words, it is important to reduce uncertainty as quickly as possible to move forward with any relationship or decision.

Innovations present us with new possibilities and raise new questions for us. Because we do not have experience with the new policy/product, we are typically uncertain how well it will work. Uncertainty is reduced by carefully considering all the information available about the innovation. "Does the innovation have some key advantages for me?

A♥ It is important to reduce uncertainty as quickly as possible to move forward with any relationship or decision. ♠A

Is it compatible with how I live? Is it simple to understand?" are key questions we ask to reduce the uncertainty. More information typically leads to rejection or adoption, either of which reestablishes a mental state of cognitive consistency by greatly reducing uncertainty.

Card talk plays a significant role in this process. The Kellogg Company encouraged housewives to play their Friend Cards and spread the news about the cereal after it gave away thousands of boxes. Kellogg also played its Advertiser Card by informing people about the product in the newspapers and later on radio. By targeting consumers using both strategies, Kellogg helped people reduce uncertainty about the product's value.

Social Pressure. We have talked extensively in this book about social pressure. It is a key component in Social Norming Theory discussed in chapter 6 focusing on persuasion. As you may recall from that theory, people are motivated to act normally or go along with the crowd. People don't want to stick out. This social pressure also drives the diffusion process. If people get the impression they will meet with peer approval for adopting an innovation or disapproval for not adopting it, they will get on board quickly. When Kellogg got the housewives involved, they put peer pressure on their friends to try the cereal. If one of your friends strongly advocates that you try something, you probably will, particularly if the cost is low. **Diffusing innovations** purposely inserts innovations in key networks to take advantage of that pressure.

The Diffusion Effect. The cumulative result of different people each being subjected to social pressure from their peers is termed the **diffusion effect**, which is a change in the social system's norms toward the innovation. Social pressure to eat toasted Kellogg's Corn Flakes®, felt individually by people in Battle Creek, Michigan, can cause a diffusion effect in the town as a whole with regard to adopting or rejecting an innovation by people who live there. Eating corn flakes became the normal thing to do.

I recently gave a seminar to a group of social club managers and told them that promoting their clubs through Facebook had become a necessity. While many resisted the idea, I suspect that most of them now have a Fan Page, because a few key opinion leaders in our seminar spoke persuasively about how Facebook works well for them. Facebook costs nothing and reaches the target audience effectively.

Opinion Leadership. Finally, as you can see from the various card games at the front of the chapter, certain people have more influence in a community than others. These people usually have the reputation for being first to try the change, read about it, and in general understand it. Since they have this reputation they are asked by their friends frequently about these innovations. When you purchased your computer, did you ask a friend or someone who was knowledgeable about computers to give you advice? Most of us who are not techies do that.

© 2012 by Junial Enterprises. Used under license of Shutterstock, Inc.

© 2012 by Golden Pixels LLC. Used under license of Shutterstock, Inc.

Opinion leadership is the degree to which an individual is informally able to influence other individuals' attitudes or behaviors about a new idea. The power of an opinion leader's influence is that it is informal and based on respect, not on positional or formal authority. That's why we ask friends about the changes we are considering. We know they are trusted and knowledgeable even if they don't hold direct power over us.

Opinion leaders often hold high positions of authority, but this is not a necessary condition for them to influence other people. One of my fellow professors is the go-to person for anyone in our department who is buying a computer because he is technologically savvy. He works frequently with high-tech equipment and talks about all the fun things his computer can do. He is an opinion leader both because he is knowledgeable and he is willing to help.

Many diffusion initiatives fail because a change agency mistakenly identifies formal authority figures as opinion leaders, when they are neither personable nor helpful. It is important to understand that typically opinion leaders are at the center of communication networks. People like the mommy blogger Bettina Elias Siegel communicate a lot with many kinds of people. It is the cumulative decisions of opinion leaders like her within a social system (like a business or network of bloggers), that make the number of adopters for an innovation really take off.

Fundamentally, innovations do not diffuse just because they are advantageous, cheaper, or compatible. They diffuse as a result of the cumulative application of the personal influence of earlier adopters on the decisions of later adopters. *Diffusion is a social process.*

Adopter Types

Innovators. We have talked about what drives the adoption of innovations. Yet, we have not talked much about the people who are the targets of innovations. What do we know about these target adopters? The key insight from years of research on this topic is that not all adopters are alike. It turns out there are several kinds of adopters, and they aren't all positive. If a company runs into the wrong kind of adopter for what it is proposing, it can have disastrous consequences.

Let's look at the group most likely to embrace change. They are the **innovators**, adventurous risk takers. They love change. They want to be the first on their block to try the new toy or embrace the new policy or try the new beer. These consumers tend to live in urban environments and to be on technology's cutting edge. However, this is a small group, representing only about 2.5 percent of a society's population. I have a colleague who is constantly reading about the latest innovations in social media applications in marketing. He uses social media like Facebook and Twitter extensively in his courses and attends conferences on social media and marketing. He is well-informed about the latest technologies, and many of us consult him about innovations for our teaching and research needs.

Opinion Leaders. The second distinct group of adopters is called **opinion leaders** and they are a larger group than the first, representing about 13.5 percent of the population. They also embrace change and are among the first to try new ideas, but they're not necessarily on the cutting edge. The key difference between opinion leaders and innovators is that opinion leaders are vocal about their interests, telling all their friends about the new products they've tried or ideas they've adopted. As a result, they usually lead or heavily influence the opinions of others who are thinking about adopting the new ideas.

A♥ Innovations … diffuse as a result of the cumulative personal influence of earlier adopters on the decisions of later adopters. Diffusion is a social process. A♠

Because of their communication skills, these people are heavily involved in social networks as well; they are Kellogg's Corn Flakes housewives and mommy bloggers. They try new things, know lots of people, are highly skilled, and have credibility with their friends.

Early Adopters. The third group of individuals is still at the front of the adoption curve because they represent about 34 percent of the population. These **early adopters** communicate with the opinion leaders but are slower to accept change. They are open to it, but they are not as emotionally invested in change as are the innovators and opinion leaders. They are more deliberate and thoughtful about what might work and not work for them. As a result, they are not as vocal about their opinions regarding the new ideas they have embraced because they have a more functional approach. They might like what the new iPad® does, but they can't necessarily describe the technological features in great detail and are uncertain how it would help them.

Early adopters are deliberate shoppers and good information managers. In playing the New Policy Communication Game, the boss would hope to have some opinion leaders among the supervisors who could be excited about the change and explain it well. More realistically, it would be best if the supervisors were at least early adopters and could be thoughtful about how the innovation would work and help people.

Late Adopters. Following these three adopter groups are two other categories of people who are not particularly excited about change. The first group that tends to reject change is the **late adopters**. These individuals represent about 34 percent of the population. They are not out scanning the horizon for things that might improve their lives. *They like what they have* or for other reasons are not interested in change. If the old stuff wears out, these individuals will be at least open to buying something better than the old thing. If they see something better than what they currently use, they tend to hold off until the price drops. People who often resist change tend to be a bit older and set in their ways, unlike people in the adopter groups who tend to be younger. These late adopters probably came to embrace the Kellogg vision of breakfast well after the first wave of adopters. These folks probably waited until everyone else was doing it and the price came down.

Laggards. Laggards comprise the final group of people, about 16 percent of the population. They not only dislike change of any kind, they actively fight it. If their TV broke they would look for one exactly like their old one, whereas a late adopter might try to find a better TV. They see change as an intrusion into their lives and an attack on their freedom. They are traditional in their orientation and are not opinion leaders of any kind. If you combine these folks with the late adopters you can see that they collectively represent 50 percent of the population. So about half the population tends to resist change and the other half embraces change.

The significance of these adopter categories for companies trying to sell new products is the need to attract young people to their brand who are more likely to embrace innovation and be open to new ideas. The Apple TV commercials show a young, casually dressed male who looks like an average college student. The PC guy he is talking to is an older-looking guy in a shirt and tie who looks stodgy and out of touch. So, college students: Apple wants you!

On the other hand, advertisers are less interested in older audiences because they have already fixed their brand preferences. Over time people grow to prefer a certain type of car, laundry soap, clothing brand, or place to shop. Trying to persuade them to change brands is difficult for advertisers, so they tend to concentrate on younger people who are just starting their adult lives and figuring out what they like. Of course, older people have more money because they've been working longer, but they are also more set in their ways. Thus, despite their economic restrictions, advertisers fight to attract younger audiences.

Forces Controlling Innovation Adoption

We now have a picture about the nature of innovation adoption, what makes adoption move more quickly or slowly, and something about the audiences that choose to adopt. Let's put this together in a larger framework to look more broadly at what it takes for an innovation or change to work successfully. Commercial innovation is controlled by three main forces: market forces, technology forces, and system forces.

Market Forces. This is the most important factor in the innovation process because without a market there is no adoption. For example, Thomas Edison invented a machine for use in the U.S. Congress and Senate that could instantly count votes that congressmen and senators made for any given legislation, and he presented it to Congress. They immediately rejected it saying, "That's the last thing we need. We don't want to know right away what the vote is." At that point Edison vowed to never again invent something unless there was a ready market for it. Markets are driven by demographics, income fluxes, prices, cultural orientations, and personalities. A refined understanding of a market is essential for success.

Technology Forces. Science and technology grow rapidly, exposing new commercial possibilities every day. If Kellogg had not researched the relationship between diet and colon cancer, he never would have invented Corn Flakes. The invention of computer chips enabled modern computing. It is vital to the economy to keep technology moving forward to ensure new products are available to stimulate the imagination of innovators who can devise creative ways to serve markets.

System Forces. These forces represent the third leg of the innovation stool. Innovations often take shape within large organizations like universities or technology corporations that can support such efforts. After a technology is introduced to the market and people have had a chance to try it, the new idea requires certain changes to improve user friendliness. If the system works well, then this feedback is quickly received and the innovation is improved. If the system is too bureaucratic and lethargic, then it ignores consumer input and ultimately fails. The W. K. Kellogg Company has always been effective at identifying changes in the marketplace and responding to those changes by coming out with new and better cereal options.

Thomas Edison.

A♥ Markets are driven by demographics, income fluxes, prices, cultural orientations, and personalities. ♠A

Results:

- If your score is 45–50 you are probably an **innovator.**
- If your score is 35–44, you are probably an **opinion leader.**
- If your score is 25–34, you are probably an **early adopter.**
- If your score is 20–24, you are probably a **late adopter.**
- If your score is 10–19, you are probably a **laggard.**

Are you surprised about your score? Most students are probably early adopters or opinion leaders. The fact that you are in college and able to take risks suggests that you are open to change and probably find change interesting and motivating. However, some of you may believe that change is about fashion and fads. Change should have a rationale to justify shifting course in some way. Reflect on your score.

Chapter Summary

- **Diffusion is about spreading the innovation to large audiences.** Diffusing a new idea requires that people hear about it from multiple communication channels, so they become interested in learning more about it. Then they must perceive that the idea is new and exciting.
- **Innovations are adopted in stages.** People must first become aware of an innovation, then express interest in it. They must be able to mentally apply it to their lives, get confirmation from a change agent that trying it would be a good idea, and then give it a trial spin before committing to it. This process is often long and tedious for marketers, but skipping steps often results in poor adoption rates.
- **The speed by which the innovation diffuses** through the target audience depends on many factors. The innovation must be perceived as new and better than the old idea. It must be compatible with what people already know, while being simple and easy to use. People must learn about the innovation from mass media channels and from people they know and trust. The social environment must support change.
- **People react differently to innovations.** At first everyone is uncertain about the new idea. Eventually that uncertainty is reduced by friends or opinion leaders, who have tried the new idea and recommended it. Diffusion is a social process.
- **People react differently to change.** While about half the population is somewhat open to change, the other half is not. Those open to change can be either very excited about it and interested, or just open to change when it makes sense. Those who resist change are generally emotionally tied to the status quo and resist change. The key in diffusing a new idea is to understand the target audience's orientation to change.

Lessons Learned

- **Know the target market.** Based on what we know about diffusing innovations quickly, the most important requirement is knowing the target audience or market for the innovation. Begin by determining whether most are early or late adopters, for example. If they are early adopters, what messages are likely to resonate with them?
- **Match innovation features to the target market.** After learning about the market, the next issue is how the innovation meets the needs of the target market. What are the innovation's relative advantages? How compatible is the innovation with current practices? Is it simple to use and understand?

- **Focus on the message.** Kellogg centered on the "modern" message since that theme was important to his target audience for Corn Flakes. By conducting marketing surveys and focus groups, it's possible to determine which messages resonate and which do not. Apple does an excellent job of branding, or creating an image of youthful intelligence and hipness that appeals to their target market.
- **Focus on the channels.** Whether the innovation is a new kind of beer, policy, computer, or cereal, the key message has to be disseminated through channels the target market values. Electronic channels are particularly effective because they get messages out through a social network created by blogging or posting information on social media sites. Interpersonal influences are also important. *Opinion leaders do most of the selling, while electronic channels do most of the informing.*
- **Focus on the process.** The diffusion process is messier than the linear stages laid out above. The typical stages of innovation diffusion are meant as a guideline for how to think about the diffusion process. For example, informing people should occur before giving out free samples. Each process is different but there must be a plan about how the diffusion effort should evolve.
- **Evaluate campaign effects.** Every diffusion campaign should be evaluated to correct and update the messages, and to update the innovation. When playing the New Policy Communication Game, the boss needs to gauge employee reaction to the new policy. If the policy is accepted, that's great, but there's likely to be some pushback or resistance. How can the policy be improved?

Opinion leaders do most of the selling, while electronic channels do most of the informing.

References

Larkin, T. J., & Larkin, S. (1994). *Communicating change: How to win employee support for new business directions.* New York: McGraw-Hill.

MacVaugh, J., & Schiavone, F. (2010). Limits to the diffusion of innovation: A literature review and integrative model. *European Journal of Innovation Management, 13,* 197–221.

Parks, M. R., & Adelman, M. B. (1983). Communication networks and the development of romantic relationships: An expansion of Uncertainly Reduction Theory. *Human Communication Research, 10,* 55–79.

Rogers, E. M. (1983). *Diffusion of innovations* (3rd ed.). New York: Free Press.

© 2012 by REDAV. Used under license of Shutterstock, Inc.

Media Learning and Entertainment Card Games

♣ Introduction

Do you remember watching a TV program with a singing purple dinosaur when you were growing up? Do you remember his name? Who was your favorite TV or movie character? If you're a female, maybe it was Princess Jasmine. For males, Spiderman might have been your hero. One of the most important sources of learning comes from the media because it gets us emotionally engaged. We are attracted to the drama— the story, the heroes, the villains. Whether we're watching movies, news, YouTube, or network shows, we consume a tremendous number of media messages.

The amount of media we consume and our normally intense emotional involvement in the action allows the media to have a significant impact on our lives. To understand this impact we need to know both what we learn from all these media messages and what effects this learning has on how we conduct our lives. To begin, consider these Media Card Games.

♣ Media Card Games

The Local News Game. If you grew up in a big city and occasionally watched the local news you may have a feel for the kinds of stories reporters cover and the style they use to tell their stories. TV reporters are assigned stories to cover that are visually appealing and able to engage the audience emotionally through some story or drama similar to a reality TV show. For example, in covering a fire or murder, playing the Reporter Card means reporting on the victims and showing how they suffered. Then, it's important to find out why this happened and who contributed to the tragedy. The reporter wants to create a drama and pull the audience into it.

The Teletubby Game. Do you remember this show? It's aimed at 1–4-year-olds and was produced between 1997 and 2001. The show involved four colorful characters with antennas sticking out of their heads and on their tummies was a TV showing real kids doing fun things. The bright colors, unusual designs, repetitive babbling dialogue, and the occasional physical comedy appealed to the young viewers. In airing the show the producers played their Kid Show Producer Card to lure young audiences (and their parents) into a learning experience.

The show sparked controversy in 1999 when the Rev. Jerry Falwell claimed that Tinky Winky, the purple character with the triangle antenna on his head, was a homosexual role model for children (King, Lugo-Lugo, & Bloodsworth-Lugo, 2010). Falwell played a Social Critic Card and claimed the purple color and Tinky Winky's triangular antenna were symbols of the gay pride movement.

The Reality TV Game. In contrast to these heavily scripted and edited media presentations is reality TV. This format is wide ranging. On one hand, there are network shows about people losing weight or surviving some game on a deserted island. While these shows use "real people," they are heavily edited to tell the story the producer wants to tell using a TV format. In spring 2010, a reality TV crew was filming a police raid on a home in Detroit. In the heat of the raid a police officer accidently shot and killed an innocent victim. In the aftermath, some questioned whether the TV crew's presence made the police officers more likely to act aggressively and play a more confrontational Police Card. The point of these unscripted videos is that individuals get to play their normal talk cards so others can see them in action.

The Scary Movie Game. Scary tales have been around for centuries. Movies do a great job of bringing these frightening experiences to life. Most of the movies that fall into this category are aimed at teens and young adults. The genre for these films is called horror movies or maybe slasher films. The formula for films such as *Scream* or *Friday the 13th* is pretty standard: A bunch of young, attractive, single people go to some remote, spooky location to party. Suddenly a really horrible-looking bad guy appears and starts killing everyone. Generally only a few good people are left with the hero saving the day by eliminating the slasher (until the next movie, of course). By playing a Scary Movie Producer Card, the producer is asking the audience to play their Scared Bystander Card and act frightened. Audiences comply, probably because scary movies are fun to watch and they allow viewers to play other games that I explain later on.

The Learning Process

Definition of Learning. In describing how we learn from media, Drs. Jennings Bryant and Mary Beth Oliver (Bryant & Oliver, 2009) present a number of authors who talk about how we learn from the media. To understand how media impact us, let's talk first about what it means to learn something. **Learning** is the active and passive acquisition of knowledge that has cognitive, emotional, and behavioral effects. **Active learning** means we intentionally pursue some knowledge that we need for some purpose. Attending this course is a good example. You need to know something about the communication process so you can perform more effectively in your career. You can also actively learn by watching the local news to get informed about the day's events.

A ♥

Learning is the active and passive acquisition of knowledge that has cognitive, emotional, and behavioral effects.

A ♠

On the other hand, **passive knowledge** acquisition is about **incidental learning** that occurs unintentionally while actively pursuing other goals. You pick up other ideas or feelings as a secondary reaction to what you are mainly interested in learning. For example, you might turn on the local news to learn about the latest demonstrations in China or Egypt because you have friends there. That's actively pursuing knowledge.

But you might passively learn something about Chinese or Egyptian culture that you didn't expect. You didn't turn on the news to specifically learn about these cultures—you picked that up while pursuing other knowledge. We learn later that this passive or incidental learning has significant effects.

How Learning Works. Whether learning is active or passive, it's useful to go into some detail about the process because it explains the effects of media messages. In general, learning occurs when we are confronted by some information that creates connections in our heads with what we already know to be true. That is, *learning is the transformation of information into knowledge.* The question is how does this transformation occur?

The transformation of information into knowledge is hierarchical in that the development of these connections is a process that moves from simple awareness all the way to using the knowledge to create something. This transformation is called Bloom's Taxonomy (Bloom & Krathwohl, 1956). Bloom believed that these steps constitute the process of how information is transformed into knowledge:

1. **Awareness.** The transformation begins when we pay attention to some sensory stimuli that are funny, colorful, or otherwise interesting. We may decide to focus actively on the stimuli to satisfy some need, or the stimuli might garner passive attention by being interesting or unusual. Kids actively sought out the Teletubby characters because they were fun and energetic. The stimuli were colorful and active, and did a good job of getting kids' attention.

2. **Understanding.** The process of understanding happens in three steps. Step 1 is called **selective exposure**. Immediately after gaining attention, only *some* of the stimuli we are exposed to become transformed into information. In other words, we don't process all the stimuli we sense. We are selective about what we process. In general, we only process, or seek to understand, what we need cognitively or emotionally, and ignore everything else. The idea is that we choose to understand some things and not others based on our needs.

Step 2 is **categorizing**. After selecting a stimulus to focus on, it becomes "information" when we perceive a sensible pattern to it by **categorizing** it in relation to what we know to be true. When a stimulus gets categorized into information, it becomes **understood** or sensible in some way. When kids turned on the Teletubby show and saw characters dancing around, they immediately understood it was a TV show; they've seen it before and it all fits into that "TV Show" category for them. Falwell's claim that Tinky Winky was passively promoting a homosexual lifestyle was only valid if viewers transformed the stimuli into information about that lifestyle. (There wasn't any evidence that kids were influenced in this way.)

© PBS/Photofest

Step 3 is **memorizing**. The final step of understanding occurs when the information is placed into memory. We remember only some of the stimuli that are transformed into information. We know from research that we tend to remember the visual information first and the verbal information second. You probably remember someone's face but perhaps not his or her name, for example. I might remember an important person's name because I tried harder to memorize it.

3. **Teaching.** Once something is understood or categorized and becomes a memory, it only stays there if the information is applied or used in some way. A good way to intensify the learning process is by asking someone to teach a lesson from what was learned. **Teaching** helps others see connections between the new information and what the person already knows to be true. When you give a speech on some topic, you are teaching others about it and helping them understand it. You're also expanding your learning by demonstrating how something works. In other words, you know the information because you can see it from many perspectives.

4. **Evaluating.** Learning about some idea or concept grows further when individuals are asked to use their knowledge to evaluate how well others understand or can apply the concepts they have learned. This evaluation process not only requires that you understand the information, it asks you to determine when others are applying it properly or improperly. For example, one of the best ways to learn how to give public speeches is to rate others' speeches. What are they doing well and not so well?

5. **Creating.** The final step of learning something is taking the knowledge and creating something new with it. The producers of the Teletubbies show relied on all the knowledge they had about child development and entertainment and pulled together a new show aimed at socializing very young children. This creative process is the ultimate demonstration of whether someone knows the information.

Understanding Entertainment

Definition of Entertainment. Now that we understand the learning process, let's explore how we satisfy the other motive we have for consuming media—entertainment. The consumption of media messages for enjoyment, relaxation, and escape without ulterior motives defines **entertainment communication**. In other words, we want to stimulate and explore our emotional side to simply feel better. It's fun to get scared, laugh at something amusing, or cry after an intense drama.

Early psychologists like Freud felt that our impulses for pleasurable experiences are repressed and that we need entertainment to express these pleasures and relieve our suffering. Later explanations focused on how media entertainment satisfies our need for fun and relaxation (see Bryant & Oliver, 2009).

Three Elements of Drama. What makes entertainment like the Scary Movie Game enjoyable is when it conforms to the three elements of good drama. First, the story must depict an **intense conflict of forces**. Drama dwells on conflict and is resolved by depicting events carried out by protagonists and antagonists who are affected by these events. The good characters are trying their best to achieve important and morally superior goals, or just prevent the bad guys from taking over. Either way, intense conflict is the first requirement of good drama.

Second, viewers must be able to **care about and relate to the characters**; they must like the good guys. And they must despise the bad guys. In the Scary Movie Game, a key element is the need for the good guys to be ordinary people who do extraordinary things in the face of unspeakable horror. We want them to demonstrate a strong moral core that we all aspire to achieve. Conversely, it is important to hate the creepy bad guys and see them as different from us. That sets up a good conflict.

In some dramas, it is possible for the good guy to convert the bad guy to achieve redemption, as Luke Skywalker did in *Star Wars* when he converted his dad from the evil Darth Vader back to the good guy Anakin Skywalker. But in slasher movies the bad guys are creepy zombies that must die.

The third element of successful drama is a **satisfying resolution** to the conflict. We want the good guys to win the large battles to save the world and the small battles associated with a marriage or relationship with someone. In the movie *Independence Day*, Will Smith first had to save the world from the ugly alien bad guys, then had to repair his relationship with his girlfriend and regain her son's trust. We want it all wrapped up in a neat package. In fact, as we learn shortly, this element of drama causes the expectation that every relational problem ends happily ever after. It happens in every movie, so we often come to expect happy resolutions to real-life problems.

Humor. Comedy is a form of drama. The only real difference is that the audience must be given cues that the events they are watching should not be taken seriously. Of course, bad guys often use hostile humor to punish the good guys, but that only intensifies the audience's dislike for the antagonists. The more common form of humor, typical in a situation comedy, involves conflict generally between a character struggling with his or her own issues and getting into weird situations, or a conflict between a couple around some funny family or relationship problem. All *Seinfeld* episodes center around issues related to Jerry and his offbeat pals.

Adam Michal Ziaja/Shutterstock.com

Romantic comedies have essentially the same formula. The couple works hard at the beginning to pursue one another, and then one person does something stupid that causes them to break up or have a crisis. Then they come back together after resolving the crisis for a happy ending.

Humor is used extensively in advertising. Research indicates that **humor makes messages more interesting** and attention getting, the first step in learning. Because people attend to humor, they're more likely to process it. Recall from chapter 6 that persuasion is more likely to occur if the audience *thinks deeply* about the message. If they are laughing, the audience is less likely to think of reasons not to like the product.

Humor enhances the user's credibility, making the message more compelling and believable. The challenge in using humor in advertising is not to make the commercial so funny that no one remembers the product. Humor can easily overwhelm any memory of the product, which doesn't help make the sale when a consumer is deciding what kind of beer or soap to buy.

Sports. The same elements that make drama entertaining also make sports entertaining. We get a great deal of enjoyment from sports when we want our team to win. They're the good guys, and the other team represents the bad guys. When the other team is a long-standing rival, it makes the drama even more compelling. Add to this the suspense, or fear of a negative outcome, and the risky play that is standard fare at big-time games— it makes us cheer harder for our noble warriors.

Regarding the effects of **sports drama**, research indicates that winning has some personal pay-off for fans. When their favorite team wins consistently, fans' self-esteem and personal confidence improves. **Gender** also impacts sports enjoyment. Women enjoy sports with more moderate levels of suspense, such as volleyball. Men want more suspenseful sports contexts such as American football. Women also prefer more artistic

© 2012 by Kzenon. Used under license of Shutterstock, Inc.

sports, such as figure skating or gymnastics, but these sports do not offer the kind of suspense that men prefer.

Suspense. Playing the Scary Movie Game is a lot of fun for many people. I really like suspenseful thrillers, particularly if they involve submarines. The drama inside that claustrophobic boat deep under the water is intense and riveting for me. I love to submit to this game, play my Audience Card, and watch till the good guys prevail.

Because participating in this Scary Movie Game causes audience members so much stress, the question is, Why do people like it so much? The obvious explanation is that it contains all the elements of drama with good guys and bad guys, so the conflict portrayed provides enjoyment. But that explanation is probably insufficient, given the amount of stress that audience members feel when consuming suspenseful content.

Research shows that the more the audience suffers along with the leading character in a scary movie, the greater the satisfaction at the end when all is resolved. The most recent explanation of this effect focuses on **emotional empathy**. Specifically, the more emotionally distraught the leading character is, the more the audience empathizes with the character and the more eager they are to relieve the character's distress.

Horror. The primary difference between horror and suspense entertainment is the different emotions that are stimulated. Suspense evokes **anxiety**, whereas horror is designed to stimulate **fear**. The elements of good drama attract people to this card game. There are a bunch of cute, innocent victims and many evil bad guys. The audience can relate to the innocent victims because they are intentionally cast to look like the target market for the films—young people.

However, audience motivations to watch horror entertainment are different than for suspense entertainment. According to research, gender differences are the driving force in making horror attractive. For example, research indicates that men enjoy horror more when they are in the company of a terrified female. Men like to show their mastery of fear—they're not afraid of some silly old slasher! Plus, he gets to comfort the terrified female and be a hero to her. Consistent with this finding, women enjoy horror movies when accompanied by a male who exhibits mastery over his fears. She enjoys it less if the guy is screaming, too; she wants a hero!

Mass Media Elements

The mass media provide a rich and diverse learning environment because the stimuli are so visceral. We like the fast-paced, colorful, engaging visuals that TV, movies, and video games provide. We have high-definition TV and even 3D-TV to sharpen the stimuli. The potential for learning is great because the stimuli are rich and powerful. The five elements of the mass communication process listed below help us understand how the media can have such a powerful impact. These elements include: professional communicators, media messages, media proliferation, diverse audiences, and audience learning.

Professional Communicators. Behind the shows you see are many people who create, produce, direct, and contribute to the shows in other ways. Pulling together a local news broadcast requires a news director, a producer, a director, on-air talent, and people to run the equipment. It is a large operation. When playing his or her News Director

Card, this person decides which stories to cover and how to cover them. The goal is to get exciting video that draws a big audience, so they can get big ratings and improve advertising sales. The Director Card is played by deciding how to stage the broadcast and pull together the various stories to create the maximum effect.

Media Messages. These professional communicators take all the knowledge they have and create messages to inform, persuade, or entertain audiences within the context of the media channels they are using. For the TV medium, the Local News Game seeks to inform and entertain while the commercials on these broadcasts seek to persuade viewers to purchase various products and services. Shows like Teletubbies that target young children are designed to achieve child development goals related to social skills and intellectual growth. In general, effective media messages must be:

- **Attention getting** by being distinctive, simple, and important to the target viewers;
- **Positively reinforcing** to ensure viewers are rewarded for consuming the messages and transforming them into knowledge;
- **Easily interpreted** in the sense that they are consistent with current beliefs and attitudes, and are simple to understand; and
- **Memorable** or able to stick with viewers so they can recall the messages and tell their friends.

Media Proliferation. The number of channels for disseminating messages seems to grow by the week! Traditional print media like newspapers and magazines have been around for a few hundred years. Electronic media like radio (first used in 1922) and television are more recent. Now people receive messages through the Internet and their smartphones. These latest developments have really shifted the scope of mass media because the Internet reduces dissemination barriers. Anyone can create a podcast or write a blog and rant about any subject.

In fact, the Internet has threatened the newspaper business because most newspaper revenue comes from advertising and classified ads. Because selling stuff is less costly on eBay, CraigsList, or Cars.com than in classified ads, people are turning away from newspapers to buy and sell things. And because targeting messages is easier online where messages are tailored to individuals' search patterns, much advertising has shifted to Google or Facebook, for example, at the expense of newspapers.

Diverse Audiences. Audiences for mass communication are heterogeneous and large. About 111 million people watched Super Bowl XLIII in 2012. In contrast, about 1 million people watch Jay Leno on the *Tonight Show* nightly. The key to understanding media is that TV shows are targeted toward specific groups. TV dramas, including cop shows, are aimed at women 18–49 because women in this age range are the primary shoppers for consumer goods. Advertisers want to reach these women. If an advertiser wants to sell beer, then that beer company will buy a sports program, since mostly men drink beer and watch sporting events.

Audience Learning. As audiences actively seek various shows, they inevitably learn a great deal. Let's take a look at the Reality TV Game. A viewer might tune into a reality police show because it's exciting to watch police conduct a drug bust, for example. That viewer might be thinking about a career in law enforcement and want to learn what it's like to be in the police force. Indirectly, the viewer might learn something about police culture and the drug culture. There might be other learning about the role of violence in society. Nevertheless, we know that people tend to learn a great deal when consuming media.

© 2012 by Sandra van der Steen. Used under license of Shutterstock, Inc.

Media Learning Effects

Now that we understand the elements of mass media, the question is, How do they combine to impact viewers? What are viewers learning as they consume their media sources? When people watch the evening news, what are they learning? When kids watch children's programs, what impressions stick with them? This next section details some of the effects of media exposure.

What Do People Learn? First, the mass media impact viewers' **attitudes**, or likes and dislikes about people and objects. For example, continuous exposure to violence impacts viewers' attitudes about real-world aggression. Viewers who see a lot of violence come to tolerate, respond more favorably to, or see as justified the actual acts of violence in the real world. Media might also change our **beliefs**, or what we think is true or false about the world. When we watch a reality TV show about cops, we are going to form some beliefs about the police culture or about the criminals they confront. Most of us don't have much experience raiding homes with guns, so we're vulnerable to forming beliefs about unfamiliar things that we see on TV.

Media impact our **feelings** and **emotions**. Because entertainment is all about stimulating our emotions, we might learn to be fearful about going out at night after repeatedly watching news programs that highlight gang violence. Or we might watch shows that calm us down when we have had a hard day. When he was young, my son watched Home and Garden TV (HGTV) on cable after a tough day at school.

People often feel alienated and despondent about society after watching many negative news stories that feature violence. Even though crime rates are down significantly across the U.S., people still believe the world is less safe today than 20 years ago. Because there are so many news media channels and producers playing News Producer Cards to sensationalize stories, the viewers' emotions and beliefs do not reflect reality, at least in the U.S.

Producers and directors playing the Scary Movie Game know that their job is to play with our emotions. What are they playing with? **Emotions** are feelings that we learn to label or define. In other words, in reacting to some specific stimuli like a scary horror movie, I might see my palms sweat, my pupils dilate, and my hair stand up on the back of my neck. Seeing all these physiological reactions, I might conclude that "I am frightened." I might observe myself staring into my child's face and conclude that "I love my son." In other words, emotions are aroused feelings that we make sense out of, or categorize, cognitively in some manner. Once we apply words that frame our internally aroused experiences, they become emotions.

Finally, the mass media can influence **behavior**. When kids identify with characters from TV or movies, a few might start to act like them or use language common to these characters. When stories appear frequently in the news, they often drive what people talk about when discussing issues of local or national importance.

This process of driving discussion is called **agenda setting** by the media. Lots of news reporting on the homeless can set the agenda for making homelessness a political campaign issue. Skilled public relations professionals advising political candidates use agenda-setting to force a debate on these issues in a way that favors their clients.

Another good example of how media influence our behavior is **advertising**. Research consistently demonstrates that advertising is effective in persuading us to buy goods and services. The more advertisers spend promoting consumer products like soap and beer, the more people are likely to buy those products. These ads and commercials are aimed at keeping the products and services *foremost in our minds* as we shop.

A♥ Emotions are aroused feelings that we make sense out of, or categorize, cognitively in some manner. A♠

Learning About Violence. We know from research (Bryant & Oliver, 2009) that violence is pervasive on TV and movies. Most movies feature violence because it gets people excited. Violence is often glamorized and sanitized. The good guys use violence to solve problems without showing many of the negative consequences of violent actions. These good guys are slick, drive expensive cars, and appear to enjoy the good life. Since violence is rarely chastised on television, frequent viewers perceive violence as an acceptable way to solve problems. Unless these perceptions are held in check by the person's own conscious thought processes, they are likely to persist.

There are generally three main effects of pervasive violent portrayals (Bryant & Oliver, 2009):

1. Individuals become increasingly **aggressive** toward others as they view a lot of violence in the media.
2. **Emotional desensitization** often occurs when viewers consume a steady diet of violence. They grow increasingly numb or insensitive to aggression in the real world and see it as more "normal."
3. Viewers of violent content increase their sense of vulnerability to becoming a **victim of a violent crime**.

However, not all types of violent depictions have the same effect on viewers. Some portrayals increase the risk of harm, whereas others decrease these risks. In essence, the context or way in which violence is depicted influences how viewers interpret and respond to televised acts of aggression. For example, in the Reality TV Game, violence is real and the consequences of these acts are seen as devastating to friends and family members. However, violence in movies is believed to be less serious. Movie violence is generally sanitized, glamorized, and viewed as justified because it's important for a drama to have the good guys shoot/beat up the bad guys. We like it; it's entertaining!

In addition to context, the **type of viewer** influences the kind of impact that media violence might have on the viewer. Some viewers are more susceptible to the harmful effects of violent media than are others. Studies show that younger children, boys, aggressive people, those who fantasize about violence, and those who believe TV violence is realistic are more at risk for learning aggression. These individuals are already more attracted to risky behavior and selectively attend to violent messages. The individual also learns to enact a broader range of violent behaviors by teaching the violence to others through re-enacting violent episodes.

These effects of consuming media violence become even more extensive when boys play violent video games like *World of Warcraft*. Such multiplayer games heighten the violent experience and become addictive over time. If we look at such games as a learning experience, it's easy to see why they are so effective. Not only do players teach one another about how to defeat powerful enemies, these games require enormous creativity in how to violently destroy enemies, which is the ultimate expression of learning. Boys most heavily impacted by these games are those who play a lot.

© 2012 by marcello farina/Shutterstock.com

Learning About Sex. Sex is another way that media garner attention. Remember that learning begins by grabbing viewer attention. When media show scantily clad men or women, viewers are physiologically programmed to focus on these images. Barriers against showing sex on TV or in the movies have disappeared in recent years so that now just about anything goes. Research indicates that the prevalence of TV sex is increasing, with over two-thirds of TV shows featuring some kind of sexual content. Much of this increase is due to the amount of sexual talk—not behavior—on television.

There is also a significant increase in the amount of sexual intercourse in the media, particularly involving characters in their teenage years. These acts are common in all kinds of TV, cable, and movie programming. Again, they get attention. Despite the proliferation of sexual messages, few programs depict the risks and responsibilities associated with sex. Few TV shows with sexual content mention safe sex or the need for thoughtful decision making associated with sexual practices. Thus, what is most likely to be learned is that sex is fun and carefree, and not necessarily associated with any kind of committed relationship.

Massive exposure to sexual content is also more likely to **desensitize** viewers to sexual indiscretions, just like massive exposure to violence numbs viewers to actual violence. This is particularly the case among male viewers who are numbed to violence and sexual indiscretion more quickly than female viewers.

There remains one unanswered question about sex in the media, that is, does exposure to sexual images contribute to early adolescent sexual activity? Recent research (Pardun, L'Engle, & Brown, 2005) suggests that it might. The study found that adolescents who view more sexual content are more likely to initiate intercourse and progress to more advanced sexual activities during the subsequent year, even controlling for characteristics that might predict these results. Heavy viewers of sex are twice as likely as light viewers to initiate sex earlier in their teen years. Parents can address these issues not by only cutting off such content but by initiating conversations about sexual behavior in relationships. Family discussions are the key.

Learning About Stereotyping. Heavy media consumers are vulnerable to stereotyping due to the nature of the medium. A 30-minute TV episode is actually 22 minutes of content and 8 minutes of commercials. In that 22-minute span the show must tell a story with a minimal amount of character development. The program producer must present a **stereotypical character**, like a typical father or criminal, for example, and let the audience fill in character traits so the producer can advance the story. Spending too much time on character development leaves less time for the story.

Another hot medium for perpetuating stereotypes is video games. Again, since character development is less important than the story or the action, game developers rely on stereotypes in their games. It should come as no surprise that a recent study of video game character images from top-selling American games showed that male characters, as you may have guessed, were more likely to be portrayed aggressively than female characters. Female characters are likely to be portrayed as scantily clad, while also showing a mix of sex and aggression. A survey of teens confirmed that male character stereotypes as aggressive and female characters as sex objects are held even by nongamers.

The problem is that when individuals have less direct contact with people who are different than themselves, they are more vulnerable to adopting media stereotypes. Research consistently demonstrates that when playing the Local News Game, producers and reporters present more crime stories of African Americans and Latinos than of whites. When viewers from any ethnic group have less direct contact with individuals from stereotyped minority groups, they are more likely to have negative appraisals of minority members. Pre-existing prejudices also play into this process.

For example, first-time visitors to the U.S. often have little direct contact with members of different U.S. minority groups, making the recent arrivals vulnerable to stereotyped media portrayals. A person from Japan who has no direct experience with Hispanics might be *more vulnerable to media stereotyping* of Hispanics than a native U.S. citizen, who likely has more knowledge of Hispanics. There are probably other cultural biases at work as well, but the stereotypical media portrayals certainly don't help the problem of racial prejudice.

Failing to overcome learned stereotypes hinders winning card games because communicators make false judgments about people in terms of their intentions, motives, and abilities. On one hand, we like stereotypes because they make communication easier; since everyone is the same you don't have to exert energy trying to discover differences. On the other hand, stereotyping focuses on inherently negative attributes and assumes that everyone who belongs to a specific group has the same flaws or quirks, from our point of view. The best strategy is to be conscious of stereotypes and work to ignore them when communicating with someone from an ethnic group other than your own.

Selective Exposure

Selective exposure is the idea that people watch what they want to watch. We select programs and content consistent with our attitudes, beliefs, interests, and personal needs. For example, my son is a history buff, so he watches the History Channel. He particularly likes shows about guns and famous battles in history. Maybe he will join the military.

To understand the selective exposure process, let's focus on TV watching. How do people make decisions about what programs to watch? This may surprise you, but research indicates that people select shows based more on what they *don't* want to see rather than on what they *do* want to see. Maybe you've done this. Most people turn on TV to watch something, and keep clicking through the channels past content they don't want to see and stopping on something that looks interesting. In other words, the choice of program is secondary to the need to simply watch something on TV.

Exposure and Involvement. Of course, there are exceptions. Sometimes people actively select entertainment programming. One of the most important factors determining the extent to which individuals are impacted by entertainment content is personal involvement or personal connection to the content.

© 2012 by Jurand. Used under license of Shutterstock, Inc.

If someone is watching a situation comedy that takes place in a hospital setting, and that viewer is a physician, then he or she is personally involved in that content. I know an emergency room physician who watches shows about ER doctors and he always comments on what the doctors do to the patients. He's involved! He constantly flips through the channels to find reruns of these shows.

One of the most popular programs on TV is *American Idol*. This show encourages people to call in and vote for their favorite contestants. This brilliant technique *dramatically increases involvement* in the content. Instead of mindlessly watching, viewers call in their preferences to determine the program outcome, and they follow their preferred entertainers from week to week. Some shows also ask people to text questions or topics of interest that the show will discuss. Entertainment show producers often develop unique strategies to increase involvement and, thus, the size of the audience that watches the program.

> *A♥*
>
> The best strategy is to be conscious of stereotypes and work to ignore them when communicating with someone from an ethnic group other than your own.
>
> *♠A*

Exposure and Mood. It's important to realize that most of the time people don't make deliberate choices about the entertainment programs they watch. Most choices are impulsive, spur-of-the-moment decisions, depending on their situation, mood, or other motives driving the individual's life at that moment. A person with a boring job might look for exciting shows, such as an action show. Conversely, someone with an intense job might want slow-paced shows for a change. People in a bad mood might select programs that are absorbing as a way to forget about their mood.

Interestingly, highly agitated, emotional individuals tend to avoid entertainment content altogether. They can't focus on anything until their agitation decreases. Once the agitation lessens, these people calm themselves further by watching comedy programs. In fact, mood plays a significant role in children's program selection. Young children who feel neglected want to watch shows that present a nurturing message rather than shows with no such message. They want to feel attached to someone and look to TV for that kind of attachment.

> When producers and reporters play their talk cards, viewers learn all kinds of things, many unintentional.

Mass Media Theories

These discussions of violence, sex, and stereotyping are meant to illustrate how attitudes, beliefs, and behaviors are learned from intense media exposure. When producers and reporters play their talk cards, viewers learn all kinds of things, many unintentional. Aside from what we know about how people learn, what theories might explain some of these media effects?

Priming Effects. One of the more interesting theories that explains how media influence behavior was developed by Dr. Leonard Berkowitz and his colleagues (Berkowitz & Rogers, 1986). The theory explains the short-term, transient impact of media violence on aggressive behavior. Berkowitz argued that the media **prime,** or stimulate, our memory, which in turn, triggers a reaction. Specifically, he contends that memory is made up of **networks** of interconnected thoughts, emotions, and action tendencies. The pathways linking these networks can be activated, or primed, by different stimuli such as seeing a violent TV show. These images prime previous aggressive thoughts, feelings, and behaviors stored in memory about that specific issue.

© 2012 by Morgan Lane Photography. Used under license of Shutterstock, Inc.

For example, my brother and I watched professional wrestling often, because early TV programming options were limited. Whenever it came on, we started wrestling ourselves, which often resulted in my older brother torturing me with the holds and slams used by the pros. My mother didn't like this, because these TV wrestling images primed our aggressive tendencies. In other words, the shows stimulated the link between our knowledge of wrestling and our brotherly quarrelsomeness for one another. By stimulating that pathway, we began to wrestle regularly. While this example is about playful boys, the priming effect becomes a tragedy when TV or movie violence primes the rare predisposed teenager to grab a gun and shoot school classmates. Priming effects are most likely to occur with heavy media exposure, lack of parental supervision, and a history of violent behavior.

Social Cognitive Theory. This theory, developed by Dr. Albert Bandura and his colleagues, focuses on the learning process that we discussed at the beginning of the chapter (Bandura, 1994). His theory takes a different tack with respect what happens from the point at which information enters our memory. The theory argues that after categorized information enters our memory it becomes a **model** for how to see other things or how to act. For example, if we see a new fashion trend or a new way of speaking, each can become a model that we use when shopping for clothes or talking with friends. Social cognitive theory contends that we act in a way consistent with that model if we are motivated to do so—*if we are reinforced either directly or vicariously* (indirectly) to adopt that new model.

The Teletubby Game is meant to encourage children to model cooperative behavior. The Teletubbies have fun playing together, so if kids see this cooperation repeatedly and like the Teletubbies, they are rewarded for being cooperative. The real insight about this theory is the idea of **reinforcement,** which is the **social learning** component of the theory. The more frequently a behavior is positively reinforced, the more likely people are to model that behavior. Because violence is so pervasive and good guys get reinforced in the movies for being violent to save the day, it becomes a learned response. Viewers begin to see violence as appropriate, and are motivated to use it when necessary because it gets rewarded.

The key difference between Priming Effects Theory and Social Cognitive Theory is that the priming effect is more limited in scope. It contends that media images prime memory connections that, in turn, stimulate behavior. The Social Cognitive Theory adds the **motivation** component to the mix. Bandura (1994) would argue that violence—or any behavior for that matter—is stimulated only when the individual is motivated to engage in that behavior. That motivation comes from seeing the pro- or antisocial behavior being positively reinforced and, thus, learned.

Cultivation Theory. While these first two theories do a good job of laying out the specific mechanisms that cause us to learn and adopt attitudes, beliefs, and behaviors stimulated by media, a theory developed by the late Dr. George Gerbner and his research team sought to explain the long-term cumulative effects of TV exposure (Gerbner, 1997; Gerbner, Gross, Morgan, & Signorielli, 1994). In developing his theory, Gerbner addressed the nature of the content that individuals consume on TV. He focused on TV because he contends that it's the most pervasive medium in our society—it is most available and most viewed.

In general, there are two basic premises to **Cultivation Theory**. First, TV is a cultural **storyteller**. Rather than the family, church, or other societal venues, TV is the major socialization agent of our time. We spend more time consuming TV and related images (on smartphones or computers) than interacting with family members or school teachers. TV creates a story or narrative about our world—it provides a dramatic model of what life is like consisting of good guys and bad guys and challenges to overcome.

Second, this Cultivation Theory argues that television delivers homogeneous stories or messages. Independent of genre, time of day, or channel, the TV message is relatively uniform. Differences are stripped away to make them simple to understand. Gerbner would certainly have supported the idea that TV presents stereotyped images of people, ideas, and events to make them easy

The more frequently a behavior is positively reinforced, the more likely people are to model that behavior.

Rather than the family, church, or other societal venues, TV is the major socialization agent of our time.

© 2012 by Subbotina Anna. Used under license of Shutterstock, Inc.

to understand. All people, ideas, and events start to look alike after a while.

Because TV programming delivers similar or uniform content to large and heterogeneous audiences, heavy viewing cultivates a shared perspective among otherwise-diverse groups. That is, repeated exposure to television cultivates a world outlook that overrides any initial differences based on demographics, personality characteristics, or environment. This **enculturation** process is called mainstreaming. Consistent with this theorizing, studies show those heavy TV viewers are more likely than light viewers to perceive the world as a mean and violent place.

Another process in cultivation is **resonance**. In some instances, television offers a double dose of reality by mirroring or reflecting viewers' direct experiences. The result of resonance is that certain cultivation effects are more pronounced or amplified when fact and fiction match. The more people watch crime shows, the more they fear being a crime victim or the more they look for criminal behavior, in order to be a part of the drama like on TV. Sometimes a show resonates with viewers so much that they want to dress like, act like, and be placed in situations like characters they are attracted to. Some young girls emulate the Twilight Vampire series.

Cultivation Theory can apply to other areas besides media violence. For instance, repeated exposure to sexual portrayals that omit the risks or responsibilities associated with mature behavior may cultivate in viewers the belief that safe sex or committed relationships are not important.

Similarly, heavy viewing of demeaning portrayals of racial minorities may cultivate prejudices and negative attitudes toward those of other ethnic groups. Perhaps Jerry Falwell had Cultivation Theory in mind when claiming that kids should not be exposed to Tinky Winky because this character cultivated homosexual beliefs.

Media Literacy Theory. A final theory that brings these other theories together, in my view, is the idea of media literacy. In his review of the **Media Literacy Theory**, Dr. James Potter (2004) indicates that the theory's basic tenet is that media images present a whole new language to viewers that must be decoded and learned for its substance and intent to be understandable. In other words, we must be media literate just as we are linguistically literate. We must have the ability and the habit of transforming media messages into their appropriate knowledge structures. We must also be able to discriminate between and accurately label a TV cartoon program and a TV cartoon commercial. If we can tell the difference, we're literate. If we can't, then we are illiterate. Let's look at the theory and see how it pulls these other theories together into a coherent framework.

Media Literacy Theory begins with the idea that messages contain two types of information between which we must be able to differentiate:

1. **Factual information** that consists of the raw, context-free truth about what the source is communicating; and
2. **Social information** that focuses on the intent of the source to inform, persuade, or entertain.

In other words, when we play the Local News Game by watching the TV news, we must first determine what's factual or true about what we are observing in the story. Does it make sense? Second, we must decide why we are seeing this message. What is the source trying to do? Is the source trying to inform us or is the source trying to persuade us to take some action? Literacy begins when we can accurately tell *what's factual and what's intentional.*

Based on this kind of discrimination, the theory further contends that the mass media present three types of messages:

1. **News,** which is intended to inform the audience about current events;
2. **Entertainment,** which seeks to evoke a pleasant or rewarding emotional experience of some kind; and
3. **Advertising,** which is intended to influence purchasing behavior.

As you know, the media like to blend these kinds of messages. Occasionally we see docudramas in which an actual event is used as the story line for a dramatic story of some kind. These shows are meant to both inform and entertain. Or we might watch infomercials that seek to inform and advertise. They are often on late-night TV and tell people about juicers or weight-loss drugs. A media literate person knows that docudramas are not real and that the facts might be fudged. The media-literate person also knows that infomercials may not tell the whole story. The new weight-loss formula is probably not the miracle cure it professes to be.

What's important about this theory is that it provides a way forward to use the valuable insights of the other theories mentioned here. It says that we must be able to accurately understand the kinds of violence we see in the media and know that this portrayed violence might prime us to act violently ourselves. We should know that watching professional wrestling is not real and not intended to incite us. We should realize that those using violence are getting rewarded because the intent of the person playing the Producer Card is to build the drama and entertain us—not to incite us to use that behavior as a model for our own lives.

We should be aware that we are vulnerable to cultivating an overly simplistic, stereotypical view of the world when we consume media that might not be accurate or productive. The bottom line is that we need to create strategies for building media literacy in our lives to see media messages as they are and to understand the cards that are being played when we consume these messages.

Strategies for Increasing Media Literacy

Understand Your Biases. The strategies most likely to be effective for increasing media literacy begin with the need to first understand our own biases that color how we interpret media messages. Are you biased against certain cultural orientations? Do you believe that police are corrupt, that women are only sex objects? Understanding our biases is important because they guide the kind of media that gains our attention. Remember: The first step in the learning process is gaining our attention. We pay attention to what we are attracted to. Many boys are addicted to video games. This attraction is a bias that colors what they consume and how they interpret it.

Gain More Personal Experiences. A second strategy for building media literacy is developing and expanding our real-world personal experiences. The more diverse these experiences are the better. Have you ever experienced true poverty where people live in cardboard shacks with dirt floors? Have you ever talked with these people? If you have,

© 2012 by Sara Berdon. Used under license of Shutterstock, Inc.

you may feel differently about them than if the only poor people you see are on TV. Do you know anyone from an Arab culture? Members of this culture are often featured in the news, yet most Americans know little about how diverse the Arab or Muslim population is. Take risks; get out and talk to people who are different than you!

Understand Media Institutions and Biases. Media institutions are organizations competing for your attention as does any other organization. A large newspaper company like Gannett Corporation owns many newspapers and TV and radio stations. What impact do their corporate identity and priorities have on how they report the news? The same conglomerate that owns the tabloid *National Enquirer* also owns the *Wall Street Journal* and Fox News. What is their **political orientation**? Does this orientation matter? More important, can you have an impact on the media? Since media are businesses, they want to have an impact and often welcome student input. Be a player and reach out!

Read More. Media institutions and concepts are complex and dynamic. They are the foundation of our democracy and they are changing rapidly. We are strong only if we are well informed about what is going on. Read a newspaper every day, write a blog, comment on others' blogs. Staying informed is the best way to stay literate. Everyone is manipulated by the media in some way. Just make sure that you understand when and how you are being manipulated.

Chapter Summary

- **Learning is both active and passive.** When we pursue information, it is active learning. When we learn something in the process of these active pursuits, it is called passive or incidental learning.
- **Learning is a hierarchical process.** Learning begins by paying attention to some stimuli, then trying to understand them. After achieving **understanding**, we try to **memorize** these stimuli. We learn even more when we can teach what we have come to understand, evaluate others with respect to this new understanding, and then create something that incorporates this understanding.
- **Media consist of many components.** To understand how media work we must focus on the **professional communicators**, the **messages** they produce, the way in which these messages proliferate though many **channels**, and the **impacts** of these messages on diverse audiences.
- **Entertainment messages are aimed at stimulating emotions.** Our emotions rise quickly and deteriorate slowly. One form of entertainment—drama—is built around conflict between good and evil. The outcome becomes more satisfying when good triumphs over evil.
- **Understanding media impact involves answering many questions.** What do people **learn** from the media? How do the media **stimulate our emotions** and change our behaviors? What **factors** influence the kinds of impact media have on us?
- **Media effects related to violence, sex, and stereotyping are most important.** The media use these three elements frequently to gain attention and promote viewer learning. Only when we understand these effects can we control them.
- **There are many theories about media impacts.** Media impact us by priming, or stimulating, our memory and triggering an emotional reaction. Media impact us when we see characters who get positively or negatively reinforced for some behavior; we want to model characters who get rewarded and avoid characters who get punished. Media also cultivate a general worldview that reality is an unsafe, dangerous place. Finally, our goal as consumers is to increase our media literacy.

Lessons Learned

Media card games teach us a lot. It's surprising how much we pick up from media messages. Let's summarize some of those lessons here:

- **Review media stereotypes in light of your first-hand knowledge.** If you listed the top 10 beliefs you have about people from cultures you have not encountered directly, it's likely that most of these beliefs came from repeated media exposure. The lesson is: Reflect thoughtfully on your beliefs before labeling someone or something you know little about from direct experience.
- **Media messages are complex.** Media messages are highly produced, and contain a lot of information. They are colorful, action-packed, and often subtle. Because they are so entertaining, they may suck us in. We may be unable to stand back from them objectively and see what they're doing to us. Consume these messages with skill and skepticism.

- **Media messages affect us in many ways.** Media messages impact our attitudes, beliefs, and behaviors. Commercials make us want to buy and to believe that we can be popular or more attractive if we do what they want. Make no mistake: These are powerful games and people with a lot of money at stake are playing powerful cards.
- **Media theories provide valuable insights into media effects.** One of the great contributions of these theories is that they provide useful insights into how and why media messages impact us so thoroughly. They tell us how they get into our heads. Armed with this information, you can now better understand these effects and approach your media message consumption with caution.
- **Media literacy is a key part of your social and intellectual development.** The goal of this chapter is to increase your media literacy. Remember, every message asks you to play a card. The advertiser plays its Company Card to encourage you to buy its products and services. In return it wants to you play your Consumer Card and buy its stuff. Do you really believe that you'll be more popular, more attractive, or a better person with more stuff? A media literate person knows the intent of these messages and can form an effective shield against unwanted influence. I hope you have formed such a shield so you can better play card games with these folks. Good luck!

References

Bandura, A. (1994). Social cognitive theory of mass communication. In J. Bryant & D. Zillmann (Eds.), *Media effects* (pp. 61–90). Hillsdale, NJ: Lawrence Erlbaum Associates.

Berkowitz, L., & Rogers, K. H. (1986). A priming effects analysis of media influence. In J. Bryant & D. Zillmann (Eds.), *Perspectives on media effects* (pp. 57–81). Hillsdale, NJ: Lawrence Erlbaum Associates.

Bloom, B. S., & Krathwohl, D. R. (1956). *Taxonomy of educational objectives: The classification of educational goals, by a committee of college and university examiners. Handbook 1: Cognitive domain.* New York: Longmans.

Bryant, J., & Oliver, M. B. (2009). *Media effects: Advances in theory and research* (3rd ed.). New York: Routledge.

Gerbner, G. (1997). Gender and age in prime-time television. In S. Kirschner & D. A. Kirschner (Eds.), *Perspectives on psychology and the media* (pp. 69–94). Washington, DC; American Psychological Association.

Gerbner, G., Gross, L., Morgan, M., & Signorielli, N. (1994). Growing up with television: The cultivation perspective. In J. Bryant & D. Zillmann (Eds.), *Media effects* (pp. 17–42). Hillsdale, NJ: Lawrence Erlbaum Associates.

King, C. R., Lugo-Lugo, C. R., & Bloodsworth-Lugo, M. K. (2010). *Animating difference: Race, gender, and sexuality in contemporary films for children.* Lanham, MD: The Rowman & Littlefield Publishing Group, Inc.

Pardun, C. J., L'Engle, K. L., & Brown, J. D. (2005). Early adolescents' consumption of sexual content in six media. *Mass Communication & Society, 8,* 75–91.

Potter, W. J. (2004). *Theory of media literacy: A cognitive approach.* Thousand Oaks, CA: SAGE Publications, Inc.

PART Five

Public Speaking Card Games

♠ Understanding the Audience's Cards and Games

♦ Preparing the Speech

♣ Delivering the Speech

© Bob Adelman/Corbis

CHAPTER Fifteen

Understanding the Audience's Cards and Games

♣ Introduction

Creating and delivering a speech has three distinct phases:

1. **Analyze** the audience and the occasion for the speech. Determine to whom you are speaking and define the expectations the audience will have for the speech. (chapter 15)
2. **Prepare** your speech including both the substance of what you want to talk about and your card talk strategies for delivering it. (chapter 16)
3. **Practice** your speech to build confidence in your ability to deliver it effectively. (chapter 17)

As you can see from this list, everything flows from a proper analysis of the audience and the occasion for the speech. In fact, we've talked about understanding and adapting to the

> **A ♥**
>
> A speech has three distinct phases: (1) analyze the audience; (2) prepare your speech; (3) practice it.
>
> **♠ A**

audience in nearly every chapter of this book. If you frame your message properly for a specific audience, you stand a better chance of achieving your message objectives.

The goal is to deliver an interesting and motivating message to the audience for some specific occasion. To do that, you need to know your audience and the occasion that brings them together. What messages will they listen to in that situation? Do they want to be entertained? Are they celebrating? Are they knowledgeable about your topic? What attitudes, values, and beliefs will they use to filter the message?

To illustrate the importance of knowing an audience, consider one of the most famous American speeches ever delivered.

The Civil Rights Speech Game. One of the most famous speeches in American history was Dr. Martin Luther King Jr.'s "I Have a Dream" speech from the steps of the Lincoln Memorial in Washington, D.C., on August 28, 1963. The occasion that brought people together was a March on Washington to mobilize America to support basic civil rights. There were hundreds of thousands of people present from all over America, and almost everyone who attended the event was there to support civil rights.

As you may know, at this point in America's history, civil rights was an important—no, it was a compelling—issue. Television was just coming of age and people saw civil rights clashes and demonstrations regularly on TV, which brought the issue into many thousands of living rooms. The leader of this movement was Dr. King, a Baptist minister from Alabama.

Dr. King faced formidable challenges in connecting not only with the audience in Washington, D.C., but with the American TV audience in the comfort of their homes. How supportive of civil rights for African Americans were Americans? Did most people agree or disagree with the civil rights movement in 1963? What kind of approach could Dr. King use, given the attitudes, values, and beliefs of most Americans at this point in history?

In this historic speech Dr. King said he had a dream that white and black children would one day walk hand-in-hand, and that sons of former slaves and sons of former slave owners would live together peacefully. Dr. King's goal on that day was to set a vision for race relations in America—to play a Vision Game that would appeal to the immediate audience in Washington, D.C., as well as to the broader U.S. population. To achieve his goal he had to select cards that would: (a) enhance his credibility as a peaceful champion of race relations; (b) allow him to use a powerful, emotional speaking style; (c) provide legitimacy to his message; and (d) encourage the audience to play a card that would make them receptive to his message.

The Banquet Speech Game. Former Michigan State University (MSU) student Kirk Cousins was the starting quarterback and the football team captain at MSU for three seasons (2009–2011). At the start of the 2011 season he was invited to give an address at a Big 10 luncheon. He represented all student athletes in the Big 10, a large athletic conference that consists mostly of Midwestern universities including MSU, the University of Michigan, and The Ohio State University.

This large event was held in Chicago, and included sports writers and media personnel, athletic directors, coaches, and players. There were more men than women in the crowd, and the average age of listeners was probably 30–35 years old. While football was the activity that brought them to the luncheon, Kirk felt he had to talk about the relationship between football and life. You can see the speech at www.youtube.com/watch?v=tp15N9BbYgY.

The audience Cousins faced was knowledgeable about sports, in general, and football in particular. Because there were some recent incidents in which football players and coaches were caught engaging in inappropriate or illegal acts, some were questioning the integrity of college football. Cousins' goal in the speech was to counter some of these perceptions, while showing that football is a privilege and a blessing. Cousins is a committed Christian, so he made several references to his faith. Later in this chapter you are asked to list the cards Cousins played in giving his speech.

♣ Card Choice in Public Speaking

The examples from both Dr. King and Kirk Cousins illustrate the importance of playing talk cards that are most likely to have a positive impact on the audience. Let's look more specifically at how card choice played out in Dr. King's speech. Dr. King had many cards to pick from in laying out his message. He was a father, a husband, a Baptist minister, a social activist, an intellectual, and a civil rights leader. He could have played several of these cards to lay out his vision. But he only had a few minutes to speak, and he had to make a big impact at this civil rights march.

The cards that made the most sense, since he had played them superbly thousands of times before, were his Minister Card and his Civil Rights Leader Card. Playing these cards met all the criteria. They enhanced his credibility since most people respected Dr. King as both a minister and a civil rights leader advocating peaceful change. People came to hear a leader lay out a vision, which he did with his Civil Rights Leader Card. By playing his Minister Card as well, he could use powerful, emotional language. Playing this second card also legitimized his message because ministers speak from a **position of moral authority,** which is important in laying out a vision associated with peace and justice.

As a result of showing both his Minister and Civil Rights Leader Cards, Dr. King asked his audience to play two cards: a Civil Rights Activist Card and a Church Congregation Card. They were hearing a civil rights speech presented as a church sermon. Congregations are receptive to the minister's message; they know that playing this card well means participating in the message and being emotionally involved with it. By playing his two main cards effectively, Dr. King kept his audience active, excited, emotionally engaged, and more willing to buy into his vision. Dr. King won his Vision Game by playing the right cards at the right time, while encouraging his audience to play cards that made them more open to his message. It was a brilliant combination for him and for America, and 50 year laters, his speech is remembered as a pivotal moment in history.

Let's explore how to conduct an audience analysis and a deliver a speech from a **card talk perspective**. What is involved in taking a card talk approach to speaking? To answer this question, let's begin with a review of some key card talk assumptions:

- **Public speakers play talk cards with their audiences.** You will always show one or more talk cards to an audience while speaking.
- **Some cards work better than others, depending on the audience and the occasion.** What cards will the audience want you to play for that occasion? Should you play those cards? How is the audience likely to interpret the topics and styles you select given their expectations in that occasion? Will they like or dislike your choices?
- **Are the cards you are asking your audience to play for that occasion helpful for making the key points of your speech?** Audiences like to play multiple cards. They may pay better attention and become more active if the speaker knows which cards the audience should play and is successful in getting them to play those cards.

- **It's generally best to play at least two or three cards during a speech.** Effective speakers like to switch talk cards regularly to keep the audience engaged. Switching from one to another also asks the audience to switch their cards, keeping them listening from multiple perspectives.

What we learn from Dr. King's Vision Game is that every great speech begins with an effective card talk strategy: What cards, topics, and styles will win the day? The simple answer is that it depends on the occasion that brings the audience together and the thoughts and feelings they bring with them to the occasion. These two concerns of speaking occasion and audience orientations are inseparable because when an audience gathers, it is for some specific occasion or purpose like listening to a friend tell a story, celebrating a loved one's life at a funeral, being entertained at a comedy club, learning from a lecture, or protesting an injustice. Let's look at these two considerations (audience and occasion) in more detail.

Occasion Considerations

Situational Constraints. Every message is delivered in some sort of context or situation. Every situation contains expectations or constraints about what cards, topics, and styles are appropriate and expected. For example, the March on Washington at which Dr. King spoke that August day was a solemn event. The marchers knew Dr. King well, and expected him to play his Leader and Minister Cards. It would have been inappropriate for him to play a Comic Card and open his speech with a joke.

In our family, my young son will sometimes barge into a serious family discussion and play a Historian Card and start talking about antique guns. We try to tell him that, first, no one wants to talk about that subject at that moment, and second, that if he wants to change the subject he should wait until the current discussion is over. My son's talk card in this scenario is ill timed.

Perhaps the most unusual situational adjustment I've ever made as an academic was at a meeting in Las Vegas. I was scheduled to give a talk on my negotiation strategies research to a group of professional divorce mediators. Just before my presentation, the event organizer asked me if I could shorten my remarks because they had scheduled a Las Vegas chorus line of dancers to perform just before me and a comedian just after my talk.

At that point I thought to myself, does the audience want a serious, detailed academic presentation just after a chorus line of dancers? Clearly, they would be in the mood for something more entertaining, I thought. So I played a Comic Card frequently during the speech and told jokes to fit in with the light-hearted entertainment of the evening. I had to play cards consistent with the situation to keep from boring the audience. They loved the speech!

Sometimes speakers play too few cards for the situation, which bores the audience. Students often make that mistake when giving speeches in class. They play only a Student Card and go through their presentation, treating it like a class assignment. Student audiences want more variety because it engages them on many levels. They might like to see a Friend Card, and have the speaker reveal some interesting personal information; they often like to see a Comic Card in which the speaker tells a humorous story about some

Effective speakers like to switch talk cards regularly to keep the audience engaged.

When you play multiple talk cards you give the audience more ways to get involved in the speech.

strange event. The audience might respond well to a Leader Card in which the student tries to recruit them for his or her cause. Variety is key!

When you play multiple talk cards you give the audience more ways to get involved in the *speech because you're asking the audience to play more than one card.* By playing a Friend Card, the speaker is asking the other students to play their Friend Cards as well. By playing a Comic Card, the speaker is asking the students to play their Comedy Audience Card. The question for the speaker is, *How can I open up the occasion to play more than one card to increase audience involvement?* More involvement means greater impact!

Message Timing. A second occasion-related consideration for any speaker is timing. Speakers must be aware of local and even national events the audience will know about that might impact how they will interpret the speech. For example, I recall a student who presented a speech in class promoting off-shore oil drilling just as the 2010 Gulf of Mexico oil spill was going on. The news media were talking night and day about what a disaster this was for the Gulf Coast. At that point, the audience would probably be unusually critical of promoting more off-shore oil drilling than just before the event. It was bad timing.

How could the student have adjusted his speech to take this timing problem into consideration? First the student could have acknowledged the oil spill and what a problem it was for the Gulf Coast. That way, the audience would know that the speaker was sympathetic to the plight of the residents and wildlife there. Second, the student could talk more about safety than he originally intended because the audience was thinking more about that issue. *Addressing audience concerns because of timing issues makes people more open to the speaker's message.*

In contrast, the timing for Dr. King's speech was excellent. For several years the nation had viewed many negative racial events on TV. Protests were violent and protestors were killed in the streets. The nation's mood called for someone to lay out a vision for how we might come together and heal our wounds. Dr. King provided that positive vision using his dream metaphor. He was only given a few minutes to speak, but like President Lincoln's two-minute Gettysburg Address, Dr. King's speech had an enormous impact on the audience. The point is that any great speaker is aware of these timing considerations and how to take advantage of them.

Background Considerations

Psychographics. Audiences always use their internal, psychological thoughts and feelings to evaluate a speech. These internal variables are called **psychographics**. These variables essentially "graph" the set of psychological orientations people use to categorize the messages as exciting or boring, informative or redundant, useful or irrelevant, for example. We know from the persuasion chapter (chapter 6) that the more precisely a speaker can graph these variables, the easier it is to select arguments and ideas that will appeal to or persuade the audience and elicit the desired response from the speech.

The key psychographic variables that come into play when audiences interpret the speaker's message include:

1. **Knowledge.** What does the audience know about your topic? Do they have a thorough background, or have they never encountered your topic and know nothing of your topic? It is important to determine their level of knowledge for two reasons. First, if they know a lot about the topic, then you don't want to insult them by reviewing what they already know. On the other hand, if they know nothing and you don't provide background knowledge, then they'll be confused.

   Second, if they know a lot about the topic and they disagree with your position, then their disagreement is likely to be more significant than if they knew only a little about the topic. It is easier to influence someone whose opinion is not well conceived. Think carefully about what your audience may know about your topic before you speak!

2. **Expectations.** Two sets of expectations are important to identify. First, what message does the audience expect to hear? Generally audiences have a good idea of what the speaker is going to talk about. If those expectations are not met, and the speaker rambles on about something else, the audience might feel used. It would be like going to class and having the professor spend the whole time talking about his or her personal problems and nothing about the course material.

Second, does the audience understand what talk cards the speaker is playing and what cards the audience is being asked to play? Audiences come to every occasion expecting the speaker to play certain kinds of cards. If they can't figure out what cards the speaker is playing, then they will be confused and react negatively to the speech.

3. **Perceptions of the Speaker's Credibility.** Based on the cards the speaker is playing, the audience judges the speaker's credibility. If you recall from the persuasion chapter, credibility consists of three judgments: The speaker must be **competent**, **trustworthy**, and **dynamic**.

For example, if the speaker is playing an Expert Card on some topic, then he or she is asking the audience to judge his or her competence—does the speaker seem to know what he or she is talking about? Does the speaker show the topics and styles expected of an expert in that area? Can the speaker be trusted? Is the person's reputation good? Is the speaker a dynamic presenter? As we know from the persuasion chapter, these judgments must be positive for the audience to focus on the speaker's message.

4. **Beliefs and Attitudes.** To review, a **belief** is an understanding about whether something is true or false. Do you believe that ghosts exist? Do you believe that smoking is bad for your health? Do you believe that seat belts save lives? An **attitude** reflects what people like and dislike. People have many attitudes about food, cultures, dress, ideas, and dozens of other things. Most of the time there are some relevant attitudes that the audience uses to evaluate the speaker's idea. These attitudes might make the audience hostile to or supportive of the speaker's topics and styles. The point is that it's imperative to understand the audience's beliefs and attitudes on your chosen topic, which they will likely use to evaluate your message.

5. **Values.** A **value** is an understanding about what's right and wrong. Generally our parents, friends, and the culture in which we were raised teach us some strong lessons about right and wrong. Do you believe that gay marriage is wrong or right? Do you believe that people should be honest and open? Work hard and honor their fathers and mothers? Culture has a tremendous influence on values as you will recall from chapter 3. Some cultures value groups over individuals, status over equality, and men's rights over women's rights. What are the core values the audience brings to your speech that may impact how they evaluate your message?

6. **Emotions.** Everyone has and expresses an infinite number of emotions from happy and sad, to love and hate, to fear and confidence. In the persuasion chapter we talked about how people who are emotionally upset are less capable of listening carefully to a message. In chapter 14 we discussed how important emotions are for the entertainment industry.

For speakers the goal is to identify what emotional reactions they want to receive from their audience and play the cards most capable of evoking these reactions. The Comic Card should make the audience happy; a Friend Card might ask the audience to be sad or excited; a Leader Card could be used to make the audience fearful. It is also important to determine what emotions the audience brings to the speech to ensure that your message does not conflict with these emotions. Again, it is vital that speakers understand these emotions and adjust to them.

© 2012 by YanLev. Used under license of Shutterstock, Inc.

Demographics. While **psychographics** are internal, individually focused variables, **demographics** are external variables that differentiate people, such as race, income, religion, education, and marital status. Demographics may have some link to a person's psychographics.

Demographics give us hints about what the audience members might know, expect, believe, and value. In other words, will younger people have different beliefs than older people? Will richer people have different attitudes than poorer people? Will people from some countries express different values than people from other countries? Will college graduates be more knowledgeable on certain topics than people who did not graduate from high school?

The following lists the most common kinds of demographic considerations:

- **Age.** Very young people, like school children, need simple and fun messages. College students don't need simple and fun, but are generally less knowledgeable about politics and current events. They do know popular culture like music and entertainment.
- **Sex.** We know from chapter 2 that men and women communicate for different reasons. They process information differently. Speaking to men-only or women-only groups requires some understanding of these cultural differences.
- **Ethnicity.** America is an ethnically diverse country and becoming more so every day. An effective speaker will tailor his or her message to the majority ethnic group, while respecting the values of people from minority ethnic groups in the audience.
- **Religion.** It may be difficult to determine if an audience comes primarily from one religion—or takes pride in having no religion—unless the speaking event is explicitly religious in nature, such as a church service, service group formed around religion, or a retreat. If the audience has a religious preference and wants you to play a Religion Card, be sure to speak knowledgeably about that religion. It's also important to realize that even if a group is not overtly religious, trivializing this topic can easily turn off your audience.
- **Education.** Better-educated audiences will appreciate more factual evidence for an idea than less educated audiences. The key for the speaker is to determine if the cards, topics, and styles are appropriate for the education level of the majority of audience members.

A♥

Demographics give us hints about what the audience members might know, expect, believe, and value.

A♠

- **Income.** People with higher incomes tend to be better educated, so the speaker should take this relationship into account when the audience's income level is known.
- **Other Relevant Demographics.** There are many other demographic features that come into play when crafting a speech strategy. A few additional features that could influence how the audience interprets a message include marital status, organizational membership, pet ownership, etc. The point is that the more the speaker knows about an audience's demographics, the better able the speaker is to predict some of the audience's most important psychographic characteristics.

After a little thought, it is readily apparent why demographics and psychographics must be considered. A group of sixth-grade Catholic school children will no doubt present different speaking challenges than a group of middle-aged men in an Alcoholics Anonymous meeting. As a speaker, you must constantly adjust your message to fit the audience!

It is possible to have similar demographic characteristics, *but very different psychographic characteristics.* For instance, consider these diverse audiences. They are all college students, but you probably wouldn't approach them in the same way: Young Republican or Democratic students, a fraternity house meeting, and a group of students working at a shelter for battered women? Similar age and education do not necessarily make for similar attitudes and beliefs. Public speakers must be careful not to make too many assumptions based on demographic characteristics. Instead, ask questions of the person who invited you to speak. Do some research, and make careful observations that reveal how the audience might react to your card choices, topics, and styles.

Speech Goals and Audience Analysis

Now that we have an understanding about the occasion and background considerations as part of audience analysis, let's look at them in relation to your speech goals. Think of your speech as climbing a four-step ladder. At the top of your ladder is commitment. You want your audience to commit to your idea, just as they committed to Dr. King's dream. But you can't get them there all at once.

There are a few preliminary steps to take, which are spelled out below. It's important to have a strategy for each step that takes into account all the occasion and background issues we've discussed to this point. Let's look at each of these four steps and think through what's needed to secure audience commitment to your ideas.

[Playing card graphic: Ace of Hearts with text:] Your speech is like a four-step ladder: commitment, awareness, understanding, attention.

1. **Attention.** The first goal of any speech is to get the audience's attention—to pull them into your world so they are with you. Let's take a look at the critical occasion and audience background issues relevant to achieving this objective:

    A. **Occasion Issues.** The occasion for your speech is a class assignment. You will present your speech to other students in a classroom. Or, if you're taking the class online, you may be presenting your speech to a group of friends or relatives. You have a specific speech assignment like a special occasion or informative speech. The first question you must answer is, "What will grab the audience's attention for that occasion?" The audience probably expects you to play a Student Card, which asks them to play their Student Audience Card.

    You have other options. You might play a Comic Card and begin by playing a funny video that sets the context for your speech. You could start with a Friend Card and tell a personal story. Other students play an Actor Card at the beginning and pretend they are acting out some cool role they saw in a movie. The key is to pick an interesting card, and then a topic on the card that is memorable and pulls in the audience.

I graded an informative speech once in which a student talked about flying squirrels. He opened his speech by playing his Pet Owner Card. He got up in front of the room and called out, "Here, Eddie! Here, Eddie!" And his pet flying squirrel crawled out of his jacket pocket on to his hand. He was so cute! He then tossed the squirrel up in the air much to the surprise of all the students! Eddie circled around in the air a couple of times, glided safely to the ground, and ran back to his owner. That certainly got everyone's attention!

The student then played an Expert Card and explained all about these interesting creatures. He also played a Friend Card, talking about how

close he was to his pet. These different cards impressed the students and pulled them into his speech. (Of course, any prop or visual aid including the use of live animals for a class speech must be cleared in advance with the instructor. It is not always appropriate.)

B. **Background Issues.** During this first step in the speech process, the audience's **expectations and speaker credibility perceptions** are the most relevant psychographic issues you must face. In a speech class the audience probably expects another typical student speech. You can violate this expectation by playing an interesting card (e.g., Pet Owner) that will get everyone's attention. Whatever card you play must also enhance your credibility, which as you recall, consists of three judgments: competence, trustworthiness, and dynamism.

During this attention step in your speech, the first judgment is about dynamism. Is the speaker interesting and motivating? Does the speaker smile and seem engaging and exciting? It takes just a few seconds for the audience to form a first impression. If you play an interesting card right away and show them you care about their involvement, that enhances your credibility and sets them up for the second step: awareness.

2. **Awareness.** The attention step gives the audience a quick glance at the general area of your speech. Now your goal is to provide some broad **awareness of your ideas** by introducing your idea in general terms to the audience. Does the theme or idea of your speech interest the audience? Will it challenge their thoughts and capture their imagination so they are eager to learn more?

A. **Occasion Issues.** Your introduction is important because it lays out the direction you want to take the audience. Is that direction appropriate for the occasion? The most significant error I've seen in speeches is that the speaker wants to accomplish too much for the occasion. In many cases, the audience isn't expecting and doesn't want too much detail. They want a general discussion that will encourage them to learn more elsewhere. You must work within your time constraints of perhaps 3–10 minutes. What can you do in that timeframe? You can switch cards during the introduction, as the flying squirrel owner did when he played both a Pet Owner and an Expert Card for an introduction. The key is to have clear, realistic, and appropriate goals for your occasion. Don't try to do too much!

B. **Background Issues.** Knowledge, attitudes, credibility, and values are particularly relevant audience issues during this introductory period. Remember, the introduction guides the direction of your speech. That direction should reflect what the audience knows about the topic. If they are well informed, then the speaker can assume some knowledge and move beyond the basics. If you believe they know nothing about it, then a more basic approach is necessary. Also, does the audience have any attitudes toward or values concerning the topic—are they for or against it in any way? If your topic is controversial (e.g., marijuana should be legalized), then you can assume the audience has formed some pro or con attitudes toward and values concerning the topic.

© 2012 by .shock. Used under license of Shutterstock, Inc.

Credibility judgments about the speaker's competence enter at this point. The introduction lets the audience judge whether the speaker seems to know something about the topic. If the introduction lays out a logical path toward the goal, the audience develops confidence in the speaker's knowledge.

3. **Understanding.** Once the audience is aware of the topic and the direction the speaker is taking, they will try to interpret and understand the ideas and arguments the speaker presents. Hopefully, this understanding will be positive and they will develop an interest in the ideas. During the speech the speaker should look for signs of interest in the audience—are they paying attention, nodding their heads, perhaps even asking questions? These are signs that the audience is trying to understand the ideas and become interested in them. What are the occasion and the background issues that may impact audience understanding of your topic?

A. **Occasion Issues.** As indicated above, sometimes timing is an issue for a speech. An audience will interpret a topic differently if it is relevant to current events. A speech about terrorism would receive a different interpretation after the events of September 11, 2001 than before that date. Timing might also impact the kinds of cards a speaker can play. I recall that after the 9/11 events, Jay Leno of the *Tonight Show* was unable to play his Comic Card on the show because the country was in no mood for comedy; we needed to heal emotionally first.

Timing can also impact the relevance of key points in your speech. If you are advocating a change in the law about some social problem and the law just recently changed and you didn't know about that, the audience will think you are uninformed and your credibility will suffer.

B. **Background Issues.** Audience **beliefs, attitudes, values,** and **emotions** play key roles in how the audience will interpret the speaker's ideas. Audiences usually have specific beliefs about

© 2012 by Monkey Business Images. Used under license of Shutterstock, Inc.

many things, particularly in this day and age when searching the Internet is so pervasive. The beliefs may not be accurate, but people will likely have them.

For example, in the flying squirrel speech, many students believed that the squirrels really flew like birds. The speaker had to explain that Eddie could not fly, he just had skin between his legs that let him glide to the ground—there's no flying!

Also, when people think carefully about a topic to understand it, they always apply their core values that guide their judgments about right and wrong. For example, what if the student gave the flying squirrel speech to a group of animal-rights advocates? Would they have been angry that the squirrel was no longer free but was held captive?

Emotions play a critical role at this point in a speech. It is generally valuable to get the audience emotionally involved in the ideas. For example, when giving his squirrel speech, the speaker played a Friend Card and told the audience a personal story about how he found the squirrel as a baby, lying on the ground injured. The student nursed the squirrel back to health by caring for it every day. That story generated a lot of sympathy for the student and enhanced his credibility as a warm, caring person.

4. **Commitment.** After presenting the main ideas in support of the speaker's theme, it's important to close with a strong commitment. The speaker wants to leave the audience well informed, excited, and possibly ready to act. How can the speaker get the audience to commit? What images, ideas, and concepts might serve as powerful closers most likely to make the speech memorable?

A. **Occasion Issues.** Dr. King's request on that August day in 1963 was to ask the audience to accept his dream of a racially transformed America. It was certainly a positive message and visually poignant as he laid out images of black and white children playing together. Creating these images was emotionally stimulating as he tried to tell us that the struggle was really about creating a better life for our children and caring about their future.

The question is always whether the speaker's request is appropriate for the occasion. What if Dr. King had closed his speech by asking people to buy his book? People would be horrified that Dr. King was using that occasion as a

> A ♥
> What if Dr. King had closed his speech by asking people to buy his book? That would have been inappropriate for the occasion and offensive to the audience.
> A ♠

sales pitch! That would have been inappropriate for the occasion and offensive to the audience.

C. **Background Issues.** The closing of a speech is important because it's the last word the audience hears. For an effective closing the speaker must take into account the audience's perceptions of his or her credibility, whether the audience has changed their attitudes, and the extent to which the speaker has touched the audience's emotions.

Hopefully, the speech will have enhanced the speaker's credibility. The audience will come to believe that the speaker is knowledgeable, trustworthy, and dynamic. If the audience holds that view, then it's likely they have also changed or strengthened their attitudes in the direction advocated by the speaker. We know from the persuasion chapter that these attitudes are a strong predictor of whether the audience intends to change their minds. If the audience shows some emotion, like enthusiasm or sympathy for example, then chances are they have changed their attitudes in the desired direction.

The most important background issue is whether the audience is able and/or willing to do what the speaker wants. If the audience thinks the topic is fine and the speaker is credible, but can't do what the speaker wants, then the speech is likely to be ineffective. The point is that the speaker has to be careful to ask for something that is within the audience's grasp.

Audience Analysis Exercise

To learn more about how speakers select cards to appeal to various audiences, answer the following questions regarding Kirk Cousins' speech at the Big 10 Luncheon:

1. **Attention/Occasion.** List the card or cards that Kirk used to gain the audience's attention. Why were they effective or ineffective in your view?

2. **Attention/Background.** Did the card that Kirk played in his attention getter seem dynamic and in what ways did it establish his credibility?

3. **Awareness/Occasion.** What was the general theme of the speech given in the introduction? Why was it appropriate or inappropriate for the occasion? What card did Kirk switch to when he presented this theme?

4. **Awareness/Background.** Do you think the audience had any knowledge about this theme or could relate to it? What specific values could Kirk assume that the audience had about his topic?

5. **Understanding/Occasion.** Were there any timing or occasion issues that could have distracted the audience? What other cards did Kirk play as he moved through his speech?

6. **Understanding/Background.** What beliefs or values did Kirk refer to that might have connected with the audience? How did Kirk impact the audience's emotions?

7. **Commitment/Occasion.** Was Kirk's closing appropriate to the occasion? What was the nature of the commitment he was seeking from the audience?

8. **Commitment/Background.** Was the closing appropriate for the level of credibility Kirk achieved during his speech? To what extent did he ask for the something the audience was able to provide?

Chapter Summary

- **A speaker's card choice must focus on audience needs.** Audiences vary in terms of how they filter and process messages. It is vital that the speaker identify significant issues that might impact how the audience will interpret the speaker's message.
- **Audiences are asked to play cards, as well.** The cards they are asked to play should challenge them. After analyzing the audience, the speaker decides to play several cards to deliver the speech. These cards also ask the audience to play the reciprocal cards. These cards should both interest and challenge the audience to keep them motivated to listen to the speech.
- **Speeches must be tailored to the specific occasions.** There are situational and timing constraints for every speech. These constraints impact what the audience wants and expects to hear in the speech. The speaker may or may not want to disregard these expectations depending on the response desired from the audience.
- **Speakers must analyze the audience's psychographics.** Every audience can be graphed in terms of their psychological orientations. Some orientations are more important at different times of the speech than others. The speaker should know which audience expectations, attitudes, values, beliefs, and emotions are most likely to determine their reaction to the speech.
- **Speakers must analyze the audience's demographics to predict psychographics.** Sometimes a good way to predict how an audience will react is to examine their demographic characteristics. Sometimes an audience that is all male, all of one ethnic group, or more economically advantaged will react differently to a message, for example.
- **Speech goals must be tailored the audience's psychographics and the speaking occasion.** It's important to have clear goals for a speech based on how the audience might react to that speech.

Lessons Learned

In this chapter, we've covered speech preparation and topic selection from the audience's perspective, with these points:

- **Speech topics should not be selected in a vacuum.** Selecting a topic that is interesting only to the speaker will not get a good audience reaction. Find a topic that the audience is excited to hear about for that occasion.
- **Speakers should listen to audience needs to adjust their goals.** Too many speeches fail because the speaker neglected to take audience interests into account. Audiences will tell you what want they want to hear if you take the time to listen to their interests.
- **Speakers who understand how to play multiple cards at multiple times are most effective.** These speakers know how to play certain cards at certain times in their speeches to elicit the best response from the audience.
- **Remember, the audience rules!** Respect them, trust them, and let them guide your speech.

Eric Broder Van Dyke/Shutterstock.com

Preparing the Speech

♣ Introduction

The last chapter asked you to focus on the audience and the occasion for speaking. In this chapter, we ask the question: What messages work best for a specific audience on a specific speaking occasion? The goal of this chapter is to walk you through the process of preparing your speech from a card talk perspective. We focus on giving informative and persuasive speeches. To get your head in the game, consider these speaking card talk games.

The Persuasive Speech Game. In 1993, Jimmy Valvano gave an emotional speech at an award ceremony. Jimmy was a famous and well-loved basketball coach whose team won the NCAA championship for North Carolina State University in 1983. When he gave this speech he was being treated for cancer and died soon after. His goal was to persuade the audience to support his cancer research foundation. Watch his speech at www.youtube.com/watch?v=HuoVM9nm42E.

The Informative Speech Game. Here is an excellent informative speech on acupuncture given by a student in a public speaking course. Focus on how she organized and developed the speech: www.youtube.com/watch?v=SRKrbXEbEvU. I encourage you to explore other speeches on YouTube to get a feel for how students prepare for and present their speeches.

Successful speaking begins by answering one simple question: *Do you care if the audience understands and is interested in anything you have to say?* If you care, then you'll do everything in your power to connect with your audience and communicate your ideas. If you play a Student Card and go through the motions, the audience will know it and will not pay attention.

Knowing how to speak in public is a powerful skill. As we learned in prior chapters, the ability to speak publicly is a key component of a Leader Card, for example. Take charge of the process and have some fun with this opportunity! Now let's walk through the eight steps you need to follow to select and develop effective messages for your audience.

♣ Step 1: Select a Topic

Select a topic that meets two criteria. First, **the topic must be interesting to you**. If *you* care about it, then your audience will see your passion and pay attention. Remember, you *must care* that your audience understands what you have to say. Did you see and hear the passion that Dr. King, Kirk Cousins (both chapter 15), and Jimmy Valvano expressed in their speeches? They were definitely interested in those topics! Indeed, the three men focused on life-changing moments; they poured their hearts into every word in speaking them.

Second, **the topic must be relevant to your audience on that occasion**. Just about any topic can be made relevant to an audience, but some topics are easier than others. Topics that audience members *understand* and are *important* to them in their daily lives are most likely to get their attention.

My son likes to talk about guns and marksmanship because he is passionate about his hobby. He might be able to inform students about guns, but most students have little to no interest in them, and many view guns negatively. So while he is excited about this topic, his classmates might find it a less compelling speech. In contrast, my other son is passionate about science fiction dramas. Most students in a typical classroom go to movies or are into dramas in some way. Relating that topic to other students might be easier.

It's difficult to find topics that all students in a class or all members of some other audience will find interesting and motivating. But it's important to make an attempt.

To help you select a topic for an informative speech, complete this exercise. Here are 10 general questions meant to uncover something that you might have strong feelings about. Answer one or more of the questions that interest you.

1. What have you purchased recently that you were excited about and why?
2. What careers or professions most impress you and why?
3. What would you do on your fantasy vacation?
4. Is there a social cause or issue you are passionate about, and why is it important to you?
5. What one question would you ask the president of the United States?
6. What one communication technology is most likely to change the way people live and why?
7. Why do so many marriages fail?
8. What should be done to preserve the institution of marriage, or should we let marriage die as a social institution?
9. How do you keep physically fit and why is that important to you?
10. What do you love to eat and why should others try it?

The speech topic must be interesting to you. ... and you must care that your audience understands.

Now focus on your answers to one or two questions you most liked. Jot down some topics underneath one or two of the questions you answered. Then indicate on a scale of 1–10 with 10 being the highest, whether the audience might find this topic interesting.

For example, you liked Question 1 because you think iPads® will change the way people live. The topics you might select for this question could be: (1) how iPads® are used as educational tools in classrooms; (2) how iPads® have changed the media entertainment industry; or (3) on a negative note, how iPads® create relationship problems for teens since they isolate themselves by focusing only on social media.

TOPICS OF INTEREST FROM YOUR ANSWERS TO THE QUESTIONS POSED ABOVE:	AUDIENCE INTEREST 1–10
1.	
2.	
3.	
4.	
5.	
6.	
7.	

Now look at your list of potential topics. Focus carefully on those you believe might be most interesting to the audience. The right topic is there, you just need to let it emerge. There are many ways to choose a good speech topic; try to find a topic that will interest both you and your audience.

♣ Step 2: Determine Your Goal

Now you have a topic. What do you want to accomplish with that topic? Notice that the speakers in both the Persuasive and Informative Speech Games had clear goals. Similarly, you should have a clear answer to the question: *Why are you speaking?* For the topic you selected, what do you hope to achieve with your speech? What specific response do you want from your audience and how will you know if you've achieved that response?

For informative speeches the goal is to have the audience understand or learn something. You could determine if they learned something by asking questions or getting them to participate in some activity. For persuasive speeches, the goal is to change the audience's mind about something, whether it's shifting policy positions or feeling stronger about an existing opinion. Perhaps you want the audience to commit to a cause or give some money to a cause.

Craft a Purpose Statement. The goal of Step 2 is to craft a **purpose statement** that is **specific, realistic,** and **results-oriented**. A specific purpose statement is most often one sentence

A
♥
You should have a clear answer to the questions: Why are you speaking ... What do you hope to achieve with your speech?
♠
A

that explains exactly what the speaker hopes to accomplish. It helps you focus your speech on one aspect of the topic. For instance, a good purpose statement would not be, "Tell people about relationships," but would be focused on, "How people initiate successful business relationships." As another example, with a general topic like skiing, the purpose statement may be the cost of skiing, the dangers of skiing, skiing fashions, or some other aspect of skiing. A specific purpose statement focuses on only one topic.

Look at the following purpose statements. Check the statements that meet the criteria listed above as being good, and check those that fail to meet the criteria as being bad.

PURPOSE STATEMENT: THE PURPOSE OF MY SPEECH IS TO …	GOOD?	BAD?
1. Make the audience laugh.		
2. Persuade audience members to wear vehicle seat belts.		
3. Inform people about cats.		
4. Persuade the audience to care more about others.		
5. Inform politicians about the dangers of high tuition costs.		
6. Inform the audience about how to start a business.		
7. Persuade the audience to join a sailing club.		
8. Help people build a stronger opinion of themselves.		
9. Train the audience on how to fire a Nerf® gun.		
10. Convince people to support a political candidate.		

There are four purpose statements in this list that are vague and are not useful for crafting a speech (1, 3, 4, and 8). The other six are fairly specific and provide a solid foundation for building a speech. Now let's look at the difference between building a purpose statement around an informative speech and a persuasive speech.

Informative Speaking. When audiences are interested in learning some kind of new information, it is called **informative speaking** or even **teaching**. Every class lecture is essentially informative speaking. The speaker's goal is to meet the audience's information needs. It is not aimed at changing the audiences' attitudes, beliefs, or behaviors. Achieving change is the goal of persuasive speaking, which we address next. Informative speaking is about helping the audience learn something.

If you recall from chapters 14 and 15, the first step in learning is ensuring the audience pays attention to the message. When they're interested in acquiring the information, they will pay attention if the message is delivered in an engaging, emotionally stimulating way. An informative speech must begin by asking how you can meet the audience's information needs in an engaging, stimulating way so they will learn the information as you intend.

If you turn the question around, would you like to hear your own speech? Is it good enough for you to listen to? If the answer is yes because you are excited about your topic and you think your information is engaging, you're halfway home. If you believe the audience will also find it engaging, then you have a foundation for success.

Persuasive Speaking. In contrast to informative speaking, **persuasion** is the process of using communication to modify the audience's attitude or behavior toward some topic.

This definition implies that there is a discrepancy between the position the speaker is advocating and the audience's attitude or behaviors.

If the audience is **hostile** and they are aware of the gap between your position and theirs, then your job is to motivate them to listen to your position. If they are **uninformed**, the gap becomes clear to the audience because you may be asking them to do something differently. Change is difficult for everyone. As we discussed above, the specific goals and purpose of a persuasive speech largely depend on the audience's viewpoint and how much the speaker can reasonably expect to change minds.

As we know from the chapter on persuasion, people must see a need for change. They must be motivated to find a solution to a problem. Persuading people to join a club or donate to a cause requires that the speaker tap into some need the audience has or some problem they are trying to solve. If the need is not apparent, then there is no need to change.

In Step 6, we develop a single topic following an outline called **Monroe's Motivated Sequence** (Micciche, Pryor, & Butler, 2000). Monroe's outline for a persuasive speech calls on the speaker to identify an audience need, propose a strategy to meet that need, and help the audience visualize how much better things will be with that solution in place.

When you watch the Jimmy Valvano speech, notice how he creates a need and then provides a solution to meet that need.

© 2012 by mangostock. Used under license of Shutterstock,Inc.

♣ Step 3: Select Your Talk Cards

The next set of choices you make in preparing your speech is determining what cards you want to play and what cards you want your audience to play. For your informative speech, what are your card choices? Let's answer this question by looking at each of the major sections of a speech:

- **Attention-Getter.** People often play a unique card to start. Kirk Cousins played a Friend Card in relating a personal story. What card did Jimmy Valvano play at the beginning of his speech? Would you be comfortable playing a Comic Card, Ethnic Card, Female Card, or Male Card for your attention-getter?
- **Awareness.** When you switch to your thesis statement, what card would be best for credibly stating your thesis? Dr. King played his Minister Card. If your topic is about a social issue, you could play a Social Activist Card, advocating for a change of some kind.
- **Understanding.** As you run through your main points you might want to switch from an Expert Card to a more personal Friend Card or a Family Member Card and tell a story.
- **Commitment.** At the end, you could switch to an Expert or Leader Card to show your expertise and convince your audience that you are a credible leader whose advice they should follow.

Card Style. The second card talk issue that's important to consider is the style you'll use in presenting the speech. Generally, you want to present a style that is: (a) friendly so the audience feels warmly about you and the topic, (b) informal so you can make the audience feel comfortable about your information, and (c) low power in that you're not trying to push the audience around in any way.

In most public speaking situations, speeches are (a) read from a prepared text, (b) recited from memory (i.e., the speech was written in advance and memorized), (c) delivered impromptu or without any prior preparation, or (d) delivered extemporaneously, where a speech is practiced in advance and brief notes are used during a presentation.

What style of card talk topics does an audience typically expect for each of these kinds of speeches?

- **Reading a speech** sends the message of low friendliness, high formality, and moderate power because written texts are formal and unfriendly. That is not a choice if you're interested in connecting with your audience.
- **Reciting a speech** is about the same as reading it. Speakers run through the script and send the same kind of unfriendly, formal messages.
- **An impromptu speech** can be friendly and informal, which is useful, but the arguments and evidence might not be convincing.
- **An extemporaneous speech** is generally best because you have taken time to prepare, but you are using your own conversational style in which you can be friendly and engaging. Use this style and speak from the heart.

Card Style and Language Use. Extemporaneous speech is more structured and formal than a normal conversation. The woman giving her informative speech on acupuncture at the beginning of this chapter illustrates this style. In contrast, the persuasive speech by Jimmy Valvano had more of an impromptu style. It was friendly and informal with jokes and lots of emotion.

For your speech it's best to *avoid excessive slang, jargon, and improper grammar* that you might use in a conversation with friends. You shouldn't play a Friend Card for the whole speech. You might play that card a time or two in your speech. But you must also play the other, more authoritative cards you've outlined, which establish a different kind of relationship with your audience. You want to be seen as the authority, the expert, and a credible speaker.

As we point out in the next chapter, public speaking requires a different form of delivery than normal speech. Conversation often contains spacers or interjections like "you know" or "like" and the use of vocalized pauses such as "uh" and "um." Effective public speakers keep things like spacers and vocalized pauses to a minimum, while adjusting their voices so they may be heard clearly by all of their audience.

A♥ For your speech, it's best to avoid excessive slang, jargon, and improper grammar that you might use in a conversation with friends. A♠

♣ Step 4: Conduct Your Research

Now you know what you want to talk about and what cards you need to be effective. To build the rest of the speech you must carefully research the topic to see what ideas and arguments will be most interesting and compelling for the audience.

Gathering Research. Imagine that you're the student preparing a speech on acupuncture like the woman playing the Informative Speech Game. That's your topic. Your goal is to inform people about the advantages and disadvantages of acupuncture so they can decide if it's useful for them. The talk cards you've decided to play are a Patient Card, a Friend Card, and an Expert Card in the course of presenting your speech. With these decisions in mind, it's time to conduct some research on acupuncture to help organize your speech.

The first step in conducting research is to brainstorm a list of questions the audience might have or issues related to your topic. This is where knowing the audience is critical, as we covered in chapter 15.

For the acupuncture example, what issues would you need to research to inform a nonmedical audience about the value of that procedure? Consider these issues that I have brainstormed:

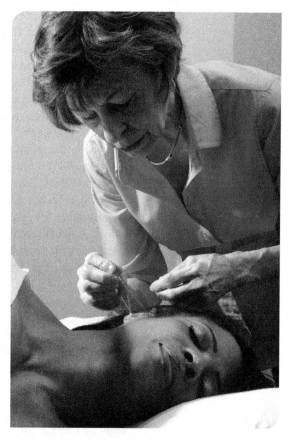

© 2012 by John Keith. Used under license of Shutterstock, Inc.

- **What is acupuncture?** How does it work? It seems strange to stick needles in people to help them get better. Does it hurt when they stick in the needles? How do they know where to stick them?
- **Who does acupuncture?** Is this a real medical specialty or an ancient practice that is not professionally certified? How can the average person determine if someone is qualified to do acupuncture?
- **Does it really work?** How successful is this procedure? Do people really get better, and are there statistics on how many people get better? How many treatments does it take to work? Will it work right away or does the patient have to wait for it to work?
- **How much does it cost?** Is the procedure covered by typical health insurance or is this some kind of experimental procedure that is unlikely to be covered? If it's not covered and someone wants to try it, how much does a typical treatment cost?
- **Who are good candidates for this procedure?** Does acupuncture cure everything or is it useful only for some things? In which areas would it be most successful?
- **How long does it take to complete one treatment?** If it takes a long time to get a treatment, is it really worth the effort?
- **What are the risks associated with acupuncture?** What are the downsides of this kind of procedure? Are there any stories about people who have had problems after doing it?
- **Are there any stories about people who have had this procedure?** There is probably some medical association that specializes in acupuncture. It probably has statistics on success and testimonials of people who have had it.
- **Where can someone go locally to get it done?** Are there any clinics in the area where someone can get this treatment? How common are these clinics and are they affiliated with conventional medical facilities?
- **Where can someone go to learn more about acupuncture?** What are some good information resources for people interested in knowing more about whether this might work for them?

Where can you go to get answers to these questions? First, understand that the **Internet** is not the only research resource! Consider gathering research in the brick-and-mortar college **library**. Start at the Reference Section and ask for help with your topic. Many libraries have specialized document sections focusing on government, medicine, or whatever topic you are exploring. The library also has many electronic databases such as **Proquest, Lexis-Nexis,** and **Blackwell-Synergy.com**. Sometimes Google searches are helpful. Use **Scholar.Google.com** for research articles.

Do not cite information directly from the Internet unless it is from an established, credible source. Instead, get the original hard copy of the information from the library. If you must cite information from the Internet—and there are topics where this is appropriate—present non-Internet sources as well.

Evidence Credibility. The credibility of the research that you cite in your work reflects on your personal credibility. Choose evidence from sources that are worthy of being cited in college-level work. For example, if you were to insert the words "effectiveness of acupuncture" in Scholar.Google.com, you would find many peer-reviewed journal articles discussing this issue. Articles that appear in medical journals would be good evidence. Wikipedia is not a good source because it can be edited by anyone and the facts are not verified. Use common sense.

Good evidence is: (a) relevant to your topic, (b) recent, and (c) reputable in that the source of the information is **identifiable** and **credible**. To gain credibility for your evidence, it's sometimes appropriate to mention how your evidence meets these three tests (relevant, recent, reputable). For example, citing the impressive qualifications of an author of an important acupuncture article shows that the article is relevant, recent, and reputable.

Citing Research. Citing other people's ideas and work is critical to researching with integrity. Using evidence to supplement or inform work that you wish to present requires citing the information's origin. In the field of Communication, we follow the American Psychological Association (APA) citation guidelines. These guidelines can be found at www.apastyle.org/learn/tutorials/basics-tutorial.aspx.

♣ Step 5: Prepare Your Thesis Statement

After completing your research you should have a good idea of what you want to say in your speech. In general, what are the main points about your topic that the audience will be most interested in hearing? Regarding the acupuncture topic, not all the questions listed above are that interesting. It is important to condense the research into some specific ideas that you believe are most important to your audience. Then you can translate these key ideas into a thesis statement.

Your **thesis statement** identies the one central idea of your speech. A good thesis is a statement, not a question or a phrase. Similar to a purpose statement, a thesis should not include slang, figurative language, or vague words. Unlike a purpose statement, a thesis statement is usually delivered to the audience. (A purpose statement is for your own reference.)

A good thesis statement meets three criteria:

1. It gives the audience a clear understanding of where the speech is going and the main point it is going to make with the audience.
2. It is what the audience will remember when the speech is done.
3. It creates the organizational structure and prefigures the speech's content so that every point and subpoint logically relate to the thesis statement.

A

Your thesis statement: (1) gives clear direction where the speech is going, (2) will be what the audience remembers, and (3) creates the organizational structure.

A

Here are five thesis statements for the informative acupuncture speech. Which one is best?

1. Acupuncture is cool.
2. Acupuncture is an effective mainstream, safe, and affordable medical procedure to manage pain.
3. Acupuncture is not as strange as it sounds.
4. Do you think acupuncture is only for tough guys? Well, you'd be wrong. It's for everybody!
5. Acupuncture is a really unusual procedure that most people don't think about, but I think it's pretty good.

Clearly, thesis statement 2 meets the three criteria outlined above (relevant, recent, reputable). It gives the audience a clear understanding of where you are going and the point you are making. It is a simple message that an audience will take with them after the speech. And it tells the audience exactly what you are going to talk about. The other thesis statements are vague and don't meet any of the three quality criteria. If you don't frame your thesis statement properly, it will be difficult to formulate the rest of your speech. So make sure you understand how to craft this statement so you can build your speech around it and accomplish your overall goal of persuading or informing this audience.

A ♥ — If you don't frame your thesis statement properly, it will be difficult to formulate the rest of your speech. ♠ A

♣ Step 6: Identify Your Key Ideas and Arguments

Your next task in building a speech is to form the ideas or arguments that will best inform or persuade your audience. Regardless of your goal (e.g., informative or persuasive speech), the structure for your main ideas and arguments comes from your thesis statement. Let's look at both informative and persuasive thesis statements and see how key ideas and arguments can be formed to support them.

Informative Speaking. Let's use the best thesis statement from Step 5 and see how it can be developed into a set of supportive ideas and arguments: Acupuncture is an effective mainstream, safe, and affordable medical procedure to manage pain.

Based on this thesis statement, there are three main points or arguments that will be used to organize an informative speech on acupuncture:

1. **Acupuncture is a mainstream, effective medical procedure.** Lots of people use it and find it effective in managing their pain when traditional medical procedures don't work.
2. **Acupuncture is safe.** There are few problems that people experience with the procedure because it is highly regulated. Physicians and practitioners must be certified to perform the procedure, and it can only be conducted in controlled clinical settings.

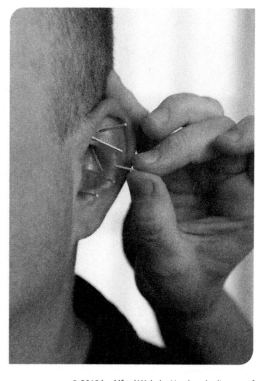

© 2012 by Alfred Wekelo. Used under license of Shutterstock, Inc.

3. **Acupuncture is affordable.** Most issues can be addressed with a few treatments, and the cost is typically less than for more complicated, traditional pain management strategies. Most health insurance plans cover it.

It is important to build your main arguments around statements that are most likely to be relevant and interesting to the audience. Perform the commonsense test. If you knew nothing about a topic like acupuncture, what would be your main concerns or fears that would either prevent or encourage you to listen to such a topic? For me, I would be concerned about whether acupuncture was effective, safe, and affordable. Your audience might look differently at the topic. That's why a strong audience analysis is needed *before* a speech is created.

Persuasive Speaking. The structure of arguments is different for persuasive speeches. Let's see how these persuasion principles are implemented in Monroe's Motivated Sequence mentioned earlier. Developed by Dr. Alan Monroe, the main idea of this model is that people need to be motivated to change their beliefs, opinions, and values. To understand how this sequence works, take a look at a persuasive form of a thesis statement constructed for the acupuncture speech: For people who have trouble managing pain, they should consider acupuncture as an effective mainstream, safe, and affordable medical procedure.

For persuasive speaking the challenge is to develop this thesis statement into a five-step organizational scheme to motivate the audience to comply with the speaker's message. Here are the five steps of Monroe's Motivated Sequence:

This final step tells the audience exactly what they must do to implement the solution.

1. **The Attention Step.** Persuading someone to change begins by trying to overcome audience apathy and direct attention to the speaker with a startling statement, a personal story, a unique visual aid, a series of questions, or a unique set of facts. For acupuncture the speaker could state statistics on how common the procedure is.

2. **The Need Step.** The goal of this step is to make the audience feel there is a need for a change. The speaker should identify a significant problem with the status quo, and how bad it is to continue on the same old path. It is often best to tell a story illustrating the problem, and then provide as many facts, examples, and quotations to make the problem real and significant for that audience. Selling the acupuncture idea to a group of students as an alternative pain management strategy might be difficult since students are generally healthy with few chronic pain problems. It is important that the audience feels the problem and sees it as real. The topic might be more persuasive to a group of older adults who have trouble managing pain with medications alone.

3. **The Satisfaction Step.** When the audience feels a need for change, they will want a solution to the problem. Any proposed solution should meet three criteria: (1) it should give evidence that the solution will work, (2) it should provide details about how it will work, thus, making it look realistic, and (3) it should be easy for the audience to implement. Make them want it and make it easy to get it. A short video showing how acupuncture works might be effective here.

4. **The Visualization Step.** It is not enough to tell the audience what they need to do to solve the problem. They must also be able to visualize the solution in action by developing *a clear mental picture* of how the solution satisfies their needs. The positive way to create a vision is to describe how much better the audience will be when they adopt the change. The negative method is to show how bad things might be if the audience fails to adopt the change soon.

5. **The Action Step.** This final step tells the audience exactly what they must do to implement the solution. What are the specific steps individuals can take to solve the problem? Whenever possible, the audience should fulfill this action step right after the speech. For acupuncture, where can they go for more information or make an appointment to try the procedure? It is best to end this step strongly with a quotation from a convincing authority figure or a story of an incident that shows how important it is to adopt the change. Some speakers like to ask the audience to sign something that commits them to the new course of action.

♣ Step 7: Organize the Speech

Now you have the pieces in place to organize your speech. You know what you're trying to accomplish, what cards you want to play, and what points you're interested in bringing to your audience. Let's put these points into a speech that will be fun and interesting to present. To accomplish this objective, first recall the four areas we explored for the audience analysis:

1. **Attention** *(What will get their attention?)*
2. **Awareness** *(What is the main point of the speech?)*
3. **Understanding** *(What are the key ideas supporting the main point?)*
4. **Commitment** *(What can convince people to commit to the key ideas of the speech?)*

We organize the speech in a way that answers these key questions. Let's look at the speech's main sections.

The Attention-Getter. The goal of the **attention-getting device** is to pull your audience into you and the topic of the speech. Effective ways to gain an audience's attention include telling a brief story, providing a startling statistic, asking a question that would appeal to the audience, showing a YouTube video, or using another visual aid. Avoid telling a joke because most jokes don't succeed unless you have a well-practiced Comic Card. What would be a good attention-getter for the acupuncture speech? Would it be appropriate to come into the speech with an acupuncture needle stuck in your cheek? That would certainly get my attention!

A Good Thesis Statement. Following the attention-getter comes the thesis statement. It is one sentence that illustrates the big picture, or the broad outline of what you want the audience to know. It gives them your presentation's main point. This statement follows the attention-getter because you want your audience to know as soon as possible what you want them to understand.

The Preview Statement. To keep your speech organized, it is important to "say what you are going to say." Specifically, while your purpose and thesis statements provide the audience with clear and concise information regarding the intent of your speech, the **preview statement** provides a clear list of the particular main points you will discuss. In essence, this list acts as a road map by providing each of your main points, in the order you will present them, so the audience obtains a mental picture of what you will talk about. It also provides a smooth transition from your introduction to your first main point.

The preview statement is several sentences long. For the acupuncture speech, you would provide two or three sentences explaining why you believe the procedure is commonplace

The preview statement provides a clear list—a road map—of the specific main points you will discuss.

and effective. Then you would move on to why it's safe and affordable. Notice how much redundancy is built into giving speeches. Good presentations are redundant because audiences need constant reminders of where the speech is going so they can follow along. Redundancy increases the chances that an audience will understand your message.

Transitions. **Transitions** signal when the speaker is moving from one point to the next, linking two ideas or issues together. It provides a conclusion to the point you are currently discussing, and segues into the next point. Transitions help the audience follow the speech's organization, and help the speech flow smoothly. Think of transitions as the connections between cars on a train. If the entire train is to make it to its destination, the links between cars must be strong.

Transitions should state both the idea you are leaving and the one you are moving to. The transition does not need to be complex. In fact, the simpler they are the better. Here are a few examples of effective transitions:

Example 1:   Now that you have a good feel for what acupuncture is, let's look at why it's effective.

Example 2:   While research and patient testimonials clearly reveal that acupuncture is effective, other studies show that it's safe as well.

Example 3:   Now that we have examined the main reasons why acupuncture is more popular than ever for managing pain, let's look at what steps we can take to find a good acupuncture physician in your area.

Signposts. Words or phrases that signal the importance of what you are going to say are **signposts**. Signposts signal to your audience that they need to *listen to and remember* what you are going to say next. You can use words to emphasize certain areas of your speech by saying something like: If you remember anything that I discussed today, it should be the following ..., or Acupuncture is a gift from the ancients that can help people today.

Using words that emphasize the importance of what you are saying can be effective, but it is the visual style or vocal emphasis you put on the words that makes the audience pay attention. Take the last example, "If you remember anything ... ." If you emphasize the word anything by saying it louder and pausing after it, you tell the audience that what you are saying next is significant. You want to get the point across that acupuncture is a gift, so you provide cues to get the audience to focus on your key point.

Speech Body. To begin writing your speech body, you need to consider how the speech will be organized and how your supporting evidence will be researched and developed. The first aspect to consider is how to organize your main points. Four of the most popular ways to organize the **speech body** include:

1. **Time Patterns:** Arranging a topic chronologically or sequentially;
2. **Topic Patterns:** Arranging a speech based on types or categories, such as types of valet services or categories of people interested in the service;
3. **Problem-Solution Patterns:** Arranging the speech by indicating a problem and then a solution; and
4. **Cause-Effect Patterns:** Indicating possible causes and then possible effects created by the causes or problems.

Conclusion. The speech's **conclusion** serves two purposes: to review the main points and to make pertinent closing remarks. Reviewing your main points is where you "say what you said." Many speakers have a hard time following this form because they feel they are being too redundant. This is untrue. Remember, your audience has never heard your speech before, so it is important to stress to them what point(s) you are making. Repeating the key points also keeps the listeners organized. Finally, *restating the main points* can serve as a signpost, telling the audience you are concluding your main remarks.

Final Statement. Your speech's final statement is likely to be the most memorable. It is *one sentence* that should not only sum up your speech, but leave a lasting impression on your listeners. Most closing statements should make the same point as the attention-getter, but should be stated by playing a different card and perhaps a different strategy. When you write your close, do not use the same technique you used in the introduction unless absolutely necessary. For example, if you played an Expert Card and used a statistic as an attention-getter, play a Friend Card and tell a personal story for the close that summarizes the key ideas in the thesis statement. It is wise to mix cards between the front and back end of the speech to make it more memorable for the audience.

The final statement of your speech is likely to be the most memorable.

♣ Step 8: Create the Outline Including Supportive Material

The most effective way to organize your speech is to write an **outline** or skeletal version of your speech. It helps you *focus* on when certain points will be stated and how much information you have to relay to the audience. You may realize after you write your outline that you have too much information (or too little) or do not have enough pertinent examples.

Good advice regarding public speaking is "Say what you are going to say, say it, and then say what you said."

Good advice regarding public speaking is "Say what you are going to say, say it, and then say what you said." Thus the standard format for such an outline is:

I. **Introduction**
    A. Attention-getter.
    B. Thesis statement.
    C. Preview statement.

II. **Body**
    A. Main Point #1.
        1. Statement.
        2. Evidence for why the statement is true.
        3. Transition to the next main point.

    B. Main Point #2.
        1. Statement.
        2. Evidence for why the statement is true.
        3. Transition to the next main point.

    C. Main Point #3.
        1. Statement.
        2. Evidence for why the statement is true.
        3. Transition to the conclusion

© 2012 by Blend Images. Used under license of Shutterstock, Inc.

III. **Conclusion**

 A. Review Main Points.

 B. Statement that explains how the main points prove your thesis and accomplish your speech goal.

 C. Closing Statement.

The outline for the persuasive speech or any other kind of speech will differ somewhat from this basic outline to reflect the speech's general goals. However, the introductions and conclusions are standard across all speech formats. It is always important to pull the audience in at the beginning, dazzle them with timely and relevant arguments in the middle, and conclude strongly with a flurry of important ideas to remember.

In a sense, outlining is a language. It has rules and standard formats that must be followed for it to be understood. To understand this "language," we must know the differences between main points, subpoints, and sub-subpoints.

- **Main points** are the major points that you are making through your speech.
- **Subpoints** contain relevant and pertinent information to support your main points. They are facts, statistics, and other supporting evidence.
- **Sub-subpoints** clarify the subpoints if necessary. Stories and examples make great sub-subpoints.

Every formal outline needs to follow this format. This format is provided in the **Appendix**. Each of these points has a standard format that must be adhered to in an outline.

After completing Step 8, the speech is ready to practice and present. Chapter 17 walks you through the steps necessary to ensure that your delivery is as compelling as the structure of your speech. The last thing you want to do is relax after outlining your speech and not practice your speech. You need to get up there with confidence and seize the opportunity to create a strong Speaker Card. This card will become your best friend in years to come.

Chapter Summary

- **The first step in preparing a speech is to select a topic** that is both interesting to you and potentially to your audience. Explore what excites you, and figure out how to pull the audience into your ideas so they share your excitement.
- **The second step is to determine your goal.** What do you want your speech to accomplish? What response do you want from the audience? When they are finished speaking, successful speakers want a specific reaction from the audience to learn how they felt about the speech. The clearer your speaking goal, the more likely it is that you'll see the desired reaction.
- **Step three involves selecting the talk cards** you believe will most impact your audience. You will be surprised at how many talk cards you hold and can play well. The goal of this book is to help you further develop the cards you currently hold, and create new ones that will be important for you personally and professionally.
- **Steps four, five, and six are essential in creating the main arguments** or talking points you need to be effective. Strong speeches are built on strong research. The audience will be looking for convincing facts. Your thesis statement will evolve from your research and careful thinking about the topic. From there you will be able to build strong ideas and arguments supporting your thesis statement.

- **In Step 7 you organize your speech, and in Step 8 you outline it.** Organizing means putting all the pieces together so you know what your message will be for your audience and what cards you must play to make the ideas compelling. That readies you to outline your speech and create the final product ready to present.

Lessons Learned

You are now equipped to prepare an excellent speech. After reading the next chapter, you'll be ready to deliver your speech. Here are some lessons learned to help you excel at preparing a speech.

- **Giving a speech is a golden opportunity** for you to develop an important personal and professional skill that will serve you well throughout your career and in personal pursuits. Seize the opportunity and have some fun with the experience!
- **We have a better chance of performing well** when we get out of our comfort zone and take some risks. Giving a class speech grants you the freedom to try something interesting and fun. Give a speech that moves out of your comfort zone and present some ideas that really interest you. Remember, you'll be listening to your own speech when you present it, so do something creative that will even impress you!
- **Successful risk-taking is always built on a solid foundation.** Preparation is essential in giving a great speech. We want the audience to be impressed with us and with our ideas. They will be impressed if we're prepared with solid facts, ideas, and an effective organization. Remember, the audience needs to be pulled in, challenged with convincing arguments, and given a path to adoption. That will happen if you're prepared!
- **Visualize yourself giving the speech and impacting the audience.** Many people experience a fair amount of anxiety when they present a speech. We talk about reducing anxiety in the next chapter, but reducing anxiety begins with visualizing yourself in front of an audience speaking confidently and successfully. Remember, everyone else faces the same challenge you do. By the end of this course you will be on the road to becoming a successful public speaker!

Reference

Micciche, T., Pryor, B., & Butler, J. (2000). A test of Monroe's Motivated Sequence for its effects on ratings of message organization and attitude change. *Psychological Reports, 86,* 1135–1138.

© 2012 by Pojoslaw. Used under license of Shutterstock, Inc.

Delivering the Speech

♣ Introduction

Delivering a speech from a card talk perspective means focusing not only on the verbal elements of the card, but the auditory and visual elements as well. In other words, a talk card not only includes what you say, but the whole picture of how you say it. The purpose of this section is to give you some tools for delivering your speech most effectively. As you develop these tools or skills you will find you are less nervous and that your speeches will flow better. To illustrate the importance of delivering a speech effectively, consider these two examples.

Prime Minister's Questions Game. One of the most skillful people at delivering speeches was England's former Prime Minister Margaret Thatcher. She was prime minister (equivalent to the American president) from 1979–1990. Thatcher was as much known for her intense delivery as she was for her powerful words.

Her nickname was Iron Lady because she never wavered from her conservative principles. See one of her most famous speeches at www.youtube.com/watch?v=okHGCz6xxiw. The occasion for her speech was the House of Parliament session called Prime Minister's Questions in which any member of Parliament can question the prime minister. These are generally confrontational events and meant more as political theater than as a serious exchange of ideas. Notice Thatcher's powerful and animated delivery style.

Persuasive Speech Game. Take a look at this student speech at www.youtube.com/watch?v=-1gVjWtwVrU. The speech does a great job of laying out persuasive arguments seeking support for the proposal to raise the teen driving age. Notice several features of her delivery. She does an incredible job of playing different cards and varying her delivery strategies to support her arguments. Her voice, appearance, body movements, and gestures are excellent at keeping the audience involved in her speech.

CHAPTER Seventeen

Speech Delivery from a Card Talk Perspective. Before we break down the elements of effective delivery, let's step back and reflect on how talk cards impact speech delivery decisions. Recall from the first chapter that card play is comprehensive. Every card talk play includes visual, verbal, and vocal elements. For example, a speaker can enhance friendliness by smiling and showing a pleasant face. More informality is communicated with pronounced body movements, such as walking around the room and making bigger gestures.

A speaker can intensify power, as Mrs. Thatcher did in her speech, by raising her voice, pointing and staring at the other person. The student who gave the persuasive speech on teen driving stayed in one place, had only a few gestures, and appeared to have a more formal style.

The point is that the goal of any **delivery strategy** *is to enhance and clarify a card's style.* Notice that at the beginning of her persuasive speech the student told a personal story about how a relative was permanently injured in a car crash. She was playing her Family Victim Card as an introductory attention-getter. She wanted to communicate a serious, formal, and powerful style with this card to get her point across. She did that by lowering her voice, having a serious facial expression, and intense eye contact. She wanted her audience to play their Sympathy Cards to both pay attention and be open to her persuasive recommendations.

Whatever delivery choices you make should *always* follow your card play strategy. The question is, How can you adjust each of the delivery elements to enhance your card style effectively? Let's review each of these elements and see how they work to express card style.

♣ Visual Card Style Elements

Physical Appearance. Because every delivery decision depends on card choices, the first place to look for guiding your personal appearance choices is the cards you plan to play in your speech. If you want to play more serious, formal cards like the Family Victim Card just mentioned, then your dress should match that formal style. In the student's speech, notice that she was formally dressed, looking like a business professional.

A more informal, casual dress style would be appropriate with a less serious topic. For example, when playing a Comic Card or a Friend Card throughout the speech, the audience would expect an informal appearance.

More informal dress and hair styles are often fun, and can be part of a clever attention-getter. I recall speeches in which students wore costumes with lots of jewelry to play an Actor Card. I have seen Superman, Spiderman, farmers, football players, and many other costumes. As a general principle, speakers should dress a little more formally than the audience when playing standard, speech-related talk cards, like an Expert Card. For men that's probably a business casual look, which means wearing a shirt with a collar. For women, that might include wearing a blouse and slacks or a skirt. Dressing up a bit shows respect for an audience and enhances the speaker's credibility.

Remember, your appearance is part of your card's style. Does it help and support the card you are trying to play, or does it conflict with your card?

A♥

A♠

The key is not to compromise credibility with inappropriate dress.

Your appearance is the first thing an audience sees, and they use it to judge your credibility. The key is to not compromise credibility with inappropriate dress.

Inappropriate dress is anything that interferes with the card the speaker is playing. Sometimes students might show too much skin or too many undergarments when they want to play an Expert Card in a formal speech. These kinds of decisions not only compromise the student's credibility, but they conflict with the student's card talk strategy. For example, can you imagine Kirk Cousins coming to his luncheon speech (chapter 15) in a t-shirt and shorts with a hat on backward and a pierced lip? Cousins wanted to play a Student-Athlete Leader Card for most of his speech, so he needed to look like one. The point is, before you give your speech, give some thought to your dress. Does it help or hurt your card talk strategy?

Facial Expressions. After your dress and physical appearance, the audience focuses on your facial expressions. They start by looking at your eyes. Then they look at the rest of your facial movements, particularly your smile and other features that communicate emotion. Let's focus first on eye movement because most speakers find this issue challenging. With just about every card a speaker plays, it is important to maintain eye contact with the audience. The audience expects you to look at them. Often speakers complain of an uninterested audience when it was actually the speaker who did not keep the audience involved by looking at them, one audience member at a time.

A ♥ *With just about every card a speaker plays, it is important to maintain eye contact with the audience.* ♠ *A*

The goal with eye contact is to look at one person at a time. Start your speech by picking someone in the class you know and looking at them for three or four seconds. Then go to the next person for a few more seconds. Sometimes it is even fun to walk toward and look directly at an individual who is not paying attention. When you make eye contact with an individual, try to maintain it for at *least three seconds*. This seems as if it would be an easy thing to do. However, during a presentation three seconds can seem like three minutes.

An easy way to accomplish this is to maintain eye contact with someone through an entire sentence that you speak. You can look up or down occasionally in your speech. But *never* spend all your time looking at the back of the room, scanning over their heads and otherwise not looking directly at anyone.

After eye contact, audiences look at facial expressions. They want to guess how you feel, and whether you're interested in connecting with them. They are looking for hints about the cards you are playing so they know which cards to play themselves. Generally, audiences focus on whether a speaker is smiling.

When beginning a presentation, the best way to warm up your audience is to smile at them. This tells your audience that you are a nice person and you are happy to be there. Studies also show that the more people smile, the more attractive they are perceived to be. Late-night TV show host David Letterman **smiles a lot**, as do all successful speakers. Remember, when you play your card, use a style that increases friendliness and some informality. Smiling goes a long way toward this goal.

Helga Esteb / Shutterstock.com

Gestures and Body Movement. Audiences prefer to see natural body movements in most speaking situations. That means the speaker's posture is relaxed and at ease. When some people are nervous, they intensify their actions by speaking rapidly and using big arm and hand gestures. Others cope with nervousness by grabbing the podium or desk and moving quickly through the speech. The idea is to control body movements and look natural to make the audience feel at ease, so they reciprocate your card talk style.

There are two kinds of body movements—**object focused** and **body focused**. Body-focused movements have nothing to do with the speech. They involve personal touching and grooming, like playing with hair, touching the nose, or wringing one's hands. These **body-focused movements** indicate nervousness. Have you ever seen anyone twirl his or her hair or engage in face touching while speaking? Those personal habits distract from the speech and show a lack of personal control.

On other hand, **object-focused movements** are deliberate gestures tied to the speech. Raising the hand to make a point or turning the head to emphasize a key issue make the speech more visually interesting. Notice that in the speeches described at the beginning of this chapter both speakers used only object-focused movements. They emphasized key points in the speech without randomly touching their hair or their faces.

You can consider blocking, or planning out your object-focused gestures at key points in the speech. When you reach an important point, you might want to raise your hand or move a few steps to the side and shift your eye contact to the other side of the room. When these gestures are coordinated, they keep the audience focused on your topic. That's one of the reasons why changing cards is effective. Shifting cards allows the speaker to also shift body movements and use different kinds of eye contact, facial expressions, and gestures to connect with the audience. Watch any of the late-night comedians like Jay Leno or Jimmy Fallon. They are good at deliberately shifting body movements to emphasize points in their comedy routines.

Learn to use your natural body movements to your advantage. Begin by identifying the body-focused movement habits that other speakers display. Count how many times they touch their faces or hair. These movements generally distract an audience. For example, if you gave your entire speech leaning on your right leg with your left hip thrown out, your audience would focus on your stance and wonder how long you could hold it without falling over. The best strategy for controlling body-focused movements is to become aware of them and consciously stopping them while speaking.

Appropriate body movements **make the speaker seem comfortable** and conversational, yet more formal than playing a Friend Card. It is a combination of an Expert Card and a Friend Card. This is a difficult mixture to get right. Think about David Letterman. He gives the audience the appearance that he is giving a formal presentation (by standing up straight) but does so in a comfortable, welcoming fashion. It almost sounds like he's talking to a friend at a

A♥ Effective speakers walk around a bit; they don't stand in one place. A♥

party. He walks around and sometimes even runs (this would not work for your speech, however), but again, not through his entire presentation. Let your personality show by playing multiple cards during your speech because that will be engaging to the audience.

Effective speakers walk around a bit; they don't stand in one place. Experiment with taking a few steps to either side or front to back. But don't pace the floor back and forth; that is distracting. If you're unsure what to do, just take a few steps and stop. The goal is to move around comfortably and naturally, and your audience will respond. During your speech it is important that you not stand in the back of the room, far away from your audience. Try also to avoid standing too close to one particular person. Stand toward the middle of the area reserved for speakers, and then move around naturally.

Finally, a word about posture. Many people slouch. They sort of hunch over and stand on one leg or put their head down. Audiences like people who stand up confidently with their shoulders back and their heads erect. Concentrate on always standing tall—it shows respect for your audience.

To review, here are the five movement elements that you must think about as you present your speech:

© 2012 by koh sze kiat. Used under license of Shutterstock, Inc.

1. **Physical Appearance:** Consistent with your card and not distracting
2. **Facial Expressions:** Smiling, friendly, and engaging
3. **Hand Gestures:** Object-focused and emphasizing key points
4. **Body Movement:** Natural and unforced
5. **Posture:** Upright and tall

Vocal Card Style Elements

Rate and Volume. The auditory component of your speaking voice gives the audience a clear understanding of the card you're playing. For most people their Friend Card has a distinct auditory style, which tends to be faster and louder than when playing a more formal card, like an Expert Card. Many students make the mistake of trying to play an Expert Card using a Friend Card style. They might talk too fast, laugh out loud frequently, and increase their volume, which discredits the importance of their content. An Expert Card requires a formal style with a slower rate of speech, less laughter, and a normal (but not soft) volume.

Concentrate on always standing tall—it shows respect for your audience.

Let's focus specifically on **speech rate** because people often think they are speaking slowly when in fact they are speaking rapidly. Look at the speech rate for the woman giving the persuasive speech referenced at the beginning of this chapter. She slowed down her speech to make a fairly dramatic style. She paused frequently to make her points. She talked about a serious topic and she wanted her audience to be serious. The speaker was playing her Expert Card, but showing some Family Victim Card, as well.

If she had spoken quickly, the audience would have been confused about the seriousness of her message and what card they should play in response. Remember, she wanted them to play their Sympathy Cards and pay attention to her message and support her cause.

It is common for individuals to speak much faster when they give their speech in class than when they practice it. The best way to control the rate at which you speak is to remind yourself: *Slow down!* Force yourself to speak more slowly than feels natural. Speaking at a **slower, natural pace** is important because it allows your audience to better understand you. It shows more of your Speaker Card than Friend Card, which typically displays a faster rate.

Volume is another speech element that many students have difficulty monitoring. If your audience cannot hear you, they cannot understand you. Many students use a soft voice when giving formal presentations. **Speak more loudly** than in a normal class presentation. For many people this is a major hurdle because they naturally do not speak loudly in a crowd, unless they are playing a Friend Card with a group of friends. A great way to learn to speak louder is to go to the room where you will give your speech and practice there. Have a friend sit in the back of the room to see if your volume is good.

For softer speakers it is even more important that you *do not look at your note cards* a lot during your speech. When your audience cannot understand you, they look at your mouth to try to lip read. If they cannot see you forming the words, they remain confused and may tune you out. Therefore, it is beneficial to have parts of the speech memorized or well-rehearsed so you can maintain good eye contact with your audience.

Pitch and Articulation. Two additional elements that students often have difficulty controlling are pitch and articulation. **Pitch** is how high or low a voice sounds; **articulation** deals with how clearly words are stated. If students use their default Friend Card for every speaking occasion, they will probably end up with a high-pitched, slurred speaking style. Friend Card speech in a crowd talking about fun topics is typically spoken at a higher pitch with some laughter. When you are playing an Expert Card, your audience expects a lower pitch that sounds authoritative. Since first impressions matter in the audience's judgment of a speaker's credibility, it's important to play an Expert or Leader Card with a lower-pitched voice.

An audience expects a clear, articulate style. Articulation quality often depends on speech pace. Friend Card speech that is spoken faster leads speakers to slur their speech. Words run together in friend-speak, so it's often not clear to outsiders what friends are saying to one another.

Remember, when playing an Expert Card, the audience wants to hear every word. They also expect words to be pronounced using a Standard English style. That means not dropping letters at the end of words, for example. I recall a friend who always dropped the "g" at the end of words ending in -ing. Goin' vs. going was common for him. It was his way of playing a Friend Card, but it hampered his perceived credibility when giving a formal presentation.

Fluency. How smooth is your speech? Do you ever insert "um" when giving a presentation? Do you use the word "like" every few words? Audiences notice disfluencies, or unnecessary words, inserted in speech. I had a high school teacher who inserted "what" every third or fourth word in his lectures. We counted the number of times he would say it and would guess ahead of time how many times he would say it. Smooth speech enhances the speaker's credibility. *It is a must* in playing an Expert Card. Students insert the word "like"

A♥
Remember, when playing an Expert Card, the audience wants to hear every word.

every third or fourth sentence when playing a Friend Card because, for some, that's how their friends talk. They want to fit in. Audiences want smoother speech. Do your best to identify any disfluencies an audience might hear in your talk and work to eliminate them.

Ethnic accents are another fluency issue. Many students taking an introductory communication course come from places in which English is a second or even third language. The student from Somalia I mentioned early in this book grew up learning Somali and Arabic. Later he learned Swahili when he lived in Kenya. After moving to the United States he had to learn English quickly. He has a bit of an accent, but it's not distracting. That's the key issue. Is the accent so distracting that it makes your speech difficult to understand?

© 2012 by William Perugini. Used under license of Shutterstock, Inc.

If you believe you have an accent that might interfere with the audience's ability to understand your speech, here are some tips to make you more understandable:

- **Speak slowly.** This is usually the biggest problem with nonnative English speakers. They play a Friend Card, speak quickly, and think the audience can understand what they're saying. Sometimes the English-speaking audience can only pick up every third or fourth word. Slow down to be understood.
- **Articulate each word.** Try not to run your words together. State each one. Sometimes that sounds too formal and unnatural. But if you take your time and pronounce each word, your audience will appreciate it.
- **Use short sentences.** Audiences have an easier time understanding someone's speech when that person uses short sentences, which are generally easier to listen to and follow. In other words, make it easy for people to understand your speech.
- **Avoid big words that are difficult to pronounce.** If you have trouble pronouncing some words, don't use them! Find other words that are easier for you to say.

Verbal Card Style Elements

In addition to visual and vocal elements of a speech, the verbal element deals with the issue of word selection. Certain cards require certain words. For example, a Friend Card often requires slang, or customized words, that only a few close pals might understand. Let's explore some word use issues and list some strategies for making effective word choices.

Slang and Profanity. Slang, or customized words for small groups, might be acceptable when playing a Friend Card at the beginning of a speech. Sometimes if it's a slang word that few people have heard, then it is appropriate to explain it. The word might even be part of the speech and be interesting for the audience. Be careful when you use slang or nonstandard English phrases of any kind. If they are an important part of the speech, they should be explained.

Avoid profanity during a student speech. It is distracting to your audience at minimum and offensive to many people. It can also compromise your credibility with the audience. When people play Friend Cards, they might use profanity. Or their

growing-up culture might have encouraged it. However, profanity has no place in a class speech.

Grammar. If you are a native English speaker, or learned formal English in school somewhere, you must have learned proper grammar. You know how to use complete sentences and verb tense, for example. When playing an Expert Card, the audience expects you to use proper grammar. If you use a Friend Card, proper grammar might not be important because friends are informal, friendly, and casual. Formal grammar is powerful. Notice that the student playing the Persuasive Speech Game at the beginning of the chapter uses formal grammar, which is an appropriate style for your speech. It's fun and important to mix cards. Just make sure that if you use improper grammar it relevant to your message.

Big Words. Using big words can be distracting to an audience if they don't understand them. If the speaker throws out big words only to enhance his or her Expert Card, the tactic may backfire. The audience may conclude the speaker is trying to show off rather than genuinely communicate. Stay clear of big words just to impress an audience. Use them if you need to, but explain them.

High-Context Language. As we learned in chapter 2, high-context language is used by individuals of the same group or culture to communicate in a short-handed, abbreviated fashion. It's insider talk that plays a specific card as a means of showing respect for the group. For example, you might play your Sports Fan Card to emphasize a point in a speech and make a reference to an American football term like "nickel defense." If the audience consists of typical college students, it is fairly unlikely they would understand such a technical term because they are probably only casual fans and not football experts. On the other hand, if you were talking to football experts, using that term would be fine. By using insider terms to non-insiders, you risk alienating the audience quickly.

Why would the audience feel alienated? Remember, card play is reciprocal. If you play an Insider Card, and the audience doesn't feel like they are insiders, then you're asking them to play an Outsider Card, which means they're not welcome and don't belong. That quickly turns off an audience. The strategy is to use low-context language in which everything the audience needs to know to understand your speech is in the speech itself. That way, everyone plays Insider Cards and feels welcome. The lesson here is to make sure everyone in your audience can understand all your terms and references!

High Power-Distance Language. Recall from chapter 2 that power-distance is all about status. Cultures having high power-distance look down on people who are not members of their social class or organization. A speaker never wants to play an Expert Card with a superior style to an audience and make them play their Listener Cards with a feeling of inadequacy. I once saw a student speaker scold an audience for not knowing something that he knew. He talked down to them. Speakers should always play their talk cards with equality of style. The speaker is neither better than nor worse than any audience member. Everyone is equal and ready to listen and exchange ideas.

Linguistic Forms. It is useful for speakers to vary the linguistic forms of their speeches. That means asking questions, making statements, stating opinions, and using any other form of speech that seems useful. Questions are a powerful tool to encourage the audience to think about something. Sometimes the speaker wants an answer to the question and sometimes the question is rhetorical, or asked simply to make a point. The answer to a rhetorical question is obvious and the speaker assumes everyone agrees. Incorporate several questions into your speech. Get your audience involved. Use the answers to make a point on some other issue later in your speech.

Switching to a question is a good way to switch cards. I have seen students use a Comic Card at the beginning of a speech, then ask a question at the end of the routine, and turn the answer into a point while playing an Expert Card. It's a good transition strategy.

Presentation Aids

At this point you have enough information to plan how the visual, vocal, and verbal elements of your speech should come together. You have good tips on how to form your talk cards for each of these three important components. Now let's turn to strategies for employing presentation aids in your speech. The main question you need to answer is whether the aid will help you play your talk cards as planned. Let's go through each of the aids and list ways to use them effectively.

Questions are a powerful tool to encourage the audience to think about something. Incorporate several questions into your speech.

Notecards. You cannot read your speech in class. *It is best to prepare* **notecards** *and deliver your speech using these cards.* A paper outline is permitted, but cards are better because they make it easier to give your speech. If you get nervous in front of your audience and start to shake, the paper outline will also shake and your audience can easily detect that you're nervous. Then they will pay attention to how much your paper is shaking rather than what you're saying.

But how should you write out notecards? Basically you want to put your outline on your notecards, but with more detail. It is important when writing out notecards to:

- Put all the important information on your notecards;
- Don't put too much on each card that might cause you to read them; and
- Include transitions on your notecards.

When creating your notecards you can highlight areas of your speech where you want to put a special emphasis. You can also draw smiley faces or something else to remind you to smile and look at your audience during your speech. Some people have even written positive thoughts in the margins of the cards to tell themselves that they will survive the speech.

Don't put whole sentences on the cards because this causes you to read them rather than to use the cards as a guide. *Your speech should not be read to your audience.* That is boring because a written speech is far too formal. Talk to us; don't read to us!

Timing. **Timing**, or pacing, yourself is important so that you finish within the required time. Often individuals speak faster when presenting a speech, so when you practice, make your *practice speech* go as long as the maximum time limit. This ensures that your *actual delivered* speech will not exceed the maximum time, and you can be reasonably certain that you will reach the minimum time requirement. Generally students who do not practice give speeches that are either too short or too long. Make sure that if you have five minutes to speak that you use nearly all of that time to connect with the audience.

Visual Aids. When a student has an interesting example to show the class or needs to make a technical point, a visual aid is useful. Notice the visual aids the student uses in playing the Persuasive Speech Game earlier in this chapter. She provides an outline of what she's going to talk about and then uses her visual aids for several other purposes as well. When used properly, **visual aids** keep the audience's attention, while helping them remember what you talked about.

The key in using visual aids is not to distract the audience. Do you remember the example of the flying squirrel in the informative speech in chapter 15? The squirrel was a visual aid. I'll bet that every student who heard that speech will remember it for a long time. Sometimes a visual aid can be too extreme. If the student playing the Persuasive Speech Game had used a graphic picture or video of a student dying in a car crash, it would have horrified many students and obscured her message. Find a few aids that make your speech visually memorable, but avoid extremes.

The best strategy is to use visual aids to make points that enhance the message. Too many aids pull the audience's attention away from the speaker and onto the visual aids themselves. They become distracting and confuse the audience. Too few aids force the audience to learn only by listening to you. Audiences retain visual information better than verbal information. Give them something interesting to look at that effectively supports your talk cards.

PowerPoint Presentations. Electronic aids like a Power-Point (PP) presentation can make a speech topic come to life for an audience. For example, one student did a speech on motorcycles and brought in a couple PP slides to highlight his speech. You might do the same for your topic because slides can make it more interesting. PP has many animation opportunities. When the slides animate, like showing the motorcycle moving, it adds interest to your speech.

The two most important issues to remember when using PP slides, or any visual aids for that matter, are: (1) they must be **clear** and **uncluttered** and (2) they need to be **practiced** before using them. If PP slides contain too much information or require the audience to read them, the audience is not going to pay attention to the speaker. The best use of PP slides is to show pictures or graphs that make simple, yet powerful points. If you could select one PP slide for your speech, what would it be and why would you use it?

Whenever you use visual aids or PP slides of any type, you must practice your speech using them. Are you introducing them appropriately? Are you focusing the audience's attention on the slide for the right amount of time? Do you pull off the slide or switch slides at the right time? Run through your speech a few times with the slides to ensure they work and have the effect you desire. Finally, what happens if the technology does not work? Do you have a backup plan?

> The key in using visual aids is not to distract the audience.

© 2012 by makspogonii. Used under license of Shutterstock, Inc.

Presentation Exercise

Take a look at this video (www.youtube.com/watch?v=KYtm8uEo5vU) and identify what the speaker does well in his speech and not so well in the areas of the visual, vocal, verbal, and presentation aids.

Name three or four cards this person played during his speech:

VISUAL CARD STYLE ELEMENTS

1. Was his dress appropriate for his cards? Why or why not?

2. Did he maintain effective eye contact? Give an example.

3. Comment on his gestures and body movement. Were they mostly object focused to emphasize key points? Give an example.

4. Were his body movements natural and engaging for the audience?

VOCAL CARD STYLE ELEMENTS

1. Comment on his speech rate—was he talking at a natural and understandable rate? Give an example.

2. Comment on his pitch and articulation. Was he understandable and not distracting? Give an example.

3. Did he use any disfluencies? Give an example.

4. Were his sentences short and did they sound conversational?

VERBAL CARD STYLE ELEMENTS

1. Comment on his use of slang and profanity. Did anything stick out to you?

2. Was his grammar consistent with his card talk strategy? Give an example.

3. Did he use sufficiently low-context language? Were there any high-context references? If so, give an example.

4. Did he ask questions and vary his linguistic form? Give an example.

PRESENTATION AIDS

1. Comment on his presentation aids. Were they consistent with his card talk strategy?

2. Comment on how well he used his notecards.

3. Comment on overall delivery quality of the speech.

♣ Overcome Your Fear of Public Speaking

Fear of public speaking often prevents speakers from selecting an engaging style to connect with the audience. Most speakers feel nervous about speaking before a group, even speakers with considerable experience. A few people believe the fear gives them a positive edge!

Communication apprehension comes in many forms and degrees of severity. A little nervousness is common and natural. If you're feeling nervous, acknowledge it to yourself, and not the audience. Avoid nervousness by preparing carefully for your speech. **Practice** is the best way to reduce speech anxiety.

It may seem uncomfortable and silly at first, but practicing a speech in front of the mirror is beneficial. Try this first, and then practice in front of friends. Make sure they give you **constructive feedback**. Practice in the room where you will give your speech, if possible. Many classrooms are open early in the morning and in the evenings. Use the classroom when it is free so you can close the door and practice your speech undisturbed.

Look for **encouraging people** in your audience. You may have some idea before you give your speech which people have been good audience members for others. If you don't know, look around just before you begin and make eye contact with a couple of people. Doing so will make you more comfortable and it will encourage these individuals to listen to your speech.

Ethics in public speaking requires that the speaker respect his or her topic and audience and always act in their best interests.

Ethics

Finally, I want to include a word about ethics. *Speakers should speak with integrity.* Whether public speakers actively inform, persuade, or entertain their audiences, they should act ethically. Ethics in public speaking requires that the speaker *respect his or her topic and audience and always act in their best interests.* No speaker should ever tell an audience or try to convince them to do something that is inappropriate or potentially not in their best interests. A speaker should never be coercive or bullying.

Sometimes speakers tell an audience something harmful without knowing it. This can happen if the speaker is poorly informed about a topic. Perhaps the speaker reads something from an unreliable source and reports it to the audience as fact. The audience will receive an incomplete picture and may try something they should not.

To prevent this kind of speaking problem, be well prepared and informed. Do the best job you can to give your audience the complete picture so they can make an informed choice. Be honest when presenting information and use reasonable evidence and valid reasoning. Conscientious public speakers ask themselves, "Will my audience receive any benefit from my speech?" and "Does my audience know how to make an informed choice about my topic/information?"

Successful public speakers are careful not to take credit for words and ideas that are not their own.

In many cases speakers feel a need to present unpleasant information to an audience because there are many unpleasant but important things going on in the world. As long as the speaker presents a reasonable perspective on these issues, then he or she is acting ethically. The speaker's job is not necessarily to be upbeat all the time. Often unpleasant cards must be played, but the cards should never be used to misdirect audiences or place them in an ethical dilemma or in a potentially abusive situation. Speakers should be prepared to answer any questions or address any concerns that they might raise by their speaking.

Lastly, ethical public speakers, like ethical writers, avoid plagiarism. Successful public speakers are careful not to take credit for words and ideas that are not their own; they tell their audience where they got their information and who inspired their words. Never copy anything word for word from a book, movie, or other source unless it's a quote that you specifically identify. Remember, ethics is credibility, and that's vital for success. It is always important as a speaker—as in life—to do the right thing and act in others' best interests!

Chapter Summary

- **Decide what cards you want to play in the speech.** That determines what cards you want the audience to play as they're listening. From those perspectives, craft the delivery strategy.
- **First major edit of your speech.** Once you have your speech drafted in either outline form or on notecards, practice the speech (perhaps on video), review it, then edit it. See how it sounds and looks by practicing *out loud*.
- **Second major edit of your speech.** Get critical feedback from someone else. Try to get as many people as possible to evaluate your speech. Have the person hearing your speech ask questions about it. Practice defending your ideas in the speech. Edit the speech based on the feedback you receive.
- **Plan appropriate visual aids.** Visual aids should help the flow of your speech and enable the audience to understand it better. They should not distract from or overwhelm the speech content. Also plan how you will handle visual aids; then make sure you practice using them. Check to ensure that the speech venue has all the necessary equipment for your speech.
- **Focus on your appearance.** What are you going to wear? Will your outfit be appropriate for the cards you want to play?
- **Plan gestures and where to stand and move strategically** to emphasize parts of your speech. An example of strategic movement would be to present the introduction in the front center of the room, move to the left side of the front of the room for the first main point, cross to the right side of the room for the second main point, return to the center for the third main point, step forward for the conclusion. Write your nonverbal plan on your speech notes as if you were blocking a drama or play.
- **Practice to become familiar with the wording of your speech.** Knowing your speech well reduces fillers and improves the flow of the presentation. Circle words you wish to emphasize and the words or phrases on which you want the audience to focus. Indicate on your notecards where you will pause in your speech to emphasize those words or phrases.

- **Time each section and the entire speech.** If you are pressed for time, you will know how long each section takes and be able to edit yourself as you speak. Keep in mind that you're likely to speak faster before a real audience. So include extra information or examples in your speech notes that can be added if you have extra speaking time. Indicate in your notes what information can be omitted if you are running out of time. Sometimes it helps to have two similar versions of the speech: short and long versions to be selected as time permits. Write **SLOW DOWN** on your notecards as a reminder if you think it will help.
- **Bring some speaking tools with you.** Bring several copies of your speech (located in different places) so if you forget the copy on your desk, you have a second copy in your backpack, on a thumb drive, and so forth. Make sure the instructor has time-cards to display so you know how much time you have remaining. Bring your visual aids and handouts ("the dog ate it" does not work in the real world), the technology you need for the venue, and water to drink. Carry a good-luck charm if you need it!
- **Nonverbal communication consists of issues** such as body movement, accents and voice styles, space use, and physical appearance. The key is to use nonverbal behaviors that *support your message* and don't distract from it. Body-focused gestures, like flicking your hair or touching your face, distract from your message. Object-focused nonverbals emphasize your message points and are useful. The key is to control your nonverbals so they add to your speech, not detract from it.

Lessons Learned

This chapter brings the entire Card Talk concept to its conclusion in delivering a speech, which is important for your future business and personal success. Here are some tips for successful speech delivery.

- **Plan the visual, vocal, and verbal elements of your speech.** Words are not enough. Delivery matters. The audience wants to see your style because they use it to determine whether they're interested in paying attention and listening to the message.
- **Show conviction.** Show that you're interested in the topic and really want to connect with the audience. It's not something you can fake. If the audience senses that you're only going through the motions, they will tune out.
- **The details matter in a speech.** This chapter went into a great deal of detail about the visual, vocal, and verbal elements of the speech. It's a lot to remember, but you have notecards and can use them to remember everything that's important.
- **Finally, and most importantly, *practice!*** Get in the room, record your speech, and get some feedback from your friends. They are going to catch lots of things that would otherwise get by you. All this preparation lets you go into your presentation feeling prepared, confident, and ready to make an impact! Good luck!

Appendix

♣ Assignment Guidelines

To ensure that your assignments throughout the semester follow the correct guidelines for content and format, make sure it agrees with the following:

Text/Page Formatting Requirements

1. Typed
2. 12-point font
3. Discernable font (e.g., Times New Roman)
4. Double-spaced lines
5. 1" margin
6. Black font
7. Printed on white, or slightly off-white, paper

Content & Structure Requirements

1. Cover page includes name, PID, section, Teaching Assistant's name, Section Leader's name, due date, title of assignment, and title of speech (if necessary)
2. Complete sentences are used for both essay and outline formats
3. Format (essay or outline) matches the assignment requirements; more specifically:
   A. Essay format assignments include multiple paragraphs and appropriate style
   B. Outline format assignments should not resemble an essay, and also:
      i. Follow a cohesive structure (roman numerals, then capital letters, then numbers, then lowercase letters)
      ii. Include the talk card analysis and audience analysis sections before the actual speech text of the outline (see below)
4. Meets page length requirement
5. Includes appropriate number of citations, both in an APA format references page and in-text citations

Talk Card Analysis Questions (Outline format assignments only)

Include talk card analysis questions for outline format assignments, formatted as follows:

I. **Talk Card Analysis**
   A. **Talk Card:** What talk card(s) do you plan on using during your speech? Why?
   B. **Content:** Generally describe the content of your talk card(s) that you plan on using during your speech.
   C. **Style:** In terms of liking, formality, and power, describe the style choices relevant to the choices of talk card(s) you made.
   D. **Audience:** What reciprocal talk card(s) are you asking your audience to play? Why? How do you think they will respond?

Audience Analysis Questions (Outline format assignments only)

Include audience analysis questions for outline format assignments, formatted as follows:

II. **Audience Analysis**
   A. **Demographics:** Describe the demographic characteristics of your audience, for example, age, sex, ethnic background, group memberships, and others. How will your audience's demographics influence your speech?
   B. **Psychographics:** Describe the biases, knowledge level, mood, attitude, needs, beliefs, goals, or wants of your audience. How will these factors affect your speech?

Paper Requirements

1. All pages are stapled together, with your cover page first, then your assignment, and lastly your grading rubric.

Sample Cover Page

Title of Speech Goes Here

William A. Donohue

A12345678

COM 100 Sec. 004

14 March 2013

TA: Erica Smith

SL: James Walker

♣ Talk Card Analysis: Part One
Essay Format Assignment

Purpose of Assignment

This assignment is the first half of a two-part assignment you will be completing this semester. Analyses of Talk Cards will help you to think more strategically about what specific strategy speakers use when giving different types of speeches. It will also help you when contemplating different ideas for speeches you may give in your professional careers by increasing your understanding of how different Talk Cards can have different impacts on audience members.

Before giving a keynote speech, skilled speakers think critically about *how* they are going to speak—not just what they are going to say within the body, or the actual wording, of their speech. For example, when the President of the United States addresses the nation, he has many different Talk Cards in his Card Deck that he can choose to play. President Obama is very skilled at combining his President Card, Leader Card, Friend Card, and sometimes a Comedian Card to effectively present his thoughts and ideas to his audience while also keeping them interested. On the other hand, you may find that your boss at work plays very different Talk Cards from those listed above. He or she will most likely spend time playing a Boss Card, but also throw in a Teacher Card or possibly a Man/Woman Card, depending on the situation.

Notice how as the goals of the persons mentioned above change, and the Talk Cards that they play also change. While the President's goals are to lead the nation and demonstrate a trustworthy and likeable personality, your boss' goals are to motivate (or possibly force) you to complete a task and get on with the day's work. When completing this assignment, think to yourself, what are the speaker's goals and how are they using the topics of their Talk Cards to accomplish these goals?

With this assignment, you will dissect a popular speech, identify what Talk Card the speaker used, and explain why that Talk Card was effective (or why it was not). For the most encompassing analysis, you should think from both the perspective of the speaker and an audience member. What was the speaker trying to accomplish that day and how was he or she motivating the audience to pursue that goal?

Directions

Read or listen to **Dr. Martin Luther King Jr.'s "I Have A Dream"** speech. Focus on *how* he speaks and his strategy instead of thinking solely about what he is saying. The speech can be easily found in text at your local library or by searching online. While reading or listening to the speech, consider the following:

Talk Card

- What **Talk Card** did Dr. Martin Luther King Jr. use when he gave his "I Have A Dream" speech?
- Is Dr. King using multiple Talk Cards during his speech? If so, why do you think he chose to do so?
- What other Talk Cards could Dr. King have played? Do you think this was a smart move, or should he have used one of the other Talk Cards you just listed? Why or why not? **How would changing the Talk Card also change the overall message?**
- What is the **style** of Dr. King's speech in terms of liking, formality, and power?

Speech Goals

- What was the **goal** of Dr. King's speech? What were the goals of the audience members who came to hear him speak? Did they have the same goals?
- Did Dr. King's Talk Card effectively supplement the goal he wished to accomplish?

Audience Analysis

- What **reciprocal** Talk Card was Dr. King trying to invoke in his audience? Think about what you learned about reciprocating Card Play in lecture. Was this effective for the goal he was trying to accomplish?
- What feelings did Dr. King invoke in his audience?
- After analyzing these facts, do you think he successfully motivated his audience? Why or why not?

Requirements

Write at least **1.5 pages** answering the above questions. This assignment should be **typed**. Handwritten assignments will not be accepted. Divide the paper into *at least* **three separate paragraphs** to answer the posed questions. The easiest way to divide this assignment into paragraphs may be to divide them based on the question categories listed above (e.g., Dr. King's Talk Card, Speech Goals, and Audience Analysis). Although it is not necessary, you may find that **quoting** specific parts of Dr. King's speech adds insight, quality, and credibility to your assignment.

♣ Grading Rubric for Talk Card Analysis: Part One
Essay Format Assignment

_____ (5)   TALK CARD questions answered appropriately

_____ (5)   SPEECH GOALS question answered appropriately

_____ (5)   AUDIENCE ANLYSIS questions answered appropriately

_____ (5)   Provides good explanations for TALK CARD responses

_____ (5)   Provides good explanations for SPEECH GOALS responses

_____ (5)   Provides good explanations for AUDIENCE ANALYSIS responses

_____ (5)   Relevant background information included from research

_____ (5)   Organization and clarity

_____ (5)   Meets mechanical requirements (typed, 1.5 pages long, etc.)

_____ (5)   Grammar (minus 1 point for every 3 errors)

_____   **Total score** (50 points)

Questions to be answered (for use by Section Leader):

Talk Card

- What **Talk Card** did Dr. Martin Luther King Jr. use when he gave his "I Have A Dream" speech?
- Is Dr. King using multiple Talk Cards during his speech? If so, why do you think he chose to do so?
- What other Talk Cards could Dr. King have played? Do you think this was a smart move, or should he have used one of the other Talk Cards you just listed? Why or why not? **How would changing the Talk Card also change the overall message?**
- What is the **style** of Dr. King's speech in terms of liking, formality, and power?

Speech Goals

- What was the **goal** of Dr. King's speech? What were the goals of the audience members who came to hear him speak? Did they have the same goals?
- Did Dr. King's Talk Card effectively supplement the goal he wished to accomplish?

Audience Analysis

- What **reciprocal** Talk Card was Dr. King trying to invoke in his audience? Think about what you learned about reciprocating Card Play in lecture. Was this effective for the goal he was trying to accomplish?
- What feelings did Dr. King invoke in his audience?
- After analyzing these facts, do you think he successfully motivated his audience? Why or why not?

♣ Talk Card Analysis: Part Two
Essay Format Assignment

Purpose of Assignment

Previously in your Talk Card Analysis: Part I assignment, you analyzed Dr. Martin Luther King Jr.'s "I Have A Dream" speech from a strategic point of view. For Part II, you will again put to work the same analysis strategies you used with Dr. King's speech, except now on a speech of your own choosing.

The speech you choose to examine can come from any perspective. For example, it can be a famous historical speech like Dr. King's, or it can be an acceptance speech for winning an award. When deciding which speech to evaluate, make sure that it is long enough to answer questions similar to those you answered in Part I.

Directions

Read or listen to the speech you chose. Focus on *how* the speaker speaks and his/her strategy instead of thinking solely about what he/she is saying. While reading or listening to the speech, consider the following:

Talk Card

- What **Talk Card** is the speaker using?
- Is the speaker using multiple Talk Cards during his speech? If so, why do you think he/she chose to do so?
- What other Talk Cards could the speaker have played? Do you think this was a smart move, or should he/she have used one of the other Talk Cards you just listed? Why or why not? **How would changing the Talk Card also change the overall message?**
- What is the **style** of the speech in terms of liking, formality, and power?

Speech Goals

- What was the **goal** of the speech? What were the goals of the audience members who came to hear the speech? Did they have the same goals?
- Did the Talk Card that the speaker used effectively supplement the goal he/she wished to accomplish?

Audience Analysis

- What **reciprocal** Talk Card was the speaker trying to invoke in his/her audience? Was this effective for the goal he/she was trying to accomplish?
- What feelings did the speaker invoke in the audience?
- After analyzing the facts, do you think the speaker successfully motivated the audience? Why or why not?

Requirements

- Write at least **1.5 pages** answering the above questions. This assignment should be **typed**. Divide the paper into *at least* **three separate paragraphs** to answer the posed questions. You may find that quoting specific parts of the speech adds insight, quality, and credibility to your assignment.

♣ Grading Rubric for Talk Card Analysis: Part Two
Essay Format Assignment

_____ (5)   TALK CARD questions answered appropriately

_____ (5)   SPEECH GOALS question answered appropriately

_____ (5)   AUDIENCE ANLYSIS questions answered appropriately

_____ (5)   Provides good explanations for TALK CARD responses

_____ (5)   Provides good explanations for SPEECH GOALS responses

_____ (5)   Provides good explanations for AUDIENCE ANALYSIS responses

_____ (5)   Relevant background information included from research

_____ (5)   Organization and clarity

_____ (5)   Meets mechanical requirements (typed, 1.5 pages long, etc.)

_____ (5)   Grammar (minus 1 point for every 3 errors)

_____   **Total score** (50 points)

Questions to be answered (for use by Section Leader):

Talk Card

- What **Talk Card** is the speaker using?
- Is the speaker using multiple Talk Cards during his speech? If so, why do you think he/she chose to do so?
- What other Talk Cards could the speaker have played? Do you think this was a smart move, or should he/she have used one of the other Talk Cards you just listed? Why or why not? **How would changing the Talk Card also change the overall message?**
- What is the **style** of the speech in terms of liking, formality, and power?

Speech Goals

- What was the **goal** of the speech? What were the goals of the audience members who came to hear the speech? Did they have the same goals?
- Did the Talk Card that the speaker used effectively supplement the goal he/she wished to accomplish?

Audience Analysis

- What **reciprocal** Talk Card was the speaker trying to invoke in his/her audience? Was this effective for the goal he/she was trying to accomplish?
- What feelings did the speaker invoke in the audience?
- After analyzing the facts, do you think the speaker successfully motivated the audience? Why or why not?

♣ Media Analysis
Essay Format Assignment

Purpose of the Assignment

This assignment is designed to challenge you to critically analyze the role of the media in daily life.

Requirements

Please select ONE of the following concepts from lecture and/or the textbook to analyze through the lens of the media:

1. Gender roles;
2. Relationship values;
3. Conflict;
4. Culture;
5. Decision-making;
6. Social identity

Please choose ONE of the following media outlets in which to analyze the chosen concept: TV, film, magazine, advertising, music, books, Internet, or video games.

Turn in at least one page of analysis. Please indicate in the analysis what type of media (i.e., TV, film) and what specific content (e.g., *Friends, Maxim Magazine,* or *Pirates of the Caribbean,* etc.) you are analyzing. Answer the following questions:

1. What specifically are we learning through the media regarding your chosen concept?
2. Are there benefits for the audience learning this concept through the media? Think critically about this question. *Explain* why or why not.
3. Are there problems with the audience learning this concept through the media? Why or why not?

Attach a copy of the article, advertisement, web site, book excerpt, etc. used in the analysis, or include a detailed account of examples, lyrics, or parts of a script.

♣ Grading Rubric for Media Analysis
Essay Format Assignment

_____ (10)   Question 1 answered clearly and completely with relevant insight and superb quality

_____ (10)   Question 2 answered clearly and completely with relevant insight and superb quality

_____ (10)   Question 3 answered clearly and completely with relevant insight and superb quality

_____ (10)   Analysis is communicated effectively

_____ (5)   Supplemental material included—must be conversation or dialogue (not a picture, article, etc.)

_____ (5)   Analyzes one of the given concepts AND uses one of the listed media (all-or-nothing)

_____   **Total score** (50 points)

♣ Special Occasion Speech
Essay Format Assignment

Speech Elements:

- Special Occasion speeches may be **formal or informal** so the word choice and language should fit accordingly. For example, some slang may be appropriate in a toast, but not in a nomination. However, the entire audience should be able to follow the speech and not be offended.
- Think about the psychographic and demographic characteristics of the audience when writing this speech. The people in the audience may affect the way you write and present the speech. For example, parents and grandparents would be present at a wedding so stories about drinking or other controversial topics may not be appropriate in a toast.

Toasts. These are used for momentous occasions such as weddings, birth of a baby, reunion of friends, successful business ventures, and anniversaries. The toasts can be personal or generic, are usually accompanied by raising glasses, and are generally short.

Eulogies. This speech is used to deliver a tribute to someone who has died. The speaker should mention the unique achievements of the person receiving the tribute and also contain an expression of loss. Further, the speaker should turn to the living and encourage them to transcend their sorrow and sense of loss, while also indicating that the audience should feel gratitude that the dead had once been among them.

Eulogies can be about you, a pet, a famous person, a family member, or even something humorous. Be imaginative!

Nominations. Nominations involve noting the occasion and significance of the award or office for which the nomination is placed. The speaker should explain clearly why the nominee's skills, talents and past achievements serve as qualifications for the award or position.

Introductions. An introduction is similar to an informative speech. The purpose is to provide the audience with information about the speaker and to ultimately, trigger interest in that person. The main elements include gaining audience attention, building the speaker's credibility and introducing the speaker's subject.

Note: Both nominations and introductions should be about a real person, but they can be a famous person or a person you know personally.

Requirements

Before the text of your speech, answer the following three questions:

1. What led you to choosing your type of speech and topic?
2. How do you think your audience feels about your topic? Will they approve, disapprove, or be indifferent?
3. What considerations will you make, both in the text of your speech and in the method you actually deliver your speech, to demonstrate the passion you have for this topic to your audience?

Prepare and present a 45 second to 1.5 minute speech of one of the aforementioned types. There is no formal structure to this speech, although you should try your best to include an introduction, body (main text), and conclusion.

♣ Grading Rubric for Special Occasion Speech
Essay Format Assignment

Written Portion (20)

_____ (9)   Questions are answered completely, clearly, and in an organized manner (3 points per question)

_____ (6)   Assignment follows one of the given options for speeches and executes the type of speech correctly

_____ (3)   Topic and written portion are interesting and engaging

_____ (2)   Grammar (0 points if more than 3 errors)

Spoken Portion (30)

_____ (5)   Clear distinction of the type of speech

_____ (5)   Executes type of speech skillfully

_____ (5)   Effective eye contact

_____ (5)   Charisma and ability to engage the audience

_____ (5)   Effective body movement and use of space

_____ (4)   Effective volume, rate of speech, and word choice for audience; avoids fillers (e.g., "um," "like," etc.)

_____ (1)   Meets time limitations (45 seconds–1.5 minutes)

_____   **Total score** (50 points)

♣ Informative Speech
Outline Format Assignment

Purpose of the Assignment

This assignment is designed to help students inform an audience about something unique and interesting, which will help build rapport between the speaker and the audience. Also, students will have an opportunity to improve skills in speaking before a small group of people.

Topic

Select a topic of your choosing for your informative speech. The topic development exercise in Chapter 16 should help you select a topic that you are excited about that your audience will also find interesting. For example, I love to read Ernest Hemmingway books and tell stories about him. I could make this topic very interesting to the class because I have visited Hemmingway's home in Key West, Florida and have some pictures. The more personal the topic is for you, the more likely you will be to get excited about it and then frame the speech to get the audience excited, as well.

Requirements

Each student will complete a written speech outline and a 4-6 minute speech to be delivered in class.

The speech outline must follow the format shown below and it must be typed. Handwritten outlines will not be accepted.

There should be at least THREE references cited in the outline and speech. The reference page and in-text citations must follow APA style. See an APA Style guide http://www.calstatela.edu/library/guides/3apa.pdf or your TA.

Note: Students must turn in a copy of the outline to their TAs prior to giving their speech. An additional copy of the outline may be used during the delivery of the speech.

♣ Informative Speech Outline

This is what your outline should look like. Use this format as your template for structuring your outline. The bolded sections **are required** for your outline.

Title: Be creative!

Topic: The idea I want to talk about is… (What is the idea or concept you have decided to talk about? Make sure you cleared your topic with your TA or Section Leader.)

Purpose Statement: To inform my audience about… (What do you want to tell the audience about the idea or topic? Is it interesting because it gives people insight about their lives, it will be helpful on family vacations, or it will help students learn more efficiently?)

I. **INTRODUCTION**
   A. **Attention getter:** Write what you intend to say to get your audience's attention. Examples: story, fact, startling statement.
   B. **Thesis Statement:** this should be a clear and specific rewording of your purpose statement.
   C. **Preview the main points:** Tell us the three main points you will be making in your speech.
      1. Main Point 1
      2. Main Point 2
      3. Main Point 3

Transition: Insert a statement linking your introduction to the body of the speech.

II. **BODY**
   A. First main point-remember only one sentence.
      1. Sub-point (You can use a definition, an example, or evidence to support your main point.) Be sure to cite your sources in your sub-points.
      2. Sub-point. Don't forget that these need to be complete sentences. The second sub-point could be an example.

Transition: Insert a comment linking your first main point to your second main point.
   B. Your second main point goes here.
      1. Just like in A (could be a definition).
      2. Could be an example like in A.

Transition: Insert a comment linking your second main point to your third main point.
   C. The last main point
      1. Again, complete sentences describing the main point
      2. Your final sub-point

Transition: Insert a comment linking the body of your speech to the conclusion.

III. **CONCLUSION**
   A. Restatement of Thesis
   B. Summary of main points
   C. Closing statement: wrap up your speech with a memorable point. You could refer to your attention getter, use a story, fact, or a quote to end your speech.

II. **Body**

    A.   There are many reasons why the owner, Jimmy Williams, thought that this second location would be beneficial to the MSU community (O'Brien, 2012).

        1.   The location by the bars is so busy at night that they don't have enough time to make deliveries, let alone answer the phone to take many delivery orders, so this new location will focus more on deliveries (O'Brien, 2012).

        2.   Where this new Jimmy's is located, the only other places that are open late for the younger students who don't go out near the bars are McDonald's and Jim's Pizza, so another late night option is perfect for this side of Long Lake Ave (O'Brien, 2012).

Transition: Now that you know why it was thought that another Jimmy's was needed, let's look at what Jimmy's has to offer.

    B.   This new Jimmy's has the same menu as the original location, with a wide variety of items.

        1.   Jimmy's is known for its "Jim-wraps," offering twelve different types of original Jim-wraps, four giant con-wraps, six chicken tender con-wraps, and four breakfast con-wraps ("Jimmy's college town," 2012).

        2.   In addition to these popular wraps, the menu includes a variety of grilled sandwiches, burgers, salads, fries, chicken tenders, mozzarella sticks, coney dogs, desserts, and much more ("Jimmy's college town," 2012).

Transition: Not only do both locations have this great menu, but business at the new location has been easily keeping up with the original Jimmy's business as well.

    C.   This second location has been doing very well so far, with business increasing each weekend as more students find out about this second location (Boyd, 2012).

        1.   Although it is open from 11 a.m. to 3 a.m. Sunday through Wednesday and 11 a.m. to 4 a.m. Thursday through Saturday, it is usually the busiest on Fridays at around 1 a.m. (Boyd, 2012).

        2.   Every time there has been a home football game this year, the new Jimmy's has been super busy, with a steady line nearly out the front doors (Boyd, 2012).

Transition: While this second Jimmy's has seen a lot of business so far, it is important to remember that it will only remain successful because of customers like you.

III. **Conclusion**

    A.   Due to its affordable menu, late night hours, and the business that the MSU community brings, this new Jimmy's continues to prove how necessary it is to have this second location.

    B.   Not only does this new Jimmy's benefit the MSU community by fulfilling more deliveries and being located in an area where there are very few places for food open late, but it also offers the same menu as the original location and stays especially busy on the weekends and on game days.

    C.   Next time your out on campus and are feeling hungry, be sure to stop by Jimmy's, offering you a quick and delicious meal at not just one, but now two Long Lake Ave. locations.

References

Boyd, K. (2012, October 6). Interview by (Name omitted) [Personal Interview]. A Jimmy's employee perspective., West Stanford, MI.

Jimmy's college town grill. (2012). Retrieved from http://jimmysgrill.com/

O'Brien, J. (2012, August 2). Jimmy's to open new location. *The State News.* Retrieved from http://statenews.com/index.php/article/2012/08/jimmys

♣ Grading Rubric for Informative Speech Spoken Portion

INTRODUCTION (8 points)

_____ (4)   Use of effective attention getter

_____ (2)   Thesis statement

_____ (2)   Preview of main points

BODY (12 points)

_____ (9)   Has 3 main points (3 points per main point)

_____ (3)   Main points are well-organized and easy to follow

CONCLUSION (5 points)

_____ (3)   Restates main points

_____ (2)   Memorable closing statement

VERBAL AND VISUAL ELEMENTS (25 points)

_____ (4)   Effective word choice, slang, acronyms, etc.

_____ (5)   Effective eye contact

_____ (5)   Charisma; engages audience

_____ (3)   Effective vocals and articulation

_____ (5)   Effective movement, posture, gestures

_____ (3)   Sources cited orally

_____ (-5)   Minus 5 points if outside time limitations (4–6 minutes)

_____ (-5)   Minus 1 point for every 3 grammar mistakes (5 point deduction maximum)

_____ **Total score** (50 points)

♣ Grading Rubric for Informative Speech Written Portion
Outline Format Assignment

_____ (3)   Title, topic, and purpose statement

AUDIENCE ANALYSIS

_____ (2)   Demographics and psychographics

_____ (2)   Verbal and nonverbal considerations

TALK CARDS

_____ (2)   Talk Card and audience's reciprocal Talk Card

_____ (2)   Content and style

INTRODUCTION

_____ (5)   Attention grabber

_____ (3)   Thesis statement

_____ (2)   Preview of main points

BODY

_____ (9)   Three clearly-stated main points that are organized and substantially different from one another

CONCLUSION

_____ (3)   Restatement of thesis

_____ (2)   Summary of main points

_____ (3)   Well thought-out closing statement

OTHER

_____ (5)   References page

_____ (2)   In-text citations

_____ (5)   Grammar and word choice

_____   **Total score** (50 points)

♣ Pro/Con Speech
Outline Format Assignment

Purpose of Assignment

This assignment provides an opportunity for you to learn more about a controversial issue and it provides an opportunity for you to practice developing strong arguments that support a particular position on a controversial issue.

Description of Assignment

You will be assigned to take either a pro or a con stance on a particular controversial topic. Another student in your section will be assigned to take a stance that is in opposition to yours on the same topic (i.e., if you are assigned to take a 'pro' stance, then the other student will be assigned to take a 'con' stance and vice-versa).

Although you will graded individually and although you will present your speeches individually, you may feel free to work with the student who will be presenting the opposing argument to compare work and to evaluate each other's rebuttal arguments.

Requirements

There are two components to the Pro/Con Speech Assignment: (1) a written component and (2) an oral/presentation component.

I. **Oral/Presentation Component:** You will have 2.5–4 minutes to deliver the speech that you create for the written component of this assignment (see requirements for the content and format of the speech below). The grading rubric contains more information regarding how you will be graded for this component of the assignment (note: see the "Spoken Portion" section of the grading rubric for the requirements). Please note that you must use oral citations during your speech (for the references that you use).

II. **Written Component:** The written component of this assignment will require you to research the controversial topic that you are assigned so that you can develop arguments **in favor of the stance (pro/con) that you are assigned**. You will be required to submit (1) an **outline** of the arguments that you develop (using the outline format provided) in addition to (2) a **references page** that will include the elements listed below.

At a minimum, your outline must include: **two main claims** (i.e., arguments) and **one rebuttal argument**. For each of your main claims, you must have **at least two subclaims**; the only exception to this is the rebuttal argument(s), which may have just one subclaim. ** Your subclaims should be developed based on your research and you will need to include **in-text citations** using **APA formatting**. The structure of your outline should follow the template provided on the next page of this handout and it must be in outline (NOT essay) format. Your outline must also conform to **all other general requirements** listed on the assignment guidelines checklist that's posted on Desire2Learn.

In addition to your speech outline, you will need to submit references page that contains **APA formatted reference entries** for each of the sources that you use (you must use **at least two sources** for this assignment). You will also need to identify **two tests of evidence for each source** and you will need to **explain why/how** the source meets each test.

Note: You must have at least **two main points/arguments** and **one rebuttal argument**. If you feel that you have time, you may include an additional main point/argument to bolster your credibility and your position IF (1) you are not just adding an additional point to lengthen your speech to meet the time limit;

and (2) all of your main points, including the additional points, are substantially bolstered by exceptional research.

Common Tests of Evidence:

- Relevance: Evidence strongly relates to the point in connection with which it is used.
- Bias: There are no strong reasons for which the source of the evidence would misrepresent the truth.
- Internal Consistency: There are no contradictions within the evidence itself.
- Corroboration: Other expert sources support this evidence.
- Reputable: The source is an expert, such as a famous professor or news station.

Pro/Con Speech Outline

I. **Introduction**
   A. **Attention grabber:**
   B. **Thesis statement:** State the issue at hand and provide a statement of the "purpose" of your speech.
   C. **Proposition:** Statement of the position that you want the audience to accept or reject.

II. **Body**
   A. **Argument #1:**
      1. **Main Claim**
         i. **Subclaim #1:** Present the first reason (piece of evidence/research) in support of the main claim of Argument #1.
         ii. **Subclaim #2:** Present a second piece of evidence/research to supports the main claim for Argument #1.
         iii. **Subclaim #3:** Present a third piece of evidence/research to support the main claim for Argument #1.
      2. **Conclusion for Argument #1:** Restate your main claim for Argument #1
   B. **Argument #2:**
      1. **Main claim**
         i. **Subclaim #1:**
         ii. **Subclaim #2:**
         iii. **Subclaim #3:**
      2. **Conclusion for Argument #2**
   C. **Rebuttal arguments**
      1. **Anticipated opposing argument #1:**
         i. **Your rebuttal:**
      2. **Anticipated opposing argument #2:**
         i. **Your rebuttal:**

III. **Conclusion**
   A. **Review of arguments:**
   B. **Implication statement:**
   C. **Closing statement:**

♣ Sample Pro/Con Speech

Minimum Driving Age should *not* be Raised to 18 Years Old

Note: Although the audience analysis and talk card analysis are not part of this example speech, the outline that you submit should include these two components.

I. **I. Introduction**
   A. **Attention grabber:** Can you imagine having gone through all four years of high school without access to an automobile? Would you have been able to hold a job if you had to depend on your parents for transportation? Now that you are in college, do you feel you would have enough time to learn to drive, if you did not already know how?
   B. **Thesis statement:** Many state legislatures are considering raising the minimum driving age to 18. This is not a good proposal, and my arguments will demonstrate why this idea is poor.
   C. **Proposition:** The minimum driving age should not be raised to the age of 18.

II. **Body**
   A. **Main Claim #1:** At the current minimum driving age of 16, teenagers are still in high school, and, more importantly, live at home. Therefore, they have ample time to learn how to drive, as well as their parents available closely by to teach them.
      1. **Evidence and research**
         i. **Subclaim #1:** Teenagers' parents are their major source for teaching them how to drive, and they are depended upon to provide guidance ("Teenage driver facts," 2008).
         ii. **Subclaim #2:** At 18 years of age, the majority teenagers are attending college, or, at least busy preparing for college ("A look at college demographics," 2006).
         iii. **Subclaim #3:** Those at a university far from home will not have time to learn how to drive, since school is the major priority.
         iv. **Subclaim #4:** Most that go away to college are not permitted to have a car their freshman year.
         v. **Subclaim #5:** At the age of 18 and at a university, teenagers do not have individuals available who could drive with them once they received a learner's permit, and, therefore, can never really learn how to drive without driving themselves, which is illegal.
      2. **Conclusion (restatement of argument #1)**
         i. Most university teenagers will be unable to obtain a driver's license due to the lack of parental teaching, strict time constraints with classes and new experiences, and the inability to have a chaperone with a learner's permit.

B. **Main Claim #2:** Teenagers between the ages of 16 and 18 need a means of getting to school, work, sports events, and social time with their friends.
1. **Evidence and research**
   i. **Subclaim #1:** Parents are the main form of transportation for individuals that do not have a driver's license ("Driver," 2004).
   ii. **Subclaim #2:** Parents cannot always be depended on to drive the teenagers everywhere.
   iii. **Subclaim #3:** Socialization is a basic need of human beings, so teenagers need a method of getting to these social events ("Three basic needs," 2006).
2. **Conclusion (restatement of argument #2)**
   i. Some of the most vital periods of growth and social experience occur when individuals are between the ages of 16 and 18, and, without a vehicle, many of these events would be extremely difficult to attend and experience.

C. **Main Claim #3:** Other more effective alternatives exist beside raising the minimum driving age to 18.
1. **Evidence and research**
   i. **Subclaim #1:** States can make driving tests more rigorous.
      a. Those with poor driving skills are more likely to cause accidents.
      b. Inexperience, not immaturity, is the leading cause of accidents.
      c. Many teenagers want to take the easiest driving test so they can easily pass and, therefore, get their license ("States should raise," 2010).
   ii. **Subclaim #2:** More severe penalties for driving infractions can be instated.
      a. Teenagers will drive more cautiously if dangerous driving is more severely punished.
      b. Instituting license suspensions or jail time will remove the bad drivers from the road.
2. **Conclusion (restatement of argument #3)**
   i. State legislatures should examine alternative options beside raising the minimum driving age to 18 years old.

D. **Rebuttal arguments**
1. Anticipated opposing argument #1: Immaturity and inexperience from young age causes driving accidents.
   i. **Rebuttal:** Being young (within reasonable limits) has nothing to do with the inability to properly operate a car. Inexperience and improper training, not immaturity, is the reason car accidents do happen to some younger individuals ("Leading causes of," 2007). Therefore, allowing teenagers to drive at age 16 and the training they receive the years before gives them the experience they need to be good drivers. Logic says start them sooner, not later (Irvine, 2008).

2. **Anticipated opposing argument #2:** Statistics show that younger drivers are more likely to get into car accidents. Teenagers account for 12% of all fatal car crashes and are 4 times more likely than others to crash ("Leading causes of," 2007).

    i. **Rebuttal:** Statistics must make sense in the context they are used. Studies show that males are 77% more likely to cause a driving accident than females. Should males, then, be prohibited from driving? ("Men 77% more, 2009). Another study shows that women over the age of 80 are 60% more likely to die in a vehicle than 16-year old men. Should maybe a maximum driving age be implemented, and not a greater minimum age?

III. **Conclusion**
   A. **Review of arguments:**
     1. At the current minimum driving age of 16, teenagers live at home. Therefore, they have ample time to learn how to drive, as well as their parents available to teach them how.
     2. Teenagers between the ages of 16 and 18 need a means of getting to social events.
     3. Other more effective alternatives exist beside raising the minimum driving age to 18.
   B. **Implication statement:** State legislatures are focusing on the wrong problems when trying to figure out methods of improving safety while driving.
   C. **Closing statement:** A greater focus should be put in preparation for driving and gaining experience on the road, rather than reducing the number of drivers on the road, when those affected need this privilege for the aforementioned reasons. For these reasons, the minimum driving age should not be raised to 18.

♣ Grading Form for Pro/Con Speech
Outline Format Assignment

Written Portion (45 points)

_____ (10)   Strong main claims (5 points per main claim)

_____ (10)   Strong subclaims/supporting evidence

_____ (10)   Strong rebuttal

_____ (5)   Two references in correct APA format, both in references page and in-text citations

_____ (5)   References page includes 2 tests of evidence for 2 different sources

_____ (3)   Organized, clear, and easy to follow

_____ (2)   Grammar (1 point if 3–6 mistakes; 0 points if more than 6 mistakes)

Spoken Portion (55 points)

_____ (10)   Main arguments are clear, effective, and backed by substantial evidence

_____ (10)   Rebuttal arguments are clear, effective, and backed by substantial evidence

_____ (5)   Arguments are presented in a logical order/manner

_____ (5)   Effective eye contact

_____ (5)   Charisma; ability to engage audience

_____ (5)   Effective body movement and use of space

_____ (5)   Effective volume, rate of speech, and word choice

_____ (5)   Uses evidence to back claims over personal opinion

_____ (3)   References are cited orally during speech

_____ (2)   Time limit (2.5–4 minutes)

_____   **Total score** (100 points)

♣ Persuasive Speech
Outline Format Assignment

Purpose of Assignment

This speech assignment is designed to help you learn how to create persuasive speeches aimed at convincing a group to support your position on an issue that is important to you.

Topic

1. This speech must be focused and created around one of the following groups. The group can either be existent or you can create one of your own:

   - Business
   - Store/restaurant
   - Organization
   - Club
   - Campus group

2. You must convince your audience to do one of the following actions:

   - Join the group
   - Donate money or something else to the group
   - Spend time with the group
   - Buy something from the group
   - Research the group
   - Develop an interest in the group

3. The group must be responding to some problem or need in society or on campus. The need/problem can be something as big as global warming or as little as there not being any good sit-down hamburger restaurants on campus.

   Have fun with the group that you would like your audience to become interested in. Be imaginative.

Requirements

Each student will complete a speech outline with **a reference page, a visual aid, and a 5 to 7 minute speech** in front of their recitation section.

The speech outline must follow the format of **Monroe's Motivated Sequence** as both instructed by your Teaching Assistant and in Chapter 16 of the textbook.

Monroe's Motivated Sequence includes the use of **persuasive devices**. Persuasive devices typically include either statistics or emotional appeals. A statistical persuasive device would motivate the audience to comply based upon current statistics of the population engaging in a harmful activity, for example. Emotional persuasive devices would typically invoke feelings in the audience, similar to those felt when you watch a commercial for adorable pets that have been abused and sheltered.

The speech outline must be typed and the visual aid must look somewhat professional. No hand-written outlines or sloppily put together visual aids will be accepted.

There should be at least **FIVE** references cited in the outline and speech. The purpose of references is to present research or other relevant information about the need for the product or service. The reference page must follow APA style.

Grading

Please review the following pages for grading.

♣ Persuasive Speech Guidelines

THIS IS WHAT YOUR OUTLINE MUST LOOK LIKE:

Note: Although this speech does not include the audience analysis and talk card analysis, the outline that you submit should include these components.

(The **bolded items** are what you should actually have on your outline.)

Name and Section Number

Title: Provide a short but interesting title for your speech.

Topic: List the name of the group you are going to speak about and a sentence or two that sums up that group.

Purpose Statement: Your purpose in this speech is to persuade. You need to provide one sentence here that describes the action you want your audience to take (e.g., Read this flyer about our store and consider stopping by the next time you need groceries!).

Audience Analysis: (Answer four questions here).

Talk Card Analysis: (Answer four questions here).

I. **Introduction**
   A. **Attention Getter:** Write a catchy attention getter to gain the audience's interest.
   B. **Thesis Statement:** This should be a clear and specific rewording of your purpose statement.
   C. **Preview Statement:** "Specifically, I am going to discuss A, B, and C."
      1. Include an additional statement describing your need/problem step (the reason your audience should develop an interest in the group).
      2. Include an additional statement describing your satisfaction/solution step (the request of what action the audience should take to develop interest in the group).

II. **Need/Problem Step:** You need one sentence here that summarizes the problem your group is directly responding to. What problem does your group solve for the target audience? Then, provide at least two good arguments and/or statements about why solving that problem is important/necessary for the target market. These are important points, so make them convincing! Please note: your group needs to be directly responding to some sort of problem or need. Therefore, if no problem or need exists that your group is responding to, then you cannot use said group.
   A. **Main Point #1**
      1. **Sub-point.** Use evidence to support your main point. Be sure to cite your sources. Do not forget that these need to be complete sentences.
      2. **Sub-point.**

Transition Sentence: Insert a sentence linking your first main point to your second main point.
   B. **Main Point #2**
      1. **Sub-point.**
      2. **Sub-point.**

Transition Sentence: Insert a sentence linking your second main point to your third main point.

    C. **Main Point #3**
       1. **Sub-point.**
       2. **Sub-point.**

Transition Sentence:

III. **Satisfaction/Solution Step:** Summarize your solution. You need to have two general suggestions for audience action. Your first will be your main suggestion (e.g., Try our valet service risk-free for 30 days!) and your second will be your secondary suggestion (e.g., Read our brochure, or check out our website at...). Give an overview of your group that is helping students solve the problems described in the needs step. Tell us when the group was founded, by whom, and why they are interested in this problem.
    A. **Main Suggestion:** (e.g., Try our valet service risk-free for 30 days!)
    B. **Secondary Suggestion:** (e.g., Read our brochure, or check out our website at...)

Transition Sentence:

IV. **Visualization Step:** Help your audience visualize how they can benefit from developing an interest in your group. Usually, this describes the key benefits the audience will receive from the solution you provide. Be effective, and be *visual!* Think about weight-loss commercials commonly shown on television and how they try to help the target audience visualize what their bodies will look like by using their product.

Transition Sentence:

V. **Action/Conclusion Step**
    A. **Action Step:** Make a specific request that the audience can do today (this is commonly very similar to the "main suggestion" from the satisfaction step).
    B. **Summary of Main Points:**
    C. **Implication Statement:** Explain how the main points prove why the problem is important enough to warrant action.
    D. **Closing Statement:** Finish with an extremely compelling wrap-up statement that ties into your attention grabber and allows your group to stick in your audience's mind.

WHAT TO REMEMBER FOR YOUR PERSUASIVE SPEECH

- You must use **Monroe's Motivated Sequence** when both writing your outline and presenting your speech.
- You must have some sort of **visual aid** (see next page).
- You must **dress appropriately** (see next page).
- The outline must be **typed**.
- Make **note cards** to help you with your main points and sub-points.
- There must be at least **FIVE SOURCES** in the outline. They should appear in three places: 1) on the references page, 2) in-text citations, and 3) cited orally when presenting your speech.

- Be creative! Try to use emotional, logical, and credible appeals. See Chapter 16 of your textbook for more information.
- This speech must be **5 to 7 minutes**.
- PROOFREAD AND PRACTICE!

Visual Aid

Create a visual aid to help your audience visualize your group or the problem that your group is responding to. For inspiration, check out typical advertisements in newspapers and magazines.

Your visual aid must be used skillfully in conjunction with other content in your speech. What this means is that you *cannot* simply hand out/show the audience your visual aid before or after the speech. It must be integrated into the speech and in a way that does not disrupt the flow of the speech.

Good visual aids:

- One-page advertisements
- Brochures
- Posters
- Poster board presentations

Unacceptable visual aids:

- Business cards
- PowerPoint/other computer presentations
- Videos
- Voice recordings

Dress Attire

For this speech, we require that you **dress appropriately**, simply for the fact that you will be simulating a situation in which you must practice persuading an audience for your professional career. You should wear something that is **business casual**. If you fail to dress appropriately, 10% of your final speech grade will be deducted from the total score.

You should NOT wear:

- jeans
- sweatpants
- shorts
- hats
- flip-flops

♣ Grading Rubric for Persuasive Speech Spoken Portion

ATTENTION STEP (3 points)

_____ (2)   Attention grabber

_____ (1)   Thesis statement and preview of main points

NEEDS/PROBLEM STEP (9 points)

_____ (5)   Identify unfulfilled needs and convince your audience that a problem exists and it will not go away on its own (build up the need)

_____ (4)   Have 2 or 3 good arguments of why there is a problem (your main points)

SATISFACTION STEP (8 points)

_____ (5)   Propose a solution that will satisfy those needs - include an organization and a clearly thought-out plan

_____ (3)   Anticipate and refute possibly audience objections to the proposed plan

VISUALIZATION STEP (5 points)

_____ (5)   Help your audience to visualize what satisfaction will mean - explain how your plan will solve the problem (visual and detailed)

ACTION STEP (8 points)

_____ (5)   dentify specific actions the audience can take—a main suggestion and a secondary suggestion

_____ (1)   Summarize and/or restate your main points

_____ (2)   Have a memorable closing statement

OTHER (41 points)

_____ (5)   Skillfully used Monroe's Motivated Sequence

_____ (5)   Use of persuasive devices (emotional appeals, statistics, logic, or credibility)

_____ (5)   Effective eye contact

_____ (5)   Charisma; engages audience

_____ (5)   Effective word choice, slang, acronyms, etc.

_____ (4)   Vocal variety employed to create emphasis

_____ (5)   Effective movement, posture, gestures, etc.

_____ (3)   Sources cited orally

_____ (5)   Visual aid attractively designed and used skillfully in speech

_____ (-2)   Minus 2 points if within 30 seconds of time limitations

_____ (-3)   Minus 3 additional points if speech is more than 30 seconds too long or too short

_____   **Total score** (75 points)

♣ Grading Rubric for Persuasive Speech Written Portion
Outline Format Assignment

_____ (3)   Title, topic, and purpose statement

AUDIENCE ANALYSIS

_____ (2)   Demographics and psychographics

TALK CARDS

_____ (2)   Talk card and audience's reciprocal Talk Card

_____ (2)   Content and style

ATTENTION STEP

_____ (3)   Attention grabber

_____ (2)   Thesis statement

_____ (2)   Preview of main points

NEEDS/PROBLEM STEP

_____ (10)   dentify unfulfilled needs—convince your audience that there is a problem

_____ (3)   Have between 2 and 3 good arguments of why there is a problem

SATISFACTION STEP

_____ (8)   Propose a solution that will satisfy those needs—include an organization and a clearly thought-out plan

_____ (3)   Anticipate and refute possible audience objections to the proposed plan

VISUALIZATION STEP

_____ (10)   Visualize what satisfaction will mean—explain how your proposed plan will rid the problem

ACTION STEP

_____ (4)   Identify specific actions the audience can take

_____ (3)   Summary of main points

_____ (3)   Have a memorable closing statement

OTHER

_____ (10)   Arguments presented logically and in an organized manner

_____ (5)   Sources cited on references page and include in-text citations

_____   **Total score** (75 points)

♣ Example Persuasive Speech

Title: "The Perfect Interruption"

Topic: The Perfect Interruption is a recently created callback service, helping people relieve themselves from those awkward situations in life. You know that one time when you were stuck in a conversation with no way out? Yeah, I do too.

Purpose Statement: Look over and review our flyer, visit our webpage, and download The Perfect Interruption Application for your smartphone and use it in those desperately awkward situations which seem unavoidable.

Audience Analysis:

A. **Demographics:** Most users of The Perfect Interruption will be both men and women ranging in ages from middle teens to the late twenties. No specific major, income, or college are need to use this application in particular. My audience will be Michigan State University students, entering their late teens, and early adulthood, making it relevant towards my speech since they are who The Perfect Interruption is marketed too specifically.

B. **Psychographics:** The types of students that would most likely be interested by The Perfect Interruption are those that like to go out in social settings in large groups of people, where there are more chances of needing to avoid someone you really do not want to talk too. Since Michigan State University is known for its academics and social setting, the mass amount of students that could potentially use The Perfect Interruption make this fact relevant to my speech. Users will have good intentions when using this product, since instead of being mean or hurtful to the person they do not want to talk to, they can simply slide away from the situation with no hard feelings.

C. **Verbal Considerations:** The verbal considerations I will need to use during my speech are the usual language that typical college students use when conversing with one another. Since I am trying to promote The Perfect Interruption though, I will need to use some sort of informative tone when speaking, letting the students know that I know what I am talking about. Knowing how to talk to a group of college students is important to make sure they will listen and not not pay attention to what I am saying.

D. **Nonverbal Considerations:** The nonverbal considerations I will need to use during my speech that are specific to my audience are eye contact, hand gestures, and a somewhat perfect posture. These three considerations are relevant to whom I will be speaking too because this shows that I know what I am speaking to them about, and confident about my product, The Perfect Interruption, making it easier for them eager to go download the application.

Talk Cards:

A. **Talk Card:** During this speech I will use my Entrepreneur Talk Card because I am telling a group of students about the product/business I created. This would be the most persuasive out of any of the other talk cards available to me because entrepreneurs create a business/product, and they usually know more about how that product works, why it was created, and how effective it is over anyone else.

B. **Content:** Five key topics that I will use with talk card to persuade my customers to buy my product is the complete knowledge about my product, my entrepreneurial abilities, management skills for a new business, my professional dress, and my financial skills that will help keep my business out of debt.

C. **Style:** My Entrepreneur Talk Card will be high in liking, I want my audience to listen and like who I am as a business person, because if they don't, this could really affect how The Perfect Interruption is perceived by them. My chosen talk card will also be formal, to show that The Perfect Interruption is not just one of those "waste of time" products, but one that is serious and has good intentions for all of its users.

D. **Audience:** I would like the audience to respond with a Customer Card to my Entrepreneur Talk Card that I use during my speech. The reason that I would like them to respond this way is because as a customer, they are more likely to want to go download The Perfect Interruption application to their smartphone after my speech is over with. Simply stated, customers are the ones that buy and use products in the marketplace.

I. **Introduction**

   A. **Attention Getter:** So here's the deal, you're at party or out with your friends, and THAT one kid from class, or high school comes up and tries to talk to you. Being a nice person, you don't want to be rude when you act like you don't want to talk to them… so what to do? The Perfect Interruption application may or may not be perfect for you.

   B. **Thesis Statement:** After downloading our application to your smartphone, you will be able to avoid all the awkward situations you could ever dream of. To find out how to download The Perfect Interruption you can look over our flyer, or you can visit our webpage for details on how to search this application in either the Android or iPhone marketplace.

   C. **Preview Statement:** Specifically, I am going to discuss why you as a young adult and student should take the time to download The Perfect Interruption to the one thing we as a generation seem to always have with us, our lifeline, our cell phones.

      1. The Perfect Interruption is not a necessity in ones life, it is simply a product that makes life simpler. It takes away the hassle of trying to get away from that one person at a social gathering that you really do not need to talk too when there is no escape route available. We all have these moments, but do we all take care of them appropriately? This is why you should download The Perfect Interruption to your smartphone.

      2. After visiting out webpage, or even reading over our flyer we would greatly appreciate it as a business and company that you at least give this application a try, and download it to your smartphone.

II. **Need/Problem Step:** The problem that The Perfect Interruption solves is simple, it takes the rude out of sitting in the conversation that you do not want to continue. It has been recorded that almost 88% of college students party on the weekends (Cha Cha, 2011). Think about all the randoms that just walk up to you and want to chat, do you really want to talk to most of them? No. What do you do when there is nothing left to do besides being mean to the innocent random? Use The Perfect Interruption. Our generation seems to live on our cell phones, not only is it a lifeline for most, it comes in handy every once in a while. The Perfect Interruption gives us as people another reason to love our cell phones.

   A. **Main Point #1**

      1. **Sub-point:** The idea of The Perfect Interruption, and how it was developed.

      2. **Sub-point:** An example of when to use this application, and how it works to get you out of that unwanted situation.

Transition Sentence: You may be thinking to yourself… is this a real life product and it is really needed? You may be surprised..

B. **Main Point #2**
1. **Sub-point:** There are many websites dedicated to describing "those awkward moments".
2. **Sub-point:** Facebook, and many dedicated pages towards plenty of awkward moment topics, but one stands out for those unavoidable moments in particular (Facebook, 2011).

Transition Sentence: Since most of the really helpful applications on smartphones cost money, we all realize that everyone needs to make a living. The Perfect Interruption is an exception to those cases, it's free of charge!

C. **Main Point #3**
1. **Sub-point:** Such a useful application is free of charge! Why this is, and the reasonings behind it.
2. **Sub-point:** The cost of The Perfect Interruption, and how this business in particular makes a profit (Miller, 2010)

Transition Sentence: Is The Perfect Interruption for you? There are a few choices for you as a smartphone and internet user.

III. **Satisfaction/Solution:** Simply stated, we as a company and business want you to download our application. In overview, The Perfect Interruption was founded in 2010 by (name omitted) after she witnessed her friends get approached by people they did not want to talk too.
A. **Main Suggestion:** The main solution for solving the occurring problem with awkward situations with people is to download The Perfect Interruption to your smartphone.
B. **Secondary Suggestion:** You can also visit our webpage, www.theperfectinterruption.com and see the interactive ways in which we have researched to avoid people, and real life stories from users of The Perfect Interruption.

Translation Sentence: The opportunity to have this electronic application is in the palms of your hands.

IV. **Visualization Step:** Downloading The Perfect Interruption will take a few moments out of your life, but the benefits from downloading this application will give you plenty non-awkward moments out at social gatherings, leaving you with plenty of time with those you actually want to be around.

Transition Sentence: There are over 45.4 million smartphone users (Mahalo, 2010), are you one of them? Now, I know you want to whip out your smartphone right now to go download The Perfect Interruption, but let me tell you how you can!

V. **Action/ Conclusion Step:**
A. **Action Step:** After the conclusion of my speech, you can go visit out website, www.theperfectinterruption.com for more details about the application, how the idea was started, and where to download The Perfect Interruption. For those with smartphones, they can go visit their local marketplace and download The Perfect Interruption by simply typing, "The Perfect Interruption" or TPI into the search bar and then clicking download, automatically putting The Perfect Interruption in your list of applications.

B. **Summary of Main Points:** The business I created is The Perfect Interruption, no one wants to be stuck in an awkward situation with some random at a social gathering, so a new application was created in hopes of getting its users out of those awkward situations without being rude. Since as a generation, us young adults survive off our cell phone, having this application on your smartphone is in its perfect convenience to you.

C. **Implication Statement:** The Perfect Interruption is the perfect application for you. Not only is is free of charge for you as a smartphone user, it also can help keep you laughing at those awkward moments you read about on Facebook, not shrugging your head when a similar story you read happened to you. Stay far away from those awkward situations by simply downloading the application, avoiding times like the terrifying example about the social gathering. Don't let that happen to you, cherish your time out on the weekends with the ones you really care about!

D. **Closing Statement:** Lets be honest, it's been proven that ignoring someone is one of top nine ways to get rid of someone that annoys you (Life Hack, 2010). Now, let's be really honest, who wants to be the one who really ignores them in such a harsh, brutal way? The Perfect Interruption is the one application you need for your smartphone, without it, you may be stuck in that awkward moment with no way out!

♣ Lecture Response Paper Quiz Questions

Lecture 1: Introduction to Card Talk

1. Card style consists of three elements. What are they?
   a. Liking, content, power
   b. Liking, relationship, formality
   c. Liking, formality, power
   d. Liking, formality, content

2. A doctor is talking to her patient in a talk game—an attempt to learn the patient's medical history. The doctor will play her Doctor Card and expects the patient to play his Patient Card. This demonstrates how card play is:
   a. responsive.
   b. reciprocal.
   c. both personal and professional.
   d. dissynchronized.

3. When can we say that a talk game is "won?"
   a. Card play is reciprocated.
   b. The signal-to-noise ratio is low.
   c. Both parties have achieved one of the three self-presentation goals.
   d. Both parties achieve their goals.

4. Britney Spears wins a Moon Man (an award) at the MTV Video Music Awards. She runs up to the podium on the stage and talks to her mom through the television broadcast, thanking her for all of her support throughout the years. Her use of the television to talk to her mother shows how a wide range of _____ exist for communication.
   a. symbols
   b. pragmatics
   c. cultures
   d. channels

5. When communicating a message in a card talk game, the source (the person sending the message) must adjust the message primarily to the person on the "other end" of the message, known as the:
   a. verbal and nonverbal considerations.
   b. receiver.
   c. source's message style.
   d. encoder.

♣ Lecture 2: Language Card Talk

1. Language can describe things we cannot see or point to (e.g. love, happiness, etc.) because language is:
   a. morphic.
   b. pragmatic.
   c. conventional.
   d. abstract.

2. Women have a far wider range of ways of expressing _____ than men.
   a. Formality
   b. Liking
   c. Content
   d. Power

3. Each of the following are characteristics of language EXCEPT:
   a. Language is symbiotic
   b. Language is symbolic
   c. Language is abstract
   d. Language is conventional

4. Taylor Lautner likes to play jokes on his friends. He went to Robert Pattinson's trailer and changed the sign on the door from "Private. No visitors welcome," to "Private? No. Visitors welcome." Later that day, hundreds of fans and photographers swarmed his trailer, interrupting his privacy. This exemplifies which element of language?
   a. Phonetics
   b. Semantics
   c. Pragmatics
   d. Syntax

5. Bob wishes to change your attitude about seat belts. He uses a variety of arguments. Bob's desire to change your attitude about seat belts using various arguments reflects which dimension of language? In other words, which dimension of language focuses most strongly on the goal one wishes to accomplish?
   a. Syntax
   b. Pragmatics
   c. Morphology
   d. Phonemics

♣ Lecture 3: Culture Card Talk

1. Individualists may place more emphasis on _____, while collectivists may place more emphasis on _____.
    a. Personal goals; friendships
    b. Group goals; personal goals
    c. "We"; "I"
    d. Group goals; friendships

2. An outsider visiting a high context culture will most likely:
    a. Not understand much of the implicit communication between members of the culture.
    b. Adapt relatively quickly to the language and rituals of the newer culture.
    c. Be more group-oriented than the individuals of the high context culture.
    d. All of the above

3. One who is a member of a caste system, a system in which social groups are distinguished into classes and where explicit differences between classes exist, is most likely:
    a. From a low power distance culture.
    b. From a high power distance culture.
    c. Collectivistic.
    d. Individualistic.

4. The stage of cultural adaptation in which one chooses to either fully participate, accommodate, fight, or flee, is known as the:
    a. Readjustment phase.
    b. Honeymoon phase.
    c. Frustration phase.
    d. Resolution phase.

5. Which of the following was NOT explicitly stated in lecture as a strategy for forming cultural interdependence?
    a. Recognizing differences between cultures
    b. Learning the rules and language of the new culture
    c. Not participating in the new culture until you are completely comfortable doing so
    d. Securing a sponsor in the new culture

♣ Lecture 4: Social Card Talk

1. Joel has high self-esteem, while Mario has low self-esteem. Joel is more likely to:
   a. use his professional cards more.
   b. avoid confrontations.
   c. follow the opinions of others.
   d. take risks in expressing attitudes.

2. Of the three interpersonal needs, which one can people live without?
   a. Inclusion
   b. Control
   c. Affection
   d. None of the above

3. Which of the following is characteristic of a high self-monitor?
   a. More "I" oriented
   b. Far less adept at modifying their behavior to meet changing situational demands
   c. Base judgments of appropriateness on external factors
   d. React generally to their underlying beliefs, attitudes, and feelings

4. Your identity is your:
   a. ability to create different talk cards and determine the games you play.
   b. collection of interests that allows you to fit in with others with those same interests.
   c. collection of attitudes and beliefs about yourself built up over your lifetime.
   d. collection of talk cards that stay constant when your other talk cards change.

5. Self-esteem is an evaluation between:
   a. what is acceptable and not acceptable.
   b. your real self and your ideal self.
   c. your identity and your behavior.
   d. each of the sub-disciplines of your self-schema.

♣ Lecture 5: Relationship Card Talk

1. Which of the following is the relationship stage in which a couple seeks potential similarities?
   a. Experimenting
   b. Contact
   c. Intensifying
   d. Integrating

2. Couples reduce uncertainty about one another through:
   a. similarities.
   b. self-disclosure.
   c. support from friends and family.
   d. becoming traditionals.

3. Susan is attractive. According to Physical Attractiveness Theory, people most likely believe that Susan:
   a. would admit that she values attractiveness in other people.
   b. was not treated with the "halo effect" when she was a child.
   c. was punished by her parents when she misbehaved.
   d. has better social skills.

4. Which was NOT discussed as a strategy for developing relationships?
   a. Respect others' interests
   b. Disclose in very large doses
   c. Learn your nonverbal habits
   d. Share control

5. Social Exchange Theory states that people seek relationships with others who:
   a. provide more rewards than costs.
   b. carry "emotional baggage."
   c. would be supported by friends and family members.
   d. are similar to themselves.

♣ Lecture 6: Persuasion Card Talk

1. Persuasion can be used to accomplish all of the following goals EXCEPT:
   a. Reinforcing current behaviors and attitudes.
   b. Promoting change.
   c. Stopping current behavior.
   d. None of the above

2. When speaking to a sympathetic audience, one of the MAIN goals of your argument must be to:
   a. Create doubts in their current beliefs.
   b. Meet their information needs.
   c. Persuade them to reinforce their current commitments with further action.
   d. Stop their current behavior.

3. All of the following are characteristic of the theory of reasoned action EXCEPT:
   a. Your perception of whether others want you to partake in the particular action.
   b. Your motivation to comply with others who want you to partake in the particular action.
   c. Whether your attitudes were changed by the speaker's message.
   d. The decision rule that you use to judge the speaker's message.

4. A shampoo company has recently chosen Tom Brady to advertise a new shampoo for men. He is not an expert on shampoo, showering, or anything of the sort. He is, however, a well-known pro football player whom many women find attractive. The shampoo company is most likely relying on which of the following theories of communication for its advertisement?
   a. Theory of reasoned action
   b. Social norming theory
   c. Central elaboration of the elaboration likelihood model
   d. Peripheral elaboration of the elaboration likelihood model

5. A campaign ad that changes individuals' perceptions of perceived norms uses which of the following communication theories?
   a. Theory of reasoned action
   b. Social norming theory
   c. Central elaboration of the elaboration likelihood model
   d. Peripheral elaboration of the elaboration likelihood model

♣ Lecture 7: Conflict Card Talk

1. Topics showing disrespect are most often:
   a. High in power.
   b. Low in friendliness.
   c. Either (both) A or B
   d. None of the above

2. Material-based conflicts are:
   a. Over things that are negotiable.
   b. Similar to identity threats.
   c. Due to threats to positive or negative face.
   d. All of the above

3. By appealing to one's negative face, you:
   a. Edify him/her in a positive or attractive light.
   b. Demonstrate that you do not wish to control him/her.
   c. Maximize positive face threats.
   d. Repair a damaged face.

4. Having a dual concern style that is high for both yourself and the other is called:
   a. Avoidance.
   b. Competition.
   c. Accommodation.
   d. Collaboration.

5. John forgets to cook Margaret dinner one night. Margaret blames this on John's forgetfulness and lack of concern for her well-being. This exemplifies the destructive conflict cycle of:
   a. Sniping.
   b. Aggressing.
   c. Personalizing.
   d. Skirting.

♣ Lecture 8: Socialization Card Talk

1. To learn about who is in charge and how decisions get made, you should ask questions about the _____ in an organization.
   a. Rewards
   b. Autonomy
   c. Structure
   d. Support

2. To learn about how emotionally supportive the climate is, you should ask questions regarding the _____ in an organization.
   a. Rewards
   b. Autonomy
   c. Structure
   d. Support

3. To learn about how much individual freedom and flexibility is in an organization, you should ask questions regarding which of the following?
   a. Rewards
   b. Autonomy
   c. Structure
   d. Support

4. To learn what behaviors are supported and what behaviors are rejected, you should ask questions regarding the _____ in an organization.
   a. Rewards
   b. Autonomy
   c. Structure
   d. Support

5. The steps of the socialization process in the correct order are:
   a. Encounter -> anticipation -> role negotiation.
   b. Role negotiation -> anticipation -> encounter.
   c. Anticipation -> role negotiation -> encounter.
   d. Anticipation -> encounter -> role negotiation.

♣ Lecture 9: Coordination Card Talk

1. Which of the following types of coordination is high in reachability?
   a. Sequential coordination
   b. Reciprocal coordination
   c. Pooled coordination
   d. None of the above

2. Coordination is the process of creating _____. People exchange both tangible resources and _____ to achieve _____.
   a. Independence; intangible resources; mutual understanding
   b. Interdependence; intangible resources; good relationships
   c. Independence; sentiment; mutual understanding
   d. Interdependence; sentiment; organizational goals

3. Which of the following is not a type of coordination discussed in lecture?
   a. Sequential coordination
   b. Literacy coordination
   c. Pooled coordination
   d. Reciprocal coordination

4. Among the types of coordination, _____ coordination is least useful in a crisis or when top-down leadership is needed.
   a. Sequential
   b. Literacy
   c. Pooled
   d. Reciprocal

5. A person who is not a member of either party but links the two groups together through interactions with both is deemed a(n):
   a. liaison
   b. isolate.
   c. aficionado.
   d. participant.

♣ Lecture 10: Decision-Making Card Talk

1. Which of the following is not a communication function that groups effective at decision-making perform?
   a. Thoroughly and accurately understanding all aspects of the problem
   b. Assessing the positive and negative consequences of alternatives
   c. Having one strong personality that plays his/her Leader Card to make all of the decisions
   d. Selecting the best alternative, then committing to implement it

2. According to your textbook, which of the following is not one of the lifecycle stages for group decision making?
   a. Discontent stage
   b. Group productivity stage
   c. Nominating a leader stage
   d. Individuation stage

3. One of the dangers in group think in making a decision is that it:
   a. Hinders the group members' willingness to disagree.
   b. Prevents the group from forming a conflict resolution plan.
   c. Disrupts the group's coordination of effort.
   d. Enhances trust and respect between group members.

4. "Social loafing" is a problem associated with which group decision-making factor?
   a. Open communication
   b. Coordination of effort
   c. Willingness to disagree
   d. Celebrating success

5. In a SWOT analysis, the letter "O" of the acronym stands for:
   a. objective.
   b. ordinary
   c. open.
   d. opportunities.

♣ Lecture 11: Leadership Card Talk

For questions 1, 2, and 3, use the following set of answer choices to answer each question:

I: Coercion   II: Referent   III: Rewards
    IV: Legitimate   V: Exper   VI: Information

1. What do choices I, III, and IV have in common?
   a. These types of power increase liking and trust in the leader.
   b. These types of power decease liking and trust in the leader.
   c. These types of power are based on respect for the leader.
   d. Both A & C

2. The Pope, the Dalai Lama, and Mahatma Gandhi are all examples of people who have built their Leader Cards using which type(s) of power from the list above?
   a. II
   b. I, III, & IV
   c. III & IV only
   d. I, II, III, IV, V, & VI

3. The power of a slave owner over his slaves demonstrates which type of power?
   a. I
   b. II
   c. V
   d. VI

4. According to your textbook, which of the following is not one of the lifecycle stages for group decision making?
   a. Discontent stage
   b. Group productivity stage
   c. Nominating a leader stage
   d. Individuation stage

5. As mentioned in lecture, "power" is best defined as:
   a. Being a great leader.
   b. Being able to get your way.
   c. The perceived ability and willingness to control outcomes.
   d. Clear leadership, closed communication, and influence.

♣ Lecture 12: Social Media Card Talk

1. Which of the following social media platforms is most beneficial for professional working and development?
   a. LinkedIn
   b. Twitter
   c. Pinterest
   d. Facebook

2. Social media has become especially important for product marketing for all of the following reasons except:
   a. It allows consumers to express their preferences and opinions about products.
   b. It provides the company important data about consumers.
   c. Some consumers want to participate in the company's story or history.
   d. Businesses are experiencing greater numbers of returns of store-bought items.

3. Research has shown that social media is able to predict real-world outcomes. Which of the following examples are consistent with this statement?
   a. Due to competition, social media commonly breaks the ties that individuals with common interests share.
   b. Activity on social media networks such as Twitter can predict how well a product sells or box-office revenues for a movie.
   c. Rates of discussion of products on social media networks are sometimes more effective at predicting how well a product sells than market-based evaluations.
   d. Both B & C

4. Hyper-personal online relationships:
   a. Remove the nonverbal cues that individuals are usually judged on in face-to-face interaction.
   b. Cause more discomfort than face-to-face interaction.
   c. Results in individuals discussing less personal topics than they would in face-to-face interaction.
   d. None of the above

5. The desire to act collectively, commonly in a large group or mob, is known as:
   a. Social sanctioning.
   b. Social intelligence.
   c. The contagion effect.
   d. Mass media marketing.

♣ Lecture 13: Diffusion Card Talk

1. The time at which a critical mass is suddenly achieved and change happens rapidly after a period of slow, gradual change is known as:
    a. The outlier.
    b. Diffusion of innovation.
    c. The status quo.
    d. The tipping point.

2. Which of the following would be typical of an individual in the confirmation stage of adopting a new product?
    a. Bill researches information about Apple computers online after visiting the Apple store
    b. Dr. Donohue sees a commercial for the iPad on television
    c. A girl asks her boyfriend if she looks good in the new jacket she just bought
    d. Your roommate buys the Shake Weight after seeing numerous commercials for it

3. One of the factors affecting speed of diffusion is compatibility. Compatibility describes:
    a. if the product has a relative advantage over other products.
    b. how familiar the new product is.
    c. how easy the product is to use.
    d. how fast the product diffuses and is adopted by users.

4. The stage of the adoption process in which you may seek additional information about a textbook rental company before you decide to rent your textbooks from them is called:
    a. the knowledge stage.
    b. the persuasion stage.
    c. the decision stage.
    d. the implementation stage.

5. The time at which a critical mass is suddenly achieved and change happens rapidly after a slow, gradual change is called:
    a. the outlier.
    b. diffusion of innovation.
    c. the status quo.
    d. the tipping point.

♣ Lecture 14: Entertainment Card Talk

1. Television promotes a view of social reality that is inaccurate, but that viewers assume reflects real life. This idea is called:
   a. Priming.
   b. Cultivation theory.
   c. Selective exposure.
   d. Satisfying resolution.

2. How do emotions physiologically function in humans?
   a. Emotions rise steadily and then drop quickly.
   b. Emotions rise in milliseconds and then deteriorate slowly.
   c. Emotions rise in milliseconds and then deteriorate quickly.
   d. Little is known about how emotions function in humans.

3. Which of the following statements regarding entertainment is true?
   a. The most successful forms of entertainment are the ones viewers can relate most closely to.
   b. The most successful forms of entertainment promote a surreal view of life.
   c. Entertainment is most successful when it does not contain characters that viewers despise.
   d. Successful forms of entertainment leave viewers to develop their own satisfying resolution to the conflict in the story.

4. The fact that television reinforces personal experiences is described in lecture as:
   a. mainstreaming.
   b. unique.
   c. resonance.
   d. direct experience.

5. The type of information or memory most easily stored and which we remember the longest is:
   a. visual memory (imagery).
   b. factual memory.
   c. information we have heard.
   d. information we have read.

CPSIA information can be obtained
at www.ICGtesting.com
Printed in the USA
LVOW02s0500021216
515254LV00001B/1/P